ROUTLEDGE HANDBO
RESEARCH METHODS IN
MILITARY STUDIES

This volume offers an overview of the methodologies of research in the field of military studies.

As an institution relying on individuals and resources provided by society, the military has been studied by scholars from a wide range of disciplines: political science, sociology, history, psychology, anthropology, economics and administrative studies. The methodological approaches in these disciplines vary from computational modelling of conflicts and surveys of military performance, to the qualitative study of military stories from the battlefield and veterans' experiences. Rapidly developing technological facilities (more powerful hardware, more sophisticated software, digitalization of documents and pictures) render the methodologies in use more dynamic than ever.

The *Routledge Handbook of Research Methods in Military Studies* offers a comprehensive and dynamic overview of these developments as they emerge in the many approaches to military studies. The chapters in this Handbook are divided into four parts: starting research, qualitative methods, quantitative methods, and finalizing a study, and every chapter starts with the description of a well-published study illustrating the methodological issues that will be dealt with in that particular chapter. Hence, this Handbook not only provides methodological know-how, but also offers a useful overview of military studies from a variety of research perspectives.

This Handbook will be of much interest to students of military studies, security and war studies, civil–military relations, military sociology, political science and research methods in general.

Joseph Soeters is Professor of Organization Studies at the Netherlands Defence Academy and Tilburg University, the Netherlands. He has published extensively in international academic journals and authored and (co-)edited several books.

Patricia M. Shields is Professor of Political Science at Texas State University, USA. She has been the editor-in-chief of *Armed Forces & Society*, the leading journal in military studies, since 2001. She has published extensively on the military.

Sebastiaan Rietjens is Associate Professor at the Netherlands Defence Academy, and a reserve major in the Netherlands Army. He has done extensive fieldwork in military operations and has published in journals and books.

ROUTLEDGE HANDBOOK OF RESEARCH METHODS IN MILITARY STUDIES

Edited by Joseph Soeters,
Patricia M. Shields and Sebastiaan Rietjens

Routledge
Taylor & Francis Group

LONDON AND NEW YORK

First published 2014 by Routledge

2 Park Square, Milton Park, Abingdon, Oxon OX14 4RN
711 Third Avenue, New York, NY 10017, USA

Routledge is an imprint of the Taylor & Francis Group, an informa business

First issued in paperback 2016

British Library Cataloguing in Publication Data
A catalogue record for this book is available from the British Library

Library of Congress Cataloging in Publication Data
Routledge handbook of research methods in military studies / edited by
Joseph Soeters, Patricia M. Shields, Sebastiaan Rietjens.
pages cm
Includes bibliographical references and index.
1. Military art and science—Methodology. 2. Sociology, Military—Methodology.
3. Military history—Methodology. I. Soeters, J., editor of compilation. II. Shields,
Patricia M., editor of compilation. III. Rietjens, S. J. H., editor of compilation.
U104.R68 2014
355.0072—dc23
2013044696

ISBN: 978-0-415-63533-2 (hbk)
ISBN: 978-1-138-20085-2 (pbk)

Typeset in Bembo
by Swales & Willis Ltd, Exeter, Devon, UK

CONTENTS

FIGURES

TABLES

CONTRIBUTORS

Manon Andres is an Assistant Professor at the Faculty of Military Sciences of the Netherlands Defence Academy. Her research topics include military families and work relations between military and civilian personnel in defence organizations.

Contact information: Manon Andres, Netherlands Defence Academy, Faculty of Military Sciences. Email: md.andres@nlda.nl

Floribert Baudet, PhD, is Associate Professor at the Netherlands Defence Academy, teaching among other things Military History, Strategy, and Historical Methodology. In 2001 he received his PhD in History from Utrecht University in the Netherlands. His dissertation focused on Dutch human rights policy with regard to Eastern Europe and Yugoslavia 1972–1989. He has published some 70 articles and books on Dutch foreign and defence policy, the former Yugoslavia, the Cold War, human rights and historical methodology. His latest book, *Het Vierde Wapen* [The Fourth Weapon], published in 2013, analyses the government-ordered build-up of the Dutch home front during the Indonesian War (1945–1949) and the early Cold War.

Email: FH.Baudet@NLDA.NL

Eyal Ben-Ari was Professor of Anthropology at the Hebrew University of Jerusalem and is now Director, the Institute for Society, Security and Peace at Kinneret College on the Sea of Galilee. He has carried out research in Israel, Japan, Hong Kong, Singapore and Sweden on various aspects of the armed forces, early childhood education and the sociology of knowledge. Among his recent books are (with Zev Lehrer, Uzi Ben-Shalom and Ariel Vainer) *Rethinking Contemporary Warfare: A Sociological View of the Al-Aqsa Intifada* (2010), (with Nissim Otmazgin) *The State and Popular Culture in East Asia* (2012) and (with Nissim Otmazgin) *Popular Culture Co-Productions and Collaborations in East and Southeast Asia* (2013).

Email: feba@netvision.net.il

Risa Brooks is Associate Professor of Political Science in the Department of Political Science at Marquette University. She researches issues related to civil–military relations, militant groups and terrorism, and is the author of *Shaping Strategy: The Civil–Military Politics of Strategic Assessment*, as well as scholarly articles and opinion pieces on terrorism and, specifically, on the phenomenon of homegrown terrorism.

Email: risa.brooks@marquette.edu

Paul F. Diehl is Henning Larsen Professor of Political Science at the University of Illinois, USA. His recent books include *International Mediation* (Polity, 2012), *Evaluating Peace Operations* (Lynne Rienner, 2010), and *The Dynamics of International Law* (Cambridge, 2010).

Contact information: Department of Political Science, University of Illinois, 420 David Kinley Hall (DKH), MC-713, 1407 W. Gregory Drive, Urbana, IL 61801, USA. Email: pdiehl@illinois.edu; phone: 217-333-9356; fax: 217-244-5712.

Daniel Druckman is Professor of Public and International Affairs at George Mason University and an Eminent Scholar at Macquarie University in Sydney Australia. Recent books include *Doing Research: Methods of Inquiry for Conflict Analysis* (Sage, 2005) and, with Paul F. Diehl, *Evaluating Peace Operations* (Lynne Reinner, 2010). Both these books received the outstanding book award from the International Association for Conflict Management (IACM). He also co-edited with Paul F. Diehl, *Peace Operation Success: A Comparative Analysis* (Martinus Nijhoff, 2013) and co-edits a book series on *International Negotiation*.

Email: dandruckman@yahoo.com

Paul C. van Fenema (Netherlands Defence Academy) holds the chair of Military Logistics & Information Systems at the Netherlands Defence Academy. He has published extensively in the field of organization studies, network value creation and information management in journals such as *MIS Quarterly, International Journal of Physical Distribution and Logistics Management, PRISM, Information Systems Journal, Information & Management, Defence and Security Analysis* and *Journal of International Business Studies*. He co-edited a number of international volumes, among which is *Managing Military Organizations* (Routledge, 2010).

Email: PC.v.Fenema@NLDA.NL

Michael G. Findley is Assistant Professor in the Government Department at the University of Texas at Austin. Research interests include political violence, international development, computational modelling, and field experiments. Recent publications appear in *British Journal of Political Science, Journal of Politics, Civil Wars, American Journal of Political Science,* and *Complexity*. His work has been sponsored by the National Science Foundation, Department of Defense Minerva Initiative, USAID, World Bank, and the Gates and Hewlett Foundations.

Email: mikefindley@austin.utexas.edu

Irina Goldenberg received her PhD in Social Psychology from Carleton University in 2004, where her research focused on interpersonal trauma, post-traumatic stress, and emotional intelligence. She joined Research and Development Canada (DRDC) in 2004 where she worked for three years in the Director of Human Rights and Diversity. In 2008 she assumed the team lead role of the Civilian Personnel Research Team in the Director General Military Personnel Research and Analysis (DGMPRA) at DRDC, and since 2011 has led the Recruitment and Retention Research Team (DGMPRA), managing the programme of research on recruitment and retention in the Canadian Armed Forces. Prior to joining DRDC, she taught in the Criminology Department at Carleton University and worked at Correctional Services of Canada. Dr Goldenberg's main research interests include recruitment and retention of military personnel, and issues related to the collaboration between military and civilian personnel in defence organizations.

Email: IRINA.GOLDENBERG@forces.gc.ca

An Annenberg Scholars Program Fellow, **Michael Griffin** teaches in the Department of Media & Cultural Studies at Macalester College. He has served as chair of the Visual Communication Studies

Division of the International Communication Association and editor of the Visual Communication Area of *The International Encyclopedia of Communication*. He writes on the history and theory of visual representation, and the use and circulation of imagery in media systems, as well as on issues of visual journalism and community media. Recent publications include: 'Visual Communication History' in *The Handbook of Communication History* (2013); 'Images from Nowhere: Visuality and News in 21st Century Media' in *Visual Cultures: A Transatlantic Perspective* (2012); 'Spectacle and Spectre: The Shifting Public Life of the Abu Ghraib Photographs,' *AugenBlick* (2011); and 'Media Images of War,' *Media War & Conflict* (2010).

Email: mgriffi1@macalester.edu

James Griffith served as an Army Research Psychologist recently retiring after 35 years of service at the rank of colonel. He also served as a supervisory statistician at the National Center for Educational Statistics, U.S. Department of Education, retiring in 2013. Dr Griffith has been involved in the design and implementation of several large-scale Army surveys examining important policies, such as the common training and deployment of company-sized units (Unit Manning System), the recruitment of retention of soldiers, and the identification and treatment of post-traumatic distress and suicidal behaviour. He has written over 60 peer-reviewed survey-based articles on a variety of topics, including cohesion; combat stress; soldier recruitment, retention, and readiness; reserve military service; and more recently, post-deployment adjustment among reservists, including post-traumatic stress, substance abuse, physical assaults, and suicidal behaviour. At present, Dr Griffith is Adjunct Faculty at University of Maryland, Baltimore County and St. Johns River State College, St. Augustine, FL, and a Research Scholar, National Center of Veterans Studies, University of Utah.

Contact information: James Griffith, 229 North Forest Dune Drive, St. Augustine, FL 32080. Email: jhgriffith@comcast.net; tel: 301-452-6026.

Jing Han is a Lecturer in the Department of Management, Mihaylo College of Business and Economics, California State University, Fullerton. Her research interest focuses on social networks, teams, and culture.

Contact information: California State University, Fullerton, Mihaylo College of Business and Economics, Department of Management. Email: jinghan@fullerton.edu

Uk Heo is a Professor of Political Science at the University of Wisconsin–Milwaukee. He is the author, co-author, or co-editor of five books. His work has appeared in *Journal of Politics*, *British Journal of Political Science*, *Political Research Quarterly*, *Journal of Conflict Resolution*, *International Studies Quarterly*, *Comparative Politics*, *Comparative Political Studies*, and others. His research focuses on the political economy of defence, international conflict, international political economy, and Asian politics.

Contact information: University of Wisconsin-Milwaukee, Department of Political Science, P.O. Box 13, Milwaukee, WI, 53201. Email: heouk@uwm.edu

Nicholas Jans is an academic and management consultant. He is a brigadier in the Australian Army Reserve and Principal of Sigma Consultancy, an Australian firm which specializes in strategic and organizational research. He has published widely in military studies journals and books.

Contact information: Nichols Jans, 17 Old Melbourne Road, P.O. Marysville, Victoria 3779, Australia. Email: sigma@virtual.net.au

Esmeralda Kleinreesink currently works as an Assistant Professor of Defence Economics at the Netherlands Defence Academy. She is also a PhD candidate at Erasmus University

Rotterdam, researching all military memoirs on Afghanistan published between 2001 and 2010 in five counties (the US, the UK, Canada, Germany and the Netherlands) to discover who these soldier-authors are, what they write about and why they say they write. In 2012, her own Afghanistan autobiography *Officer in Afghanistan* was published by Dutch publisher Meulenhoff.

Email: LHE.Kleinreesink.01@NLDA.NL

Yagil Levy is Professor in the Department of Sociology, Political Science and Communication at the Open University of Israel. His main research interest is in the theoretical and empirical aspects of civil–military relations. He has published six books, three of them in English, in addition to a co-authored book and a textbook, and has authored over 70 academic articles, chapters and papers.

Email: yagil.levy@gmail.com

Jan-Bert Maas is a PhD candidate at the Netherlands Defence Academy and Tilburg University. His research focuses on the assimilation and use of information systems and the impact of such systems on their users. He is also interested in knowledge management during the post-implementation phases of information systems. Jan-Bert's work has been accepted for and presented at conferences and workshops, including the Academy of Management Annual Meeting and the International Conference on Information Systems.

Email: JGGM.Maas@NLDA.NL

William Maley is Professor and Director of the Asia-Pacific College of Diplomacy at the Australian National University, and taught for many years in the School of Politics, University of New South Wales, at the Australian Defence Force Academy. He is author of *Rescuing Afghanistan* (London: Hurst & Co., 2006), and *The Afghanistan Wars* (New York: Palgrave Macmillan, 2002, 2009); edited *Fundamentalism Reborn? Afghanistan and the Taliban* (New York: New York University Press, 1998, 2001); and co-edited *From Civil Strife to Civil Society: Civil and Military Responsibilities in Disrupted States* (Tokyo: United Nations University Press, 2003); and *Global Governance and Diplomacy: Worlds Apart?* (New York: Palgrave Macmillan, 2008).

Email: william.maley@anu.edu.au

Min Ye is an Associate Professor in the Department of Politics and Geography, Coastal Carolina University. His research interests include international conflict, foreign policy analysis, East Asian politics, and formal modeling. He is the author or co-author of articles published in *Studies of Conflict and Terrorism, Korean Journal of Social Science, Journal of Political Science Education, Journal of Political Science, Korean Observer, Pacific Focus,* and *Foreign Policy Analysis.*

Contact information: Department of Politics and Geography, P.O. Box 261954, BRTH 344, Coastal Carolina University, Conway SC 29528. Email: mye@coastal.edu; tel: 843 349 2208.

René Moelker is an Associate Professor of Sociology at the Faculty of Military Sciences of the Netherlands Defence Academy. His work in military sociology focuses on military families, veterans and civil–military relations.

Email: R.Moelker.01@NLDA.NL

Brenda L. Moore is an Associate Professor of Sociology at the State University of New York at Buffalo. Researching in the fields of race and ethnic relations, military sociology, gender, and social stratification, she is author of the books *To Serve My Country, To Serve My Race: The Story* *of the Only African American WACs Stationed Overseas during World War II* (NYU Press, 1996; reprinted 1998); *Serving Our Country: Japanese Women in the Military During World War II* (Rutgers University Press, 2003); and some journal articles and chapters on the subject. She is currently working on a project which examines military sexual assault from a socio-historical perspective.

Contact information: Brenda L. Moore, PhD, Associate Professor, Department of Sociology, University at Buffalo, SUNY, 430 Park Hall, Buffalo, N.Y. 14260; Voice: (716) 645-8470; Fax: (716) 645-3934; Email: socbrend@buffalo.edu

Björn Müller-Wille is the technical director of the Uruzgan and Helmand monitoring and evaluation programmes, the latter of which he led as team leader for more than two years. He is also senior lecturer at the UK Royal Military Academy.

Contact information: b.mullerwille@googlemail.com

Celestino Perez Jr. is an active-duty Lieutenant-Colonel in the United States Army. A veteran of Operation Iraqi Freedom (March 2007–June 2008) and Operation Enduring Freedom (January 2011–July 2011), he has served in a variety of command and staff positions as an armour officer and strategist. He has a BS from the United States Military Academy at West Point and a PhD from Indiana University at Bloomington. From 2002 to 2005, he taught political theory in the Department of Social Sciences at West Point. He currently teaches political science, strategy, and military planning at the U.S. Army Command and General Staff College at Fort Leavenworth, KS. He has published articles and book reviews in *Armed Forces & Society, Military Review,* and *Perspectives on Politics.*

Contact Information: Celestino Perez Jr., perez.celestino@gmail.com

Rene G. Rendon is Associate Professor of Acquisition Management in the Graduate School of Business & Public Policy at the Naval Postgraduate School, Monterey, CA. He received his DBA from Argosy University, Orange County, California. His teaching and research interests lie in the areas of contract management, purchasing and supply management, and project management. His recent journal publications appear in *Journal of Public Procurement, Journal of Purchasing & Supply Management,* and *Journal of Public Affairs Education.*

Contact information: Rene Rendon, Naval Postgraduate School, Graduate School of Business and Public Policy, Monterey, California, 93943, United States. Email: rgrendon@nps.edu

Sebastiaan Rietjens, an engineer by training, is an Associate Professor at the Netherlands Defence Academy, and a reserve major in the Netherlands Army. He has done extensive field-work in military operations and has published accordingly in international journals and books. His main focus of interest is on civil–military cooperation, effectiveness of military operations as well as military and humanitarian logistics. He co-edited a volume on civil–military cooperation (Ashgate, 2008) and a special issue on defence logistics (*International Journal of Physical Distribution and Logistics Management,* 2013).

Contact information: Sebastiaan Rietjens, Netherlands Defence Academy, Faculty of Military Sciences, MPC 55A, PO BOX 90.044, 3509 AA, Utrecht, The Netherlands. Email: basrietjens@gmail.com

Chiara Ruffa is Assistant Professor at Uppsala University, Department of Peace and Conflict Research. After receiving her PhD from the European University Institute in 2010, she has been a research fellow at the Belfer Center for Science and International Affairs, Harvard Kennedy School of Government between 2010 and 2012. Chiara's research interests lie at the crossroad between security studies and military sociology with a focus on qualitative empirical research, mainly ethnography and comparative case study. For her PhD thesis, which she is currently turning into a book manuscript, Chiara has conducted extensive field research in Southern Lebanon and Afghanistan embedded with several different NGOs, civil society actors and Western and non-Western armies. Her work has been published in journals such as *Comparative European Politics, Security and Defense Analysis, Armed Forces & Society, Small Wars and Insurgencies, Security Studies* (forthcoming), and book chapters in several edited volumes.

Email: chiara.ruffa@pcr.uu.se

Jan-Kees Schakel specializes in collaborative networks that are formed to head problems that none of the partners can head (as easily) on their own. In his work he focuses on coordination under pressure and innovation. He works as a programme manager for the Dutch National Police for the development of a national operational coordination centre, and he is member of the Knowledge, Innovation, and Networks-Research Group of the VU University Amsterdam.

Email: jankeesschakel@me.com

Patricia M. Shields is a Professor of Political Science at Texas State University. She has been a military studies scholar for over 35 years and has published articles and book chapters on topics such as military recruitment, the expeditionary mindset, peacekeeping, women in the military, military families, socioeconomics, the equity of the draft, military sociology and Maria Von Clausewitz. She has been the editor of *Armed Forces & Society* since 2001. She also, along with Nandhini Rangarajan, has written an innovative research methods text *A Playbook for Research Methods: Integrating Conceptual Frameworks and Project Management*.

Contact information: Patricia M. Shields, 601 University Drive, Department of Political Science, Texas State University, San Marcos, TX 78666. Email: ps07@txstate.edu

Currently residing in Tartu, Estonia, **Eric A. Sibul** is from an Estonian background but was born and grew up on the eastern seaboard of the United States. He has been on the directing staff at the Baltic Defence College in Tartu since January 2006, largely dealing with topics related to military theory and military history. He has a PhD in History from the University of York in the United Kingdom, where his dissertation focused on the US Army Transportation Corps operation of the Korean National Railroad during the Korean War 1950–1953. He has an MA in History from San Jose State University in California. He also studied business administration at Golden Gate University and has his BA from the Pennsylvania State University in International Affairs with minors in History and Geography. Dr Sibul's military experience includes service in the US Navy and previous employment experience includes teaching at Central Texas College (history and business administration), Kutztown University (history) and in the Republic of Korea Army's professional military education programmes. He is also a certified firefighter and rescue technician in the State of Pennsylvania. Dr Sibul writes on a wide array of topics including military history, military theory, military logistics, naval affairs, business history, management, transportation policy and professional military education. He has also lectured in the cyber security program at the University of Tartu.

Email: Eric.Sibul@bdcol.ee

Keith F. Snider is Professor of Public Administration and Management in the Graduate School of Business & Public Policy at the Naval Postgraduate School, Monterey, where he teaches courses in Defense Acquisition Management and Policy. His PhD is from the Center of Public

Administration & Policy at Virginia Tech. His recent journal publications appear in *Journal of Purchasing and Supply Management*, *Journal of Public Affairs Education*, and *Armed Forces & Society*.

Contact information: Keith Snider, Naval Postgraduate School, Graduate School of Business and Public Policy, Monterey, California, 93943, United States. Email: ksnider@nps.edu

Joseph Soeters holds the Chair of Management and Organization Studies at the Faculty of Military Studies at the Netherlands Defence Academy. He is also a part-time Professor of Organizational Sociology at Tilburg University. His work includes comparative studies of organizational and military culture, multinational military cooperation, and effectiveness of military operations including 'evidence-based soldiering'.

Email: JMML.Soeters@nlda.nl

Associate Professor **Jeremy M. Teigen** (PhD University of Texas, BA University of Wisconsin) is the Director of the Political Science major at Ramapo College and teaches courses on American Government and Electoral Phenomena. His research specializes in elections, political participation, the politics of military service, and political geography. He has published articles in *Social Science Quarterly*, *Armed Forces & Society*, *European Security*, *Political Communications*, *Political Geography*, and *Political Research Quarterly*. Professor Teigen is also a former Fulbright scholar. His research has been featured in media coverage of American elections, in sources such as the *New York Times*, NPR, *US News and World Report*, *The Weekly Standard*, and others. He went to college on the GI Bill after serving in the US Air Force.

Email: jteigen@ramapo.edu

Pascal Vennesson is Professor of Political Science at the S. Rajaratnam School of International Studies (RSIS), Nanyang Technological University and at the University Panthéon-Assas, Sorbonne University, Paris. His research and teaching lie at the intersection of the fields of international relations and strategic studies. He recently published 'War under transnational surveillance: Framing ambiguity and the politics of shame', *Review of International Studies* (FirstView Article, April 2013); 'Soldiers drawn into politics? The influence of tactics in civil–military relations', (with Chiara Ruffa and Christopher Dandeker), *Small Wars and Insurgencies*, 24(2), 2013.

Email: ispvennesson@ntu.edu.sg

Travis A. Whetsell is a PhD student at the John Glenn School of Public Affairs at the Ohio State University. Between 2010 and 2012, he was managing editor of *Armed Forces & Society*. He has published book chapters and articles in *Administration & Society* and the *American Journal of Public Administration*. His award-winning master's capstone paper evaluated a programme which addressed child support issues among veterans. His current research interests include the philosophy of science, research design and methodology.

Contact information: Travis Whetsell, John Glenn School of Public Affairs, 1801 College Rd, The Ohio State University, Columbus, Ohio 43210, USA. Email: travis.whetsell@gmail.com

Ina Wiesner is Research Fellow at the Bundeswehr Academy for Information and Communication in Berlin, Germany. She received her PhD in Political and Social Sciences from the European University Institute. She recently published *Importing the American Way of War? Network-Centric Warfare in the UK and Germany* (2013) and is the editor of *German Defence Politics* (2013). Her research interests include the sociology of military technology, German military transformation and methodology in the social sciences.

Email: ina.wiesner@yahoo.com

Joseph K. Young is Associate Professor of Public Affairs at American University. Research interests include terrorism, political violence, and computational modelling. Recent publications appear in *Journal of Politics*, *Civil Wars*, *International Studies Quarterly*, *Journal of Peace Research*, and *Perspectives on Politics*. His work has been sponsored by the National Science Foundation, Department of Defense Minerva Initiative, and the National Consortium for the Study of Terrorism and Responses to Terrorism (START).

Email: jyoung@american.edu

PREFACE

This *Handbook of Research Methods in Military Studies* emerged out of our desire to fill a gap in the scholarly study of the military. As an institution relying on men, women and resources provided by society, the military is often studied by scholars from traditional, separated disciplines: Political Science, Sociology, Anthropology, History, Psychology, Administrative Sciences and Economics. The knowledge and scholarship of these studies is rich in diversity and often seems disconnected (the stories of soldiers and computational modelling). The techniques and norms of empirical methods are one way the field is tied together. The tie, however, is implicit. Our hope is that this *Handbook* makes these connections explicit and knits the field together in fruitful ways. As most military scholars are trained in their discipline and do not have a source which captures the methodological diversity and unique challenges of studying the armed forces, this *Handbook* hopes to fill this void.

Given this ambition, the *Handbook* aims to provide a comprehensive and dynamic overview. The dynamic and comprehensive nature is represented by the expansion and diversification of methodologies that have been applied to the empirical study of the military. Hence, quantitative techniques have been assisted by new computer technologies and software. At the same time qualitative techniques have become more sophisticated and accepted as most appropriate for certain types of research questions. The new technological facilities are likely to bring the various streams of research together, at least to some extent. It is our goal to highlight these trends.

This *Handbook of Research Methods in Military Studies* enables us to demonstrate the current richness of empirical military studies as well as the various methodological approaches and techniques that have been applied in military studies over the years. In fact, we aim to combine both goals, which is to provide an overview of current methodologies and the way they have been used in the military realm. The *Handbook* is designed to support graduate level military academic education. It is, however, not a replacement for in-depth study of any particular technique.

We are grateful to Routledge, in particular Andrew Humphrys and Annabelle Harris, for providing us the opportunity to publish this *Handbook* and for their continuous help during the whole project. We have enjoyed the unrelenting support of our copy editor at Routledge.

We, of course, also thank our colleagues and friends from all over the world who were willing to engage with us on this project by supplying their talent and energy in writing one or sometimes more chapters. While working on the project, we guess, all of us learned a lot, which has been a joy in itself throughout the process. This is the work of all of us, and we hope it will be used by many.

Joseph Soeters
Patricia M. Shields
Sebastiaan Rietjens

PART I

Getting started and seeing the context

1

INTRODUCTION

Joseph Soeters, Patricia M. Shields and Sebastiaan Rietjens

What is special about studying the military?

Military organizations and the profession they spawn are unique. The military dispatch their personnel to far-flung places throughout the world. These men and women are asked to risk their lives in the service of the state, for higher purposes, and in so doing suffer, sometimes even after a mission is over. Military organizations and the people within them are tasked to do something extraordinary. Militaries are also unique because they frequently conduct their business in an atmosphere of secrecy. Sometimes a military organization does not want to reveal its actions because it is not always good at what it does, or because it now and then behaves unethically, especially towards the people in its area of operation (e.g. Soeters et al. 2010).

These characteristics demonstrate that studying the military is valuable and difficult at the same time. Researching the military is valuable and in fact indispensable because the use of violence, the military's core business, is probably one of the most unpredictable and impactful forces in social dynamics. Further, a society's armed forces use collective sources such as the taxpayers' money and hires citizens who could have earned their salaries elsewhere in the economy, under less threatening circumstances. For all these reasons the voters and taxpayers – ordinary people in society – have every right to know what military organizations are doing.

Doing research in any organization is difficult (e.g. Bryman 1988). However, studying the military is probably more complex because, more than other organizations, the military is a world on its own, an island within society-at-large on which its inhabitants work and live together. Getting access, particularly if one is not a regular inhabitant of that island, usually is no easy game to play. On the other hand, if one is a regular inhabitant, it may not be easy to do research either, because the organization wants some control over the diffusion of information about itself. Therefore, military organizations often manage the timing of the release of the research and occasionally, when a study is unflattering (but not a threat to security), inhibit or delay publication. Besides, national or regional security concerns can affect the diffusion of research findings. Studying the military is also difficult because its impact and presence can be felt along a continuum of scale. It can range from the causes of war to the stories of soldiers. Sources of data can range from sophisticated, international, longitudinal databases to intimate stories of soldiers. Methods of military studies are truly dynamic.

Taken all together, one can observe a societal and political push to know and an organizational tendency, however slight, to hide. Given this possible tension, the methodology of studying the military is defined by idiosyncrasies, relating to the specific work itself and accessibility barriers (e.g. Caforio and Nuciari 2003). These unique characteristics provide ample rationale to devote a specific volume to the methodologies of studying the military and the way it tries to achieve its main goals: prevention, containment and resolution of conflict. This *Handbook* can be seen as an addition to a recent volume on qualitative methods in military studies (Carreiras and Castro 2012).

What this book is, and what it is not

This *Handbook* focuses on the methodology of research that is in use in the social, behavioural, economic, political and administrative sciences. It is a social science introduction to the broadly defined intricacies of studying the military. Therefore it does not deal with issues that are particularly suited to the technical sciences, such as the study of *Markov Chains, knapsack* problems or linear programming in operations research. Of course, these problems are of large importance in the military, but they fall outside the scope of this book. Nor is this *Handbook* a statistical textbook on scale construction, measurement and (model) testing, or a volume devoted to methodological recipes for ensuring reliability, validity, the construction of representative samples, and the like.

Clearly, to become a fully trained military researcher one needs to do a bit more than working with this volume. One would need to master general aspects of research methods that extend beyond the military context. In fact, this *Handbook* assumes a basic knowledge of research methods and practices – developing a research question and conceptual model, designing a research set-up, and knowing about data collection and analysis – before it can be valuable to its readers (e.g. Bryman 2012; Shields and Rangarajan 2013). As such, this book is intended to be used at the graduate or the advanced undergraduate levels, like other books dealing with research within one specific sector, such as education or organizational research (Cohen et al. 2011; Buchanan and Bryman 2009).

While this book is not about technical sciences or statistical methods, it is not devoted to epistemological questions or the history of science either. Hence, issues concerning the possibilities, varieties and limitations of developing knowledge will only be discussed occasionally when the topic demands it. Frankly, we think that many distinctions and even controversies or debates about how to do research and acquire knowledge, have become cliché-ish, stereotypical, polarized or even obsolete (e.g. Boëne 2008). With other authors we think it is about time to leave the 'paradigm wars' behind.

Stressing the interpretative strength of qualitative studies over 'positivist' methods disregards the fact that in 'positivist' studies, such as surveys or experimental studies, interpretation – the search for 'meaning' – is as important as it is in, for instance, social constructivist studies (e.g. Whetsell and Shields 2014). Also contrasts between objectivist and subjectivist, or between naturalistic and artificial, research seems less and less relevant today. An important distinction in social science research may, however, be the use of words only (=qualitative) versus the use of words, numbers and their interrelations (=quantitative). This is the main distinction that we have used while structuring the book.

But most likely, even the distinction between qualitative and quantitative research methods, may be exaggerated these days (Bryman 2012; Moses and Knutsen 2012). The idea that quantitative research is about large Ns, cross-case analysis and inferential statistics and that qualitative methodology is about within-case analysis only (Goertz and Mahoney 2012) seems increasingly less relevant. For example, new computer-aided procedures aimed at identifying, selecting and counting words in the analysis of interviews and other texts bring a quantitative and comparative dimension to what has previously be seen as a purely qualitative methodology. Also the study of historical texts such as in archives may change in such direction due to the rapidly increasing digitalization of sources. The same applies to new developments in the study of visual data. Convergence of the various streams of research is likely to occur thanks to new technological facilities and the broader and open-minded training of junior researchers today.

In this book we aim to be pragmatic and interested in empirical research questions. This volume contributes to research methods by examining the key nexus between the military context and the path to quality social science research on the military. We take the military in the broad sense of the word, including the study of military operations, their effectiveness in conflict prevention, containment and resolution, people's behaviour in those operations as well as the military's general context such as the development of conflicts. This type of empirical work is not something new: there is some history as we will now show.

Predecessors

Most contemporary social scientists who study the military point to the Second World War as the starting point of their self-aware field. During WWII this occurred when American sociologists and social psychologists received the assignment to conduct empirical research among the 8 million American enlisted men and women at war. In numerous paper-and-pencil, cross-sectional sample-surveys the researchers, led by the social scientist Samuel Stouffer, examined attitudes of, in total, about half a million soldiers. These attitude measurements pertained to a multitude of issues such as adequacy of training, food, clothing and equipment, the quality of leadership, individual and group morale, and beliefs about the enemy.

On the basis of the survey results four volumes consisting of 1,500 pages were published (a.o., Stouffer et al. 1949a; Stouffer et al. 1949b). These proved to be highly influential in the development of teaching sociology and social psychology in future decades. More importantly, on the basis of these studies a number of personnel policies were developed in the military, which were related among others to racial integration, the introduction of the Expert and Combat infantrymen's badges, the elaboration of pay scales, leave and promotion policies, food and clothing standards, and so forth. According to military historian Joseph Ryan (2013), Stouffer through his empirical research did perhaps more for the everyday soldier than any general officer could have hoped to accomplish.

The permanent theoretical contributions of these studies lie in the development of new insights with respect to the importance of (morale in) the primary group, the significance of perceptions of obligation, justice and fairness, officers' performance and the impact of reference group behaviour, more specifically feelings of relative deprivation (Merton and Lazersfeld 1950). The value of these insights goes beyond the study of military and war, as they pertain to behaviour of, and among, people everywhere in the world. The researchers also pursued and elaborated data analysis procedures by delving more deeply into the giant databases. There were even specimens of experimental research about attitude change based on message characteristics.

Another example of research from the Second World War that has been inspirational for this *Handbook* is Ruth Benedict's work. She authored a number of reports on the national cultures of a number of countries that American troops would liberate and occupy for some time, including the Netherlands for instance (van Ginkel 1997). The Pentagon wanted to know more about the host-nationals in the countries where they were about to occupy. The most important in this connection is her 1946 study about Japan, a year in which roughly half of million American soldiers were in Japan as part of the occupation. Once published, this book – *The*

Chrysanthemum and the Sword – became an instant classic. Benedict received her important perspective through fieldwork conducted among Japanese people who were interned in the USA during the war. In 1944 and 1945 Japan clearly had not been accessible to Americans, let alone American anthropologists working for the US military. Benedict's study is a prime example of creative and highly relevant qualitative empirical research in military studies; just as the *American Soldier* her work has laid the foundation for the development of empirical social research in the decades after the war had ended.

Set-up of the *Handbook*

Following up in this all-inclusive tradition of empirical research on the military, this volume aims to be broad in scope and practical in use. Its scope ranges from getting access to the field and discussing 'who's in charge' to – at the end of the day – reflecting on ethical dimensions, the development of new theories and publishing along a continuum, which includes high-standing academic outlets or the opposite, focused policy reports. This in fact is the project cycle in research.

Additionally, this volume aims to be broad by giving full attention to all sorts of methodological approaches, ranging from archival and historical studies to conducting case studies and in-depth interviewing as forms of qualitative research methods, and to quantitative approaches such as surveys, (quasi-)experiments, computational modelling and the use of business analytics.

This broad approach, displayed in the different chapters, may be conducive to advocating methodological pluralism, eventually merging into the use of mixed methods in the study of the military. The most experienced researcher, we think, is she or he who is capable of choosing from, and in fact using, the whole toolkit of methodologies, dependent of the type of problems, research questions, design and context of a study-in-being. Sometimes, often in fact, this may lead to using a number of research methods in one study simultaneously. Such mixed methods – or blended methodologies, if you wish – are likely to lead to a better understanding of the phenomena under study (Bryman 2012; Tashakkori and Teddlie 2010). It will lead to stronger validity and credibility of the findings and it will include more diverse perspectives, more context and more opportunities to explain and illustrate what has been found. Mixed methods require a broad approach to research design, and that is what we want to provide in this *Handbook*.

Taken all together, the 27 chapters have been divided in four parts:

- The first part is about getting started and seeing the context, and it consists of six chapters including this introductory chapter, respectively about gaining access to the field, ownership of the research, reflexivity, doing military research in conflict environments and studying host-nationals.
- The second part is about qualitative methods, counting nine chapters dealing with respectively historical research, archival research, process tracing, participant observation, in-depth interviewing and oral history, qualitative data analysis, visual social research, the study of auto-narratives and the use of the Internet for research purposes.
- The third part is about quantitative methods, containing nine chapters as well, on respectively survey research, longitudinal studies, multilevel analysis, cross-national research, experimental studies, computational modelling, assessing the military's effectiveness and business analytics.
- The final part is about finishing a research project, comprising three chapters referring to ethics, theory development and doing practical research and publishing in military studies.

Because methodological issues can easily turn into abstract arguments and debates, we have chosen to present a well-published book or article as an illustrative study opening to each chapter. The main findings and methodological characteristics of each study are presented in a textbox, at the beginning of each chapter.

These illustrative studies range from war in ancient history via actions during the Second World War to the recent operations in Iraq and Afghanistan and current UN peace operations. Also included are examples of studies that relate to the military organization and community as well as to the military people when they are not in operation. Next, studies pertaining to the political and social context of military actions as well as the development of violent conflicts are used as illustrations of specific methodological topics. Finally, also topical studies concerning the use of Internet and big-data-mining facilities are illustrated in a textbox.

Hence, this volume provides knowledge on studying the military in two ways: by providing methodological know-how and concerns and by presenting a gamut of important empirical studies on the military that have been published over recent decades, in all parts of the world. The reader will, consequentially, learn about using methodologies in a military context but also about the military itself.

We are truly grateful that so many researchers from all over the globe, including Australia, Canada, China, Denmark, France, Germany, Israel, Italy, the Netherlands, South Korea and the USA, were willing to contribute to this book. This broad representation of authors has contributed to the book's international outlook and usefulness. As to the authors' affiliation with the military, there is the whole gamut of experiences. Many of the authors work closely with the military either as active duty or retired personnel, or they are employed as civilians for the military in one way or another. Others are scholars without a military affiliation. Thus we bring a variety of experiences and perspectives to the problem of research methods in military studies. We are all, however, committed to a fair treatment of the subject taking into account the need to balance involvement and detachment, which is the appropriate way to conduct research, we believe.

References

Benedict, Ruth (originally 1946/1989). *The Chrysanthemum and the Sword: Patterns of Japanese Culture*, Tokyo: Tuttle Publishing.

Boëne, B. (2008). 'Method and substance in the military field', *Arch. Europ. Sociol.*, 49(3): 367–398.

Bryman, A. (ed.) (1988). *Doing Research in Organizations*, London: Routledge.

Bryman, Alan (2012). *Social Research Methods* (4th edn), Oxford: Oxford University Press.

Buchanan, D.A. and A. Bryman (eds) (2009). *The Sage Handbook of Organizational Research Methods*, Thousand Oaks, CA: Sage.

Caforio, G. and M. Nuciari (2003). 'Social research and the military', in G. Caforio (ed.), *Handbook of the Sociology of the Military*, New York: Kluwer, pp. 27–58.

Carreiras, H. and C. Castro (eds) (2012). *Qualitative Methods in Military Studies: Research Experiences and Challenges*, London and New York: Routledge.

Cohen, Louis, Lawrence Manion and Keith Morrison (2011). *Research Methods in Education* (7th edn), London and New York: Routledge.

Goertz, G. and J. Mahoney (2012). *A Tale of Two Cultures: Qualitative and Quantitative Research in the Social Sciences*, Princeton, NJ: Princeton University Press.

Merton, Robert K. and Paul F. Lazersfeld (eds) (1950). *Continuities in Social Research: Studies in the Scope and Method of 'The American Soldier'*, Glencoe, IL: Free Press.

Moses, Jonathan W. and Torbjørn L. Knutsen (2012). *Ways of Knowing: Competing Methodologies in Social and Political Research* (2nd edn), Houndmills: Palgrave Macmillan.

Ryan, Joseph W. (2013). *Samuel Stouffer and the GI Survey: Sociologists and Soldiers during the Second World War*, Knoxville, TN: University of Tennessee Press.

Shields, Patricia and Nandhini Rangarajan (2013). *A Playbook for Research Methods: Integrating Conceptual Frameworks and Project Management*, Stillwater, OK: New Forums Press.

Soeters, Joseph, Paul van Fenema and Robert Beeres (eds) (2010). *Managing Military Organizations: Theory and Practice*, London and New York: Routledge.

Stouffer, Samuel A., Edward A. Suchman, Leland C. DeVinney, Shirley A. Star and Robin M. Williams Jr. (1949). *Studies in Social Psychology in World War II: 'The American Soldier'; Vol. 1: Adjustment during Army Life*, Princeton, NJ: Princeton University Press.

Stouffer, Samuel A., Arthur A. Lumsdaine, Marion Harper Lumsdaine, Robert M. Williams Jr., M. Brewster Smith, Irving L. Janis, Shirley A. Star and Leonard S. Cottrell (1949). *Studies in Social Psychology in World War II: 'The American Soldier'; Vol. 2: Combat and Its Aftermath*, Princeton, NJ: Princeton University Press.

Tashakkori, A. and Ch. Teddlie (eds) (2010). *The Sage Handbook of Mixed Methods in Social and Behavioral Research*, Thousand Oaks, CA: Sage.

Van Ginkel, Rob (1997). *Notities over Nederlanders* [Notes on the Dutch], Amsterdam and Meppel: Boom.

Whetsell, T.A. and P.M. Shields (2014). 'The dynamics of positivism in the study of public administration: A brief intellectual history and reappraisal', *Administration and Society* (online).

2

GETTING ACCESS
TO THE FIELD

Insider/outsider perspectives

Eyal Ben-Ari and Yagil Levy

C. Lutz (2002) *Homefront: A Military City in the American 20th Century*. Boston, MA: Beacon.

Many issues of gaining access to the field are illustrated in Lutz's *Homefront* (2002). The volume, representing the author's first foray into the study of "things military," argues that the United States is a country "made" by war preparation. Lutz focuses on Fayetteville, North Carolina, and neighboring Fort Bragg, the largest army base in the United States. She uses a rich array of sources gathered over a period of six years – among them tens of interviews and numerous conversations with military personnel and civilians, official records, and journalistic accounts – to undergird her analysis. Despite her critical tone, Lutz presents human portrayals of soldiers and of people who live in and around the city.

This book is an ethnographic history of the relations between Fort Bragg and Fayetteville and the volume richly evokes the development of the city by situating it in wider social, economic, and political developments. Yet, this is also a volume on militarization and its implications for noncombatants who are not directly or visibly caught up in war making or war preparation. Lutz argues that since the end of World War II the United States has undergone a process of militarization and that the symbiotic couple of Fayetteville–Fort Bragg is a microcosm of this process. She shows how militarization is strongly related to the country's inequalities (along race, class, and gender lines) by being a huge employer and a very significant political actor. Thus, she suggests that scholars use the concept of "militarization," which avoids a focus on the discrete event of war and draws attention to broader processes of war preparations and their implications.

A key metaphor in the book – and related to the kind of knowledge that Lutz produces – is that of an unseen process underlying reality around the globe, what she calls the "invisible world of America and its military." This process is invisible because of secrecy laws, actively complicit corporate media, and the difficulties of tracing far-flung connections that do not seem to be directly implicated in war making or in preparations for war. Lutz makes a very good case for how "we" (meaning Americans, but her point could apply to members of other societies) have been taught

(continued)

(continued)

to look at the implications of war almost exclusively for combatants and how secrecy laws, certain histories, and taken-for-granted notions of war as being directly related to the military have hidden many developments from notice.

Some methodological issues related to the volume are worth noting. First, like many researchers, Lutz does not provide much information about her access to the field in the methodological sense of creating contacts, negotiating her way into the camp and the city, or the understandings that she reached with her informants about publication. Perhaps this situation ensued because she is wary of being identified as a scholar enabled by the military; she nevertheless had access to the archives of Fort Bragg and talked to numerous military personnel. Second, because Lutz argues that we are witness to an inexorable trend toward militarization, she has problems explaining changed attitudes to the use of force and violence. Thus, for example, although aware of the antimilitarist tradition in the United States, she does not really theorize its impact on militarization or how processes of militarization have been contested during different eras. Third, there is a clear, but implicit, ideological bias at base of her volume. Lutz is highly critical of US government policies and the role of the United States around the globe. For the purposes of our analysis the question is what kind of knowledge is she producing? Fourth is the American-centrist approach in a study focused exclusively on the United States and written for American readerships. This focus raises questions about gaining access to an academic field as a field of knowledge marked by certain actors that belong to the military and wider security establishment.

Introduction

Gaining access to the field of military studies implies two types of entrées: the organizational or institutional kind that involves being admitted into a large-scale bureaucracy and the epistemological one of encountering a certain field of knowledge. We argue that both are interrelated and can best be understood via the understanding that all research is a social activity. This point implies examining both the unique features of the armed forces as a large-scale organization headed by powerful national elites focused on "national security," and the particular kinds of knowledge that are created in and around the social institution charged with the use of organized (if at times contested) violence (Boëne 1990).

Epistemology and the sociology of knowledge

The critiques of Lutz's volume lead us to an appreciation of the epistemological issues involved in getting access to a field in the sense of how knowledge is acquired and produced, or the conditions of possibility of knowledge about the military. Specifically, the critical approach that Lutz undertakes is related to the kind of understanding of the armed forces and the processes attendant upon them that she argues for. To be sure, research does not always start with scholarly self-awareness of its goals or implications or indeed of the biases implicit in it since these most often emerge during the process of inquiry. Yet it is important to attempt and clarify these themes since they frame the kinds of knowledge that is produced and the relations (if at all) negotiated between the military and scholars upon entry for research purposes.

The German philosopher Jürgen Habermas provides the key for starting our analysis. In his *Knowledge and Human Interests* (1971), Habermas offered a typology of what he termed *knowledge-constitutive interests*, each expressed in a particular type of scholarly inquiry each of which can be exemplified in the study of the military. The first is *technical interest* in the prediction and control of the natural environment that aims at tying knowledge-production to controlled observation and testable general explanations yielding the *empirical-analytic* sciences. This kind of knowledge was dubbed the engineering model of military sociology by Moskos (1988), a knowledge oriented to seeking explanatory laws by which politicians or senior commanders can better control the actions of the armed forces. Concretely, this kind of knowledge has been produced by independent scholars in universities and a variety of in-house research agencies established primarily by psychologists around the world after WWII (Boëne 2000: 160). This kind of knowledge was spearheaded by an alliance between psychology and the military, and the governing idea was of military social science as social engineering that meets the urgent functional needs of the forces and based on (straightforwardly) applying universal theories to the military (Boëne 2000).

Most studies of the military or of civil-military relations belong to this category of empirical-analytic sciences (sometimes funded by security related agencies), such as those focused on enlistees' motivations and propensity to serve, reengineering of the social makeup of the ranks to promote diversity management, models of civilian control that imply the best practices to discipline the military (Feaver 2003), cohesion, leadership, primary groups, morale, race relations, and communication and persuasion (Capshew 1999; Boëne 2000: 199; Segal 2007: 49). Scholars even provide advice about how to frame the use of force to muster support despite mounting casualties (Gelpi et al. 2009). In general, research which is turned into applied knowledge is guided by technical interests, and this typifies much of the work done by military academies and the research units of militaries and defense ministries.

In a different manner, *practical human interest* in establishing consensus makes use of the cultural-hermeneutic approach relying on interpretive methods. Assuming that social life is constituted by social actions, and actions are meaningful to the actors and to the other social participants, the scholarly task is interpretation of the meanings of social actions. It aims at attaining reliable intersubjective understanding established in the practice of ordinary language to assure channels of communication, by expanding possibilities of mutual and self-understanding in the conduct of life. The search for this kind of knowledge is what Moskos (1988) calls the enlightenment model of the sociology of the military.

Some ethnographic research exemplifies this hermeneutic mode (Yanow 2006). Along these lines, given anthropology's long-term preoccupation with the broadly "cultural" aspects of social life, Lutz analyzes how the links between violence and the military are concealed or naturalized. In a related manner, understanding the language, action, symbols of military personnel (rather than searching for predictive models) has often enriched the study of military organizations by showing how soldiers and civilians create and recreate meanings centered on the armed forces (Simons 1997; Ben-Ari 1998; Hawkins 2001; Hockey 1986; Rubinstein 2008). Indeed, given the strong stress on the political arrangements that characterize the military, many studies rooted in political science and political sociology have done little to explore the cultural imagery and practices by which the militaries of the technologically advanced democracies handle their relation to violence.

In contrast to the former two sets of interests, the third category is *emancipatory interest* that makes use of *critical theory*. Its goal is to achieve emancipatory knowledge by counteracting the oppressive effects of the social construction of knowledge (assuming that science is a product of social activity). Critical thinking identifies constraining structures of power, such as relation of dependence that unreflectively appear as natural (Elias 1956). Thus, at once sympathetic to the soldiers and civilians that Lutz talked to she nevertheless maintains sufficient distance from her subjects to wage a strong critique of the hugely influential military through being a dominant employer, a key political player and framing issues of national security. As she explains, militarization is at once a set of discourses legitimating the use of force, the organization of large standing armies, and the higher taxes or tribute used to pay for them.

Many of the social scientific studies of the military bearing this kind of critique began to be produced from about the mid-1960s in the wake of the Vietnam War and the associated peace and student movements of the time. From that time, and primarily within sociology and anthropology and parts of political science, critical studies of the armed forces began to appear. In this sense, Lutz's analysis follows the investigations of such sociologists as Tilly (1992) or Giddens (1985), who argue that war and the institutions of war making are integral to the creation of states and to the mobilization of social resources. Such scholars have done much to uncover the main social and, especially, political mechanisms – recruitment, taxation, and propagation of ideologies of citizenship, for example – by which war has become part and parcel of the very dynamics of contemporary countries. Accordingly, critical thinking in the domain of civil – military relations has traditionally focused mainly on the rise of tacit forms of militarism and their contribution to the construction of power relations. Also important are studies about the role of the military in entrenching ethnic relations and gender relations. Similar are studies uncovering the military role in reproducing the hierarchy in society due to the hurdles in converting military service into social status (Krebs 2006; Levy 1998).

Gaining access to the armed forces for research: A sociology

Researchers of large-scale organizations are often met with concealment, harassment, or obfuscation, since their presence is often unwelcome (Spencer 1973: 91). What lies behind such attitudes? Along the lines of our appreciation that research is a social process, we analyze the characteristics of the military as a particular kind of social entity that bears at best an ambivalent attitude to external research.

Our starting point is that the armed forces are *like* any large-scale organization that is bureaucratized, centralized, secretive, masculinized, led by national elites, and preoccupied by its public imagery and *unlike* most other organizations in that it deals with the use of organized violence as part of national security. From their perspective, the greatest risk posed by researchers is the potential leakage of information and knowledge to the outside where the military organization has much less control and which may harm it or individuals within it. As such, not only are senior commanders or civilian decision-makers related to the military powerful and literate agents who read what scholars write about the security establishment (Gusterson 1997: 17), but they may also use a variety of formal and legal frameworks to limit access to the organization including formal and informal ones centered on national security.

From the perspective of researchers, the root problem of access to the military centers on the how the knowledge they potentially create (intentionally or unintentionally) may impact the armed forces (Spencer 1973). It is for this reason that researchers may encounter numerous difficulties. First, they may encounter bureaucratic rigidity because they do not fit into the regular administrative classifications and are independent of the regular bureaucratic hierarchies. Thus Williams (1984) relates how researchers of the US Army during WWII had an ambiguous and precarious status and thus had a constant need to negotiate their position that was usually dependent on local commanders. Second, research findings may threaten individual military careers by uncovering mistakes (or worse) since researchers are in a position to observe things outsiders cannot. For example, surveys of troops' view of their commanders may have harmful effects on the possible promotion of the latter (Williams 1984). Third, the knowledge researchers create may pose wider risks to the power and image of the military institution. That is why, according to the experience of the authors of this chapter, the Israel Defense Force limits scholar's access to information covering the social composition of the military. Information of this kind may tarnish the military's image as equally representing the Israeli Jewish society. About 40 percent of respondents in a survey conducted among military sociologists in 20 countries reported sensitive topics, which were not allowed to be investigated (Caforio and Nuciari 2006: 40). Since the military controls access to information and individuals, external researchers must negotiate their access with a host of gatekeepers such as military censors, security officials, military spokespersons, public relations officers, or local commanders of units. Here it would have been helpful to learn about the difficulties that Lutz encountered in her research project since these difficulties in and of themselves may contain insights about her argument about the militarization of society in the United States.

While any external investigator (be they a journalist, civilian governmental official, or lawyer (Irwin 2011)) may encounter these problems from the perspective of academic investigators, among the most important gatekeepers (and ones that have potentially much to lose) are internal researchers. In fact, given the potential risks represented by external academic actors it is not surprising that armed forces around the world are typified by the establishment of "in-house" research arms and at times a wariness of publishing their findings outside of it. For example, most of the social research carried out within the government offices in charge of defense in France are used for internal purposes as decision-making and "of course, reports are not available for outside users" (Thomas 2000). In many countries such as Austria, Italy, or Israel furthermore only a small amount of the research carried out by the military or Ministries Defense is published openly (Caforio 2000; Maman, Rosenhek and Ben-Ari 2003). The end of the Cold War has brought about a more open attitude in regard to the study of most of the European armed forces and indeed the attitude in some of these institutions is very laid-back in regard to publication. But, when compared to other social institutions the general tendency is still towards *relative* closure (Dandeker 2000; Soeters 2000). The situation in most countries perhaps stands in contrast to Germany, where, by law, great autonomy has been put in place to assure inquiries through publicly available publications, an independent ability to set part of its research agenda and membership of its researchers in international scholarly associations (Klein 2000).

Given the core expertise of the military in the use of organized violence a host of justifications for limiting or controlling access are used by gatekeepers. First, since the armed forces are responsible for the safety of researchers in combat areas they may invoke danger as a limiting factor on access and mobility (Ben-Ari et al. 2010; Williams 1984). Thus civilian researchers are generally not allowed outside the wire of the camps they visit in Afghanistan. Second, given the still highly masculinized nature of combat units, a further restriction is often placed informally on female researchers (Sion 2004). Third is the problem of the legitimacy of the researcher as perceived by gatekeepers: since the military is closely associated with national security some military actors may questions researchers' authority to do research and potentially criticize the armed forces. In this respect, as Irwin (2011) makes clear, researchers who have served previously in the military are often granted easier access. In this regard, it would have been very useful to learn if Lutz encountered any such problems in here research. The very fact that she was an external researcher from a prestigious academic institution (the University of North Carolina at Chapel Hill) may have sometimes hindered her in gaining access to informants or alternatively opened doors since they would have liked their story to be recorded and heard by such a scholar.

Polymorphous engagement and contracts

Sociologically, gaining access to research within the armed forces, as any large organization, is a process involving negotiations and dialogues with gatekeepers over various issues and resistances (Reeves 2010). One excellent example is Lomsky-Feder's (1996) essay on the problems of a woman entering the masculine world of the military. In her research conducted on veterans of the Yom Kippur War in October 1973 she initially assumed that being an Israeli and contemporary of her male interviewees she would be easily allowed to enter conversations about their experiences of the war. However, she found that she was treated as a stranger and outsider. It was only gradually that she understood that taking the role of the stranger actually aided her access since it placed her in a situation where she was allowed to ask very basic, taken-for-granted questions and that her interviewees easily moved into "teaching" her about the military and about war.

Gazit and Maoz-Shai (2010; Castro 2013; Navarro 2013) take her insights further to show that the intricacies of studying an armed force "at home" (of one's own nationality) as the majority of researchers on the military do, carry some rather peculiar complications. They conceptualize the effects of the dynamic positioning of researchers in four social fields: the academic, the military-security, gender, and the ethno-national whose influence changes throughout research. Each of these fields dictates different expectations about the outcome of investigations. For instance, they show that many academic disciplines are populated by scholars who carry expectations that research be critical. Furthermore, when researchers and respondents share similar ethno-national affiliation and military experiences, the dichotomous relations between them break down and give way to a dense web of mutual expectations about shared concerns, the critical positioning of scholars and the problems of constantly negotiating access to the field.

The process of gaining access often begins with assorted formalities that have increasingly burdened research due to the growing legalization of social life and the juridification of the military. Requirements include submitting proposals and parleying with ethical, institutional and risk management review boards. This general trend that characterizes contemporary social and human sciences leads, as Lincoln (2005) argues, to scholarly conservatism and an emphasis on the production of Habermas' first kind of knowledge. Formal procedures also include obtaining funds from varied sources as university bodies, public or private foundations, government ministries or the military itself. Since many of these entities approve funding for proposals that are low risk in the sociological sense they too may lead to a conservative research orientation since many scholars cannot provide funders with answers at the beginning of research about its results or indeed about where their investigations will lead them. Indeed, one of Lutz's insights about the blurred lines between what are popularly seen as separate military and civilian spheres emerged only through the process of gaining access to the city and the camp she studied. Thus for instance, she underscored the complex manner through which employment, shopping opportunities and land ownership in the city were dependent on the dynamics of the military camp.

Next take social and organizational positioning of researchers upon entry and during the first stage of research. They may find themselves slotted into or negotiate their way into various relations with the armed forces. These include active military roles such as a psychiatrist at military hospitals or research psychologists at various military centers. Then there are roles combining teaching and research functions in military academic institutions (Ender 2009; Tomforde 2011) or dual appointments in military academies and civilian universities (De Waard and Soeters 2007). The great advantage of these positions is that they allow relatively unobstructed access to troops and a greater willingness of local commanders to cooperate since they are seen as part of the team. Next is research specifically commissioned by the armed forces but carried out by external civilian academics (Segal and Segal 1993), research that is externally funded but enabled by the military (Simons 1997; Winslow 1997), or investigations carried out by coalitions between external scholars and in-house researchers (Ben-Ari et al. 2010). Finally, entry may be facilitated through guarantors who are "friends" of the military like Irwin (2011) who gained access through a senior commander that she knew or Sion (2004) who was assisted by one of her PhD supervisors who taught at the Netherlands Defence Academy.

The processual character of any research involves a number of other issues. Once inside there is a need to respond as honestly as possible to gatekeepers' concerns such as being receptive to their suggestions and demonstrating academic suitability. The problem here, as we noted, is that many insights only emerge during the research process and thus necessitates further dialogues. It is for this reason that some researchers – presumably like Lutz – have found that gradual entry is profitable since once a modicum of trust is built between them and the informants or other authorities they can proceed further. Indeed, at all stages of the process access to participants and data needs to be continually renegotiated.

Each mode of access carries advantages and penalties. At the personal level, once one has created relations with informants or local gatekeepers, researchers may feel that they "owe" them something for their goodwill and hence possibly self-censor their findings. Similarly, any enablement by the military risks the creation of knowledge that could not be otherwise created but may come at the cost of limits on publication and official censorship (Ben-Ari 2011). In other words, gaining official permission for entry into the military may lead to an acceptance of the military's agenda but also access to data that would otherwise not be forthcoming. Similarly, the hierarchical nature of the military makes sure that once an order is given to provide access research instruments can be applied rather straightforwardly but the disadvantage is that data elicited through this mode of entry – say a questionnaire administered by a commanding officer – may not reflect true attitudes and researchers will receive the "party line." Thus the route of access is itself part of the limits and advantages of the research process.

It is for these reasons that some scholars use only externally available data for research on the military: public records, historical archives or journalistic reports. In this spirit, the social backgrounds of Israeli casualties were documented by using public sources as a means to bypass the need to problematically collaborate with the military (Levy 2007: 117–128). The use of external sources, however, does not mean that scholars using them hold emancipatory or critical views. Thus for example, Lewy (1980) used data from the US Congress to offer suggestions about improving the American army's effectiveness after Vietnam. The disadvantage of the use of only external sources is, of course, that scholars may miss crucial internal aspects of the armed forces, while the advantage is a much more autonomous position vis-à-vis the military establishment. As the case of mapping Israeli casualties shows, autonomy may compensate for lack of information. Of significance here is the fact that part of the information researchers report about is related to the interests of different groups (including the military organization) to withhold it.

In order to be able to maintain a critical distance from the armed forces, we follow Gusterson (1997) who suggests a polymorphous engagement: interacting with informants and gatekeepers across a range of sites (including ones belonging to the virtual and popular culture worlds), and collecting data eclectically form a disparate range of sources in different ways. The idea is keeping one's mind open to a variety of research strategies *and* modes of access. Such engagements should be placed within a wider model of ongoing exchange between scholars and the military about creating and adjusting expectations about the conditions of research, funding, and knowledge produced.

Our suggestion is thus in terms of access to the field, to think not only about formal contracts with the armed forces but about informal ones in which the mutual expectations of researchers and representatives of the military are discussed and agreed upon along the *whole* process of investigation.

Conclusion: Gaining entry while maintaining distance

In our endeavor to gain access to the study of the armed forces, we argue for a constant awareness – reflexivity in a more contemporary vein as explained in Chapter 4 of this *Handbook* – of the multiple issues that are involved. This move entails being clear about the dual route we undertake: into the institution or organization and into a specific field of knowledge. Accordingly this chapter has focused both on the implications of the administrative path into the military and the negotiated character of this trail *and* the different assumptions at base of the kinds of knowledge that is produced by researchers of the armed forces.

Concretely, researchers need to be clear about principles and the implications of our scholarly practices in regard to the military as they may change and emerge throughout a whole project. In this regard, perhaps their greatest challenge is to make an intentional effort to maintain a critical edge, not to become an advocate for organizational interests or legitimizing the powers that be. In this endeavor they are aided by the character of scholarship as a public discipline devoted to open discourse. The very need to publish work in scholarly journals and books and to present findings in workshops and conferences (within and outside the various relevant disciplines), as indeed this volume itself, forces researchers to constantly reflect about their own assumptions and positions.

References

Ben-Ari, Eyal (1998) *Mastering Soldiers: Conflict, Emotions and the Enemy in an Israeli Military Unit.* Oxford: Berghahn.

Ben-Ari, Eyal (2004) Review Article: The Military and Militarization in the United States. *American Ethnologist* 31(3): 340–348.

Ben-Ari, Eyal (2011) Anthropological Research, and State Violence: Some Observations of an Israeli Anthropologist. In Laura A. McNamara and Robert A. Rubinstein (eds) *Dangerous Liaisons: Anthropologists and the National Security State.* Santa Fe, NM: School of Advanced Research Press, pp. 167–184.

Ben-Ari, Eyal, Zeev Lehrer, Uzi Ben-Shalom and Ariel Vainer (2010) *Rethinking Contemporary Warfare: A Sociological View of the Al-Aqsa Intifada.* Albany, NY: State University of New York Press.

Boëne, Bernard (1990) How Unique Should the Military Be? A Review of Representative Literature and Outline of Synthetic Formulation. *European Journal of Sociology* 31(1): 3–59.

Boëne, Bernard (2000) Social Science Research, War and the Military in the United States: An Outsider's View of the Field's Dominant Tradition. In Gerhard Kummel and Andreas D. Prufert (eds) *Military Sociology: The Richness of a Discipline.* Baden-Baden: Nomos, pp. 149–253.

Caforio, Giuseppe (2000) Military Sociological Research in Italy. In Gerhard Kummel and Andreas D. Prufert (eds) *Military Sociology: The Richness of a Discipline.* Baden-Baden: Nomos, pp. 116–127.

Caforio, Giuseppe and Marina Nuciari (2006) Social Research and the Military: A Cross-National Expert Survey. In Giuseppe Caforio (ed.) *Handbook of the Sociology of the Military.* Boston, MA: Springer, pp. 27–58.

Capshew, James H. (1999) *Psychologists on the March: Science, Practice and Professional Identity in America, 1929–1969.* Cambridge: Cambridge University Press.

Castro, Celso (2013) Anthropological Methods and the Study of the Military: The Brazilian Experience. In Helena Carreiras and Celso Castro (eds) *Qualitative Methods in Military Studies: Research Experiences and Challenges.* London: Routledge, pp. 8–16.

Dandeker, Christopher (2000) Armed Forces and Society Research in the United Kingdom: A Review of British Military Sociology. In Gerhard Kummel and Andreas D. Prufert (eds) *Military Sociology: The Richness of a Discipline.* Baden-Baden: Nomos, pp. 68–90.

De Waard, Erik and Joseph Soeters (2007) How the Military Can Profit from Management and Organization Science. In Giuseppe Caforio (ed.) *Social Science and the Military.* London: Routledge, pp. 181–196.

Elias, Norbert (1956) Problems of Involvement and Detachment. *British Journal of Sociology* 7(3): 226–252.

Ender, Morten (2009) *American Soldiers in Iran.* New York: Taylor and Francis.

Feaver, Peter D. (2003) *Armed Servants: Agency, Oversight, and Civil-Military Relations.* Cambridge, MA: Harvard University Press.

Gazit, Nir and Yael Maoz-Shai (2010) Studying-Up and Studying-Across: At-Home Research of Governmental Violence Organizations. *Qualitative Sociology* 33(3): 275–295.

Gelpi, Christopher, Peter D. Feaver, and Jason Reifler (2009) *Paying the Human Costs of War: American Public Opinion and Casualties in Military Conflicts.* Princeton, NJ: Princeton University Press.

Giddens, Anthony (1985) *The Nation-State and Violence.* Cambridge: Polity.

Gusterson, Hugh (1997) Studying Up Revisited. *Political and Legal Anthropology Review* 20(1): 114–119.

Habermas, Jürgen (1971) *Knowledge and Human Interests.* Boston, MA: Beacon.

Hawkins, John Palmer (2001) *Army of Hope, Army of Alienation: Culture and Contradiction in the American Army Communities of Cold War Germany.* New York: Praeger.

Hockey, John (1986) *Squaddies: Portrait of a Subculture.* Exeter: Exeter University Press.

Irwin, Anne (2011 Military Ethnography and Embedded Journalism: Parallels and Intersections. In Laura A. McNamara and Robert A. Rubinstein (eds) *Dangerous Liasons: Anthropologists and the National Security State.* Santa Fe, NM: School of Advanced Research Press, pp. 127–144.

Klein, Paul (2000) Sociology and the Military in Germany. In Gerhard Kummel and Andreas D. Prufert (eds) *Military Sociology: The Richness of a Discipline.* Baden-Baden: Nomos, pp. 44–54.

Krebs, Ronald R. (2006) *Fighting for Rights: Military Service and the Politics of Citizenship.* Ithaca, NY: Cornell University Press.

Levy, Yagil (1998) Militarizing Inequality: A Conceptual Framework. *Theory and Society* 27(6): 873–904.

Levy, Yagil (2007) *Israel's Materialist Militarism.* Madison, MD: Rowman and Littlefield/Lexington Books.

Lewy, Guenter (1980) The American Experience in Vietnam. In Sam C. Sarkesian (ed.) *Combat Effectiveness.* Beverly Hills: Sage, pp. 94–106.

Lincoln, Yvonna S. (2005) Institutional Review Boards and Methodological Conservatism: The Challenge to and from Phenomenological Paradigms. In Norman K. Denzin and Yvonna S. Lincoln (eds) *The Sage Handbook of Qualitative Research.* Thousand Oaks, CA: Sage, pp. 165–181.

Lomsky-Feder, Edna (1996) A Woman Studies War: Stranger in a Man's World. In Ruthellen Josselson (ed.) *Ethics and Processes in the Narrative Study of Lives.* Thousand Oaks, CA: Sage, pp. 232–242.

Lutz, Catherine (2001) *Homefront: A Military City in the American 20th Century.* Boston, MA: Beacon.

Maman, Dani, Zev Rosenhek and Eyal Ben-Ari (2003) The Study of War and the Military in Israel: An Empirical Investigation and Reflective Critique. *International Journal of Middle Eastern Studies* 35: 461–484.

Moskos, Charles (1988) *Soldiers and Sociology.* SLA Marshall Lecture. Washington, D.C.: US Army Research Institute for the Behavioral and Social Sciences.

Navarro, Alejandra (2013) Negotiating Access to an Argentinean Military Institution in Democratic Times: Difficulties and Challenges. In Helena Carreiras and Celso Castro (eds) *Qualitative Methods in Military Studies: Research Experiences and Challenges.* London: Routledge, pp. 85–96.

Reeves, Carla (2010) A Difficult Negotiation: Fieldwork Relations with Gatekeepers. *Qualitative Research* 10(3): 315–331.

Rubinstein, Robert A. (2008) *Peacekeeping under Fire: Culture and Intervention.* Boulder, CO: Paradigm Publishers.

Segal, David R. (2007) Current Developments and Trends in Social Research on the Military. In Giuseppe Caforio (ed.) *Social Science and the Military.* London: Routledge, pp. 46–65.

Segal, David R. and Mady Wechsler Segal (1993) *Peacekeepers and Their Wives.* Westport, CT: Greenwood Press.

Simons, Anna (1997) *The Company They Keep: Life Inside the US Army Special Forces.* New York: Free Press.

Sion, Liora (2004) *Dutch Peacekeepers: Between Soldiering and Policing.* Doctoral thesis, The Free University of Amsterdam.

Soeters, Joseph L. (2000) Military Sociology in the Netherland. In Gerhard Kummel and Andreas D. Prufert (eds) *Military Sociology: The Richness of a Discipline.* Baden-Baden: Nomos, pp. 128–139.

Spencer, Gary (1973) Methodological Issues in the Study of Elites: A Case Study of West Point. *Social Problems* 21(1): 90–103.

Thomas, J.P. (1989) 'Recent Defence-Related Social Research in France'. In J. Kuhlmann (ed.) *Military Related Social Research: An International Review.* Munich: Sozialwissenshaftliches Institut der Bundeswehr, pp. 67–72.

Tilly, Charles (1992) *Coercion, Capital, and European States, AD 990–1992.* Cambridge, MA: Basil Blackwell.

Tomforde, Maren (2011) Should Anthropologists Provide Their Knowledge to the Military? An Ethical Discourse Taking Germany as an Example. In Laura A. McNamara and Robert A. Rubinstein (eds)

Dangerous Liaisons: Anthropologists and the National Security State. Santa Fe, NM: School of Advanced Research Press, pp. 77–100.

Williams, Robin M. (1984) Field Observations and Surveys in Combat Zones. *Social Psychology Quarterly* 47(2): 186 192.

Winslow, D. (1997) *The Canadian Airborne Regiment in Somalia: A Socio-Cultural Inquiry*. Ottawa, ON: Ministry of Public Works and Government Services.

Yanow, Dvora (2006) Thinking Interpretively: Philosophical Presuppositions and the Human Sciences. In Dvora Yanow and Peregrine Schwartz–Shea (eds) *Interpretation and Method: Empirical Research Methods and the Interpretive Turn*. Armonk, NY: M.E. Sharpe, pp. 5–26.

3

GETTING ON THE SAME NET

How the theory-driven academic can better communicate with the pragmatic military client

Nicholas Jans

Charles Moskos (1977) 'From institution to occupation: Trends in military organization', *Armed Forces & Society* **4(1): 41–50.**

Moskos's seminal paper hit an important nerve, both within the scholarly community and the military institution itself. Its central thesis continues to shape the scholarly discourse and it has had an arguably profound influence on the way Western military leaders think about organisation and conditions of service.

In what became known as the 'Moskos thesis', the article contrasts two 'ideal models' of military organisation. At one pole was the Institutional model. This conceived of membership based on a common identity and core competencies, motivated by 'psychic income' at least as much as by conventional remuneration. At the other extreme, the Occupational model was legitimised in terms of the marketplace. It saw self-interest as being the core of the employment arrangement, with reward systems based on market demand and skill level; work performed by military personnel working alongside civilians; and grievances settled via the mechanisms of industrial relations and trade unions.

Each time one reads the Moskos article, one is struck by certain features. It is clearly written, with a minimum of sociological jargon. It addresses an issue – that of attracting, motivating and keeping service personnel – of permanent strategic concern. It introduces a simple and memorable frame of reference, one that helps academics and practitioners alike to make sense of the myriad complex interactions within the military institution. Finally, it presents its argument in terms of narrative rather than statistics. In all these ways, it is a model of how to communicate research in ways that improve the chance that it will be noticed and acted upon.

What has transpired more than three decades on? On the one hand, two of the thesis's three features – quasi-market based remuneration and functional integration of civilian and military organisational elements – can be seen at every hand in contemporary military organisations. However,

(continued)

(continued)

these sit fairly comfortably alongside many of continuing traditional institutional features. At the same time, the brief experimentation with military trade unionism in a number of Western military institutions has petered out.

For the most part, the balance between the Institutional and the Occupational has been achieved by strengthening certain core institutional features so as to compensate for any excessive influence that occupationalism might have on professional values. Alerted by the Moskos thesis, the institution found ways to accommodate rather than resist social trends. In the famous phrase from a classic novel, its approach was that 'If we want things to stay as they are, things will have to change'. Thus it improved leadership practices and developed more imaginative socialisation, while continuing its traditional emphasis on building social cohesion and institutional identity.

One may speak a language even if it is not one's native tongue.
(Michael Mosser 2010: 1078)

An important and neglected issue

The communication of scholarly research findings is part of the 'sense-making' process within the academic community. Academics conduct research and attend to other scholars' research in order to improve their understanding of how things work and to identify what questions need to be explored (as well as to improve their promotion chances). They focus on methodological soundness and appropriate interpretation, communicating their findings according to well-established and familiar structures. However, what scholars often tend to overlook – blinkered perhaps by familiarity with the conventional forms of their own disciplines – is the extent to which these forms inhibit communication of the value of the research for practitioners wanting to learn from scholarly discourse. While the scholar might be interested in 'puzzles', the pragmatic client is much more interested in 'problems' (Mosser 2010: 1078; Weick et al. 2005; Lawler 1985). As part of this process, practitioners often draw on a very wide range of information sources, attending to each to according to its utility. And if they often overlook scholarly research as part of this process, this is generally less the fault of the practitioner than it is of the scholar.

Some scholars rail against this, blaming the practitioner's lack of perspective and openness to ideas. However, others argue that the scholarly community does itself a disservice when it is excessively 'purist' about its choice of research problems, analytical methods and means of communication, and that the solution to any communication problem lies much more with scholars than with practitioners. Consistent with this second line of argument, this chapter outlines a number of simple but powerful ways in which the theory-driven academic can better communicate with the pragmatic military client.

Military culture: Institutional perspective of 'research'

An important but subtle foundation for the whole issue is concerned with military culture, so the argument begins with a brief discussion of culture and its influence on how people think about important and complex issues.

Culture can be thought of as a coherent view of the world and of thinking about and making sense of that world. Culture manifests itself in 'a complex system of elements – language, symbols, stories, myths, heroes, artefacts, norms, beliefs, values, and practices – that are shared by and shape the identity of a group or community . . . [and which] coalesce and mutually support each other in meaningful patterns' (Potorowski and Green 2012: 273). This results in a worldview that is shaped by mutually supporting beliefs into patterns or 'mental models'.

A fundamental reason for lack of communication between academics and military practitioners is that each camp tends to adhere to different tacit beliefs and thus different theories of justification or worldviews (Potorowski and Green 2012: 273). While scholars will generally be guided by so-called *correspondence theory*, with its emphasis on scientific method and appropriate criteria for conclusions that are justifiable versus those that are not, military practitioners tend to take a *coherentist* view of the world. The coherentist view of the world regards the justification of a given belief as being at least in part contingent on its compatibility with other beliefs, many of which may be deeply tacit and derived from the influence of cultural norms. Within the military, this tendency is reinforced by the value placed by practitioners on qualities that are often difficult to describe and objectively analyse, for example values, relationships and character (Soeters 2000).

Three particular features regarding how culture is shaped in military organisations are worth noting. First, the adoption of explicit and implicit rules and norms is strongly shaped by 'what works', especially in times of crisis (Schein 2010). These rules are passed to new members as a ready framework for interpreting and interacting with the environment, and thus become deeply embedded even if the organisational reality shifts significantly. Thus, for example, the Australian Army has always found its professional identity in the warrior role at the regimental-or-lower level at the tactical level of warfare. Australian soldiers of all ranks put a high premium on the 'professionalism of small things': on the mastery of myriad routine and minor details, each perhaps petty in itself but profound in their combination (Jans and Schmidtchen 2002). Australian soldiers thus came to think of themselves as 'artisans of war', personified by the lightly equipped but highly adept warrior operating in a small team, doing the job with professional nonchalance, choosing to give loyalty to the institution through loyalty to local leaders as expressed in the strong social bonding in the small group, and worrying little about the higher ramifications of the campaign. For officers, battalion or regimental command is the professional ideal, essentially because the responsibilities involved are much more meaningful than those at higher command levels. In contrast, because of its larger size and strategic responsibilities, the US Army has always operated at a higher level of military operations, and hence professionalism is expressed in broader terms. Officers aspire not only to unit command but also to higher command appointments. Similarly, the distinctive historical circumstances associated with other military institutions will invariably have shaped their practices and norms and worldviews (Soeters 2000).

The second factor that distinctively shapes culture in military organisations is its career system. The career system contains a number of features that shape and reinforce particular ways of looking at the world (Jans and Schmidtchen 2002). The military career requires members to adopt particular values and then rewards performance to the extent to which it personifies such values. Career advancement thus depends on the demonstration of values-in-action, with the result that those in charge will further reinforce the process by creating institutional forms that are consistent with their values. Further, the high rate of job rotation to which military officers are subjected (Jans and Frazer-Jans 2004) tends to increase their levels of pragmatism and concern with 'what works' in 'our context'.

Career practices and their parent, institutional culture, also shape 'expertise' and the way that it is defined within the military profession. Not surprisingly, experts tend to be better at sense-making and problem diagnosis than non-experts (Chi 2006; Schön 1983). They also identify exceptions to a rule more often because they ignore less relevant surface features, conceptualise problems in terms of their deep structure, and identify what key information is missing. However, even experts have shortcomings. For example, experts can be over-confident, bound by their disciplinary training when diagnosing problems in offering solutions, and not as flexible and adaptable as one might expect – in part because they often see more costs and risks than benefits in being open to the perspectives outside their particular expertise boundaries (Weiss and Shanteau 2012). Further, because expertise in the military is attained by steady progression, there is a strong link between expertise and its twin, 'professional judgement', on the one hand, and rank, on the other. Reliance on rank as the indicator of expertise becomes particularly important when problems are complex and where professional judgement is seen as a major strategy for dealing with such complexity. But such reliance can be fraught with pitfalls, especially when – as tends to happen – those at the top of the military profession comprise a highly homogeneous group, of similar age and similar career and educational experiences.

The situation is far from intractable, however. As the next section shows, military practitioners who are considering research evidence look for certain features in such research (relevance, alignment with and support for cultural norms, and stemming from a 'reliable source'). Scholarship is thus likely to be welcomed to the extent to which it has such features.

Institutional reaction to scholarly research

Relevance

Practitioners in all fields, military and civilian, tend to welcome and attend to scholarly research to the extent to which it is seen as being 'relevant' (Giluk and Rynes-Weller 2012; Lueng and Bartunek 2012), especially in terms of its association with 'core business'. Military practitioners are likely to pay close attention to research that addresses operational issues (doctrine, tactics, weapon systems, equipment and logistics) or basic motives for serving (such as are represented by the Moskos institutional-occupational thesis). The reception will be somewhat less enthusiastic for research that investigates areas tangential to core business, such as the work in staff organisations (Jans and Schmidtchen 2002). And the reception will be unlikely to be even more than lukewarm for research that seems to be concerned with issues outside the institution's day-to-day ambit.

The example of the Moskos institutional-occupational thesis was introduced in the text box to this chapter as an example of how scholarly research can be made relevant. Another example, but of research seen as not being of significant relevance, relates to that which focuses on the activities of organisational elements that are not part of the military career mainstream. Thus while the Australian Army has welcomed the work of research on leadership in operational units (Grisogono and Radenovic 2011; Mueller-Hanson et al. 2007) because it deals with a challenging and highly relevant and topical issue, it has been less receptive to research on leadership in staff organisations (Jans and Harte 2003). This is because the Australian military places a lower cultural value on staff work compared to the 'true work' done in the operational and command spheres. Another factor in such acceptance is pragmatic appreciation of the feasibility of acting on its findings. Issues associated with practice in mainstream units can be readily dealt with because of the continuity within such units, in contrast to the discontinuity and the resulting periodic losses of 'corporate memory' that stem from the continual job rotation of officers within staff areas.

Alignment with and supportive of cultural norms

Research that presents an implied threat to the professional identity of the warrior or prestige of the 'expert practitioner' is also likely to be resisted – for example, when such research draws conclusions contrary to long-standing practices and cultural norms or to the views of 'expert practitioners' (Potorowski and Green 2012). Conversely, research will be welcomed if it is seen to be consistent with or sympathetic to cultural norms (as in the example of the US Army's reception of the Moskos thesis).

This threat/anxiety issue is particularly likely to arise when research findings are contrary to those that the practitioner expects or hopes to emerge. People's expectations and indeed their hopes can influence what they believe is possible or 'true' (what is 'common sense') and thus their reaction to any particular piece of research is often shaped in part by such expectations (Bastardi et al. 2011; Lord et al. 1979; Nickerson 1998).

For example, a consultancy study of Australian Army reservists' remuneration and conditions of service (Jans et al. 2001) found that junior reservists placed little importance on remuneration as a motivator, and considerable weight to the opportunities afforded by military training for personal fulfilment, adventure/stimulation and career development. The modelling that was central to the research method showed that junior reservists would be comfortable with losing the tax-free element of their reserve pay – and thus with receiving lower net remuneration for their time and efforts – in exchange for more meaningful training and for more operational service opportunities. However, when they were presented with the findings, senior reservists rejected them on two grounds. First, they argued that the findings were contrary to common sense: they simply could not comprehend how someone would willingly accept a remuneration arrangement that put less money into their pockets (i.e. untaxed versus taxed military pay). Second, senior reservists argued that tax-free pay should not be lightly put aside because of its symbolism as a tangible indicator of the value placed on reserve service by society. In this conflict between the 'rational' and the 'cultural', the cultural factor (perhaps inevitably) prevailed. However, a retrospective consideration suggests that this was probably the appropriate decision – not because of its 'not making sense' (because this did make perfect sense to those at the junior levels one) but because it was consistent with the special status of military reserve service in society.

Findings from a 'reliable source'

The source of research findings is another factor that affects the attention they get amongst practitioners. Most cultures give greater reliance to the perspectives of insiders than of outsiders, however 'expert' (Cialdini and Goldstein 2004; Weiss and Shanteau 2012). A further issue is the type of problem in question. Expert advice on 'complicated' problems (i.e. those where there is a 'right answer' and 'right approach' that an expert can determine) will tend to be accepted on its merits, regardless of its source. But the situation becomes different when a problem shift from 'complicated' to 'complex' (i.e. to one in which there is no single 'right answer' that an expert can work out and apply, and which thus requires 'judgement'). In such cases people tend to rely on advice from representatives of the social majority rather than from a minority, however supposedly expert (Madhaven and Mahoney 2012). The tacit assumption here is that the insiders bring a more valid perspective because they can, at least implicitly, place the findings in the context of cultural values (Gino and Moore 2007).

This issue arises particularly when the research concerns a question that is part of a broader constellation of issues, for example the above illustration with respect to Australian Army reservists' pay. Again, the practitioners' reservations result often from their lack of confidence that the researcher has appropriate comprehension of this broader constellation or of the 'strategic' context and hence cannot be expected to appreciate its full implications (Madhaven and Mahoney 2012).

For example, an important factor in Charles Moskos's acceptance within the military was the credibility he possessed because of his career experiences. Moskos had been drafted into the US

Army as an enlisted soldier in the late 1950s and he used the experience wisely and shrewdly in his subsequent dealings with the military institution. His service experience had taught him the forms by which senior people expect to be approached, and so his subsequent communication with them – however informal – was always respectful and reflective of his understanding of his status as a civilian versus their status as senior professionals; and he had always been an assiduous networker even as a private soldier. Finally, his experience in the ranks (as an enlisted soldier rather than as an officer) conferred on him a certain tacit 'grass-roots' credibility. This was strengthened by his making frequent visits to service personnel in operational areas, from Vietnam through to Bosnia and then Iraq and Afghanistan. His shrewd and broadly informed observations of what he saw and heard in such places were valued by his many senior champions in uniform in the Pentagon and the like. And it kept him in touch with the evolving military culture.

Bridging the gap between research and practitioner acceptance

Of the many things ways of bridging the gap between social science research and practitioner acceptance, three in particular are proposed as having utility in communicating with military practitioners.

Using research to develop relevant frames of reference

The first and probably most important recommendation is to use research findings to enhance practitioners' understanding of the situations that they face. Lawler (1985) proposes that the best way for academics to contribute to improving practice is not by producing facts but presenting simple but valid ways of organising and thinking about the world (what he calls 'frames of reference'). As he puts it, managers and practitioners 'constantly want to know what happens to Y if they do X and they also want to know the best way to change organisations' (Lawler 1985: 10). Similarly, Mitroff (1985) urges researchers to get below what seems to be going on at an organisation's surface in order to understand the frames of reference used by executives in their decision-making processes. And Schön (1983) observes that, given that managers typically face situations characterised by uncertainty, complexity, instability, uniqueness and value-conflict, 'useful research' will be that which focuses on framing and clarifying problems as much as on exploring ways to solve them. (An important side-effect of taking a frame-of-reference approach is that such an approach will also help researchers to understand the institution from the practitioner's perspective.)

Moskos's model of institutional-occupation is a clear example of the value of focusing research on a frame of reference. The I-O thesis gave practitioners and academics alike a comprehensible and comprehensive way of making sense of a range of issues. It encompassed a wide range of organisational issues and processes, including professional values, conditions of employment, professional development, recruitment, and even leadership styles; and all done within the neat rubric of the institutional-occupational paradigm. It was a way of strategically viewing all of these factors in a way that was flexible, simple and powerful. Little wonder that it hit such a nerve.

A somewhat different way of thinking about the 'frame of reference' issue is in respect to research *methods* as opposed to research *findings*. It sometimes happens that a particular methodology can stimulate the pragmatic client to think about issues in a fresh and useful way. Such an example happened with a series of research programmes initiated in Australia in the late 1990s (Jans et al. 2001; Jans 2006). This research introduced the military institution to a modelling process that came from a collaboration between researchers involved in the twin fields of marketing and HR, a collaboration that had produced a hybrid methodology called 'employee choice modelling'. The method allows employees' decisions about employment issues to be simulated, modelled and quantified. This not only enhanced the rigour of such research but also involved a shift from focusing on the somewhat nebulous areas of feelings and attitudes onto the more tangible and useful factors of choice and behaviour. Another benefit was to bring examination of the practical issue of making policy analysis trade-offs to a more systematic level, including providing policymakers with easy-to-use aids for decision-making. However, notwithstanding the ready practitioner acceptance of the method, this would not have been possible had not the methodology first captured their attention by its obvious relevance for investigating long-standing personnel problems.

Involving practitioners and researchers in each other's areas

Another way of building closer intellectual connections between scholars and practitioners is to include practitioner representatives in the research process or to embed researchers within practitioner organisations. This can be done, for example, by incorporating such engagement into the curricula of staff colleges and the like. Course members at such educational institutions could be involved in the processes of framing, researching, and communicating such research. In doing so, they will often learn much as well as contribute, with such involvement also helping to clarify the practitioners' perspectives and to enhance the acceptability of the subsequent findings (or simply even to get clearance to study the issue in the first place).

For example, it is likely that a major reason for the penetration of the Moskos model came from his credibility, his networks and his many opportunities to communicate with middle- and senior-level officers at military educational institutions. The I-O thesis served as a major vehicle for his and other military sociologists' entrée to service academies and other institutions of higher learning. Here they had the opportunity to convey their views and to share their understanding of the sociological basis of military organisations with the future leaders of the world's largest and most influential military establishment. In turn, these future leaders would have been instrumental in passing those views and values to both their own institution and to their counterparts in other countries.

Embedding researchers within practitioner organisations can be achieved by, for example, having a 'scholar in residence' scheme at senior headquarters or, as in the Moskos example, having a small team of scholars regularly present and leading discussions on relevant research topics and findings at headquarters or educational institutions. The idea is for the practitioner to become familiar with the potential contribution of past or existing research for ongoing problem-solving. Mosser (2010) notes the way that this has been done in the US Army, with the involvement of soldier-scholars such as John Nagl, David Kilcullen and H.R. McMaster on the personal staffs of influential generals. He also draws attention to the Minerva Initiative, a university-based social science basic research programme recently initiated and sponsored by the Department of Defense. In a speech that outlined the Minerva Initiative in April 2008, Secretary Robert Gates compared it to the US National Defense Education Act that increased funding to universities at almost every level in the late 1950s but which in return required scholarly support for the Cold War effort against the Soviet Union.

Communicating more imaginatively

The final suggestion relates to the way that research findings are communicated. Experienced researchers characteristically report results in terms of the standard format of introduction, objectives, method, findings, discussion and conclusions, with appropriate emphasis on hypoth eses and statistics. However, while this works well in the academy, the same cannot be said for the client audience. For this audience, stories and narratives tend to be more effective and engaging ways of communicating (Sachs 2012), particularly if they resonate culturally.

This extends to the general context as well as to the examples addressed here. A research report based on the analysis of case studies is one of the main strategies for improving researcher– practitioner communication suggested by contributors to the recent *Oxford Handbook of Evidence-Based Management* (Giluk and Rynes-Weller 2012; Lueng and Bartunek 2012; Madhaven and Mahoney 2012; Potorowski and Green 2012). Moreover, such an approach is certainly central to the success of most of the better selling books in the management-leadership field.

Again, Moskos was adept at this particular style. It is notable that his seminal paper contains not a single statistic. Instead, it concentrates on telling the story through example and discussing the implications of the institutional-occupational paradigm in narrative form. (And this was the written medium: in face-to-face communication, he was even more engaging.) The extent to which this reflected his approach in general is illustrated by his instructions to contributors to the conference in 1985 at the U.S. Air Force Academy that resulted in his book on the international experiences of institutional-occupational military employment (Moskos and Wood 1988); he stressed in his guidance the need to include case studies and stories as much as, and as well as, statistics. (In fact, he was quite happy to get papers that were based on case studies and stories without recourse to statistical evidence.)

In the same vein, a recent study on Australian military strategic leadership (Jans et al. 2013) used case studies copiously and avoided statistical tables and the like. Each of its chapters began with a one-page case study drawn from a relevant Australian military example, with the issues contained by the case study then used to illustrate the points made in that chapter.

Conclusion

The issue of academic–practitioner communication is one that has the keen attention of scholars beyond the field of the military application of the social sciences. The sources for this chapter have come from diverse fields that included organisational and medical studies as well as the military. The clear message is that, if we wish our research findings to have more impact, we as scholars need to develop broader and more flexible modes of researching and communicating.

All scholars who desire 'relevance' for the research can learn from Charles Moskos's prag-matic approach to academic–practitioner communication. He took advantage of his time in uniform as a conscript, an experience that undoubtedly gave him a well-tuned ear for commu-nicating with the military institution at all levels, as well as an outsider–insider's perspective on its major sociological issues.

The general argument extends to the acceptance of more sophisticated research methodol-ogy. As the academy finds ways to increase the relevance of its research findings and research topics to the pragmatic military practitioner, scholars are likely also to find ways to improve practitioner awareness of and appetite for research methods that go beyond interview surveys and the simplest of statistical analyses.

This chapter has been tackled in the spirit of addressing things that I wish had been drawn to my attention much earlier in my career. The pragmatist in me had always been drawn to the practical application of whatever findings I and my colleagues produced for the military institu-tion. And if my track record in terms of getting attention from the military practitioner is less than stellar (as is attested by some of the examples given herein), it is probably because for too long I paid insufficient attention to the old adage of 'keeping it simple, stupid' – always remembering that 'simple' doesn't mean 'simplistic'.

The suggestions made herein for improving the degree to which the pragmatic practitioner will take notice of the theory-driven academic – suggestions that include focusing focus on frames of reference, recruiting practitioners for communicating research teams, and communicate findings in narrative as well as or in lieu of statistical form. If we as scholars want our research to be noticed, we need to play by the rules of the practitioner as much as by the professional conventions of the academy. In short, it's up to 'us', not to 'them'.

References

Bastardi, A., Ulmann, E.L. and Ross, L. (2011) 'Wishful thinking: Belief, desire and the motivated evaluation of scientific evidence', *Psychological Science*, 22: 731–732.

Chi, M.T.H. (2006) 'Two approaches to the study of experts' characteristics', in K.A. Ericsson, N. Charness, P.J. Feltovitch and R.R. Hoffman (eds) *The Cambridge Handbook of Expertise and Expert Performance*, Cambridge: Cambridge University Press, 21–30.

Cialdini, R.B. and Goldstein, N.J. (2004) 'Social influence: Compliance and conformity', *Annual Review of Psychology*, 55: 591–621.

Giluk, T. and Rynes-Weller, S. (2012) 'Research findings practitioners resist: Lessons for management academics from evidence-based medicine', in D. Rousseau (ed.) *The Oxford Handbook of Evidence-Based Management*, Oxford: Oxford University Press, 132–145.

Gino, F. and Moore, D.A. (2007) 'Effect of task difficultly on use of advice', *Journal of Behavioural Decision Making*, 20: 21–35.

Grisogono, A.M. and Radenovic, V. (2011) 'The adaptive stance – steps towards teaching more effective complex decision-making'. Paper presented at the International Conference on Computational Science, 2011, Boston, MA.

Lawler III, E. (1985) 'Challenging traditional research assumptions', in E. Lawler III, A. Mohrman Jr., S. Mohrman, G.Ledford Jr. and T. Cummings, *Doing Research That Is Useful for Theory and Practice*, San Francisco, CA: Jossey Bass, 1–17.

Lord, G.C., Ross, L. and Lepper, M.R. (1979) 'Biased assimilation and attitude polarisation: The effects of prior theories upon subsequently considered evidence', *Journal of Personality and Social Psychology* 37: 2098–2109.

Lueng, O. and Bartunek, J. (2012) 'Enabling evidence-based management: Bridging the gap between academics and practitioners', in D. Rousseau (ed.) *The Oxford Handbook of Evidence-Based Management*, Oxford: Oxford University Press, 165–180.

Jans, N.A. (2006) 'Evaluating HR DSS Predictions for Navy PQ and Sailor Categories Following the Introduction of Financial Incentives for Continued Service', presented at the bi-annual conference of the International Military Testing Association, Surfers Paradise, October 2006.

Jans, N.A. with Schmidtchen, D. (2002) 'The Real C-Cubed: Culture, Careers and Climate and How They Affect Military Capability'. Canberra Papers on Strategy and Defence, No. 143, Australian National University.

Jans, N.A. with Harte, J. (2003) 'Once Were Warriors? Leadership, culture and organisational change in the Australian Defence Organisation'. Centre for Defence Leadership Studies, Australian Defence College.

Jans, N.A. and Frazer-Jans, J.M. (2004) 'Career development, job rotation and professional performance', *Armed Forces & Society*, 30: 255–278.

Jans, N.A., Frazer-Jans, J.M. and Louviere, J.J. (2001) 'Employee choice modelling: Predicting employee behaviour under varied employment conditions', *Asia-Pacific Journal of Human Resources*, 39: 59–81.

Jans, N. A., Mugford, S., Cullens, J., and Frazer-Jans, J. M. (2013) *The Chiefs: A Study of Strategic Leadership*, Centre for Defence Leadership Studies, Australian Defence College (http://www.defence.gov.au/adc/docs/Publications2013/TheChiefs.pdf)

Madhaven, R. and Mahoney, J.T. (2012) 'Evidence-based management in "macro" areas: The case of strategic management', in D. Rousseau (ed.) *The Oxford Handbook of Evidence-Based Management*, Oxford: Oxford University Press, 79–91.

Mitroff, I. (1985) 'Why our old pictures of the world do not work anymore', in E.E. Lawler et al. (eds) *Doing Research That Is Useful for Theory and Practice*, San Francisco, CA: Jossey Bass, 18–35.

Moskos, C.C. (1977) 'From institution to occupation: Trends in military organization', *Armed Forces & Society* 4: 41–50.

Moskos, C.C. and Wood, F. (eds) (1998) *The Military – More than Just a Job?* Elmsford Park, NY: Pergamon-Brassey's.

Mosser, M.W. (2010) 'Puzzles versus problems: The alleged disconnect between academics and military practitioners', *Perspectives on Politics* 8: 1077–1086.

Mueller-Hanson, R.A., Wisecarver, M., Baggett, M., Miller, T. and Mendini, K. (2007) 'Developing adaptive leaders', *Special Warfare*, July–August: 28–32.

Nickerson, R.S. (1998) 'Confirmation bias: A ubiquitous phenomenon in many guises', *Review of General Psychology* 2: 175–220.

Potorowski, G. and Green, L. (2012) 'Culture and evidence-based management', in D. Rousseau (ed.) *The Oxford Handbook of Evidence-Based Management*, Oxford: Oxford University Press, 272–292,

Sachs, J. (2012) *Winning the Story Wars: Why Those Who Tell – and Live – the Best Stories Will Rule the Future*, Boston, MA: Harvard Business Review Press.

Schein, E. (2010) *Organisational Culture and Leadership*, 4th edn, San Francisco, CA: Jossey-Bass.

Schön, D. (1983) *The Reflective Practitioner: How Professionals Think in Action*, London: Temple Smith.

Soeters, J.L. (2000) 'Culture in uniformed organizations', in N.M. Ashkanasy, C.P.M. Wilderom and M.F. Peterson (eds) *Handbook of Organizational Culture and Climate*, Thousand Oaks, CA: Sage Publications, 465–483.

Weick, K.E., Sutcliffe, K.M. and Obstfeld, D. (2005) 'Organizing and the process of sensemaking', *Organization Science* 16: 409–421.

Weiss, D.J. and Shanteau, J. (2012) 'Decloaking the privileged expert', *Journal of Management and Organization* 18: 300–310.

4

REFLEXIVITY

Potentially "dangerous liaisons"

Eyal Ben-Ari

Eyal Ben-Ari (1998) *Mastering Soldiers: Conflict, Emotions and the Enemy in an Israeli Military Unit.* **Oxford: Berghahn Books.**

Mastering Soldiers is an ethnographic study of an infantry battalion of the Israeli Defence Forces in which the author served for eight years. As an officer in the unit and a professional anthropologist, the author was ideally positioned for his role as participant observer. During the years he spent with his unit he focused primarily on such notions as "conflict," "the enemy," and "soldiering" because they are, he argues, the key points of reference that form the basis for interpreting the environment within which armies operate. Relying on anthropological approaches to cognitive models and the social constructions of emotions, the author offers an analysis of the dynamics that drive the men's attitudes and behavior. In addition to his participation in staff meetings, he observed training exercises, took notes during conversations with his fellow reservists, and conducted 30 interviews.

Examining the soldiers' use of language, the author identifies three folk models they use to interpret and act within military life. These models – based on the machine metaphor, the brain metaphor, and the rhetoric of emotional control – comprise a more complex cognitive schema of combat. The utility of these taken-for-granted models is apparent in descriptions of battles, and especially in providing points of reference for appraising and prescribing soldierly behavior. For example, since lack of emotional control may impede the completion of military tasks, according to this schema the soldierly ideal is composed and confident behavior under pressure. Ben-Ari contends that troops subscribe to this schema and that it is common not only throughout the IDF, but in all Western military institutions. However, he also shows that differences exist, between the IDF and other Western militaries primarily in the ways in which enemies are dehumanized: while they are objectified in the Israeli military context, during certain periods they were demonized by forces such as the Americans in the Pacific and Vietnam Wars.

Throughout the volume and in the appendices Ben-Ari provides reflexive explanations about his methods and positions within the battalion and in Israeli society. The appendices methodically

(continued)

(continued)

describe and explain the field methods used and the procedures utilized in analyzing data. These depictions elucidate the principles of the ethnographic approach he uses. Specifically, Ben-Ari explains how ethnographic work should be carried out through seeking multiple sources of data, awareness of the social location of the researcher in terms of the information gathered and the actual interview schedules, observational techniques and use of documents used. In addition he gives details about the methodology of interpretation through describing how he created detailed indexes of his field notes and literature review and compared the categories derived (and the data included) in order to explore hypotheses.

Criticisms of the volume include first, that the amount of data he provides to undergird arguments about the wider significance of the volume such as the relationship between citizenship, military service, and masculinity is insufficient. Second, his suggestions that the IDF has developed a rational and humane policy toward enemy civilians is unsupported by evidence, reducing the usefulness of his analysis for those concerned with employing military forces in peacekeeping and peace-imposition roles. Third, and more relevant to this chapter, he does not pay enough attention to the wider political and economic framework that produced not only the models he describes but also the conditions of extended military occupation and oppression.

Introduction

Any piece of social research, whether qualitative or quantitative, should spell out its methodological tools: its route into the field, methods for gathering data, means of interpreting this data, and the textual representation chosen. Such descriptions – reflexive comments – are important because they allow readers to evaluate the limits and benefits of the study. Such descriptions are not straightforward, however, since any research activity is never simply only scientific or scholarly. It is also expressive of a presupposed social and cultural world to which the research project belongs (Salzman 2002). Hence an adequate account of research – a reflection about it – should take into account and report about the epistemological and political forces that condition it (Whitaker 2000). Discussions of the concept of reflexivity grew out of these understandings of the social character of research.

At its most basic, reflexivity is consciousness about being conscious (Myerhoff and Ruby 1982). Processes of reflexivity – thinking about our thinking – loosen us from habit and custom and turn us back to contemplate ourselves and our actions. Once researchers take into account their role in their own productions – something perhaps experienced as exhilarating or frightening or both – they may achieve a greater originality and responsibility than before, a deeper understanding at once of themselves and of their subjects. From the perspective of this chapter, reflexive knowledge about researching the military contains not only data but also information about how it came into being, that is, the processes by which it was created (Myerhoff and Ruby 1982). Though the term may appear fashionable (particularly within anthropology and qualitative sociology), the idea of reflexivity is actually very old such as in storytelling found in all cultures. While reflexive stories are also told in the academic world, they are usually found in more informal settings such as coffee sessions during conferences. It is not surprising then that in many older academic texts, one sometimes finds reflections about research in the marginal parts of volumes such as prefaces, acknowledgements or forewords (Ben-Ari 1995).

Finlay (2002) suggests that there are varieties of reflexive practices, each of which provides different opportunities and challenges. These include: *introspection* or internal contemplation as a springboard for more generalized understanding about the (social) world; *intersubjective reflection* is based on the idea of mutual negotiation between researcher and researched; *shared collaboration* entails a much more conjoint activity in which participants are enlisted as co-researchers in a cycle of mutual reflection and experience; *social critique* involves acknowledging the power imbalances between participants that are brought into the research process so that opportunities are opened for a link to wider issues (such as social inequalities); and *discursive deconstruction* engages the attention of researchers to the ambiguity of meanings in language and how these impact modes of presentation. Whichever version is used by researchers, the idea is to turn the subjectivity of the researcher from a problem into an opportunity (Finlay 2002: 212).

Higate and Cameron (2006) argue that while the concept of reflexivity has been used for decades in the social sciences its impact on studies of the military has been marginal because of the prevailing assumption that researcher bias can be neutralized by adhering to the traditional positivist model of sociological research. Indeed, the title of this chapter is taken from a recent volume attempting to systematically reflect about the problematic relations researchers have with the armed forces (Ben-Ari 2011). Along with previous scholars, Higate and Cameron argue that researchers can gain much by reflecting on the process of doing research and in "writing in" the authors where appropriate into the texts. Their focus in studies of the military is on the motivations for research, how access to the sample was negotiated, and the criteria stipulated by funders. In this respect, there are disciplinary differences in the degree to which reflexivity is openly talked and written about, with psychology and political science probably less amenable than anthropology or qualitative sociology (Higate and Cameron 2006). Since much of military sociology and social-psychology and parts of political sociology are dominated by what Moskos (1988) calls the engineering (rather than the enlightenment) model of research (aimed at making the armed forces more effective), it is not surprising that almost all of the studies carried out during the decades following World War Two are not marked by a high measure of reflexivity. Rather, it seems, as Higate and Cameron go on to contend, most published research has been "cleaned-up" for analytical closure in the sense of the messy processes of research having been swept away. By messy processes they refer to the blind alleys scholars encounter, the constant application and discarding of data that is relevant or irrelevant to the analysis, and the testing and rejection of hypotheses that do not appear in the published text.

For all of the advantages of reflexivity, the concept and associated practices have come under legitimate critiques. First, too much reflexivity may devolve into amateur forms of self-analysis that may end up as little more than self-indulgence or methodological self-absorption (Salzman 2002). This potential is expressed in a tendency among some scholars to reflect on their work and their place in it rather than to do the work (Hatch and Wisniewski 1995: 131). Second, researchers should be wary of assuming that all of their realistic self-awareness and honest disclosure are available to consciousness and assume that people present themselves with no ulterior motive (Salzman 2002: 610). Third, and by extension, by saying we are reflexive as scholars researchers may mark themselves as postmodern or post-positivist thereby as belonging to certain (progressive) camps within the disciplines and in this way make a plea for academic prestige rather than advance research (Salzman 2002; Whitaker 2000).

In achieving thoughtfulness about research, Higate and Cameron (2006: 222; also Carreiras and Castro 2012) argue for the need for reflective auto-ethnographies. These enhance transparency and accountability and provide opportunities for exploring such issues as personal motivations for accepting grants from military funders, or interviewing a "captive" sample of respondents, some of whom may be subordinate and deferential to the wishes of a researcher perceived as more powerful than they. But how does one become reflexive? In order to answer this question the chapter is divided into three sections to prompt readers to reflect on the whole process of research (that is, not only the stage of gathering data). In any case, I do not provide an exhaustive list of issues that should be taken into account, but rather inform readers about how to go about being reflective. Indeed, given the focus of this chapter I have begun with my own first book about the military and I will intentionally use examples taken from my own studies. Finally, while many comments are oriented towards qualitative projects, along with recent thinking (Carter and Hurtado 2007) the chapter also addresses quantitative studies. Indeed, one thrust of the chapter is to suggest thinking innovatively about bridging methods between the two traditions of research in the social science

Reflexivity in gathering data

Biographical aspects of researchers such as values, employment, personal status or key social attributes like age, gender, and ethnicity are all relevant for choice of a topic and field, the process of gaining access to it, and actions within it. While this is true of any social research, the specific characteristics of the military as a large-scale, hierarchical, masculanized, and secretive organization frames such considerations. The essays by Higate (2003) and Hockey (2003) are good examples of how autobiographical issues are brought into analyses of the peculiarities of military life.

Social positioning and social attributes

In considering reflexivity one needs to take into account some of the following issues. For instance, the inbuilt suspicion of outsiders found in any large-scale organization is intensified by the armed forces being "the" organization associated with national security. Hence, such biographical attributes as being a veteran or closely allied with the armed forces help base one's legitimacy and overcome initial misgiving upon entry (see Chapter 2). Furthermore, because the armed forces are still a highly masculanized organization, gender may impede or facilitate rapport with soldiers. But following Lomsky-Feder (1996), women may actually have an advantage in studying soldiers because being "ignorant" they can ask many questions about taken-for-granted matters. Similarly, in some contexts such as the British one, class is important since if the researcher is middle-class he or she may be hampered in gaining access to certain groups labeled as working-class. And, because the armed forces are an extremely hierarchical organization, the level at which researchers enter could limit the willingness of the researched to cooperate since researchers may be identified as a means for organizational control or as stooges of commanders. Hence, it is important to keep in mind that even in the simple act of handing out questionnaires researchers may be unaware of how the answers obtained are framed by context: for example, are they handed out by or in the presence of senior or junior NCOs or by officers?

Personal features and interpersonal dynamics

Personal qualities such as willingness to understand others' point of view or the ability to listen aid one in research. This point is especially important in regard to sensitive issues such as the use of violence by troops or relations with "enemy" civilians. In all of my projects about the Israeli military I tried to be as non-judgemental as possible in interviews and conversations. Furthermore, if researchers understand that research is a social activity the similarity to psychotherapy may be instructive in terms of gathering data. Just as psychotherapists use reactions to themselves as data about patients, so researchers may benefit from seeing themselves as data-generating instruments who make explicit the process by which their interactions with others is a means to gather data (Russell and Kelly 2002). Put by way of example, resistance to external researchers may be indicative of wider resistance to military authority or to specific individuals in command positions. But researchers need to be forewarned that their individual impressions are not knowledge about the people studied. Rather their insights must be constantly and systematically triangulated against other sources of data.

Ethics and motivation

Gaining access to, and gathering data within, the field involves reflection about the ethical dimensions of research about the military, especially in conflict zones or near them (Wood 2006). Such questions as "are we doing harm?" and "to whom?" are especially important in such contexts since they touch upon the role researchers may have in armed conflicts (or peace-keeping) and our commitment to them. In this sense, reflecting about motivation is crucial here since, for instance, prior commitment either to making the military more effective or critiquing its actions may actually blind researchers to important questions: both political and analytical. Hence in many quantitative projects a priori motivated by a desire to improve military performance may stand in the way of understanding how research is carried out within specific political and organizational contexts (Ben-Ari 2012). To put this point by way of example, many studies of the Israeli military that apply available social psychological theories pertaining to leadership, discipline or cohesion miss the wider political situation of a military occupation that influences the behavior of soldiers. Similarly it would be beneficial for researchers to think about how quantitative projects in the military as in many large organizations are considered more scientific, as more legitimate ways gain access and obtain funding. Thus, even if one wants to make a contribution to the armed forces, even critically, this may dictate (at least partially) the methods chosen for gathering data: for instance, quantitative tools may be more persuasive in regard to studying inequality in the military.

Reflexivity in analysis

A rather extensive scholarly literature has been published about data analysis in both the quantitative and qualitative traditions. In terms of reflexivity the idea is to explicitly think about how theories "create" certain facts or actors. In other words, the challenge is to think about the deeper assumptions of the analytical frameworks wielded. An excellent introduction to issues of reflexivity in research is Becker's (1998) monograph whose subtitle is "How to Think about Research While You're Doing It." His argument is that there are various means we can use in order to be both more creative and more critical of our analyses. These include the purposive creation of imagery to guide research, for example thinking about the military as composed of social movements led by charismatic leaders or as a constant assembly of ad-hoc units like high-tech companies. Also the development of concepts for organizing findings (for instance, going outside our disciplines to literature, art or cultural studies for the concepts they use to organize their material) may be conducive to improve one's creativity and reflective thinking. The same applies to converting one's line of reasoning (such as thinking not about what the findings tell us about the question we have asked but what questions the findings can answer). What is common to all of his suggestions is that they necessitate a constant reflection about research.

Specifically, researchers may want to take into account the following kinds of issues (Brewer 2000: 132–133). First, the wider relevance of the setting and the topic for the kinds of analytical lenses one chooses to use. Once this has been clarified one can move on to asking about how empirical generalizations are made: is the setting or population representative of a wider class of phenomena? Or, is the setting a case study framed within an exploratory study or aimed at theoretical innovation? Second, researchers may pay attention to those parts of the topic that have been left unresearched, discussing why these choices have been made and what implications follow from these decisions for the research findings. This can lead to discussing negative cases falling outside the general patterns and categories employed to structure the findings. Third, it is important to make clear the grounds on which the categorization system that has been used to interpret the data is developed. This should enable one to identify clearly whether this is an indigenous one used by respondents themselves, or an analyst-constructed one, and, if the latter, making explicit the grounds which support this view. Finally, and this will relate to the next section, it makes sense to discuss rival explanations and alternative ways of organizing the data (see Chapter 26 on theory development).

My experience may be instructive in this regard. When I began to analyze my data I used a combination of categorical and narrative analyses. I both categorized the data in my field notes and focused on a few key interviews that seemed to me especially revelatory because they appeared to be "rich" in terms of their understandings. The categorization was an emergent one (something similar to creating an index for a book). I created categories for individuals and groups (units or informal small groupings), places and activities, and analytical classes based on my initial interest in cognitive schemas used by troops. The latter especially developed during analysis and I found myself going back to the index of categories to refine it. Moreover, during writing I continuously returned to my field notes to check whether my understanding was supported or not by other data: data elicited in contexts other than formal interviews (observations, casual remarks, or meetings, for instance) or the one found in secondary sources about the IDF and other military establishments for the same reasons. The manner in which I proceeded was a sort of circle of activities – in a sort of hermeneutic circle - that involved a movement between data, theory, provisional interpretation, data, theory, and reinterpretation. While this was a rather solitary endeavor, whenever possible I engaged colleagues in discussion of my categorization.

It is here that issues of validity (the extent to which a test measures what it is supposed to measure) and reliability (the extent to which measurements are repeatable) come up. For instance, in regard to validity, I understood, my kind of research has clear advantages because it permitted me to assemble complementary and overlapping measures or indicators of the same phenomenon. Indeed, many qualitatively minded scholars try to maximize validity, and to a certain extent reliability, through the use of an eclectic mix of research operations. Reliability usually means the ability to replicate the original study using the same research instrument to obtain the same results. Much qualitative work is said to be difficult because there is a lack of standardization. Each social scientist, as it were, is said to write his or her own story, and there is little to guarantee that several social scientists will report the same story. In this sense, approaches like mine are probably not replicable. However, this does not preclude the possibility that researchers report their findings and their methods in a way that can be appraised by other scholars. Thus the issue is less that of replicability but rather that of transparency in providing enough information about the methods of collecting data/evidence so that readers can appraise how the data was collected and assess possible biases.

Two issues I faced may be instructive in terms of the kinds of reflection I embarked on. One focused on whether my membership in the unit was not a sign of methodological weakness? Like the role of any researcher, so my position presented strengths and weaknesses, because, of course, knowledge is always relative to the knower. To be sure, the advantages of participation in the unit centered on being closest to the way military meanings are "naturally" actualized and my ability to use my native understandings of soldiering as a resource. Yet the major disadvantage, it may be argued, is the lack of proper "distance" from the unit and very basic (emotionally loaded) issues such as masculine identity, citizenship, militarism, or nationhood. Ultimately then the strength of my work was predicated on my ability to achieve a reflexive stance: an ongoing effort not to rely only on introspection but to record, describe, analyze and formulate my findings in a way that would allow them to be critiqued by others.

What methods did I use to achieve this distancing? Briefly, one approach involved an inspection of the language used in the Israeli military to uncover the meanings attached to military service, what Finlay (2002) calls discursive deconstruction. For example, the translation of army terms into English prompted me to face their Hebrew connotations. In this respect, the IDF (like all armies) has its own rather specialized language ranging from formal jargon and acronyms through to vernacular idioms and slang. While I am usually fully bilingual between Hebrew and English, I found myself making extensive efforts to translate and thus to find the exact meanings of terms. The next method of distancing had to do with deliberate attempts to defamiliarize my material. I did this by relating my material to theoretical formulations elicited in other contexts. For example, I linked my data to explanations of small group formation in the American army in Korea and Vietnam and to the Wehrmacht in the Second World War, to feminist examinations of gender identity among policemen, or to the social scientific study of embodiment and of emotions. All of these operations forced me to reflect about my data from a more detached vantage point.

Reflexivity in writing

As part of the emphasis on reflexivity along the whole research process, the chapter now moves on to the writing stage. Atkinson (1990) illustrates how the believability of a research report is not a given that just comes with the data. It is formed through the researcher's use – *within* an academic text – of a variety of literary devices and narrative strategies that depict rhetorical figures, use descriptive vocabulary to evoke the scenes within which these characters live their lives and which rely on the selection of appropriate illustrative material. Indeed, as Richardson (1990: 131) states "No matter how we stage the text, we – the authors – are doing the staging." More prescriptively, writing should actually accompany the whole research process. No matter if we call the text accompanying the project a research diary (Hughes 2013) or research journal (Watt 2007), the idea is that by recording things researchers create an objective form that can be then inspected and used for (self)discovery. In other words, one may benefit from looking at writing as a method of reflection and inquiry that constantly accompanies any empirical study.

Writing during research

One way to reflect on writing is to think more systematically about the kinds of texts created during research. Hughes (2013) distinguishes four types of notes while doing research: *observational notes* that are essentially descriptive of an encounter or setting and contain as little interpretation as possible but as reliable as one can construct them; *methodological notes* for reflecting on the methodological aspects of research and the researcher's actions in undertaking an interview, observation and so forth (for example, thinking about how an interview went or what was one's role within it); *theoretical notes* about initial explanations of what the data is telling you; and *analytic memos* where one tries to bring several inferences together such as reviewing the theoretical notes and beginning to see recurrent themes in the data or initial attempts to link analysis to the literature in a field. Personally, as in all my research projects, I keep a chronological journal and a host of reflective notes within one text to which I later add transcriptions of taped interviews. What I found important is that the very act of writing already forced me to be much more explicit not only in regard to descriptions but also my implicit biases and thoughts. The added advantage here is that writing involves – especially for younger scholars – constant exercises in creating texts that often ease the final writing of the final product.

The final text

In considering the design of the final text (a book, article or report, for instance) disciplinary differences are prominent. With the turn to reflexivity, especially in disciplines producing ethnographies, has come a greater openness to experimentation in textual strategies, narrative devices and modes of presentation of research data (Richardson 1990). Ellis and Bochner (1996: 30) comment that using creative genres of writing in the social sciences can help mobilize social action or evoke participatory experiences through imagination and storytelling. In regard to the military it is true that at least some of our subjects may read what we say so that we must balance the critical distance we create with creating spaces within our texts for the subjects to speak back (Gusterson 1997). In my ethnography of the Israeli infantry battalion, providing the voices of the soldiers was also important in order to let readers evaluate the inferences I was drawing from them. At the same time, reflection about textual experimentations should not be limited to qualitative projects. It can also refer to questions of how to display data – such as through using investigational charts, diagrams, photos, or idea maps – other than narrative that innovatively allow readers easy access to the descriptive or analytical parts of the argument (Watt 2007: 95).

I have always looked for good models in writing. Such models from writings about the military include, for instance, Griffin's (2010) use of the actual documents used by US counterinsurgency forces in Iraq and Afghanistan as part of the Human Terrain System; Schirmer's (1998) integration of organizational charts and photographs into her ethnography of the Guatemalan military; or Rubinstein's (2008) depictions of insignia worn by peacekeepers. In my ethnography, I experimented textually by interweaving the analytical chapters with interludes that included definitions from military dictionaries, a letter the battalion commander wrote after a deployment or excerpts from personal observations in the field.

Readerships

The manner by which we construct our texts is directly related to our imagined readerships. For most psychologists textual choices are relatively easy since they have very few degrees of freedom in the articles they pen. When I wrote about my military experience I found myself writing for a plurality of audiences but with only one text. I imagined addressing three readerships: fellow social scientists interested in the military (most prominently sociologists, social-psychologists and anthropologists), scholars interested in "things military," and a vague category of "concerned" Israelis. This mix of audiences was difficult to handle since each group, I thought, had different expectation about analysis and approach. For fellow social scientists I offered an ethnography using concepts from cognitive anthropology. Moreover, because much of military sociology and social-psychology are dominated by quantitatively oriented researchers, I added methodological appendices to my ethnography (and was roundly criticized by one anthropological reader for being too apologetic). For scholars and generalists interested in "things military," I extended an in-depth study of one of the prime examples of military units – a combat battalion – but, in contrast to most texts about the military which are written from the point of view of senior commanders, I brought in the voices of ordinary soldiers and junior officers. Finally, for concerned Israelis I was advancing an analysis of a central institution in our society and which has figured prominently in the lives of many of its Jewish citizens. Indeed, this was a period when scholars in the humanities and social sciences were preoccupied with deconstructing Israeli militarism.

Having said that, however, addressing a multiple readership is probably easier in a book rather than via an article published in a specific journal. When writing for a journal, then, it is useful to look at the journal's web site to understand who the intended audience is. This may considerably aid scholars in formulating the problem and methods accordingly.

Conclusion: Collaborative reflexivity

This chapter explained that reflexivity in research – thinking about and discussing how we create knowledge – implies a range of issues covering all stages of a project: choosing a topic, gaining access to the military, gathering and creating data, analyzing it, and finally writing a publishable or reportable text. While reflexivity has not been a key feature of research into the military it can provide means to think critically and innovatively about studies, be they qualitative or quantitative. Reflexivity seems to be of especial importance in regard to the military because it is a central institution in most societies, continues to receive significant amounts of material and non-material resources and above all is "the" organization charged with the use of legitimate, if sometimes contested, use of organized violence.

Perhaps it is fitting to end this chapter with a plea for more collective team research, which has a built-in potential for a significant measure of reflexivity. Such collaborative research is one in which the findings or arguments of one scholar are continually challenged by other team members or by informants. The advantage of such designs lies in examining personal responses and interpersonal dynamics, opening-up for discussion unconscious motivations and implicit biases among researchers; empower others to contribute or even join forces; evaluate the whole research process, method and outcomes; and enable public scrutiny of the integrity of the research project (Finlay 2002: 225). Such groups can take a variety of formal or informal forms such as cooperative research groups, pairs of researchers from diverse disciplines, graduate students led by a senior researcher or various one-off seminars or meetings to appraise a project. I have had quite successful experiences with such projects as joining an Austrian cultural studies scholar in research into the Japanese armed forces, heading teams led by another senior researcher and myself with graduate students in studying the Israeli military or informal study circles of about 15 individuals that regularly met every three weeks to discuss ongoing academic projects about the military. Above all these cooperative endeavors carry the following message: embrace the social aspect of research and explicitly use interactions among team members on your way towards becoming reflective practitioners (Argyris and Schon 1996: 157) of the social scientific study of the military.

References

Amit, Vered (2000) Introduction: Constructing the Field. In Vered Amit (ed.) *Constructing the Field*. London: Routledge, pp. 1–18.

Argyris, Chris and Donald Schön (1996) *Organizational Learning II*. Reading, MA: Addison Wesley.

Atkinson, Peter (1990) *The Ethnographic Imagination*. London: Routledge.

Becker, Howard (1986) *Writing for Social Scientists*. Chicago, IL: Chicago University Press.

Becker, Howard (1998) *Tricks of the Trade*. Chicago, IL: Chicago University Press.

Ben-Ari, Eyal (1995) On Acknowledgements in Ethnographies. In John Van Maanen (ed.) *Representation in Ethnography*. Thousand Oaks, CA: Sage, pp. 130–164.

Ben-Ari, Eyal (1998) *Mastering Soldiers: Conflict, Emotions and the Enemy in an Israeli Military Unit*. Oxford: Berghahn Books.

Ben-Ari, Eyal (2011) Anthropological Research, and State Violence: Some Observations of an Israeli Anthropologist. In Laura A. McNamara and Robert A. Rubinstein (eds) *Dangerous Liaisons: Anthropologists and the National Security State*. Santa Fe, NM: School of Advanced Research Press, pp. 167–184.

Ben-Ari, Eyal (2012) What Is Worthy of Study about the Military? The Sociology of the Armed Forces in Current-Day Conflicts. Paper Presented at a Conference on *Conflict, Peace and the Production of Knowledge*, Exeter Centre for Ethno-Political Studies' Workshop, University of Exeter.

Brewer, John D. (2000) *Ethnography*. Buckingham: Open University Press.

Campbell, Donald T. (1988) *Methodology and Epistemology for Social Science*. Chicago, IL: Chicago University Press.

Campbell, Elaine (2001) Interviewing Men in Uniform: A Feminist Approach? *International Journal of Research Methodology* 6(4): 285–304.

Carreiras, Helena and Ceslo Castro (eds) (2012) *Qualitative Methods in Military Studies: Research Experiences and Challenges*. London: Routledge.

Carter, Deborah Faye and Sylvia Hurtado (2007) Bridging Research Dilemmas: Quantitative Research Using a Critical Eye. *New Directions for Institutional Research* 133: 25–35.

Denzin, Norman K. (1997) *Interpretive Ethnography*. Thousand Oaks, CA: Sage.

Ellis, Carolyn and Arthur P. Bochner (eds) (1996) *Composing Ethnography*. Walnut Creek, CA: Altamira Press.

Finlay, Linda (2002) Negotiating the Swamp: The Opportunity and Challenge of Reflexivity in Research Practice. *Qualitative Research* 2(2): 209–230.

Fruhstuck, Sabine and Eyal Ben-Ari (2002) "Now We Show It All!" Normalization and the Management of Violence in Japan's Armed Forces. *Journal of Japanese Studies* 28(1): 1–39.

Gazit, Nir and Yael Maoz-Shai (2010) Studying-Up and Studying-Across: At-Home Research of Governmental Violence Organizations. *Qualitative Sociology* 33(3): 275–295.

Goodall, H.L. (2000) *Writing the New Ethnography*. Walnut Creek, CA: Altimera Press.

Griffin, Marcus B. (2010) An Anthropologist among the Soldiers. In John D. Kelly, Beatrice Jaregui, Sean T. Mitchell and Jeremy Walton (eds) *Anthropology and the Global Counterinsurgency*. Chicago, IL: Chicago University Press, pp. 215–229.

Gusterson, Hugh 1997 *Nuclear Rites*. Berkeley, CA: University of California Press.

Hatch, J. Amos and Richard Wisniewski (1995) Life History and Narrative: Questions, Issues, and Exemplary works. In J. Amos Hatch and Richard Wisniewski (eds) *Life History and Narrative*. London: Falmer, pp. 113–135.

Higate, Paul (2003) "Soft Clerks" and "Hard Civvies": Pluralizing Military Masculinities. In Paul Higate (ed.) *Military Masculinities*. Westport, CT: Praeger, pp. 27–42.

Higate, Paul and Ailsa Cameron (2006) Reflexivity in Researching the Military. *Armed Forces & Society* 32(2): 219–233.

Hockey, John (2003) No More Heroes: Masculinity in the Infantry. In Paul Higate (ed.) *Military Masculinities*. Westport, CT: Praeger, pp. 15–25.

Hughes C. (1997) Mystifying through Coalescence: The Underlying Politics of Methodological Choices. In K. Watson (ed.) *Educational Dilemmas*. London: Cassell, pp. 413–420.

Hughes, Christina (2013) *Developing Reflexivity in Research*. Warwick: University of Warwick, Department of Sociology. Available online at www2.warwick.ac.uk/fac/soc/sociology/staff/academicstaff/chughes/hughesc_index/teachingresearchprocess/reflexivity.

Lincoln, Yvonna S. (2005) Institutional Review Boards and Methodological Conservatism: The Challenge to and from Phenomenological Paradigms. In Norman K. Denzin and Yvonna S. Lincoln (eds) *The Sage Handbook of Qualitative Research*. Thousand Oaks, CA: Sage, pp. 165–181.

Lomsky-Feder, Edna (1996) A Woman Studies War: Stranger in a Man's World. In Ruthellen Josselson (ed.) *Ethics and Processes in the Narrative Study of Lives*. Thousand Oaks, CA: Sage, pp. 232–242.

Mauthner, Natasha and Andrea Ducet (2003) Reflexive Accounts and Accounts of Reflexivity in Qualitative Data Analysis. *Sociology* 37(3): 413–431.

Moskos, Charles (1988) *Soldiers and Sociology. SLA Marshall Lecture*. Washington, D.C.: US Army Research Institute for the Behavioral and Social Sciences.

Myerhoff, Barbara and Jay Ruby (1982) Introduction. In Jay Ruby (ed.) *A Crack in the Mirror*. Philadelphia, PA: University of Pennsylvania Press.

Punch, Keith F. (1988) *Introduction to Social Research: Quantitative and Qualitative Approaches*. London: Sage.

Richardson, Laurel (1990) *Writing Strategies*. London: Sage.

Rubinstein, Robert A. (2008) *Peacekeeping under Fire*. Boulder, CO: Paradigm Publishers.

Russell, Glenda M. and Nancy H. Kelly (2002) Research as Interacting Dialogic Processes: Implications for Reflexivity. *Forum: Qualitative Social Research*. 3(3) [Open Journal]. Available online at www.qualitative-research.net/fqs.

Salzman, Philip Carl (2002) On Reflexivity. *American Anthropologist* 104(3): 805–813.

Schirmer, Jennifer (1998) *The Guatemalan Military Project*. Philadelphia, PA: University of Pennsylvania Press.

Sullivan, Mortimer A., Stuart A. Queen and Ralph C. Patrick Jr. (1970) Participant Observation as Employed in the Study of a Military Training Program. In William J. Filstead (ed.) *Qualitative Methodology*. Chicago, IL: Markham Publishing, pp. 91–100.

Watt, Diane (2007) On Becoming a Qualitative Researcher: The Value of Reflexivity. *The Qualitative Report* 12(1): 82–101.

Whitaker, Mark P. (2000) Reflexivity. In Alan Barnard and Jonathan Spencer (eds) *Encyclopedia of Social and Cultural Anthropology*. London: Routledge, pp. 470–473.

Wood, Elisabeth J. (2006) The Ethical Challenges of Field Research in Conflict Zones. *Qualitative Sociology* 29(3): 373–386.

5

DOING MILITARY RESEARCH IN CONFLICT ENVIRONMENTS

Björn Müller-Wille

Helmand Monitoring and Evaluation Programme (HMEP). Although not classified, access to HMEP findings remains limited to official use only. More information can be requested at www.helmandmep.info

HMEP forms part of the multinational and multi-agency Helmand Provincial Reconstruction Team (PRT) and is designed to help improve the effectiveness of stabilisation and development programmes in Afghanistan. Since 2009, HMEP has supported the planning process within the PRT, tracked progress against plans (How well are we doing?) and provided evidence for what interventions are most likely to generate desired results (Are we doing the right things?).

HMEP is innovative in that it does not assess the effect of military efforts in isolation. Instead, it asks how the military and other agencies collectively achieve desired higher-level objectives. The organisational link of HMEP to the planning section within the PRT means that more attention is placed from the start on the question of how progress can be monitored and evaluated, obliging agencies to clarify the logic of planned interventions, which in itself improves plans. HMEP produces all source assessments drawing on information from the military, civilian agencies and open sources. In addition, it also performs its own primary collection of data. Since October 2010, HMEP has conducted the largest quantitative survey in Helmand as well as a large number of in-depth interviews. This has allowed HMEP to produce quarterly reports and formulate recommendations that have influenced strategic decision-making and planning.

The main challenges HMEP faced include:

- The development of a clear, logical and assessable theory of change that brought the logic of different agencies together, to some degree reflecting different (occasionally conflicting) ambitions and agendas (Church 2006: 34). Moreover, the higher-level objectives HMEP focuses on generally tend to be less precise and tangible than lower level ones (often intentionally). Military plans remain particularly challenging, as they normally do not clearly outline the logic between first, second and third order effects, let alone the assumptions on which this logic is based.

> - Setting up systems to validate that interviews are not falsified and that the selection method of interviewees is followed.
> - Presenting results and setting priorities in a fashion that is useful to a broad range of stakeholders.
>
> HMEP modelled regressions to find out which interventions are most likely to generate support for the government. While confirming that the provision of core state functions does indeed improve the legitimacy of the state, it found the emphasis on the justice sector much more promising than services topping the list of things respondents wanted the government to focus on such as education and health.

Introduction

This chapter seeks to outline the specific challenges that researchers encounter in conflict environments. While few of these are unique to research in life threatening conditions, they tend to be exasperated here. The chapter is structured around the chronological order research projects normally follow. It sets out by highlighting issues around the tasking, i.e. the formulation of the research question, followed by matters arising around the research design and planning, collection of data, the analysis and finally issues related to the dissemination. The content reflects a practitioner's view and is centred on the author's own experience of such research and each section seeks to outline the challenges, possible solutions and what shortcomings remain even after such solutions have been applied. Although the military itself constitutes the object of some research (e.g. assessments of how headquarter structures operate or how soldiers react to stress), the bulk of research in conflict environments is focused on the effects of military activities on the operational environment. This chapter focuses on the latter, i.e. research aimed at informing an ongoing intervention.

Tasking: Formulating the research question

Constituting the starting point of research projects, the formulation of research questions is critical. In conflict environments, the military itself often functions as a gatekeeper enabling studies of itself and the effects it generates. The following three aspects are of particular interest: researchers' dependence on the military, the military's limited ability to formulate precise and achievable questions and institutional and personal motivations and drivers determining what questions the military chooses to pursue.

Dependence: Gatekeepers decide what research can be pursued and by whom

A key limitation researchers in conflict environments face is to obtain access to the research object. Whoever controls access can determine what research questions may be effectively pursued, by whom and by what means. At home, researchers may circumvent limitations in access imposed by the military by contacting military staff directly. In hostile environments, access is much more limited and controlled. Unless foreign researchers engaged in the geographical area prior to the conflict (for this see e.g. Giustozzi 2009), it is likely that they will depend on other institutions to facilitate physical access and provide costly security arrangements. Normally, government agencies and IGOs, including the military, or NGOs, think tanks and the like provide such entry. Local researchers, who could potentially operate more independently, are often drawn to these institutions too, not least for financial reasons. As a result, these gatekeepers fund, facilitate and in one way or another control the bulk of research.

Despite this, there are also several international studies that were carried largely without depending on such outside support. In Afghanistan many of such studies focused on the insurgency (see e.g. Giustozzi 2009; Van Bijlert 2009; Farrell and Giustozzi 2013).

In general dependence does not simply mean that researchers are less free in determining research questions. More often than not, the gatekeepers determine both the research agenda and select what researchers they will task (fund). As a result, most research is demand-driven and little, if any, primary research conducted independently without direct support from the gatekeepers, each one of which pursues its own interests. While this also applied to HMEP, the programme was designed to support decision-making of an institution that encompassed a large range of military and civilian agencies from several countries. As a result, it pursued research questions in relation to the higher objectives pursued by all agencies, assessing the effect of their combined efforts and thus collective interests.

Clarity: Gatekeepers are often not proficient in commissioning research

The clients' limited ability to formulate clear and achievable research questions is another concern. One reason for this is that most military staff do not have research backgrounds and are used to task subordinates who are equally methodologically illiterate and uncritical. It is very common that researchers are provided with a general topic rather than with clear terms of reference and a specific research question.

The rotation of personnel, resulting in limited expertise, is another weakness. Those formulating terms of reference and commissioning research tend to spend a limited amount of time in theatre. If they return to theatre, they rarely do so in the same capacity. This means that many are inexperienced in their specific new role and have limited knowledge about what the organisation already knows.

As other researchers, the HMEP team had to spend much time negotiating with the client to establish clear and achievable research questions.

Relevance: Gatekeepers have good reason to avoid the most important research questions

Arguably the most serious shortcoming of research in hostile environments is to be found in what research questions are *not* pursued. Most funding for research is linked directly to individual institutions, each one of which makes a specific, but limited, contribution to the overall intervention, and requiring specific decision-making support. At best, questions focus around each funding institution's specific concerns, and aim at improving its contribution. At worst, research supports personal career ambitions and institutional interests. Generally, overarching questions that would be most useful for the combined effort of all involved tend to be ignored. It is for instance rare that comprehensive conflict assessments, outlining the main actors and their interest, conflict dynamics and the resilience of local institutions, are commissioned, let alone repeated and updated at a later stage.[1] This means that the problems the intervention in its entirety is seeking to address are poorly analysed, systematically discussed or understood. In reality, research tends to be compartmentalised and 'solution', rather than 'problem' focused. Institutions tend to focus research on issues directly affecting their activities and rarely ask if or how their activities contribute towards shared strategic aims of the collective of intervening actors, for example towards a resolution of the conflict/problem. The focus tends to be on how they can improve what they do (doing things right), rather than asking, if they are focusing on the right issues (doing the right things). This focus on lower level objectives also means that the vital overarching questions often remain unformulated (OECD 2012: 29; De Coning and Romita 2009: 2; Stabilisation Unit and DCDC 2012: 2).

One reason why organisations avoid questions about whether they 'do the right things' is that they may not like the answer. There is little incentive to fund research that may indicate that efforts make little difference. Quite the contrary, many institutions consciously avoid such questions. It is rare to see the military on operations really embrace these questions, and use findings to intentionally adapt and add more value. This even applies to multinational head-quarters that have been set up and designed to last but a few years, where one might expect institutional interests to be less prevalent.

Another reason is that it is generally difficult for many people and institutions to see their own activities and the environment in which they operate from the outside. One can only assess if the institution pursues the best course of action by looking at it from a position that is somewhat detached from the institution itself. People often find it difficult to look at themselves and their institution through a new lens. The lack of well-developed and documented theories of change makes it even more difficult (Stabilisation Unit and DCDC 2012: 1). Personal incentives reinforce this tendency. Most people like to do a good job, ideally one that their superiors understand and appreciate to gain promotion or other benefits. They will therefore stay in their comfort zone and focus on producing what *their* part of an organisation normally does, can digest, comprehend and appreciate. For the military, this often means that research tasks are formulated based on the interests of a specific subset of organisation, for example a branch of the headquarters.

A third reason can be found in the time lines of such research. Assessing what impacts or what contributions (military) activities make to higher-level objectives normally requires time (Rietjens et al. 2011). However, research that comes to fruition over longer periods, thus, only benefiting successors, is generally avoided. This is not necessarily a result of planned and conscious decisions, but rather because superiors tend to face a number of immediate concerns and questions they want addressed. Thus, daily short-term (tactical) concerns crowd out long-term (strategic) ones. An organisation that rotates on a six monthly basis will understandably view research that takes four months to complete as long-term project. Those that take more than six months are often not even considered, and if they are, they require buy-in from successors to be completed.

The position of HMEP in the PRT is very helpful in this respect. Exploring the progress of a combined effort, rather than that of an individual programme, and in a situation where progress (or failure) cannot be attributed to a single actor, institutional interests played a very limited role in the design of the research framework. While some agencies wanted to add research questions, and some occasionally took issue with findings, HMEP was never told to shy away from exploring any questions.

Improving research by asking basic questions about the problems we seek to solve

In short, research conducted in hostile environments generally takes the commissioning organisation and its activities as a starting point rather than the problem(s) the intervention as a whole is trying to address. It tends to focus on issues that are easily understood by the institution's staff, and normally centres around how the institution can improve what it does (efficiencies) rather than trying to examine if the institution delivers what is most needed (effectiveness), and all of this within relatively short time frames. These limitations do not just shape research questions, but also the research design and the methodologies applied.

To improve the situation, staff in headquarters, ideally supported by researchers, should start with a discussion of what fundamental and basic questions they and their successors collectively need to answer to understand the problem their intervention is trying to address and then work out priorities and who can contribute in what way to answer them over certain periods of time. For HMEP such conversations proved crucial, making long-term research projects more easily achievable, producing data sets spanning over several years, and delivering products that contribute both to a better understanding of the problem and inform strategic decision-making with a view to improving the intervention as a whole.

Research design and planning

Planning and designing research in conflict environments is inherently difficult. Security concerns accentuate most of the uncertainties researchers normally face, at the same time as additional challenges occur.

Lack of baseline data

One considerable hurdle in the design phase is that data generally is scarce, out of date or lacks accuracy (see e.g. Glenn and Gayton 2008). The host nation often has little capacity to generate data and what little exists will be based on uncertain assumptions or extrapolations. In some cases, elements of the host nation government may even have an interest in inaccurate data, as it might decrease their opportunities for rent seeking and possibly even shift the power balance. Population data is a good example. In Afghanistan, for instance, a proper census might potentially change election results.[2] Nevertheless, even without any resistance to produce accurate data, displacement is likely to make population data unreliable. Often older baseline figures are not based on a thorough census either. As a result, circular situations often arise in which the research design is based on assumptions that will be informed and refined by the resulting research findings.

For surveys, for instance, HMEP found it challenging to design a representative sampling frame, as no population data is available. By asking respondents about how many people live in their household/compound, its surveys themselves informed population estimates and refined the sampling frame of subsequent surveys. In short, much research requires considerable collection of primary data, which, especially in the case of quantitative methods, is required for an adequate research design.

When access to data is scarce, the close relationship with gatekeepers offers key advantages. The first advantage is that these institutions tend to be supportive of the research they commission. A crucial form of support is that staff offer their own time for conversations, make documents available as well as share findings and sometimes even the underlying raw data from previous research. Often researchers do not just obtain information from the commissioning institution but also access to staff and data from other partner organisations. A particular feature of conflict environments is that the number of institutions working alongside the military tends to be relatively limited. Most of them are government or IGO funded, often organisationally linked (e.g. in Provincial Reconstruction Teams), generally cooperative and mutually supportive. This means that a large proportion of the pool of existing research and data tends to be readily available for researchers, allowing them to draw on, and constructively add to, existing knowledge. HMEP certainly benefited from being part of this establishment, giving desk officers from other agencies the confidence to apply pragmatic approaches to the sharing of data, often shortcutting cumbersome bureaucratic processes.

Uncertain access to data

The limited and often unpredictable prospects of collecting primary data also pose further constraints. To begin with, the uncertainties related to the changing security situation make it difficult to estimate timelines, methods, required resources and costs for the collection of data. When budgets are fixed, delays and increased costs in the collection phase are likely to eat into the assessment resourcing, and thus the scope and quality of the analysis of the data. Often, the only way to find out what data can be collected, when and how is to try it. It is therefore likely that researchers have to adapt the research plan and design as they experience unforeseeable hinders. In the worst case, research questions have to be adapted.

In reverse, those commissioning and undertaking research often have strong preconceived ideas about what methods of data collection are feasible and reliable. This can lead to a research design that accepts more compromises than needed and that discounts methods that are more sophisticated, before they have even been tested (Mansfield 2013: 12). This was for instance the case for HMEP when exploring ways to study the political economy in the Taliban-controlled desert areas. Here survey techniques proved more promising than expected, and key informants proved more willing to be interviewed than anticipated. As a result, more emphasis could be put on these methodologies and some research questions expanded. Yet, other research questions had to be dropped, either because they were based on preconceived ideas that were proven inapplicable, or because their pursuit would have require more resources and involved more risk.

Where access is limited, researchers either depend on others to provide the security and enable access, for example by accompanying patrols, or they have to rely on local staff for the collection of data (see also Sriram et al. 2009). Both solutions are associated with problems of their own.

Letting internationals collect data

The option of collecting data themselves does not just put the researcher at greater risk. It also influences sample selection, size and biases. The dependence on the provision of security means that dedicated resources (transport or protection) may be re-assigned, thus delaying or completely denying the collection of data during the researcher's time in theatre. It is rare that security resources are exclusively devoted to ensure that a particular research project can be conducted as planned. Normally, research is added to patrol movements that primarily pursue other tasks, while facilitating some research. This makes any random and representative samples, for example in the case of interviews, impossible. Instead, sampling points (and respondents) are often selected based on where opportunities arise. The method also effects what sample size can be collected. It is certainly impossible to select samples randomly in this way, which excludes quantitative approaches. That is not to say that qualitative approaches are inappropriate or fail to add value. Just as quantitative methods, they do nevertheless have limitations. While adding much narrative and explanations, one should not treat such findings as representative for the population as a whole. Researchers also need to be aware of how the presence of an armed escort, or in some cases even armed researchers, is likely to influence interviewees' responses (social desirability bias). This approach clearly limits what questions can reasonably be asked. For instance, it is highly likely that respondents will express more positive views about accompanying international forces than they would under other circumstances. HMEP only used international staff to conduct selected key informant interviews.

Letting local staff collect data

The use of local staff for collection of data may overcome some of the constraints mentioned above, but the dependency on intermediaries creates new worries. Duty of care is an important factor easily overlooked. While local researchers may have better access to sources than international staff, they may also be more dependent on the extra income the collection generates. Those commissioning researchers must therefore not put undue pressure on local nationals to take unnecessary risks. It is also important to ensure that local collectors can contact researchers, possibly via an intermediary, in case they run into problems with government authorities or international forces. HMEP used local staff extensively, and exclusively for quantitative interviews.

In reverse, local collectors have strong incentives to avoid risks by fabricating data, collecting it in different locations or from different people, or by different means than intended. A rigorous validation framework is therefore essential. However, even when balancing risks adequately and operating with honest and willing local nationals, researchers should run pilot studies to establish what collection methods are likely to work. To ensure the best possible outcome, one should first test the preferred collection framework, for example random sampling, and then adapt ambitions. Too ambitious collection methods are likely to force local nationals into dishonesty.

Researchers are likely to find it challenging to find qualified local staff, especially in societies with low literacy levels. The most qualified segment of the population is generally in full time employment (often working for internationals) and not available for *ad hoc* work or unwilling to undertake it. If one could draw on this group of people, for example teachers, research would generate unintended negative consequences, for example by undermining education efforts. Thus, the recruitment pool of sufficiently qualified people is often limited. This means that the qualification standards may have to be lowered or that people have to be brought in from other geographical areas. Both are likely to influence the quality of the collection. The former, because staff will have limited ability to adhere to given instructions and document findings, the latter because non-locals often do not have the same access to contested geographical areas or key informants. Training sessions that convey an understanding of methods and offer the opportunity to practice the collection are essential. Digressions from instructions may well result from lacking knowledge rather than from a conscious choice to cheat. However, training is unlikely to fully compensate for a lack of basic schooling. Delivering and monitoring such training is often impeded by cultural and language barriers. In general, it is also difficult to find local staff with the experience and qualifications to manage collection teams, again somewhat reducing the quality of the collection and recording processes, and possibly of the data provided.

Gatekeepers are willing to take risks and accept research constraints

While institutions commissioning research are generally well aware of all these constraints and challenges, they are not necessarily discouraged by them. Many are willing to take the risk of commissioning research that may not be possible to undertake, and to adapt ambitions to what is possible as limitations become apparent. Not only is there a greater need for flexibility regarding collection methods, coverage, methods of analysis, timings and sometimes even regarding an adaptation of the research question for research in conflict environments. It is probably more prevalent too. HMEP was certainly allowed to explore what research was feasible.

Collection of data: When the plan hits reality

As indicated above, researchers in conflict environments must expect and prepare for disruptions during the collection phase, often created by security or logistical challenges. It is important to offer collectors alternative approaches, such as alternative sampling points or methods they can use to obtain the data sought if the initial plan fails. This does not just require that alternatives are thought of in advance, but also that researchers are in continuous contact with collectors and clients to agree on alterations and to undertake corrections. All changes must also be recorded as they influence the data set and how it can reasonably be used.

Independent validation is essential

If researchers themselves do not collect data, independent processes validating the collection methods are required. This is particularly important if contracted local nationals or subcontracted organisations undertake the collection. In absence of control measures, incentives to 'cheat' are likely to outweigh advantages gained from adhering to a rigorous collection process. HMEP's experience from the field demonstrates that businesses have limited incentives to set up appropriate (and costly) internal validation processes and to detect and reveal more than marginal shortcomings. As there are often few or no alternative providers, researchers do well not to trust arguments that the provision of a quality product is in the business own long-term interest. It is worth noting, however, that the mere existence of an independent validation procedure is likely to reduce fraudulent behaviour.

Taking survey techniques as an example, conventional validation techniques are often easier to use than technical solutions. While GPS phones or other technologies can track interviewers' movements effectively, HMEP could not use such equipment as it would endanger interviewers and mark them out as collaborators with the international community. The preferred conventional validation method consists of call backs, where validators contact a respondent after the interview to confirm that the interview took place and ideally by asking a set of control questions from the survey questionnaire. To allow for such call backs, one must either obtain respondents' contact details (which they may not be willing to provide) or opt for selection procedures that, if repeated, would identify the same respondent. The most common approach is to use the accommodation as a selection criteria (house or compound) and a clear raster defining who in the household should be interviewed. Physical call-back visits can validate both the application of the selection criteria and that the interview took place. Results from the validation will inform decisions on how the obtained data can reasonably be used and what conclusions can be drawn from it. In some cases small adjustments may be sufficient, while a complete re-collection of data may be required in others.

Delays

Delays in the collection are common. It is therefore important that a system is set up in which the collected data is recorded and entered into a database straight after they have been obtained during the collection phase. This will ensure that collection issues are identified early, for example misunderstandings regarding how interviews should be recorded or conducted, allowing for adjustments and possible recollection in time. If research findings are to inform decisions at a particular time, researchers can also use the already available data to a certain extent to draw preliminary conclusions and refine them, once the full data set has been received.

Language barriers

Language barriers and translation issues may also come to bear during the collection phase. The most obvious problem with translations is that researchers often lack the language skills to undertake the translation itself or judge its quality. Perfect translations do not exist. Even when performed by highly skilled professionals they cause friction and require some interpretation and compromise. This is why a re-translation rarely results in the original wording. The people used for translation services in support of researchers in conflict environments are normally not trained professional translators and are not in full command of English. As a result there is more room for misunderstandings, misinterpretations and over simplifications. Researchers need to take this into account when designing questionnaires and offer explanations, ensuring that instructions are clear, simple and unambiguous. Moreoever, they need to resist the temptation to over interpret responses and nuances, in order to reach more distinct conclusions and recommendations.

Managing the above risks for text translations is relatively easy. Researchers should draw on a team of translators that control and proof read all material. Regarding oral translations, risks for mistakes are generally higher. Normally translators have less time for reflection and reach the point of exhaustion faster. In such cases recordings of conversations prove very useful, as they capture how questions have been translated and record full answers, not just translated ones. HMEP found an increase in quality if others than those interpreting during an interview produced transcripts.[3]

Assessment: Verification and triangulation of results

The challenges outlined above limit the confidence researchers can have in collected data and in validity of the conclusions drawn based on it. As in other areas, researchers should always seek to verify results drawing on data and information from a range of sources. However, the scarcity of data often makes this particularly difficult in conflict environments (Stabilisation Unit and DCDC 2012: 2). It also increases the risk of so-called circular reporting, as other, seemingly independent sources, often draw on the same source. Population data is a good example. In the absence of reliable and up-to-date census data, many institutions undertake efforts to model population figures. However, almost all of them will take what official data there is as a starting point and partially base calculations on the same data set. This means that the flaws contained in the official data transpires all demographic estimates which comparisons are unlikely to reveal.

Frequently, resourcing prevents the collection of additional data for 'triangulation'. This may invite researchers to seek validation of their results in similar exercises run by others. Again, survey research offers a good example. Often survey data from one organisation is compared with that from another covering the same geographical area. This comparison is all the more attractive, if the questionnaire design is similar, making a comparison of results relatively easy. While interesting and useful, this approach offers limited scope for proper validation, partially because the method used to obtain the data is too similar, and partially because such data tends to be delivered by the same provider. Nevertheless, HMEP found that more rigorous alternatives sometimes prove difficult as other, independent qualitative or quantitative research is unlikely to examine the same questions in the same area during the same period.

Even if such alternatives exist, researchers may not be aware of it. Although the willingness to share data has markedly improved over the last decade, classifications combined with a plethora of computer systems that do not speak to each other pose a considerable hindrance (see also Mitchell 2009). Even if researchers have the required clearance and access to workstations, they need to familiarise themselves with and search for information in several differently organised systems. As an example, at least seven separate IT systems are used in the Helmand PRT alone. Short tour lengths often mean that information is saved in an inconsistent manner or that procedures change over time. Consequently, researchers often rely on personal relationships to become aware of research and data that may be useful. These informal relationships also prove most useful for the coordination at the planning stage of research conducted in different organisations.

Another severe limitation is that many organisations only save research reports, not the raw data on which they are based. This is particularly common when the collection and analysis is outsourced. This means that collected information that could have proven useful is not available.

In the end, researchers in conflict environments often have to rely on single source or 'similar' source data than those in more stable environments. At the same time, proper 'triangulation' is arguably even more desirable in conflict zones than elsewhere due to the increased uncertainty during the collection phase (UNDP 2009: 110).

One core problem researchers face is the trade-off between validation and triangulation of findings on the one hand and the timely delivery of the analysis on the other. For research intended to inform decision-making, the timely delivery will normally weigh heaviest. In that case, researchers need to take particular care to emphasise the limitations of their approach.

Presentation of results: Methodological illiteracy and dangerous products

The presentation of results is arguably just as important as the findings themselves. At best, the message is easily understood, tailored to the audience's information needs and convincing (Jans 2014, Chapter 3 this volume). At worst, products can be misleading or misinterpreted. Problems arise both on the side of researchers and on the side of audiences.

Misleading presentation of results

Military staff produce much research in theatre themselves. By no fault of their own, many of these professionals have but rudimentary methodological knowledge, which influences the quality of products. A common problem is the confusion of qualitative and quantitative approaches. Like others, the branches of intelligence, information operations, psychological operations and other military staff are often interested in representative statistics on the population's perceptions, behaviour or other socioeconomic data (see also Rietjens et al. 2011). Thus, questionnaires are devised and put to the local population by patrols or uniformed specialists accompanying them. Results are then processed in headquarters and presented in the form of graphs outlining what proportion of the population has what characteristic.

While understandable and tempting, this approach is problematic for two reasons. To start with, sample sizes tend to be limited and the selection is rarely random. This means that the confidence levels achieved are low and the margins of error high. Hence, without knowing it, military staff often present results that are very unreliable and by no means representative. Identifying trends over time based on such data is impossible. Changing the intervention based on such loose data is irresponsible, not to say dangerous.

Moreover, the temptation to produce quantitative data means that the opportunity to undertake qualitative research that can offer important explanations, narratives, ideas and insights is missed (Glenn and Gayton 2008). In short, considerable resources are allocated and risks taken to produce useless data, and chances to collect data offering further critical insights are wasted.

More methodologically proficient researchers also find themselves forced to simplify findings. Results are often ambiguous, with conflicting narratives and different variables pointing in different directions and displaying geographical and other variations. Hence, researchers not only have to choose what relationships in a data set they explore, but also which of the results they present and how. Properly caveating findings, for example with probabilities or methodological limitations, is also challenging as most decision-makers find it difficult to properly make sense of them. Generally, the question is not so much about what researchers present, but also what they leave out and why.

Clients' unrealistic demands and misinterpretation

Understandably, decision-makers can be frustrated when presented with too many caveats when they want clear answers. Rather than having to make sense of all findings themselves, they often prefer researchers to tell them what the findings 'really' mean. Hence, researchers can feel pressured to present clear and simple recommendations to prove 'useful'. The problem is that research into complicated (and interesting) questions, such as how best to improve local security or how to generate support for host nation security forces, is based on models and simplifications that need explaining, adding to the caveats outlined in the paragraph above. In addition, one can rarely infer causality with full certainty from the facts examined when studying questions relating to such higher-level objectives. While researchers can establish associations between different variables and assume what changes have or would contribute to a certain development, findings remain uncertain (DFID 2012: 38), again adding to the caveats. As outlined above, it is rarely practical for researchers to outline all limitations of their research in presentation material. When choosing what caveats and limitations to include, they should bear in mind they risk taking on the decision-making function themselves, without the client's knowledge, if they do not make key limitations and assumptions clear.

Given that the amount of research produced in conflict environments remains very limited, and that decision-makers have little time, they have a tendency to disregard caveats and to use whatever data and findings are available. The argument 'some data is better than no data', frequently results in an overreliance and trust in data and findings that is inappropriate.

One way out of this dilemma is to ensure that research projects focus on a single research question broken down into explicit sub-questions, and to examine it using different approaches. Such focus studies are likely to generate results that are more reliable and prove more useful. However, this requires the client to be precise in their terms of reference, to have the courage to, and take the responsibility for focusing resources on a particular issue, thus, disregarding other interesting questions.

Conclusion: Improving research of the military in conflict environments

Many common research challenges are exacerbated in conflict environments. While most external factors lie beyond the influence of researchers (although their findings may bring about positive change), they have to adapt to the restrictions posed by insecurity. However, researchers and their military gatekeepers can achieve much by improving their relationship. Assuming that the research ultimately seeks to improve the intervention (rather than pursuing institutional or personal interests), some simple changes would be particularly beneficial.

The commissioning of research should be centralised within headquarters to ensure a sensible allocation of research resources. This should involve discussion across headquarters about what questions are relevant. In a first step, the headquarters needs to establish what it (and its successors) collectively needs to know about the conflict their campaign is to address. A better understanding of the problem lays the foundation for an improved intervention logic. In a second step, they need to think about how research can contribute towards testing and refining their theory of change and earlier research findings.

Researcher advisers should be involved in this process from the start to elaborate on what key questions can reasonably be pursued, how, following what time lines and to what costs. Based on these considerations and on what is already known, a priority list of research questions can be produced, each one broken down into sub-questions, and the collection and analysis resourced (including military means). This more systematic approach to research would ensure clearer tasking throughout the organisation and that research projects collectively could be aggregated into a more useful whole.

This would increase clarity of the aim of research, improve its focus to what is most relevant and ensure that good use is made of the resources available.

Notes

1 Exceptions to this are the periodic civilian assessments that were carried out by the Liaison Office in Uruzgan Province (see e.g. TLO 2009, 2010; Rietjens 2011).
2 The last official, but incomplete, population census in Afghanistan was undertaken in 1979. Although mentioned in the Bonn Agreement in 2001, a full census had still not taken place by 2012. The Afghanistan Population and Housing Census (APHC) was cancelled and replaced by a Socio-Demography and Economic Survey (SDES), rolled out in 2011 and planned to be completed in 2014.
3 For more information on the use of interpreters, see e.g. Van Dijk et al. 2010.

References

Church, C. and M.M. Rogers (2006). *Designing for Results: Integrating Monitoring and Evaluation in Conflict Transformation Programs*. Washington: SFCG. Available at: http://www.sfcg.org/programmes/ilt/ilt_manualpage.html.

De Coning, C. and P. Romita (2009). *Monitoring and Evaluation of Peace Operations*. New York: International Peace Institute.

DFID (2012). Broadening the range of designs and methods for impact evaluation. Working Paper 38. Available at: www.gov.uk/government/uploads/system/uploads/attachment_data/file/67427/design-method-impact-eval.pdf

Farrell, T. and A. Giustozzi (2013). 'The Taliban at war: Inside the Helmand insurgency, 2004–2012'. *International Affairs*, 89(4): 845–871.

Giustozzi, A. (ed.) (2009). *Decoding the New Taliban: Insights from the Afghan Field*. New York: Columbia University Press.

Glenn, R.W. and S.J. Gayton (2008). *Intelligence Operations and Metrics in Iraq and Afghanistan*. Washington, DC: National Defense Research Institute.

Jans, N. (2014). 'Getting on the same net: How the theory-driven academic can better communicate with the pragmatic military client'. In: J.M.M.L. Soeters, P.M. Shields, and S.J.H. Rietjens (eds) *Routledge Handbook of Research Methods in Military Studies*. Abingdon: Routledge.

The Liaison Office (TLO) (2009). *Three Years Later: A Socio-Political Assessment of Uruzgan Province from 2006–2009*. Kabul: TLO.

The Liaison Office (TLO) (2010). *The Dutch Engagement in Uruzgan: 2006–2010, A TLO Socio-Political Assessment*. Kabul: TLO.

Mansfield, D. (2013). All bets are off! Prospects for (b)reaching agreements and drug control in Helmand and Nangarhar in the run up to transition: Afghanistan Research and Evaluation Unit Case Study Series. Available at: www.areu.org.af/UpdateDownloadHits.aspx?EditionId=621&Pdf=1302%20Opium%2023%20Jan-Final.pdf.

Mitchell, P.T. (2009). *Network Centric Warfare and Coalition Operations: The New Military Operating System.* London: Routledge.

OECD (2012). *Evaluating Peacebuilding Activities in Settings of Conflict and Fragility: Improving Learning for Results.* DAC Guidelines and References Series, OECD Publishing. Available at: http://dx.doi.org/10.1787/9789264106802-en.

Rietjens, S.J.H., J.M.M.L. Soeters and W. Klumper (2011). 'Measuring the immeasurable?: The effects-based approach in comprehensive peace operations'. *International Journal of Public Administration,* 34(5): 329–338.

Rietjens, S.J.H. (2011). 'Between expectations and reality: The Dutch engagement in Uruzgan'. In: Hynek, N. and P. Marton (eds) *Statebuilding in Afghanistan: Multinational Contributions to Reconstruction.* London: Routledge, pp. 65–87.

Sriram, C.L., J.C. King, J.A. Mertus, O. Martin-Ortega and J. Herman (eds) (2009). *Surviving Field Research: Working in Violent and Difficult Situations.* Abingdon: Routledge.

Stabilisation Unit and Development, Concepts and Doctrine Centre (DCDC) (2012). *Joint Doctrine Note 2/12, Assessment.* Shrivenham: UK Ministry of Defence.

UNDP (2009). Handbook on planning, monitoring and evaluating for development results. Available at: http://web.undp.org/evaluation/handbook/documents/english/pme-handbook.pdf.

Van Bijlert, M. (2009). 'Unruly commanders and violent power struggles: Taliban networks in Uruzgan.' In: Giustozzi, A. (ed.) *Decoding the New Taliban: Insights from the Afghan Field.* New York: Columbia University Press, pp. 155–178.

Van Dijk, A., J.M.M.L. Soeters and R. de Ridder (2010). 'Smooth translation? A research note on the cooperation between Dutch service personnel and local interpreters in Afghanistan'. *Armed Forces & Society,* 36(5): 917–925.

6

STUDYING HOST-NATIONALS IN OPERATIONAL AREAS

The challenge of Afghanistan

William Maley

M. Van Bijlert (2009) 'Unruly commanders and violent power struggles: Taliban networks in Uruzgan', in Antonio Giustozzi (ed.), *Decoding the New Taliban: Insights from the Afghan Field*. London: Hurst and Co., pp. 155–178.

Decoding the New Taliban puts on display a number of approaches to understanding post-nationals in Afghanistan, from which militaries could readily profit. Two of the contributors to this edited collection have military experience of their own, but of very different kinds. Dr David Kilcullen, now a well-known writer on counterinsurgency and author of *The Accidental Guerrilla*, was formerly a lieutenant-colonel in the Australian Army. On the other hand, Mohammad Osman Tariq Elias was a *mujahid* in the Afghan resistance in the 1980s. All the other contributors are long-standing observers of Afghanistan who can claim the kind of familiarity with the situation on the ground that is often denied to those who see the country only on short-term rotations. As an edited collection, the book puts on display different interpretations of both the circumstances leading to the re-emergence of the Taliban, and the significance of this particular phenomenon. In this way, it allows for the kind of contestation of ideas that can allow knowledge to build up. The editor has set out not to impose a particular line of argument upon his contributors, but rather to find contributors who will have interesting arguments to advance.

Martine van Bijlert's study of Taliban networks in Uruzgan provides a good example of how one can go about navigating the methodological complexities of studying host-nationals in Afghanistan. The fundamental technique that she has used is what one might call *immersion*: as she puts it, the analysis in the chapter 'is based on conversations over a period of several years with tribal leaders, commanders, villagers, government officials and NGO workers, who either are from Uruzgan or spent considerable time working in the province'. Two elements are central to such an approach. One is *linguistic skill*. Bijlert, a former Dutch diplomat, has an excellent command of Afghan languages. The other is *time*. In contrast to some military personnel whose efforts to study

(continued)

(continued)

host-nationals have been hampered by short postings, this author has been able not only to accumulate a substantial knowledge base, but also to establish trusting relationships with local informants in a way that can be difficult for militaries who are perceived as players in local politics by virtue of the power that they can exercise.

Beyond the technique of immersion, van Bijlert displays one other skill that is of critical importance, namely an ability to conceptualise. A real challenge in studying host-nationals in Afghanistan is that one can be overwhelmed by an avalanche of information which can hinder rather than assist understanding. On the one hand, she makes effective use of terms that Afghans in Uruzgan themselves deploy to characterise their social worlds. On the other, she makes equally effective use of Western terms such as revenge, rivalry and opportunity to explain Taliban behaviour.

Introduction

The study of host-nationals in Afghanistan raises a number of serious issues for the military. If one accepts the Clausewitzian understanding of strategy as the harnessing of military force to the realisation of political objectives, then an understanding of the context – social, political, and economic – within which political objectives are located becomes essential if the objectives of a military deployment are to be realised. Yet the skills that may be required in order to undertake the kind of analysis that this involves often do not figure prominently in the curricula of military academies, and may require an understanding of the complexities of social anthropology that even a highly skilled scholar may struggle to attain. All this creates for military forces a major set of challenges. And in few theatres of operation can these challenges have been more acute than in Afghanistan.

One of the reasons why this is the case is that Afghans typically live simultaneously in a number of different social worlds. The world that they choose to inhabit can shift on a daily basis, depending upon the incentive structures by which people are confronted. Thus, even analyses which pay lip-service to familiar bases of social organisation that are typically discussed in the Afghan context, such as tribe, ethnic identity, sectarian identity, gender, class, or physical location, can do less than justice to the way in which individuals trying to survive in a hostile environment can shift their affiliations or manipulate their identities as a way of securing some degree of protection. As a result, host-nationals in Afghanistan should not be considered in any respect a fixed category. Rather, they take on a kaleidoscopic character that reflects the shifting foundations of Afghan politics and society. The aim of this chapter is to explore some of the dimensions of these complexities.

Objectives of studying host-nationals

The inclination to study host-nationals is very much a product of particular forms of modern armed conflict. Ruth Benedict's famous study *The Chrysanthemum and the Sword* (Benedict 1946), based on an analysis during the Second World War of Japanese writings, provides a notable early example. Where set-piece battles are fought between organised military forces, the citizens or residents of the countries in which the battles are being fought often appear as little more than extras in the performance, peripheral to the outcomes of the battles themselves. Such battles, however, by no means exhaust the range of activities for modern militaries in the territories in which they are deployed. More and more conflicts since the end of the Second World War have pitted insurgents, resistance movements, or other armed groups against professional uniformed militaries, often in circumstances in which the asymmetries of 'hard' power are manifest, and the real struggle is a political one for the loyalty and support of the population at large. This was particularly the case in such well-known conflicts as the Chinese Civil War in the years before the fall of Peking in 1949, and the phase of the Vietnam War that concluded with the fall of Saigon in 1975. In each of these cases, substantial and well-organised armed forces had very significant roles to play, but ordinary people also played important roles in shaping the outcomes of the struggles. A key consequence has been a proliferation of serious scholarly and military literature concerned with guerrilla warfare, counterinsurgency, and the ways in which the 'hearts and minds' of target populations can be won (see Kaplan 2013). This requires attention to the peculiarities of local populations that generals of earlier times could safely overlook. But that said, host-nationals can be studied with a number of different objectives in mind, of which five are particularly important.

First, host-nationals may be studied simply with a view to *gathering information* relating to their beliefs, affiliations, and character. There is no doubt that information of this kind can potentially be of considerable benefit to military forces, but the danger that obviously arises is that there may be an almost infinite range of data-points that must somehow be processed to make them meaningful. Here, it is useful to bear in mind the distinction that the philosopher Karl Popper used to draw between the 'bucket' and the 'searchlight' theories of knowledge (Popper 1972: 341–361). The weakness of the former is that it puts the accumulation of data at the centre of the enterprise, whereas as Popper rightly argued, it is theory and theoretical presuppositions that provide the searchlight that allows such a mass of data to be scrutinised, processed and managed. Unless one can make sense of information, it will be of little value.

Second, host-nationals may be studied with a view to facilitating the *exercise of domination* over people, territory or political relations. There are all sorts of respects in which the capacity of militaries to exercise domination is central to the hope of realising military objectives. If populations remain fractious, if territory remains insecure, and if plotting against military forces is a routine activity in the areas in which they are deployed, then the prospects that military force will be able to deliver meaningful political objectives are likely to be poor. Yet it is very difficult to exercise domination over people or in an environment that one does not understand. For this reason, there is at least a threshold level of comprehension that needs to be met if the attempt to work in a complex environment is not to collapse.

Third, one may study host-nationals in order to help *enhance the legitimacy of the deployed forces and their mission*. A legitimate mission – one that enjoys generalised normative support – is more likely to secure cooperation from informed and authoritative locals than is one which is regarded with scepticism. Furthermore, a legitimate mission will be better placed to pursue a range of activities to consolidate what gains have flowed from the use of kinetic force. Yet to build legitimacy, it is necessary to understand what *kinds* of factors are relevant in the eyes of the local population. Skill and speed in the execution of reconstruction projects, for example, will do little to build legitimacy if the key criterion of legitimacy for locals relates to the religious values to which the deployed military forces are committed. There is no substitute for a fine-grained understanding of these complexities.

Fourth, it can be useful to study host-nationals in order to improve one's understanding of what the likely consequences of particular actions might be. For example, in the Afghan province of Uruzgan, Australian forces became strongly involved in supporting a particular militia leader, Matiullah Khan (see Schmeidl 2010; Maley 2011a: 131–132). A closer study of the social environment in which he was operating might have prompted a degree of caution. Matiullah is a member of the Popalzai tribe of Durrani Pushtuns. The favouritism shown to him has had the effect of alienating non-Popalzai Durranis, non-Durranis, and non-Pushtuns alike. While Australian forces remained deployed, the situation was unlikely to spiral out of control, but fireworks are likely as the international presence winds down.

Finally, those militaries that wish ultimately to extract themselves with some dignity from a theatre of operations may find it useful to understand how to co-opt diverse local actors into the wider projects that militaries are seeking to advance (see Kitzen 2012). If this is done success-fully, it may ease the process of exit.

Challenges for the social sciences and humanities

When one embarks on the study of host-nationals, a number of disciplinary approaches are available. One obvious point of departure is provided by the lessons of *political science*. In a narrowly institutional sense, political science may not offer that much to the soldier in the field, although an understanding of the wider political context within which ordinary Afghans position themselves is undoubtedly important. Where political science is valuable in particular is in focusing attention on power relations as a central dimension of people's lives. In highly institutionalised political systems, such as one finds in developed Western democracies, ordinary people may be able to live their lives comfortably without paying too much attention to power relations. In Afghanistan by contrast, where individuals have struggled for decades to cope with the consequences of institutional failure, an understanding of power relations and dynamics is likely to be crucial to people's capacities to navigate the complexities of everyday life. This applies not only to the power relations in particular localities, but also to the complex interac-tions between the centre and periphery in Afghanistan, since formal institutional maps may do little to capture the reality of power exercised on the basis of personal relationships and affinities (see Barfield 2010: 302–311).

In the analysis of social power, *social anthropology* is at least as important a discipline as politi-cal science, and it is perhaps not surprising that a number of the most significant writers on Afghanistan have been anthropologists: Louis Dupree, Pierre Centlivres, Robert Canfield, Nazif Shahrani, Ashraf Ghani, Thomas Barfield, and Alessandro Monsutti. The writings of such schol-ars are perpetually instructive, and a number of them remain major contributors to our under-standing of contemporary Afghanistan. Social anthropology, by focusing on the multifarious interactions of rules, roles, relations and resources, can supply more-nuanced accounts of com-plexity than the macro approach of political science has to offer. The difficulty for social anthro-pologists is that their research methods tend to rely on extensive fieldwork and interaction with the populations that they study. While Afghanistan now provides wonderful opportunities for research of this kind, all too often the perceived risks of allowing young researchers into the field, combined with the difficulty of obtaining insurance to provide them with protection, prompts universities in particular to tread with excessive caution when considering whether to give staff or students permission to travel (see Maley 2011b).

Another approach, arguably a subset of social anthropology, involves the detailed study of *culture*. The idea of culture is a complex one, and embraces not only beliefs that are held within a population – mythological, religious, ideological, historical or scientific – but also the embodi-ment of beliefs in literature, tradition and conventions, norms and rules. Since 2001, both qualitative and survey analyses have provided valuable insights into the beliefs and attitudes of ordinary Afghans, Nonetheless, because the idea of culture is complex, it needs to be handled with caution when one is attempting to explain social and political behaviour. First, it is dan-gerous to assume that the shape of social and political institutions is simply an outgrowth of pre-existing cultural patterns. In the real world, a range of causal factors can contribute to the shape which institutions take, and culture is only one of these (Pateman 1971). Second, all too frequently one encounters analyses which looked at the behaviour of political actors as evidence of culture. This runs the risk of contaminating with circularity one's attempted explanation of behaviour: if one is seeking to explain behaviour, one cannot do so by reference to an explanatory variable of which behaviour is an element. Third, within any given territory, there may be a multiplicity of cultural patterns on display. This is certainly the case in Afghanistan, with over 50 identified ethnic groups (see Orywal 1986; Schetter 2003), and many other cross-cutting bases of networking and stratification. This can make the use of a single 'cultural advisor' somewhat perilous, no matter how insightful a particular individual may be (see Sieff 2013).

Since beliefs and attitudes tend to be communicated in natural language, there is much to be gained through the study of the *semantics of the languages of host-nationals*. This is particularly a problem for militaries, since the interpreters whom they are typically in a position to recruit may well be competently bilingual for the discussion of most routine matters, but need not necessarily have much sense of the complex cultural scripts that can pervade the subtleties of linguistic interaction (see Wierzbicka 1997, 1999; Goddard 2011). Afghan languages are rich with metaphor, allusion, and embodied cultural mores (Kieffer 2011), and can usefully be mined to shed light on the complexities of the micro-societies in which they are used. Interpreters can also have interests of their own to protect, and these can distort messages in both directions. There is no easy solution to this problem, but it pays to bear it in mind.

Finally, one should never lose sight of the importance of what Michael Polanyi called 'tacit knowledge'. As Polanyi famously put it, 'we can know more than we can tell' (Polanyi 1966: 4). The capacity of the mind to integrate in a subliminal fashion a whole range of data-points underpins this insight. In this vein, the eminent political scientist T.H. Rigby counselled that one should never underestimate the value of simply wandering around to pick up the 'smell and feel' of a situation. But that said, this is not a capacity that comes readily to beginners. It is readily detectable in specialists on Afghanistan who have spent years studying the country and its people. It is much harder to inculcate in a young soldier on his or her first deployment, especially if security concerns throw up barriers to interaction with ordinary people. Here, the impact of so-called 'green on blue attacks' stretches well beyond the immediate victims: by eroding trust, such attacks undermine the ability of foreign soldiers to get to know the people with whom they are working.

The burden of history

Hegel's warning that the owl of Minerva spreads its wings only when dusk is falling highlights the dangers of seeking to learn too much from history. Nonetheless, history can be a useful companion when one seeks to make sense of complex circumstances that confront one in unfamiliar environments. But that said, the so-called 'lessons of history' do not come neatly packaged. Indeed, Sir Karl Popper famously observed that history has no meaning, but he went on to say that we can give it a meaning (Popper 1966: vol. 2: 278). The challenge is to make sure that we do not draw erroneous lessons or rely on false analogies (see Khong 1992).

Afghanistan is unfortunate to have been oversupplied by its history with analogies that can easily mislead. Its history is one littered with military encounters. The cover of a recently published (and estimable) book states that the 'so-called first war of the twenty-first century actually began more than 2,300 years ago when Alexander the Great led his army into what is now a sprawling ruin in northern Afghanistan' (Holt 2012). The nineteenth century witnessed a number of military encounters between Afghan and foreign forces that have shaped perceptions of the Afghan theatre of operations to this day. The First and Second Anglo-Afghan Wars of 1839–1842 and 1879–1880 seem in particular to have left a substantial burden of preconceptions and images that can surface with little notice in Staff College presentations on Afghanistan and in lectures by military historians. On a number of occasions, this writer has sat through such lectures awaiting with mounting trepidation the inevitable resort to the verse of Rudyard Kipling: 'When you're wounded and left on Afghanistan's plains . . . '. There is of course no harm in learning the history of earlier wars in Afghanistan, but one needs to show appropriate caution. Robert Johnson, concluding an excellent study of Afghanistan's military history, warns that 'we should be extremely circumspect of the historical record as a means to glean lessons for current operations' (Johnson 2012: 301).

In particular, there are dangers in adopting approaches to Afghanistan which mirror the worst excesses of Orientalism. The idea of Orientalism is a complex one (Said 1978; Barkawi and Stanksi 2012), but at its most basic it involves reducing complex actors to stereotypical 'others' to whom notions of rationality are alien given the potency of the raw emotions and drives that are seen as shaping their behaviour. Such thinking can prompt analyses of the most spurious kind. For example, the conflict between 1992 and 1995 that caused ruinous damage to the southern suburbs of Kabul was frequently depicted as an inexplicable upsurge of ethnic hostility, profoundly irrational, and evidence that Afghans were congenitally prone to the reckless use of violence as a way of achieving their objectives. One writer described it as a 'vicious squabble' (Fergusson 2010: 9), as if the conflicting parties were ill-disciplined children. But such an interpretation was always suspect (see Maley 2009: 162), and a recent meticulous study shows how the behaviours of the various combatant parties were strongly political in character and reflected a high degree of rationality (Christia 2012: 57–100).

Orientalist views of Afghanistan do the country a disservice by depicting it as frozen in time, with any attempt at moving forward doomed to inevitable failure. Those who cleave to this view may well be influenced by the well-documented failure of communist modernisers in the late 1970s to have any positive effect on the environment in which they were working. This, however, is an unfortunate analogy, which de-authenticates the current generation of young Afghan modernisers who are very different from their predecessors. The modernisers of the 1970s were driven by a crude variant of Marxist ideology. By contrast the modernisers of the twenty-first century are very much a product of globalisation. Processes of globalisation have affected Afghanistan more dramatically than virtually any other country in the world. Below the surface, Afghanistan is experiencing profound changes. An Asia Foundation survey in 2012 found that 80 per cent of respondents had a functioning radio in their households, 71 per cent a mobile phone, and 52 per cent a television, with television access reaching 40 per cent even in rural areas (Asia Foundation 2012: 171). Furthermore, as of 2010, an estimated 68.3 per cent of the population was under the age of 25 (Afghan Public Health Institute 2011: 19). Militaries would do well to avoid images of Afghans as white-bearded tribal leaders disconnected from the wider world.

Human terrain analysis

One approach to the study of host-nationals has been embodied in the so-called 'human terrain system' (HTS). In an article published in the *Military Review* in 2005, McFate and Jackson argued that the US Department of Defense 'should create and house an organization of social scientists having strong connections to the services and combatant commands. The organization should act as a clearinghouse for cultural knowledge, conduct on-the-ground ethnographic field research, provide reachback to combatant commanders, design and conduct cultural training;

and disseminate knowledge to the field in a useable form' (McFate and Jackson 2005: 20). An initial pilot study was followed by the deployment to Afghanistan of a first team in February 2007, and in 2010 the programme was made permanent. The achievements of the human terrain system are difficult to assess: there has been no serious, comprehensive open-source appraisal of its achievements. Two major problems, however, severely compromised the human terrain team approach.

First, the impetus to develop a human terrain system for Afghanistan ran into major difficulties in the sphere of professional ethics. Like many social sciences, the discipline of anthropology has developed an elaborate code of ethics to govern the responsibilities of members of the anthropology profession in their dealings with the subjects of their research. Shortly after the first human terrain teams were deployed in Afghanistan, the American Anthropological Association issued a statement criticising the Human Terrain System Project. The statement raised a number of concerns, but three were particularly potent. First, it noted that 'anthropologists work in a war zone under conditions that make it difficult for those they communicate with to give "informed consent" without coercion, or for this consent to be taken at face value or freely refused'. Second, it noted that as members of HTS teams, 'anthropologists provide information and counsel to U.S. military field commanders. This poses a risk that information provided by HTS anthropologists could be used to make decisions about identifying and selecting specific populations as targets of U.S. military operations either in the short or long term'. Third, it noted that because 'HTS identifies anthropology and anthropologists with U.S. military operations, this identification – given the existing range of globally dispersed understandings of U.S. militarism – may create serious difficulties for, including grave risks to the personal safety of, many non-HTS anthropologists and the people they study' (American Anthropological Association 2007; see also Forte 2011). All these propositions could be debated, but they proved sufficient to scare many professional anthropologists away from any engagement with the program.

Second, declining security in Afghanistan has made it harder for human terrain teams to operate with any degree of safety, or without endangering their interlocutors (Gezari 2009). To the extent that human terrain teams become associated in the minds of ordinary Afghans with wider military operations, the likelihood diminishes that ordinary people will cooperate actively with the teams if the ultimate outcome of the struggle for Afghanistan's future remains uncertain. Furthermore, lives have been tragically lost within the teams themselves. In 2008, Michael Vinay Bhatia, a fine scholar with an excellent record of research (see Bhatia 2007; Bhatia 2008; Bhatia and Sedra 2008) was killed when the vehicle in which he was travelling struck an improvised explosive device in Khost. And in November 2008, Paula Loyd was doused with petrol and set on fire in the village of Chehel Gazi, and subsequently died of her injuries in January 2009 (Constable 2009). These deaths again have had the effect of undermining the appeal of programmes of this kind for professional anthropologists: there are safer ways in which those interested in Afghan society can pursue their interests.

Intelligence analysis

Another device for enhancing an understanding of host-nationals is military intelligence. This has a very long history in the operations of states, with Queen Elizabeth I having drawn on an expert intelligence service headed by Sir Francis Walsingham. In modern times, intelligence has underpinned the planning of military operations at both strategic and tactical levels, and in addition, resources have been effectively devoted to deception operations and counterintelligence as partners of mainstream intelligence analyses. In a counterinsurgency environment, understanding host-nationals is an important element of intelligence activity, differing from human terrain analysis principally through its reliance on permanent military personnel, whether uniformed or not, in contrast to contracted anthropologists and social scientists. Intelligence information comes in a number of different forms, including 'human intelligence', obtained from human sources, and signals intelligence, obtained through the interception of electronic communications.

While it is difficult to generalise, a critical analysis of US intelligence gathering in Afghanistan suggests that there has been significant room for improvement. In a January 2010 study, Flynn, Pottinger and Batchelor identified a number of systemic flaws in US intelligence capabilities. They opened with the following damning passage:

> Having focused the overwhelming majority of its collection efforts and analytical brainpower on insurgent groups, the vast intelligence apparatus is unable to answer fundamental questions about the environment in which U.S. and allied forces operate and the people they seek to persuade. Ignorant of local economics and landowners, hazy about who the powerbrokers are and how they might be influenced, incurious about the correlations between various development projects and the levels of cooperation among villagers, and disengaged from people in the best position to find answers – whether aid workers or Afghan soldiers – U.S. intelligence officers and analysts can do little but shrug in response to high level decision-makers seeking the knowledge, analysis, and information they need to wage a successful counterinsurgency.
>
> (Flynn et al. 2010: 7)

They also highlight the insidious effects of new means of packaging information:

> The format of intelligence products matters. Commanders who think PowerPoint storyboards and color-coded spreadsheets are adequate for describing the Afghan conflict and its complexities have some soul searching to do. Sufficient knowledge will not come from slides with little more text than a comic strip. Commanders must demand substantive written narratives and analyses from their intel shops and make the time to read them. There are no shortcuts. Microsoft Word, rather than PowerPoint, should be the tool of choice for intelligence professionals in a counterinsurgency.
>
> (Flynn et al. 2010: 23–24)

There are ethical as well as technical concerns surrounding intelligence gathering as well. One recent press report alleges that women taking part in a sewing project were used without their knowledge to pinpoint the locations of Taliban dwellings (Kelly 2013). Such manipulation goes well beyond what would ever be permitted for academic researchers, and may help explain why many observers remain sceptical about the purposes that can motivate military attempts to study host-nationals.

Coping better

The two previous sections paint a somewhat-dispiriting picture of achievement in the area of studying host-nationals in Afghanistan since 2001. While there is no magic solution to the problems that have confronted human terrain analysis and intelligence gathering, there are a number of options available that deserve consideration as ways of improving performance on the ground.

First, longer deployments can enhance the opportunity for soldiers to develop a better understanding of the environment in which they are operating. This proved to be a serious problem with the so-called Provincial Reconstruction Teams (PRTs) in Afghanistan. All too often, it was just at the point where trust was beginning to be established that a scheduled rotation of troops occurred, removing from the theatre of operations the very people that locals had at last been getting to know (Yaqub and Maley 2008: 10–11). Furthermore, short deployments compromise organisational memory, which can be critical for effective organisational performance (Mahler with Casamayou 2009: 205–207).

Second, there is a need for improved education and training for forces deploying to countries such as Afghanistan. A number of military forces have training programmes that incorporate discussion of cultural awareness, but these face a number of problems. There is no single 'Afghan' culture, but rather a range of diverse cultural practices that can be encountered in different parts of the country. As one observer has put it, 'Afghanistan is home to different ethno-linguistic and tribal communities and each group adheres to and cherishes its unique traditions and way of life' (Emadi 2005: 135; see also Nojumi et al. 2009). There is therefore a risk that if, for example, cultural awareness training has been conducted by people familiar with Tajik communities from the north, soldiers will be ill-prepared for deployment in areas where the population is more mixed.

Furthermore, the environment within which cultural awareness training takes place before troops are deployed differs in subtle ways from what they will encounter in the field. The Australian Federal Police, for example, has built an entire village near the headquarters of its International Deployment Group designed to simulate the circumstances that deployed police are likely to encounter when they are sent overseas, and training sometimes includes interaction with migrants and refugees who have come from the country in which the deployment is to occur. But there is an inevitable difference between the approach of those who are recruited to assist such endeavours, and real locals in a country such as Afghanistan. Afghans in Afghanistan are entangled in a complex power game which gives their interactions with international forces a strategic dimension. Foreigners invite manipulation by locals, especially if the foreigners are powerful but lack any deep understanding of what is going on around them. In addition, it is one thing to be told about cultural mores: it is another thing to respect them in practice (Nordland 2012), and if foreign forces are increasingly seen as occupiers rather than liberators or partners, their margin for error in cultural understanding will likely be very narrow.

Third, for reasons that have been obvious since the time of Socrates, it is important that there be structures of analysis that allowed different views about host-nationals to be advanced and contested. The danger in a theatre of operations such as Afghanistan is that information will be stove-piped, and that particular items of received wisdom will acquire a status within organisations and bureaucracies that they do not deserve. Skilled management of operations requires a flexible awareness of the operating environment, and this is not always easy to secure. In part, this is because political leaderships in the United States and within NATO have proved incapable of articulating a clear overarching vision for the mission, leaving personnel on the ground to muddle through in areas where strategic guidance is required. In such circumstances, oversimplified precepts can easily become a substitute for strategic logic. But it also reflects an ineluctable tension between hierarchy as an organisational principle within militaries, and the contest of ideas as a dominant principle within research communities. This is not an easy gap to bridge.

Conclusion

The preceding sections of this chapter have documented a range of challenges in studying host-nationals, both for militaries in general, and for militaries in Afghanistan in particular. Military organisations may not be well trained or well structured to do a good job, and the complexity of the analytical tasks involved may overwhelm even the best of analysts. There are a range of identifiable steps that might be taken to address these problems, but the barriers to taking them may prove significant, and there is always the risk that by the time the need for more effective approaches is recognised, a mission may already be mired in controversy, which provides a less-than-perfect environment for seeking to overcome such deficits.

Is a fine-grained analysis of host-nationals always necessary? Arguably not. Although the idea of common sense is itself a complex one (Rosenfeld 2011), in some circumstances common sense may be all that one needs in order to sense approaching danger, especially at the strategic level, and direct oneself towards wiser pathways. As an example, the circumstances surrounding the US invasion of Iraq in March 2003 come to mind. No one should have been surprised when things began to go awry. Iraq had long been dominated by a Sunni Muslim minority, in a country where the majority of the population consisted of Shiite Muslims. The overthrow of the existing elite, followed by democratisation, required very careful handling. These changes held out the prospect of consigning the former rulers and their sectarian supporters to the position of a permanent minority, in circumstances in which for the new rulers and their associates, the temptation to engage in revenge would be all too understandable given the former regime's abominable record of human rights violations (see Hiltermann 2007). It was therefore blindingly obvious that the former elite would most likely engage in spoiler behaviour, something facilitated by its ready access to the weaponry of the Iraqi armed forces. One simply did not need to be a specialist on the culture, society or politics of Iraq to be able to identify this danger, and it was an indictment of the judgement of US political leaders that they seem not to have given it a moment's thought.

As an act of foolishness, this was on a par with invading Russia as winter approached, the mistake that proved catastrophic for Napoleon in 1812 and Hitler in 1941. And it was by no means an isolated case: the parallels with earlier strategic misjudgements in Vietnam are rather obvious (see Brodie 1973). In the real world, however, choices for armed forces in the field tend to be more complicated, with both risks and opportunities, both costs and benefits, being associated with the various options that one confronts. It is in this world of grey, where one does not enjoy the luxury of black-or-white choices, that the skills required for careful analysis of social complexity come into their own. As long as militaries inhabit a complex world, they will need the mental and analytical tools to cope with such complexity.

References

Afghan Public Health Institute (2011) *Afghanistan Mortality Survey 2010*, Calverton, MD: Afghan Public Health Institute, Central Statistics Organization, ICF Macro, Indian Institute of Health Management Research, and World Health Organization.
American Anthropological Association (2007) *American Anthropological Association's Executive Board Statement on the Human Terrain System Project*, Arlington, VA: American Anthropological Association.
Asia Foundation (2012) *Afghanistan in 2012: A Survey of the Afghan People*, Kabul: The Asia Foundation.
Barfield, T. (2010) *Afghanistan: A Cultural and Political History*, Princeton, NJ: Princeton University Press.
Barkawi, T. and Stanski, K. (eds) (2012) *Orientalism and War*, New York: Columbia University Press.
Benedict, R. (1946) *The Chrysanthemum and the Sword: Patterns of Japanese Culture*, Boston, MA: Houghton Mifflin.
Bhatia, M. (2007) 'The Future of the Mujahideen: Legitimacy, Legacy and Demobilization in Post-Bonn Afghanistan', *International Peacekeeping*, 14(1): 90–107.

Bhatia, M. (ed.) (2008) *Terrorism and the Politics of Naming*, New York: Routledge.

Bhatia, M. and Sedra, M. The (2008) *Afghanistan, Arms and Conflict: Armed Groups, Disarmament and Security in a Post-War Society*, New York: Routledge.

Brodie, B. (1973) *War and Politics*, New York: Macmillan.

Christia, F. (2012) *Alliance Formation in Civil Wars*, Cambridge: Cambridge University Press.

Constable, P. (2009) 'A Terrain's Tragic Shift: Researcher's Death Intensifies Scrutiny of U.S. Cultural Program in Afghanistan', *Washington Post*, 18 February.

Emadi, H. (2005) *Culture and Customs of Afghanistan*, Westport, CT: Greenwood Press.

Fergusson, J. (2010) *Taliban: The True Story of the World's Most Feared Guerrilla Fighters*, London: Bantam Press.

Flynn, M.T., Pottinger, M. and Batchelor, P.D. (2010) *Fixing Intel: A Blueprint for Making Intelligence Relevant in Afghanistan*, Washington, DC: Center for a New American Security.

Forte, M.C. (2011) 'The Human Terrain System and Anthropology: A Review of Ongoing Public Debates', *American Anthropologist*, 113(1): 149–153.

Gezari, V.M. (2009) 'Rough Terrain', *Washington Post*, 30 August.

Goddard, C. (2011) *Semantic Analysis: A Practical Introduction*, Oxford: Oxford University Press.

Hiltermann, J.R. (2007) *A Poisonous Affair: America, Iraq, and the Gassing of Halabja*, Cambridge: Cambridge University Press.

Holt, F.L. (2012) *Into the Land of Bones: Alexander the Great in Afghanistan*, Berkeley and Los Angeles, CA: University of California Press.

Johnson, R. (2012) *The Afghan Way of War: How and Why They Fight*, New York: Oxford University Press.

Kaplan, F. (2013) *The Insurgents: David Petraeus and the Plot to Change the American Way of War*, New York: Simon & Schuster.

Kelly, J. (2013) 'Afghan Women Duped into Spying for NATO', *The Times*, 25 March.

Khong, Y.F. (1992) *Analogies at War: Korea, Munich, Dien Bien Phu, and the Vietnam Decisions of 1965*, Princeton, NJ: Princeton University Press.

Kieffer, C.M. (2011), *Tabous, interdits et obligations de langage en Afghanistan: Éléments du vocabulaire de la vie privée en terre d'Islam*, Wiesbaden: Dr. Ludwig Reichert Verlag.

Kitzen, M. (2012) 'Close Encounters of the Tribal Kind: The Implementation of Co-option as a Tool for De-escalation of Conflict – The Case of the Netherlands in Afghanistan's Uruzgan Province', *Journal of Strategic Studies*, 35(5): 713–734.

McFate, M., and Jackson, A. (2005) 'An Organizational Solution for DOD's Cultural Knowledge Needs', *Military Review*, July August: 18–21.

Mahler, J.G. with Casamayou, M.H. (2009) *Organizational Learning at NASA: The Challenger and Columbia Accidents*, Washington, DC: Georgetown University Press.

Maley, W. (2009) *The Afghanistan Wars*, New York: Palgrave Macmillan.

Maley, W. (2011a) 'PRT Activity in Afghanistan: The Australian Experience', in N. Hynek and P. Marton (eds), *Statebuilding in Afghanistan: Multinational Contributions to Reconstruction*, New York: Routledge.

Maley, W. (2011b) 'Risk, Populism, and the Evolution of Consular Responsibilities', in J. Melissen and A.M. Fernández (eds), *Consular Affairs and Diplomacy*, Leiden: Martinus Nijhoff.

Nojumi, N., Mazurana, D. and Stites, E. (2009) *After the Taliban: Life and Security in Rural Afghanistan*, Lanham, MD: Rowman & Littlefield.

Nordland, R. (2012) 'Culture Clash with Afghans on Display at Briefing', *New York Times*, 6 September.

Orywal, E. (ed.) (1986) *Die ethnischen Gruppen Afghanistans: Fallstudien zu Gruppenidentität und Intergruppenbeziehungen*, Wiesbaden: Dr. Ludwig Reichert Verlag.

Pateman, C. (1971) 'Political Culture, Political Structure and Political Change', *British Journal of Political Science*, 1(3): 291–305.

Polanyi, M. (1966) *The Tacit Dimension*, Chicago, IL: University of Chicago Press.

Popper, K.R. (1966) *The Open Society and its Enemies*, Princeton, NJ: Princeton University Press, vols 1–2.

Popper, K.R. (1972) *Objective Knowledge: An Evolutionary Approach*, Oxford: Oxford University Press.

Rosenfeld, S. (2011) *Common Sense: A Political History*, Cambridge, MA: Harvard University Press.

Said, E. (1978) *Orientalism*, London: Routledge & Kegan Paul.

Schetter, C. (2003), *Ethnizität und ethnische Konflikte in Afghanistan*, Berlin: Dietrich Reimer Verlag.

Schmeidl, S. (2010) *The Man Who Would Be King: The Challenges to Strengthening Governance in Uruzgan*, The Hague: Netherlands Institute of International Relation *Clingendael*.

Sieff, K. (2013) 'Nebraska Kebab-Maker Has Advised Seven U.S. Commanders in Afghanistan', *Washington Post*, 29 March.

Van Bijlert, M. (2009) 'Unruly Commanders and Violent Power Struggles: Taliban Networks in Uruzgan', in Antonio Giustozzi (ed.), *Decoding the New Taliban: Insights from the Afghan Field*, London: Hurst & Co., pp.155–178.

Wierzbicka, A. (1997) *Understanding Cultures through Their Key Words*, New York: Oxford University Press.

Wierzbicka, A. (1999) *Emotions across Languages and Cultures: Diversity and Universals*, Cambridge: Cambridge University Press.

Yaqub, D. and Maley, W. (2008) 'NATO and Afghanistan: Saving the State-Building Enterprise', in Robin Shepherd (ed.), *The Bucharest Conference Papers*, Washington, DC: German Marshall Fund of the United States.

PART II

Qualitative methods

7

HISTORICAL RESEARCH IN THE MILITARY DOMAIN

Floribert Baudet and Eric A. Sibul[1]

Thucydides (1881) *History of the Peloponnesian War*. Translated into English, to which is prefixed an Essay on Inscriptions and a Note on the Geography of Thucydides, Volume 1. B. Jowett translator. Oxford: Clarendon Press.

Some time during the Peloponnesian War (431–404 BC) exiled Athenian general Thucydides (c.460–395) decided to write the history of this fratricidal war between Athens, Sparta (Lacedaemon) and their allies. His work is notable not only for its exploration of human nature as such (exemplified in the Athenian treatment of the Melians) but also for its attempt to establish strict standards in evidence-finding and analysis. As such his work may be considered the first scholarly book on (military) history, although some of his methodology – notably his decision to include fictionalized speeches (expressing what the actor may have said or even should have said) – differs dramatically from what is customary today.

'[1.20] Such are the results of my enquiries, though the early history of Hellas is of a kind which forbids implicit reliance on every particular of the evidence. Men do not discriminate, and are too ready to receive ancient traditions about their own as well as about other countries. (. . .) [3] There are many other matters, not obscured by time, but contemporary, about which the other Hellenes are equally mistaken. For example, they imagine that the kings of Lacedaemon in their council have not one but two votes each, and that in the army of the Lacedaemonians there is a division called the Pitanate division; whereas they never had anything of the sort. So little trouble do men take in the search after truth; so readily do they accept whatever comes first to hand.

[1.21] Yet any one who upon the grounds which I have given arrives at some such conclusion as my own about those ancient times, would not be far wrong. He must not be misled by the exaggerated fancies of the poets, or by the tales of chroniclers who seek to please the ear rather than to speak the truth. Their accounts cannot be tested by him; and most of the facts in the lapse of ages have passed into the region of romance. At such a distance of time he must make up his mind to be satisfied with conclusions resting upon the clearest evidence which can be had . . .

(continued)

(continued)

[1.22] As to the speeches which were made either before or during the war, it was hard for me, and for others who reported them to me, to recollect the exact words. I have therefore put into the mouth of each speaker the sentiments proper to the occasion, expressed as I thought he would be likely to express them, while at the same time I endeavoured, as nearly as I could, to give the general purport of what was actually said. [2] Of the events of the war I have not ventured to speak from any chance information, nor according to any notion of my own; I have described nothing but what I either saw myself, or learned from others of whom I made the most careful and particular enquiry. [3] The task was a laborious one, because eye-witnesses of the same occurrences gave different accounts of them, as they remembered or were interested in the actions of one side or the other. [4] And very likely the strictly historical character of my narrative may be disappointing to the ear. But if he who desires to have before his eyes a true picture of the events which have happened, and of the like events which may be expected to happen hereafter in the order of human things, shall pronounce what I have written to be useful, then I shall be satisfied. My history is an everlasting possession, not a prize composition which is heard and forgotten.'

As transpires from the preceding quotes from what is arguably the first scholarly book on military history, Thucydides' *History of the Peloponnesian War*, since time immemorial soldiers have turned to history to understand war. It is the original discipline to conduct systematic study of military affairs. But, dealing with past events of any type history as a discipline is also inherently broader, and more diverse than the study of any other area of human activity. As such it is different from other fields of military studies and it has developed several peculiarities, methodological and other. These will be the focus of this chapter.

Although other approaches to military affairs have developed since Thucydides wrote his book, military history has endured in value and importance. It serves a broad group of needs and interests that at times may be contradictory. Among other things it forms the foundation for military theory and military doctrine; doctrine is rooted both in theory and history (Vego 2011: 61). While history serves as a foundation for military theory and doctrine guiding future military operations, it does not and cannot predict the future. However, it does provide a methodology for military lessons learned and serves to help understand probable future trends in the warfare and operating environment. The US Joint Force Command's study *Joint Operating Environment 2010* notes, 'As war at its essence is a human endeavor, then it follows that one of the most effective ways to understand human nature is by a close consideration of history. As such, rather than futuristic vignettes, the *Joint Operating Environment* uses history as a principal way to gain insight into the future' (US Joint Forces Command 2010: 5). Historical analysis is useful on all levels of the conflict spectrum from high-intensity conventional war to low intensity stability operations. When faced with a growing insurgency in Iraq, the United States and its coalition partners began to look at 'best practices' in counterinsurgency in order to understand the nature and continuities of insurgencies and what could be judiciously and appropriately applied from historical experiences to defeat the insurgency in Iraq (Sepp 2005: 8).

As military history provides insight into the enduring nature of war as well changes in its character, it is the bedrock of professional military education and professional development for the profession of arms. This is self-evident: physics is not studied without an awareness of Newton, Faraday and Einstein, and the psychologist needs to know who Freud and Jung were and what they thought and did. Advanced professional military education uses historical case studies in much the way that business case studies are used in graduate business education, that is, as a decision-making exercise to build professional judgement (Wyly 1993: 259). After all, 'the human mind is not designed to learn from lists of characteristics, traits, and attributes. Rather, it was designed to learn from experience' (Gudmundsson 1984: 29).

Experience, however, is a unique problem for the profession of arms. A military officer may be called to exercise his or her central duties such as command in wartime, only once in a life-time. Sir Michael Howard gives the analogy of Olympic athletes who spend their life practising on for an Olympic championship on which the fortune of his or her entire nation depends. Moreover, with the complex problem of running a military unit in peacetime with its admin-istration, discipline, maintenance and supply of an organization the size of a fair-sized town, it is easy to forget what the unit is being run for – the conduct of war. Therefore if there are no wars at present, a military practitioner is almost compelled to study past wars, that is, to study military history (Howard 1961: 6–7).

Military history also serves to further unit cohesion and helps in developing and placing into context professional concepts. The study of history enables military practitioners to see how military affairs have related to the larger concerns of their nations throughout the ages. Military history allows them understand the interaction of the various forces that have shaped their pro-fession and permits the practitioner to view current problems in the perspective of decades and centuries rather than months and years (Van Riper 1994: 51).

As war affects society broadly, the greater value of military history is to society as a whole. The availability of good military history may even help the common citizen think intelligently about military affairs. It has even been argued that 'the better educated we are historically, the less likely we are as a country to make stupid mistakes' (US and World News Report 2008). However, not only when working towards the realm of general civilian education and popular culture, the military history researcher must guard against an excess of what Michael Howard describes as 'myth-making' or the creation of an image of the past, through careful selection and interpretation, to encourage patriotic feeling, or to create support for a political regime (Howard 1961: 3). Others have argued against 'camouflaged history' – history that makes you look good, but is at odds with historical reality (Liddell Hart 1972: 27). Then what is history, past events – or a record of what happened in the past?

History and historiographical trends: Limits to historical knowledge

'History' in popular usage has carried two very different meanings. It has often been used to designate the sum total of human activities in the past. Seemingly important events in contem-porary times or even victory of a sports team in a championship are described as 'history being made'. A more focused common usage looks upon this history as a record of events rather than the events themselves. In this vein, history may be regarded as the record of all that has occurred within the realm of human consciousness. The task of the historian can be considered as recon-structing as far as may be possible, the past thoughts and activities of humanity (Barnes 1963: 3). However, the historian cannot possibly hope to cover all human activity in any degree of success and hence the study of history involves the selection of a topic and a somewhat arbitrary elimination of its borders cutting off connections with the universal. Within these arbitrarily established borders there is a selection and organization of information in a systematic approach. This selection is influenced by the historian's frame of reference. The frame may be a narrow sectional, national, or limited group conception of history or it may be broadly influenced by the prevailing social, political and intellectual trends of the contemporary time. Whatever the nature of the frame, it is there and exists in the mind of the historian. It may inadvertently lead him or her to turn a blind eye on some aspects or to exaggerate the importance of others.

History writing on war and the deployment of armed forces also often reflects the peculiarities of a given military culture or establishment. Though war is widely and long recognized as an utterly messy and chaotic activity, militaries as institutions attempt to maintain a 'culture of order' (Lind et al. 1989: 26). That culture, embodied in ranks, saluting, uniforms and drill, is largely a product of style of warfare that reached its apex in the eighteenth-century 'column and line' infantry with armies having centralized command under a single general, king or aristocrat. From the time of the Napoleonic Wars to 1945 the Prussian–German way of dealing with this contradiction of military order versus battlefield chaos has been outwardly maintaining the traditional culture of order while developing a decentralized command system and education for leaders to adapt to a disorderly battlefield. Other powers went different routes to maintain the culture of order on the battlefield, for instance by attempting to make war a science and postulating that there were immutable laws or principles of war governed by Marxism-Leninism, as the Soviets did. The United States Armed Forces during the First World War began treating the conduct of war as an industrial process as in a large automobile assembly plant. Decision-making was centralized as it was in a large manufacturing plant and the complex phenomenon of war was broken down into interchangeable parts, much like an assembly line, where military commanders could make decisions based on standard principles and achieve statistically predicable results (Vandergriff 2002: 41–44). Appointed in 1899, Secretary of War Elihu Root, an early devotee of scientific management ideas of Frederick Taylor and Harrison Emerson, paved the way for their introduction to the US Army. However, it was Major General William Crozier, Chief of Ordnance from 1901 to 1918, and for a time the President of the Army War College, who introduced scientific management in earnest to the US Army. In the interwar year the army became steeped in the theory and practice of scientific management (Sibul 2012: 160). After the military reform movement in the late 1970s and 1980s in the United States in the wake of the Vietnam War, the US moved away from the industrial process approach and towards the Prussian–German approach of decentralized command and treating war as a complex and chaotic phenomena where those who are able to best adapt in the chaotic atmosphere are successful (Kiszely 2005: 41).

All these different approaches to war affect and have affected the military historians' frame of reference. Soviet military historians operated under the guidance of Soviet military science while American military historians often framed military history studies within terms of standard principles of war and saw military success in terms of superior firepower and defeating enemies through attrition by using superior materiel resources. Even if the outlook of the society and of military establishments has changed, old habits tend to linger on (Muth 2011).

This being said, military history as a scholarly endeavour has changed much in scope since the Napoleonic Wars when it was indistinguishable from general history. Nowadays, it can be divided into three general strains: the study of operational affairs, the study of administrative and technical issues, and the study of the relation between the military and society. The study of operational or combat aspects includes military strategy and tactics, logistics and leadership including campaign studies and operationally oriented biography. Administrative and technical studies focus on the functional and professional activities of the armed forces, organization and doctrine, education and training, procurement and materiel development in peacetime and in war. The military and society approach looks at the broadest spectrum of military affairs throughout the cycle of war and peace, including the military's relationship to society as a whole, addressing such themes as culture, politics, the civilian economy, women and war and minorities in military service and on social histories of elements of the enlisted ranks and the non-commissioned and commissioned officer corps. To the extent civilian universities take an interest in military history, the 'war and society' approach, as opposed to the other two more traditional branches in military history, has acquired some academic standing (Chambers 1991: 405–406; Yerxa 2008: 5). In terms of basic methodology the varieties are quite similar though.

Whatever the scholarly and historiographical preferences and whatever the nature of the frame of reference, these two guide the attempts of the historian to put history in a smaller manageable slice and to put chaotic events into a systematic order. But as Charles A. Beard, perhaps the greatest of American historians, cautioned, 'History is chaos and every attempt to interpret it otherwise is an illusion' (Beard 1934: 228). Even though the ultimate goal is to tell history 'as it really was', historians and their readers should be aware that it is historians that order and structure the past.

For the military historian this structuring presents a special challenge as war in essence is the most chaotic of activities and still the historian must reduce it and systemize it to make the study of it useable. On this, Howard notes, 'Some attempt must be made to sort order out of chaos; that is what historians are for. But we would do well says the sceptical academic, not to take this orderly account even for an approximation to what really happened; much less base any conclusions on it for the future' (Howard 1961: 5).

Pursuing historical research: Methodological considerations

Central to any successful historiographical endeavour is of course the formulation of a research question. This question may be inspired by the needs of today, or by an interest in past events as such. In any case, in formulating a research question the researcher will have to take into account the historiography on the matter, which will serve both as a body of reference and, through the gaps, shortcomings and inconsistencies in it, as a justification for further research. Historians may also turn to a theory and apply this to a historical subject. Unlike political and social scientists, in many if not most cases historians do so implicitly and one can only distil their frame of reference, or the theory they subscribe to, from the way they construct their narrative and from their conclusions. The decision of whether or not to explicitly use theory as an analytic device also has consequences with regard to the way historical researchers present their findings. We will get back to that later on.

The first step after formulating a research question is to decide on a research strategy. The researcher may want to limit himself to books and articles only, or may want to interview witnesses (assuming they're still around), or use a combination of both. He or she will also have to decide on the advisability of conducting research in archives. Since archival research is time-consuming, this decision involves a trade-off between the time available and the possible gains to be expected from spending it in an archive, i.e. novel and unexpected findings that shed a fundamentally different light on the subject: archival research offers the possibility of correcting well-established but erroneous views. Of course it may also confirm earlier hypotheses. This is the main reward of conducting archival research, apart from getting 'the feel' of a certain period or issue.

By necessity the decision to conduct archival research is somewhat of an educated guess, based on both past experience and a thorough analysis of what has been written on the subject before. Before embarking on archival research, the researcher will have to identify gaps and inconsistencies in the existing body of literature that may warrant additional research in archives. This said, time constraints generally advise against large-scale archival research. The researcher normally ends up combining and challenging insights of other scholars. This may produce valuable new views but there is some sterility in this approach given that researchers comment on analyses of primary sources that they haven't studied for themselves. Arguably, archival research produces a greater familiarity with the subject leading to a more fruitful contribution to the academic debate and even present-day practices or decision-making, but time constraints often makes this impractical.

As part of this first step – and this applies to any historical enquiry that involves archival research – the researcher is to identify the main institutional bodies involved, locate their paper trail (the written remains of their activity), establish its size and the way in which it is organized. He should also try and locate whatever private archives have been left by persons involved – these may contain documents that are no longer in public archives or that offer a more personal view. He may also want to find out whether persons involved in the matter are still living. Interviewing them involves another set of methodological challenges that will be discussed elsewhere in this volume.

Then – but partly coinciding with the first step – the researcher is to find out which regulations pertain (as to access and right to publish) and obtain the required permissions if any. It is advisable to build good relations with the officials (in public archives) or relatives (when conducting research in private archives) especially since in the case of the latter, access is granted on the basis of trust or interest, rather than on the basis of any formal regulation. This also poses a risk – access may be withdrawn at any time and accordingly the researcher may end up as a hostage of sorts.

Having met the conditions outlined above, the researcher who decides to conduct archival research will have to work through the material in an organized systematic way. What we know about the past is based on sources that do not simply list all that happened. Instead, they are rife with conjecture, interpretations, (un)intentional simplifications and hidden agendas. Historians, nonetheless, must base their accounts on those sources since they have nothing else to go by. This requires the mastering of the heuristic tools of the historian – the application of criteria to establish the veracity of the sources. One may think of such methods as close reading and textual analysis, but also of specific abilities such as the ability to read hand-written documents and foreign languages. In any case it requires knowledge about the functioning of the organization under scrutiny (Tosh 2009).

A well-formulated question, i.e. one that not only defines topic and time-span but also clearly specifies what the researcher wants to know, channels his or her efforts. Still, it may sometimes be advisable to apply a broad sweep instead of a narrow one. Depending on the nature of the research question, a random start though highly costly in terms of time and effort, may produce interesting finds and, because of the fact that it cuts across the hierarchical logic of the institution, surprising insights as well. It is costly because it takes considerable time to master the material and develop a coherent view. At the same time, one of its benefits may be that the researcher is not adopting the reasoning of the institution. He or she may wander off the well-trodden paths to find amazing sights.

This wandering off is also one of the main pitfalls involved in archival research. Given that most scholars will have deadlines of sorts even when there *is* time, time is limited. The danger is that the researcher unknowingly may get carried away without any prospect of finding this true gem. He or she will end up with a pile of notes on a variety of subjects but nothing truly useful. A challenge of a different nature is the assumption that all that was done and thought is recorded. The challenge is twofold: it will lead the researcher to continue looking for material that in fact doesn't exist, and poses the risk of attempting an in-depth analysis to the point of becoming irrelevant. Knowing when to stop looking and start writing may therefore be the most daunting task for a historian.

Writing history

Perhaps more so than any other discipline history seems deceptively simple, but writing good history is difficult. The explanatory force of historians' accounts is not rooted in theory, but in the ability to convincingly present a story. Writing history is about narrative skills as much as it is about conducting research and analysing the findings. Still, there are a few demands every historian is expected to live up to. Some national historical associations have developed ethical codes that are to ensure this, and in recent years appeals were made to further expand the professional standards these codes contain (De Baets 2008). Basically, the historian is required to present a truthful interpretation of past events based on *verifiable* sources. It is inexcusable to invent sources, as much as it is to quietly ignore sources that contradict the historian's view. But within these parameters historians are found to have considerable leeway – it is perfectly admissible to downplay the importance of such sources, albeit on the basis of valid arguments.

There are no clear limits as to what is considered acceptable 'poetic licence', which hasn't really solved the problem as to how far a historian may go in interpreting thoughts, acts and ideas. On what grounds do we conclude that there is a causality between two thoughts or events? As a result scholarly debates in history are not only about historical events but even more so about interpretation. Theory may provide well-needed help, although in most cases historians do not make their assumptions explicit.

A related challenge is how to know that an interpretation actually is truthful. Not only will every historian be confronted with the methodological questions of the admissibility of filling the gaps and reading between the lines, they also face the risk of anachronism and bias. Anachronism involves a linear projection of modern conceptions on past actors. Since modern historians are convinced that change, especially in mindsets, is the essence of history, anachronism is considered a deadly sin. Both anachronism and a lack of awareness of it may reduce the value of (military) history for military organizations. Bias may also obscure a fruitful analysis. It may be the result of existing historiography (as discussed above) and its existence may be shown through archival research, but archives being the product of human activity, they themselves also contain bias.

Knowing about the risk of anachronism and bias is not the same as acting on it. It takes hard thinking to understand the past. Professional (operational) military historians analysing armed conflict and the decisions taken in it, often combine two mutually exclusive epistemological theories. They do so perhaps unwittingly, as many historians do not address the theoretical fundaments of their craft on a daily basis. Historians hope to experience and then evoke in others a so-called 'historical sensation', an epiphany-like phenomenon that instils a deeper, intuitive, understanding of the true nature of past events, that was first defined by historian Johan Huizinga in the early 1900s (Ankersmit 2005). By and large they also apply R.G. Collingwood's theory of re-enactment. Collingwood's main concern was causality and his theory was based on the fundamental rationality of man. Actions imply thought, and thought underlies action. The historian's 'main task is to think himself into this action, to discern the thought of its agent' (Collingwood 1994; Helgeby 2005: 10). In Collingwood's view thought is the only element of the past that leaves identifiable traces of some sort. It is thus the only element that can be retrieved – all else is lost forever. 'The history of thought, and therefore all history, is the re-enactment of past thought in the historian's own mind' (Collingwood 1994: 215). This re-enactment requires hard thinking (Inglis 2009: 215–216).

The idea of the fundamental rationality of man is somewhat awkward, and may already be hard to sustain when analysing peacetime decisions, or decisions made during stabilization operations. It is outright misguiding when analysing battles, where there is an interplay of intentions, chance, and fear, of rational and irrational, even subconscious, factors. While it may be true that intuitive and impulsive actions cannot be re-enacted the way rational decisions might, limiting ourselves to only Collingwood's theory would preclude the possibility of fruitfully analysing these vital ingredients in warfare. To leave them out is inadmissible, however. To take an example, the ability to intuitively 'read' a battlefield, or a situation, is a vital asset for command-ers at every level. Such an intuitive understanding is equally invaluable for a historian, however problematic this may be from a rationalist epistemological point of view.

Actual and potential pressures

When analysing history, certain pressures may occur. People who witnessed the events under discussion may be approached for an interview, which offers a *couleur locale* that is often absent from the more sterile and formal documents in public archives. Oral history, i.e. talking to witnesses, may also enhance the credibility of the analysis, but problems will arise when wit-nesses argue that their personal recollection is correct and the researcher's analysis is not (Moore 2014, Chapter 11 this volume). Unfortunately, recollections do not simply depict events as they unfolded, but are also influenced by their outcomes. The brain is also not a running CCTV recorder; it tends to forget, misplace, distort, ignore and deny, but individual or even collective memory and scholarly analysis may and in fact do coexist. The historian offers an analysis at a higher level of aggregation while the benefit of hindsight gives him the opportunity to access sources such as records of the adversary that were not available to witnesses. It does mean, though, that the historian should be able to provide documentary evidence for every statement he or she makes.

This last demand may be problematic in view of changes in technology. For example, in current operations, hard copy paper orders and reports no longer predominate. In Iraq and Afghanistan coalition commands have tended to conduct the majority of their planning and communications via the Internet (often by chat and email), resulting in a large number of opera-tional documents being temporarily stored on computer servers. If historians have access to computer systems this actually presents some advantages, with some planning and the right soft-ware, historians now can data-mine the servers and storage media for key documents describing any and all aspects of the operation studied (Visconage 2006: 35–36). These servers are acces-sible to security-vetted historians, but historians outside the chain of command will have to wait until this material is declassified. As the archival protocols for electronic material are still work in progress in most countries, future historians may find considerable gaps in information if and when key documents, presentations and messages have been deleted.

The wider issue of how the development of digital humanities will affect the way today's and tomorrow's military historians work will not be addressed in this contribution. It has been argued that practitioners of digital humanities place too much emphasis on tools and data, and that the tendency towards 'technological determinism' needs to be balanced by more attention to methodological and epistemological considerations (Zaagsma 2013). In view of this, these developments deserve more space than can be offered in the context of the present volume.

In recent years there has been an interesting development in that the historian may actually be on locale and gather material largely as events are taking place; this is the case for instance of field historians of the US Army and Marine Corps. This is a clear indication of the value accorded to historical enquiry. Historians thus employed are expected to operate independently and to do their job without getting in the way of the units or operations, whatever their nature, they are documenting (Visconage 2006: 35). The most important for the field historian is gain-ing the trust and support of the commander as the commanders set the tone and facilitate the ability of the historian to gather information to tell the unit's history. Through the commander the historian can gain access to key subordinates and primary staff officers, and be allowed to attend staff meetings, conference calls and other historically significant events. Of course, such a historian is bound by operational security and his or her work might be used only on command level for analyses and declassified at a later time. In order to have the trust of commanders, operational understanding and ability to accomplish the task in a hazardous environment, field historians are usually serving military personnel or retired officers with academic credentials. For armed forces using purely academic historians or ones with minimal military background to chronicle and analyse contemporary operations, the challenge of gaining trust of field commanders is even more difficult and can be accomplished by only the most talented of individuals.

There are some complications. Even for a historian in the chain of command or a retired trusted old military hand, the work produced often is dependent on the outlook of the commander towards the field of history. Some commanders will be action-oriented and time-pressed in their demands on the historian wanting rapid reporting of lessons identified in time for next phase of the operation, while other commanders see history largely as a public-relations exercise to build the historical 'myth' of his unit or command being flawlessly efficient and effective. The pressure is more for press-release type stories of the unit's accomplishments and material for the next chapter of the official history. In this case the effect can be what Sir Basil H. Liddell Hart described as 'camouflaged history'. Such history can engender a false military confidence – leading to greater operational failures (Liddell Hart 1972: 27).

Concluding remarks

Arguably a historian working for a military or defence organization is not at freedom to be fully critical of its leadership, especially of officers who are still serving under current doctrine and policy. However, the historian can still write critical history. Helmuth Von Moltke the Elder under whose supervision the German General Staff produced an official history of the Franco-Prussian War, gave the following advice on that work which is still relevant today for writing and using official histories: 'We must be able to read between the lines. The History produced by our General Staff is the best that has been written of the last war. It is valuable for all to study and requires to be read between the lines, seeing that criticism of persons are always expressed in it with finest tact, while the historical truth, as far as it can be ascertained, is always there' (quoted in [Anonymous] 'War as a Teacher of War' 1902: 607).

While military institutions, as discussed earlier, have a culture of order, it is, however, largely a myth that civilian academics have far more academic freedom than historians in a military chain of command. On many North American and European university campuses, academics have the 'political correctness Sword of Damocles' hanging over them (Sibul 2011: 78–80), and 'army historians, of course, can point out that there are prevailing trends and fashions that academic historians up for tenure violate at their professional peril' (Sandler 2001). Misuse of history occurs in both worlds. William S. Lind, a historian who was a key figure in the post-Vietnam military reform movement, records several instances where elements in the US Army senior leadership exerted pressure on historians to attack the emerging maneuver warfare concepts, or critical studies as such (Lind 2005).

Political pressures, debates on reforms and changes in concepts, doctrine and technology can put special pressures on the historian within a military bureaucracy, because he or she can become involved in encouraging and resisting change based on historical evidence. As history is a storehouse from where 'the number of possibly relevant "facts" is infinite', they can be 'cherry picked' and arranged to argue for whatever is in some faction's self-interest (Howard 1961: 7). The risk is of course that such enquiries will be utterly one-sided and won't offer real guidance.

While methodology has made great moves forward, and we would no longer consider as adequate some of the methods he applied, Thucydides' ambition is as relevant as it was 2,500 years ago, 'But if he who desires to have before his eyes a true picture of the events which have happened . . . shall pronounce what I have written to be useful, then I shall be satisfied. My history is an everlasting possession, not a prize composition which is heard and forgotten.' The ideal of the historian is to conduct historical analysis clear of prejudice and preconceptions no matter what bureaucratic and political pressures are (Baudet 2013). Ultimately it is also the best interest of the institution, which he or she serves.

Note

1 The authors wish to thank Henk de Jong (NLDA) for his comments on an earlier version of this chapter.

References

Ankersmit, F.R. (2005) *Sublime Historical Experience*, Stanford, CA: Stanford University Press.

Anonymous (1902) 'War as a Teacher of War'. *United Service: A Quarterly Review of Military and Naval Affairs* 6(3): 604–632.

Baets, A. de (2008) *Responsible History*, New York: Berghahn Books.

Barnes, H.E. (1963) *A History of Historical Writing*, New York: Dover Publications Inc.

Baudet, F.H. (2013) 'Some Thoughts on the Utility of the Past to the Military'. *Air and Space Power Journal – Africa and Francophonie* 4(4): 4–14.

Beard, Ch.A. (1934) 'Written History as an Act of Faith'. *The American Historical Review* 39(2): 219–231.

Chambers, J.W. (1991) 'The New Military History: Myth and Reality'. *Journal of Military History* 55(3): 395–406.

Collingwood, R.G. (1994) *The Idea of History* [1946], Revised edition with lectures 1926–1928, edited by Jan van der Dussen, Oxford: Clarendon Press.

Creveld, M. van (1990) *The Training of Officers: From Military Professionalism to Irrelevance*, New York: The Free Press.

Ewers, J. (2008) 'Why Don't More Colleges Teach Military History? Despite Its Enduring Public Appeal, and a Country at War, the Subject Gets Little Respect on Campus'. US News and World Report, 3 April 2008. Available at www.usnews.com/news/articles/2008/04/03/why-dont-colleges-teach-military-history?page=1).

Gudmundsson, B.I. (1984) 'Instruction at the Basic School'. *Marine Corps Gazette* 68(2): 29.

Helgeby, S. (2005) *Action as History: The Historical Thought of R.G. Collingwood*, Exeter: Imprint.

Howard, M. (1961) The Use and Abuse of Military History. A Lecture given by Michael Howard at the Royal United Services Institution (RUSI) on 18th October 1961 (typescript).

Inglis, F. (2009) *History Man*, Princeton, NJ: Princeton University Press.

Kiszely, J. (2005) 'Thinking about the Operational Level'. *RUSI Journal* 150(6): 38–43.

Liddell-Hart, B.H. (1972) *Why Don't We Learn from History?* London: Allen & Unwin.

Lind, W.S. (2005) 'Wreck It and Run'. *Counterpunch*. Available at www.counterpunch.org/2005/06/01/wreck-it-and-run (accessed 20 August 2013).

Lind, W.S. 'The Ugly'. On War #149 – *Defense and the National Interest*. Available at www.dnipogo.org/lind/lind_1_25_06.htm.

Lind, W.S., Nightingale, K., Schmitt, J.F., Sutton, J.W. and Wilson, G.I. (1989) 'The Changing Face of War: Into the Fourth Generation'. *Marine Corps Gazette* 73(10): 22–26.

Moore, B.L. (2014). 'In-Depth Interviewing'. In: J.M.M.L. Soeters, P.M. Shields and S.J.H. Rietjens (eds) *Routledge Handbook of Research Methods in Military Studies*. Abingdon: Routledge.

Muth, J. (2011) *Command Culture: Officer Education in the US Army and the German Armed Forces 1901–1940 and the Consequences for World War II*, Denton, TX: University of North Texas Press.

Riper, P.K. Van (1994) 'The Use of Military History in the Professional Education of Officers'. *Marine Corps Gazette* 78(2): 48.

Sandler, S. (2001) 'U.S. Army Command Historians: What We Are and What We Do'. *Perspectives on History* 39(4): 24–27.

Sepp, K.I. (2005), 'Best Practices in Counterinsurgency'. *Military Review* 85(3): 8–12.

Sibul, E.A. (2011) 'Military History, Social Sciences, and Professional Military Education'. *Baltic Security and Defence Review* 13(1): 71–99.

Sibul, E.A. (2012) 'The Military and the Management Movement'. *Baltic Security and Defence Review* 14(2): 147–180.

Thucydides (1881) *History of the Peloponnesian War.* Translated into English, to which is Prefixed an Essay on Inscriptions and a Note on the Geography of Thucydides, Volume 1. B. Jowett translator. Oxford: Clarendon Press.

Tosh, J. (2009) *The Pursuit of History*, London: Routledge.

US Joint Forces Command (2010) *Joint Operating Environment 2010*, Norfolk, VA: US Joint Forces Command.

Vandergriff, D.E. (2002) *The Path to Victory: America's Army and the Revolution in Human Affairs*, Novato, CA: Presidio Press.

Vego, M. (2011) 'On Military Theory'. *Joint Forces Quarterly* 62(3): 59–67.

Visconage, M.D. (2006) 'Getting It All Down: Marine Field Historians in Operation Iraqi Freedom'. *The Leatherneck* 89(6) 34–37.

Wyly, M.D. (1993) 'Teaching Maneuver Warfare'. In: R.D. Hooker (ed.) *An Anthology: Maneuver Warfare*, Novato CA: Presidio Press.

Yerxa, D.A. (2008) *Recent Themes in Military History: Historians in Conversation*, Columbia: University of South Carolina Press.

Zaagsma, G. (2013) 'On Digital History'. *BMGN – Low Countries Historical Review* 128(4): 3–29.

8

RETRIEVING WHAT'S ALREADY THERE

Archival data for research in defense acquisition

Rene G. Rendon and Keith F. Snider

J.R. Fox (1974) *Arming America: How the U.S. Buys Weapons.* **Cambridge, MA: Harvard University Press.**

Arming America is a comprehensive analysis of how the USA acquires major weapons and other military systems for national defense. It provides a deep understanding of why defense acquisition seems so problematical, with many weapons programs experiencing cost overruns, schedule delays, and performance shortfalls. In explaining the sources and manifestations of these problems, *Arming America* covers a wide range of topics, including acquisition's stakeholders – Congress, industry, and the Department of Defense (DOD) – and the complex managerial, political, and legal environments in which they operate. Making sense of the often-convoluted relationships among these stakeholders in such an environment is daunting, but Ron Fox meets the challenge with a classic work that remains highly relevant in almost every important aspect.

Fox writes as the quintessential "pracademic," having served in several DOD acquisition-related positions, most notably as the Assistant Secretary of the Army for procurement, while on leaves of absence from Harvard Business School. Drawing on his personal experiences in DOD, Fox also relies on a broad range of archived data sources, including Congressional reports and testimonies; reports from the General Accounting Office (GAO; now Government Accountability Office); DOD budgetary and cost data; internal DOD policies on acquisition; and defense industry data (e.g. Moody's, Standard and Poor's, and Forbes' data). Fox's skillful use of these data sources illustrates the variety of topics and methods that hold promise for research in defense acquisition.

While having the advantage of inside-the-Pentagon access to much acquisition data, Fox adroitly uses several publicly available data archives, including Congressional testimony, auditor reports, and industry databases. In recognizing his data's limitations, Fox employs straightforward and simple methodologies, and he avoids an overreliance on any one data source. For example, in his chapter comparing defense industry to private industry, Fox eschews hypothesis testing through statistical analysis of financial data in favor of a triangulated approach using several data sources. He prefers simple graphical and tabular comparisons of financial metrics such as debt/equity ratios and bond ratings, and he reinforces these with tables and graphics of figures from DOD contract awards. He also incorporates relevant commentary from trade journals, government reports, and interviews of industry leaders. The result is a multi-faceted, nuanced, and compelling interpretive analysis, which contrasts markedly from the highly technical methods and cramped conclusions too often found in strictly quantitative studies.

Arming America is pragmatic rather than conceptual. Fox pursues richly contextual descriptions and explanations for how acquisition works (or doesn't work). He portrays a system characterized by participants with poorly aligned incentives and disincentives, and by features that both cause problems and resist reform. These features are evident in a range of issues, from strategic issues of DOD-Congressional relationships to tactical issues of vendor selection. Underlying these issues is the pervasive environment of uncertainty (thus risk) inherent in pursuing advanced weaponry for use in constantly evolving scenarios, whether terrorist-style attacks by Afghan insurgents or missile attacks from North Korea.

Arming America appeared 40 years ago, but its findings remain valid. Fox concluded that large-scale structural changes were necessary to address acquisition's fundamental problems, but he doubted that America had the political will to effect those changes. Time has proved him right. While many reforms have been attempted, little of substance has changed, and U.S. defense acquisition remains as troubled as ever.

Introduction

Among the functions of national governments, defense acquisition, the activities that provide equipment and services to armed forces for the conduct of military operations, attracts much scrutiny (Kausal 1999; 2000). Controversy is evident in seemingly perennial debates surrounding the rationales, strategies, and tactics for acquisition; consensus is elusive on many questions. For example, what is the proper military strategy for any nation, and what capabilities and resource investments are needed for success in any given strategy? What is the proper relationship between a nation's military forces and the industries that equip them? What is the proper contribution of defense industry to a nation's economy? How is a proper level of transparency and accountability achieved in this unique civil-military activity? Such a wide range of important policy and management issues makes defense acquisition a compelling topic for social science research.

What data are available to support such research, and how might they be used? This chapter documents and describes some of the principal sources of archival data and research techniques used to support defense acquisition research. The goal is to provide useful information for potential researchers on:

- types of data available
- sources of data
- issues with access to and use of the data
- illustrations of research methods, which draw on these data.

Background

Data types

Archival acquisition data may be structured or unstructured. Structured data are well defined and often organized in tabular form, which enables graphical, statistical (e.g. time series), or other quantitative analysis. Most acquisition data, however, exist as unstructured information in text-heavy documents like contracts, narrative reports, and policy documents. These typically lend themselves to interpretive, critical, or other qualitative analyses, such as those found in *Arming America*. Quantitative methods that employ content analysis, textual analysis, and data mining using document search engines may also be useful (Zhao et al. 2010).

Data sources

At present, two major forces shape the demand for and generation of defense acquisition data. The first is a managerial emphasis: data on acquisition-related actions are collected, stored, and used by acquisition managers in order to accomplish those actions more efficiently. The second is a political-legal emphasis: data are collected and made available to officials and the public in order to promote values like accountability, probity, and transparency in acquisition processes. These two forces indicate the main sources of archival data.

The agencies that acquire products and services for the military usually maintain extensive document files of unstructured information on procurement actions, such as solicitations, bids and proposals, contract awards, modifications, and closeouts. Nowadays, acquisition agencies in most nations use paperless "e-procurement" systems to promote efficiency, equity, and transparency. The acquisition authority in Singapore's Ministry of Defense (MOD) is typical in its use of a government-wide e-procurement system (GeBIZ) that is open to the general public. The MOD uses the system to post solicitations for defense contracts for public viewing, and prospective firms use the system to search for and submit bids on suitable work. Notices of contract awards are also usually publicized via these e-procurement systems (Singapore Government 2013).

Such data from acquisition agencies might then be obtained by a variety of means by a variety of entities and used for a variety of purposes, each of which may result in the generation of additional archival acquisition data. Here are some examples:

- An acquisition agency is required to provide to its higher authority a periodic report on contract actions, including summary statistics; these are then consolidated and publicized for all defense agencies or perhaps for the entire national administration.
- A defense agency reports its anticipated contract awards to the defense budgeting authority, which then uses those in preparing future defense budgets.
- An independent government audit agency is directed to investigate a contract action or series of actions and provide a report to defense leaders or to the national legislature.
- An agency publicly announces a major contract award, which then is reported on by news media or a private watchdog group.
- Influenced by any of the above, national leadership or the legislature promulgates acquisition-related laws, regulations, and other policy, which then become part of the archives of institutional acquisition data.

These scenarios indicate that the promising starting points for researchers to seek archival defense acquisition data are the data repositories of the entities mentioned above. Forty years ago, Fox relied on paper files from many such entities to write *Arming America*. Today, of course, most of those entities have searchable organizational web sites with links to pages with relevant data. In each of these scenarios, the data that are generated and archived will vary between structured or unstructured, depending on their purpose and use.

Data challenges

For a variety of reasons, little attention is given to scholarly research on defense acquisition (Albano et al. 2013; Snider and Rendon 2012), and so little data have been collected for that purpose. Researchers thus have the challenge to understand the purposes for which archival acquisition data are collected, how those purposes affect the quality and quantity of the data, and how to make their research questions and methods compatible with those data. To illustrate, Table 8.1 shows publicly available data on four of NATO's approximately 350 contracts awarded during the last half of 2012. While this type of information might serve a transparency purpose, it is clearly inadequate for examining many interesting research questions, such as whether NATO procurement processes allow for adequate competition among vendors in member states, or whether small and medium-sized enterprises have adequate opportunities to sell products and services to NATO.

Restrictions on access to acquisition data represents a second challenge. As expected with national security matters, sensitive data are classified, especially regarding new weapons capabilities, technologies, and employment, and thus available only to relatively few within the defense establishment. Further, the structural arrangements for government contracting often restrict access to data through the safeguards they provide for any sensitive vendor information. As a result, proprietary data ("trade secrets") and documents such as a firm's business plan, marketing strategy, and salary structure are accessible only by those acquisition officials who need them to judge whether the firm should receive a contract award. Thus, unless researchers obtain the same sort of insider access that Fox enjoyed in writing *Arming America*, they will find it difficult to obtain acquisition-related data that are not already publicly available.

Archival defense acquisition data in the USA

The remainder of the chapter focuses on archival data in the USA. While most other liberal democracies collect data and information with a view towards acquisition reform, no other nation has such extensive archival data as the USA. A primary reason is the high cost of collecting data and maintaining archives; the USA, with its large defense investments, can most readily afford to do so. No other nation is likely to have all of the types of archival data found in American sources; for example, no other country has a system comparable to the Federal Procurement Data System-Next Generation (FPDS-NG; discussed below). While many nations have some archival data (e.g. e-procurement systems; auditor reports), it is unlikely that any has types of archival data that are not also found in the USA.

As might be expected, availability of the Department of Defense's (DOD's) acquisition data ranges from unrestricted to highly restricted. The discussion here addresses only data that are

Table 8.1 Extract of NATO purchase orders during the period July–December 2012

Contractor	Country	Value (EUR)	Purpose
Aerazur – Zodiac Aerospace	France	109,640	Fixture, lighting
Aero Precision Industries Inc.	USA	264,332	Procurement of parts
Agilent Technologies	Italy	348,501	Supplies for fixed wing aircraft
Agusta Westland Ltd.	Great Britain	1,001,332	Supplies for helicopter

Source: NATO Support Agency (NATO 2013).

Note: The threshold value for reporting an award was EUR 76,800 in 2012.

publicly available and have searchable web sites that are easily found simply by entering the organization's name in any Internet search engine.

DOD makes vast amounts of data and information publicly available via the Defense Technical Information Center (DTIC), to which most institutional libraries have access. DTIC's products are searchable by its site search engine, as well as by web search tools such as Google Scholar. DTIC contains budget documents, DOD policies, reports and theses written by students at various DOD schools, and many other defense-related publications.

Structured data

Sources of archival structured data include program data and contract data (Table 8.2); these are both from government sources.

Program data

The Selected Acquisition Report (SAR) is DOD's principal report to Congress on cost, schedule, and performance information for a major acquisition program. A SAR provides up-to-date estimates on program status in relation to baseline estimates. A variance between the baseline and current estimate may be either favorable or unfavorable. SARs are submitted on an annual basis, with quarterly reports required for programs experiencing significant cost growth. While the SAR contains other-than-cost information, for example, unstructured narrative text descriptions of program events, progress, and plans, most of its data elements are related to cost. SARs provide total program cost estimates that account for a variety of activities, including research and development, procurement, military construction, and other acquisition-related operations and maintenance costs. Anticipated inflation rates are also taken into account. In addition, the SAR provides data on approved future levels of funding for each major acquisition program.

Table 8.2 Sources of structured data

Source of data	Examples of data	Example of research using the data
Selected Acquisition Report (SAR) http://www.acq.osd.mil/ara/am/sar/index.html	Program Narrative Highlights Program Acquisition Cost Program Cost Changes Program Funding Status	In Drezner et al. (1993) SAR cost data are used to quantify cost growth in acquisition programs and to identify factors affecting cost growth. Bolten et al. (2008) use SAR cost data for 35 major acquisition programs to identify sources of cost growth, which included errors in estimation and scheduling, government decisions, and financial matters.
Federal Procurement Data Systems-Next Generation (FPDS-NG) (www.fpds.gov)	Top 100 Contractors Report; Small Business Goaling Report	Lloyd (1988) uses FPDS data to analyze alternate dispute resolution in contract appeals.
Federal Business Opportunities (FEDBIZOPPS) (www.fbo.gov)	American Recovery and Reinvestment Act (economic stimulus) Reports	Benner et al. (2010) use FEDBIZOPPS data are used to analyze how much stimulus funding was budgeted for health intervention and comparative effectiveness research.

Because SARs are used to monitor program status, they emphasize changes from the previous SAR. Clearly, cost variances may occur for a variety of reasons; for example, costs will increase or decrease if the procurement quantity changes. The SAR categorizes cost variances according to several causes, including variances caused by inflation index changes, by changes in the procurement quantity, or by changes in the procured item's attributes. Most of the extant quantitative research that analyzes causes for the perennial problems in defense acquisition in the USA has focused on cost variances in acquisition programs and thus has employed archival SAR data. While Fox used some SAR data in *Arming America* (1974: 364–365), the RAND Corporation publications represent the most significant body of work of this type (see examples in Table 8.2).

While the level of detailed data that are captured in annual SARs enables rich possibilities for quantitative research, researchers must understand its limitations. Hough (1992) described several issues with SAR data, for example, varying interpretations across programs of how to define and present data elements. Further, reporting requirements occasionally change, for example, as in 2006 when Congress revised the requirement for programs to report variances from their original baselines in addition to any updated baselines (Schwartz 2010).

Contract data

The aforementioned FPDS-NG is the central repository for all federal government contracting actions, including DOD actions, above the micro-purchase threshold (currently $3,000). The FPDS-NG provides summary data for contract awards by federal government executive agencies. It also provides archives of several standard annual reports, such as the *Top 100 Contractors Report* and the *Federal Procurement Report*, the data from which allow analysis of federal contracting according to geographical location, market segment, and other factors (FPDS-NG 2013).

FPDS-NG also contains archives of raw procurement data in extensible markup language for all federal procurement actions from 2004 to the present. While these archives represent a tremendous potential source of research data, the FPDS-NG web site cautions:

> The [XML] archives are intended for use by users who have a great deal of experience with procurement data, XML technology, and large volumes of data. Use of the archive data without a complete understanding of the business processes, rules and regulations, and system information increases the risk of flawed analysis.
>
> (FPDS-NG 2013)

Finally, Federal Business Opportunities (FEDBIZOPPS) is the official federal government electronic portal for contracting officers to publicize notices of proposed contract actions over $25,000. FEDBIZOPPS is tailored for use by either buyers or vendors, but researchers who seek information on specific contracting actions would find it a potentially valuable resource. While much of its content is unstructured data (see below) in the form of solicitations and award notifications, FEDBIZOPPS also contains significant archival structured data on certain high-profile areas of acquisition, for example, contracts awarded as a result of the 2009 economic stimulus program (US Congress 2009).

Unstructured data

Next, various sources of unstructured data are discussed – both governmental and non-governmental (Table 8.3). Most of these sources conduct studies or investigations related to defense acquisition and provide reports summarizing their findings. As demonstrated by Fox in *Arming America*, they are excellent secondary sources for acquisition-related research.

Table 8.3 Sources of unstructured data

Source of data	Examples of data	Example of research using the data
Government Accountability Office (www.gao.gov)	High-Risk Series; Defense Acquisitions: Assessments of Selected Weapon Programs	Gansler (2011) uses secondary data from Assessments of Selected Weapon Programs to evaluate the performance of industry in managing acquisition programs and to recommend changes in government policy and practices to protect critical technologies.
	Contract Management: Coast Guard's Deepwater Program Needs Increased Attention to Management and Contractor Oversight, GAO-04–380, March 9, Washington, DC: Government Accountability Office	Brown et al. (2010) apply principal-agent theory to the case of the Coast Guard's controversial Deepwater project.
	Comptroller General Legal Decisions and Bid Protests	Maser and Thompson (2010) conduct statistical analysis of bid protest data to test various hypotheses (e.g. that small vendors are more likely than large to protest contract awards).
		Rogerson (1989) uses secondary data from the Comptroller General report on defense contractor profitability to test a theory that observed changes in firms' stock market value infers the size of the estimated profit from the awarded production contract.
Congressional Research Service (https://opencrs. com)	Chadwick, S.H. (2007) *Defense Acquisition: Overview, Issues, and Options for Congress*, CRS Report for Congress. Washington, DC: Congressional Research Service	Kratz and Buckingham (2010) use secondary data to analyze threat versus capability-based planning.
DOD Inspector General (DODIG) (http://www. dodig.mil/pubs/index. cfm)	Department of Defense Inspector General (2009). *Summary of DOD Office of Inspector General Audits of Acquisition and Contract Administration*, Report D-2009–2071, Washington, DC: Author	Rendon et al. (2012) use DODIG reports on contracting deficiencies to analyze services acquisition management practices across Army, Navy, and Air Force installations.
RAND Corporation (www.rand.org)	Chow, B., Silberglitt, R., and Hiromoto, S. (2009) *Toward Affordable Systems-Portfolio Analysis and Management for Army Science and Technology Programs*, Monograph MG-761, Santa Monica, CA: RAND Corporation	Dacus (2012) uses secondary data to argue that DOD should implement simple metrics when assessing the technological maturity of defense acquisition programs.

Center for Strategic and International Studies (www.csis.org)	Center for Strategic and International Studies (CSIS) (2001) 'Technology and Security in the Twenty-First Century: U.S. Military Export Control Reform,' *A Report of the CSIS Military Export Control Project*, Washington, DC: CSIS, p. 4	Lavallee (2003) analyze European countries' difficulties in securing export control licenses from the U.S. Department of State.
Institute for Defense Analysis (www.ida.org)	Arnold, S.A., McNicol, D.L., and Fasana, K.G. (2008) *Can Profit Policy and Contract Incentives Improve Defense Contract Outcomes?* IDA-P-4391. Alexandria, VA: Institute for Defense Analyses	Callahan et al. (2011) study the public policy effects of cash flow subsidies on defense contractors' capital expenditures and cost of debt from 1978 to 2009.
Project on Government Oversight (POGO) (www.pogo.org)	Project on Government Oversight (various years). *National Security Investigations: Wasteful Defense Spending Reports*	Thorpe (2010) refers to a series of POGO reports in her discussion on the characterization of defense contract allocation for weapons expenditures as wasteful and abusive.
Citizens Against Government Waste (CAGW) (www.cagw.org)	Finnigan, T. (2006) *All About Pork: The Abuse of Earmarks and the Needed Reforms*, Washington, DC: Citizens against Government Waste	Rubin (2007) uses CAGW data in critiquing an increase in the Congressional practice of spending on special interest group programs.

Government sources

The main governmental investigative entities for acquisition matters include the Government Accountability Office (GAO) and the DOD Inspector General (DODIG). The GAO, headed by the Comptroller General, is the watchdog agency of Congress. It investigates issues related to public management and, as part of its evaluation of government programs, issues reports on those evaluations. The *Assessments of Selected Weapon Programs* summarize the GAO's analysis of cost, schedule, and quantity data on DOD's major defense acquisition programs obtained from SARs. Its *High Risk* reports summarize its observations in areas judged as high risk in their vulnerabilities to fraud, waste, abuse, and mismanagement. Unstructured data from the GAO also include the legal decisions by the Comptroller General on settlements of vendor bid protests and claims. The DODIG is the principal advisor to the Secretary of Defense on matters pertaining to fraud, waste, and abuse. The DODIG's staff conducts audits and investigations and, like the GAO, issues reports on the results of these activities.

An agency within the Library of Congress which works exclusively for Congress, the Congressional Research Service (CRS) provides policy and legal analysis on a wide range of complex government topics, including defense acquisition. The CRS does not conduct audits or investigations but rather relies almost exclusively on secondary sources to produce its analyses for members of Congress and their staffs. Reports, testimonies, and other publications from the GAO, DODIG, and CRS are accessible to the general public on the respective agency websites, each of which includes advanced textual search features and links to other research resources.

Non-government sources

Several non-profit organizations conduct research and analysis on public policy and decision-making, including defense acquisition. The RAND Corporation is a federally funded research and development center (FFRDC) that has long been active in acquisition studies. The Center for Strategic and International Studies (CSIS) conducts research, analysis, and develops policy initiatives focusing on defense and security; regional stability; and global challenges and issues. Finally, the Institute for Defense Analyses (IDA) operates three FFRDCs that conduct scientific and technical research on national security issues, including acquisition-related issues. Research products for each of these organizations are archived and accessible at their respective web sites.

Two non-profit watchdog groups publish significant information on acquisition. The Project on Government Oversight (POGO) investigates corruption, misconduct, and conflicts of interest throughout the federal government. Citizens Against Government Waste (CAGW) is a nationally recognized source for information on government waste. CAGW publishes the *Congressional Pig Book Summary* containing "the most glaring and irresponsible pork-barrel projects in the 13 annual appropriations bills and their sponsors" (CAGW 2013).

Finally, a few universities have dedicated programs to promote and conduct acquisition-related research; examples include the Center for Public Policy and Private Enterprise at University of Maryland, and the Acquisition Research Program at the Naval Postgraduate School. Such entities typically publish research products on their own searchable web-based repositories, though most may also be accessed through DTIC or a search engine such as Google Scholar.

Other types of archival acquisition data

Two other important types of data deserve some attention: those related to budgeting for acquisition programs, and those that document and describe acquisition-related policies. These may be found in a variety of sources (Table 8.4), and they contain a mixture of structured and unstructured data.

Table 8.4 Other types of archival acquisition data

Type	Source(s)	Example research project
Budgetary documents:		
• DOD Budget Submissions	DTIC (http://dtic.mil) DOD Comptroller (http://comptroller.defense.gov)	Davis, J. (1995) documents how extensive oversight of the program's annual budgets by
• Congressional Hearings and Enactments	DTIC (http://dtic.mil) THOMAS (http://thomas .loc.gov)	Congressional committees from 1982 to 1995 created significant turbulence in the program and nearly caused its cancellation.
Policy documents:		
• Federal Acquisition Regulation (FAR)	FAR Site http://farsite.hill.af.mil/	Dillard, J. (2003) analyzes and critiques
• DOD Policy Issuances	Policy Vault http://www.acq.osd.mil/dpap/	DOD's imposition of increasingly onerous reporting requirements
• Federal Statutes	Defense Acquisition Portal http://dap.dau.mil THOMAS (http://thomas.loc.gov)	for acquisition programs.

Budgetary documents

An extensive amount of data is generated each year when DOD prepares and submits its annual budget request, which is then incorporated into the President's Budget to be submitted to the Congress each February for its consideration. The DOD budget request includes, for each program, detailed supporting documentation that explains and justifies the rationale for the program and for the budget needed for execution. Annual budget documentation provides a deep level of context for any individual procurement action. For example, the supporting documentation for the Navy's procurement of the Tomahawk missile in fiscal year (FY) 2013 includes:

- the number of missiles to be procured (196)
- the required FY 2013 budget ($308.97M)
- the projected annual quantities to be procured and budgets through FY 2017
- a summary description of the program's history, current status, and plans
- a breakdown of the major cost elements (e.g. hardware, software, logistical support)
- information on the major contracts (e.g. vendor, contract method and type)
- missile production rates
- the vendor's delivery schedule (Comptroller 2012).

Such information is presently archived and publicly available from FY 2000 for all major acquisition programs in various stages of development.

For any program, the budget documents should provide sufficiently detailed information so that the Congress will approve the program's budget for the upcoming FY. The documents contain semi-structured data with defined elements in tabular formats, as well as unstructured data consisting of narrative text.

In response to DOD's budget submissions, Congress begins its annual process of hearings and debates leading to passage of laws that authorize and provide appropriations for defense acquisition programs (Candreva 2008). Records of deliberations and decisions are contained in Congressional hearings, reports, and various versions of the legislation, including the final enacted version signed into law by the President. All of these are archived and available in the Library of Congress THOMAS site and consist almost entirely of unstructured data and information. These documents provide Congressional direction on major acquisition programs as well as the actual amounts approved for any acquisition effort. For example, the FY 2008 DOD appropriations legislation approved $339 million for the new Littoral Combat Ship (US Congress 2007a: 12), while the defense authorization legislation for the same year contained a provision that DOD may employ only a fixed-price type contract for construction of the Littoral Combat Ship (US Congress 2007b: 27).

Policy documents

In light of the apparent failure of various acquisition reform initiatives over the past half-century, scholars have recently begun to take an interest in acquisition policy as a research topic (see for example Fox 2011; Dillard 2007). The general line of inquiry is to examine the artifacts of reform-minded policy, such as statutes, federal regulations, and internal DOD procedures, in relation to some defined outcomes so as to assess a policy's effects. Acquisition-related policy documents are typically publicly available – legislative documents via THOMAS, and historical DOD documents through DTIC.

Challenges: An example

The analysis by Maser and Thompson (2010; see Table 8.3) of protests of DOD contract awards illustrates some of the processes and challenges of using archival data. This study sought to identify misalignments in DOD's management practices which create conditions conducive to errors – whether actual or perceived – that lead to protests. While Maser and Thompson (2010) relied heavily on interviews with knowledgeable contracting and industry officials, they first established an empirical foundation that used both structured and unstructured archival data on DOD contracts and protests. This foundation illuminates the general context and trends of DOD contract protests with information such as the distributions of protests by the: numbers of bidders; dollar value and duration of contracts; sizes of winning and protesting firms; revenues of winning and protesting firms; and type of contract output (e.g. product, service). Maser and Thompson also used this data to test several hypotheses, including the likelihood of a contract protest in relation to: the number of bidders on a contract; the bidders' size; the complexity of the contracted effort; and the type of contract (fixed-price or cost-reimbursable). The retrieval and use of these data are summarized in the following sections.

Structured data

Due to the magnitude and complexity of the data collection effort (many contracts awarded by several DOD agencies to numerous firms over multiple years), Maser and Thompson relied mainly on a commercial data mining web application, FEDMINE.US™. This tool 'aggregates data from various disparate but authoritative federal government data sources . . . with full details on each transaction for all federal contractors . . . ' (FEDMINE.US™ 2013). They obtained additional and confirmatory data from several of the structured data sources described above, including FPDS-NG and FEDBIZOPPS (2010: 81).

While most of these data were available in spreadsheet formats produced by FEDMINE.US™ and FPDS-NG, Maser and Thompson (2010) undertook a significant coding effort to convert the data to simpler, more usable forms. For example, they categorized a firm as either small or large based on its annual revenue and number of employees, which were presented in terms of dollars and headcounts, respectively. To give another example, they reduced the wide range of contract outputs (e.g. missiles, cargo vehicles, information systems, medical services, construction) to just three categories – weapons, products, or services. As a final example, they simplified the multiple contract types to the two major categories – fixed-price and cost-reimbursable.

Unstructured data

Maser and Thompson relied on narrative texts of protest cases from the GAO, as well as from lawsuits brought before the Court of Federal Claims by disgruntled bidders. They used the 'Advanced Search' feature of the GAO website to identify and extract relevant protest cases (e.g. those involving DOD agencies). They read the GAO protest cases and coded them according to whether the protest was viewed favorably or was denied. As with the structured data, some simplifying assumptions were made. For example, if several firms protested the same contract award, Maser and Thompson treated that case as one protest. Because of the need for legal skills in interpreting the cases decided by Court of Federal Claims, several law school students were engaged to assist in coding (2010: 79–81).

Based on their coding of both structured and unstructured data, Maser and Thompson (2010) conducted both ordinary least squares (OLS) and logistic regression to test the hypotheses mentioned above. For the OLS regression, the dependent variable was the protest rate in each month during their time period of interest (2004–2009); independent variables included firm size, contract type, number of bidders, contract output, and several others. The logistic regression tested 65,000 DOD contracts awarded during these years, with the dependent variable for each contract action as dichotomous, that is, either protested or not (2010: 49). Here Maser and Thompson encountered the challenge of capturing and reflecting data for all of the independent variables; indeed, they were able to obtain data on only some variables of interest. As Maser and Thompson noted in their methodology section, "Missing information [in FPDS-NG and other databases] is a significant problem" (2010: 81).

Had Maser and Thompson ended their study with this statistical analysis of archival data, it would have limited utility because of its simplifying assumptions and data limitations. As mentioned earlier, however, they also conducted a series of interviews with experts in contracting and protest resolution. As an integrated research effort, the interviews and the statistical analysis provide a valuable addition to the literature of contracting and defense management.

Summary and conclusion

The purpose of this chapter was to document and describe the principal sources of archival data on defense acquisition. While it focused on the USA, most other developed nations will have at least some similar data sources that are accessible from their MOD websites, as well as from sites that house their national government e-procurement systems. It discussed the unique nature of defense acquisition data. That is, some data are publicly available as part of the government's promotion of transparency, probity, and accountability, while other data may be controlled for security's sake, with limited access for research purposes. The chapter discussed sources of unstructured and structured data, along with budgetary data and policy documents, as well as examples of scholarly research that have drawn from those data sources.

Defense acquisition involves programs that are often fraught with cost, schedule, and performance problems. The costs, risks, and government oversight of these programs create a target-rich environment for scholarly research and investigation. Knowing how to navigate the terrain of the archival data landscape will equip the serious investigator to successfully conduct research on defense acquisition in any nation.

References

Albano, G., Snider, K. and Thai, K. United States (2013) "Charting a course in public procurement innovation and knowledge sharing," in G. Albano, K. Snider and K. Thai (eds) *Charting a Course in Public Procurement Innovation and Knowledge Sharing*, Boca Raton, FL: PrAcademics.

American Institute of Aeronautics and Astronautics (AIAA) (2013) Online. Available at www.aiaa.org (accessed March 12, 2013).

Benner, J.S., Morrison, M.R., Karnes, E.K., Kocot, S.L., and McClellan, M. (2010) "An Evaluation of Recent Federal Spending on Comparative Effectiveness Research: Priorities, Gaps, and Next Steps," *Health Affairs*, 29(10): 1768–1776.

Bolten, J., Leonard, R., Arena, M., Younossi, O., and Sollinger, J. (2008) *Sources of Weapon System Cost Growth: Analysis of 35 Major Defense Acquisition Programs*, Monograph MG-670, Santa Monica, CA: RAND.

Brown, T.L., Potoski, M., and Van Slyke, D.M. (2010) "Contracting for Complex Products," *Journal of Public Administration Research and Theory*, 20(suppl 1): i41–i58.

Callahan, C.M., Vendrzyk, V.P., and Butler, M.G. (2011) "The Impact of Implied Facilities Cost of Money Subsidies on Capital Expenditures and the Cost of Debt in the Defense Industry," *Journal of Accounting and Public Policy*, 31(3): 301–319.

Candreva, P. (2008) "Financial Management," in R. Rendon and K. Snider (eds) *Management of Defense Acquisition Projects*, Reston, VA: AIAA.

Citizens Against Government Waste (CAGW) (2013) Online. Available at www.cagw.org (accessed March 12, 2013).

Comptroller (2012) *Fiscal year (FY) 2013 President's Budget Submission (Navy)*, Justification Book vol. 1, Weapons Procurement, Navy, February. Online. Available at www.finance.hq.navy.mil/FMB/13pres/WPN_BOOK.PDF (accessed July 29, 2013).

Comptroller (2013) *DOD Financial Management Regulation 7000. 14-R*. Online. Available at http://comptroller.defense.gov/fmr/index.html (accessed July 29, 2013).

Dacus, C.L. (2012) "Improving Acquisition Outcomes through Simple System Technology Readiness Metrics," *Defense Acquisition Research Journal*, 19 (4): 444–461.

Davis, J. (1995) Congressional Budget Oversight of the Military Strategic and Tactical Relay (MILSTAR) Satellite Communications System, Fiscal Years 1982–1995, Master's thesis, Naval Postgraduate School, Monterey, CA.

Defense Acquisition University (DAU) (2011) *Defense Acquisition Guidebook*. Online. Available at http://at.DOD.mil/docs/DefenseAcquisitionGuidebook.pdf (accessed July 29, 2013).

Dillard, J. (2003) *Centralized Control of Defense Acquisition Programs: A Comparative Review of the Framework from 1987–2003*, Report No. NPS-AM-03–003, Monterey, CA: Naval Postgraduate School.

Dillard, J. (2007) *From Amorphous to Defined: Balancing the Risks of Spiral Development*, Acquisition Research Program Report, NPS-AM-07–002, Monterey, CA: Naval Postgraduate School.

Drezner, J., Jarvaise, J., Hess, R., Norton, D., and Hough, P. (1993) *An Analysis of Weapon System Cost Growth*, Monograph MR-291, Santa Monica, CA: RAND.

Federal Procurement Data System – Next Generation (FPDS-NG) (2013) *Reports*. Online. Available at https://www.fpds.gov/fpdsng_cms/index.php/reports (accessed July 29, 2013).

Fox, J.R. (1974) *Arming America: How the USA Buys Weapons*, Cambridge, MA: Harvard University Press.

Fox, J.R. (2011) *Defense Acquisition Reform, 1960–2009: An Elusive Goal*, Washington, DC: United States Army Center of Military History.

Gansler, J.S. (2011) *Democracy's Arsenal: Creating a Twenty-First-Century Defense Industry*, Cambridge, MA: MIT Press.

Hough, P. (1992) *Pitfalls in Calculating Cost Growth from Selected Acquisition Reports*, RAND Note N-3136-AF, Santa Monica, CA: RAND.

Kausal, T. (1999) *A Comparison of the Defense Acquisition Systems of France, Great Britain, Germany, and the United States*, Fort Belvoir, VA: Defense Systems Management College Press.

Kausal, T. (2000) *A Comparison of the Defense Acquisition Systems of Australia, Japan, South Korea, Singapore, and the United States*, Fort Belvoir, VA: Defense Systems Management College Press.

Kratz, L. and Buckingham, B.A. (2010) "Achieving Outcomes-Based Life Cycle Management," *Defense Acquisition Review Journal*, 53: 45–66.

Lavallee, T. (2003) "Globalizing the Iron Triangle: Policy-Making within the US Defense Industrial Sector," *Defense & Security Analysis*, 19(2): 149–164.

Lloyd, R.E. (1988) "Alternative Dispute Resolution in Federal Contracts: The Irony of Process," *Policy Studies Journal*, 16(3): 542–561.

Maser, S.M., and Thompson, G.F. (2010) *Understanding and Mitigating Protests of Department of Defense Acquisition Contracts*, Acquisition Research Program Technical Report WIL-CM-10–164, Naval Postgraduate School, Monterey, CA.

Maser, S.M. and Thompson, F. (2011) "Mitigating Spirals of Conflict in DOD Source Selections," *Defense Acquisition Research Journal*, 18(2): 160–175.

North Atlantic Treaty Organization (NATO) (2013) *NATO Support Agency Contract Awards*. Online. Available at www.nspa.nato.int/PDF/Procurement/Jul12-Dec12.pdf (accessed July 29, 2013).

Rendon, R.G., Apte, U.M., and Apte, A. (2012) "Services Acquisition in the DOD: A Comparison of Management Practices in the Army, Navy, and Air Force," *Defense Acquisition Research Journal*, 19, 1 (61): 3–32.

Rogerson, W.P. (1989) "Profit Regulation of Defense Contractors and Prizes for Innovation," *The Journal of Political Economy*, 97(6): 1284–1305.

Rubin, I. (2007) "The Great Unraveling: Federal Budgeting, 1998–2006," *Public Administration Review*, 67(4): 608–617.

Schwartz, M. (2010) *The Nunn-McCurdy Act: Background, Analysis, and Issue for Congress*, Washington, DC: Congressional Research Service.

Singapore Government (2013) *Government Electronic Business (GeBiz)*. Online. Available at www.gebiz.gov.sg (accessed July 29, 2013).

Snider, K.F. and Rendon, R.G. (2012) "Public Procurement: Public Administration and Public Service Perspectives," *Journal of Public Affairs Education*, 18: 327–348.

Thorpe, R.U. (2010) "The Role of Economic Reliance in Defense Procurement Contracting," *American Politics Research*, 38(4): 636–675.

US Congress (2007a) *Department of Defense Appropriations Act*, H.R. 3222, 110th Congress, January 4, Washington, DC: United States Government Printing Office.

US Congress (2007b) *National Defense Authorization Act for Fiscal Year 2008*, H.R. 1585, 110th Congress, January 4, Washington, DC: United States Government Printing Office.

US Congress (2009) *American Recovery and Reinvestment Act*, Public Law 111–115, 111th Congress, February 17, Washington, DC: United States Government Printing Office.

Zhao, Y., Gallup, S. and MacKinnon, D. (2010) *Towards Real-Time Program Awareness via Lexical Link Analysis*, Acquisition Research Program Report NPS-AM-10–174, Monterey, CA: Naval Postgraduate School.

9

PROCESS TRACING IN CASE STUDIES

Pascal Vennesson and Ina Wiesner

I. Wiesner (2013) *Importing the American Way of War? Network-Centric Warfare in the UK and Germany.* **Baden-Baden: Nomos.**

Military organisations regularly face the challenges and dilemmas of innovation. The longbow, the airplane, the computer as well as the mass army or amphibious warfare are technological and conceptual innovations that altered the conduct of war. They also reshaped military organisations leading, in some cases, to the creation of new combat arms or concepts of operation while, in others, to modest adaptations or even to deliberate resistance. The military uses of cyberspace, counterinsurgency, drone campaign strikes and Network-Centric Warfare are at the heart of the politics of military innovation at the beginning of the twenty-first century. They may durably affect operational planning, resource allocation, procurement decisions, training, and organisations. Yet surprisingly little is known about the factors that explain success and failure in military concept adoption. Why do some military organisations successfully incorporate new technologies or ideas while others do not?

Importing the American Way of War? examines the adoption by the British and German armed forces of Network-Centric Warfare (NCW), a concept based on the networking of relevant military units to achieve combat superiority. After being developed by US military officers in the late 1990s, the idea of networking sensors, commanders, and shooters to achieve greater mission effectiveness quickly spread to other military organisations. By 2001, a number of militaries started to emulate this innovation – albeit in different ways and with uneven results. What are the factors that account for differences in the adoption of NCW? To answer this question, Wiesner develops a small-N structured-focused comparative analysis and uses process tracing as an analytical tool to open the 'black box' that lies between initial conditions for the adoption of a military innovation and the eventual outcomes.

Process tracing helps to carefully reconstruct and compare the sequences of events constituting the process through which the relevant actors in each country became aware of NCW, used the concept and implemented it. It becomes possible to identify, and explore, the causes and consequences of differences in timing and pace, as well as differences in concept and implementation faithfulness. In doing so, she draws descriptive and causal inferences from various pieces of evidence that formed part of the temporal sequence of events. While the British military started to embrace NCW early in 2001 and introduced the concept rather quickly, the German military paid closer attention to NCW later in 2004 and proceeded slowly with its adoption. Further differences appeared with regards to concept faithfulness. Britain tailored NCW to fit its military culture and its operational needs. By contrast, despite a profound difference in military culture with the US and distinct security challenges, the German NCW concept essentially copied the US original. Finally, the assessment of implementation faithfulness revealed that, in the UK, the conceptual ambitions and the eventual adoption output lay close to each other. In the German case, however, implementation contradicted not only the conceptual outline, but also operational realities. Framed by an institutionalist argument, this study establishes that a different emphasis on military effectiveness and societal legitimacy in each country led to the different adoption processes and outcomes. In the case of NCW adoption, the British military was an efficiency maximiser whereas the German military was a legitimacy maximiser.

Introduction

Process tracing, succinctly defined as a method designed to 'identify the intervening causal process . . . between an independent variable (or variables) and the outcome of the dependent variable' (George and Bennet 2004: 206), is one of the most important analytical tool in case study research, particularly for within-case analysis (Mahoney 2012: 571; Goertz and Mahoney 2012: 100–114). The goal of this chapter is to present and discuss process tracing in military studies. Specifically, we address three questions: What is process tracing and how does it relate to other methods employed by social scientists? What is the purpose and added value of process tracing in military studies? How is process tracing in case studies actually conducted? We argue that process tracing is a valuable analytical tool for researchers interested in analysing the specifics of one case (or a small number of cases), in finding generalisable patterns and in making theoretical arguments. We start our chapter by locating process tracing in current social sciences methodology. We point out its value for explaining unique and outstanding events that often are interesting for scholars of military studies. We then discuss the utility of process tracing. Finally, we reflect on the actual uses of process tracing in case study research.

Process tracing and case-oriented research

Ways to study military affairs

With the exception of normative peace research and critical security studies, the majority of social science research conducted in the fields of military studies, such as peace and conflict studies as well as security studies, share a broadly positivist meta-theoretical foundation. Most researchers seek to uncover causal relationships or they engage in testing general hypotheses, or propositions, about causal relationships. The three most common methodological approaches in this regard are the statistical method, experiments and the case study method (Bennett and Elman 2006: 457). Scholars using statistical methods analyse large-N observational data-sets to infer about the relations between outcomes and conditional factors. Researchers also use experiments to assess cause-effect relationships in a controlled environment (see also Chapter 20 by Teigen). Yet there might be circumstances in which experiments are not feasible either for practical or ethical reasons. Likewise, scholars might consider that statistical analysis is insufficient, for example if they are interested in unique, outstanding events such as wars, battle outcomes or specific political and military decisions. They may also seek to explore the impact of certain factors on military organisations (for example the end of conscription) or the causes of specific outcomes (success and failure in war) that cannot be observed in a large number of cases. Moreover, some scholars are dissatisfied with the statistical method's bracketing of the social settings which frame their unit of analysis, the specific case that they want to examine. They believe that context matters. Finally, the statistical method has been criticised for producing assumption about causal relationships between two variables when in fact all it is able to show is their covariation (Gerring 2008). Both in order to establish the existence of a causal link and to understand the character of the causal relationship researchers most likely turn to qualitative methods (Goertz and Mahoney 2012: 101f.).

In these situations, case study research is the method of choice. In general, scholars employing qualitative methods are not interested in 'the net effect of a cause over a large number of cases, but rather how causes interact in the context of a particular case or a few cases to produce an outcome' (Bennett and Elman 2006: 458). Depending on their research interest and on the availability of empirical resources, researchers select a small number of cases, sometimes even one single case. The case study approach is the 'detailed examination of an aspect of a histori-cal episode to develop or test historical explanations that may be generalizable to other events' (George and Bennett 2004: 5). Like the researchers who use statistics or experiments, those who use case studies (and share a positivist meta-theoretical preference) aim at making inferences about cause-effects relationships that hold generalisable claims.

Originating in the field of cognitive psychology in the early 1970s, and later expanded and reformulated notably by the political scientist Alexander George, process tracing is one way of conducting case studies (George and Bennett 2004; Bennett and Elman 2006). We define process tracing as a technique designed to re-construct causal processes with the aim of developing or evaluating theoretical propositions about what accounts for an outcome in the specific phenomenon under study. Process tracing helps to uncover the links connect-ing outcomes and antecedent factors. It is common to ask whether there is any difference between process tracing and historical explanation (Bennett and George 2001: 144–152; George and Bennett 2004: 208–209, 224–230). While process tracing shares some of the basic features of historical research, historians and social scientists differ in the type of process tracing that they conduct and in their emphasis. Generally, historians are more interested in using process tracing to explain particular historical events in nearly all of their complexities, whereas social scientists seek to explain specific cases and establish generalis-able causal patterns across cases or categories of cases. What distinguishes process tracing by social scientists is that usually one of their goals is to test, refine and develop theories (although historians at times also use process tracing for these goals). They seek to uncover patterns and causal mechanisms that ultimately lead to a theoretical approach being rejected, refined or confirmed.

Process tracing has often been used, implicitly or explicitly, in the field of military studies to explain diverse phenomena, for example, the adaptation of armies to changing circumstances during the course of conflicts for which they are initially unprepared (Nagl 2005), the adoption of military concepts by military organisations (Farrell 2002), the production of knowledge and ignorance within, and by, military organisations (Eden 2004), or weapon-systems procurement decisions (Tessmer 1988). In these and other areas of interest, process tracing helps to establish cause-effect relationships and to uncover causal mechanisms; thus helping to specify how a certain outcome was brought about. A causal mechanism is:

> A link or connection in a causal process. In the relationship between a given independent variable and a given dependent variable, a causal mechanism posits additional variables, sometimes called intervening variables, that yield insight into how the independent variable actually produces the outcome, including the sequence through which this occurs. Compared to the original causal relationship that the scholar is considering, the causal mechanism is often located at a more fine-grained level of analysis.
>
> (Seawright and Collier 2004: 277)

Process tracing is useful to establish causal-process observations (distinguished from data-set observation), 'an insight or piece of data that provides information about context or mechanism' (Collier et al. 2010: 184). These observations about contexts and processes provide an alternative source of insight into the relationships among the explanatory variables, and between these variables and the dependent variable. Through process tracing, the researcher can assess not merely the presence or absence of an antecedent but the logic of the association between antecedents and outcomes (Steinberg 2007: 191–193; Falleti and Lynch 2009). By helping to establish such causal-process observations, process tracing provides a distinctive leverage in causal inference. Statements about covariation and causal mechanisms differ in that the latter is richer in content, embedded in context and thus depicting a more comprehensive view of a particular event. Exploring causal mechanisms allows understanding how variables might be related (Gerring 2008). By establishing the causal sequence of events the researcher can prove that X in fact anteceded Y. By uncovering how, in a specific case, X brought about Y, or, to what degree and in what way X influenced Y and how other factors influenced the process the researcher might furthermore be able to develop a theoretical argument about how – in general – X causes Y, thus eliminating rival hypotheses derived from competing theories. Finally, alternative explanations are considered by outlining the process tracing expectations of a range of explanations and then considering the evidence in the light of these theoretical propositions. The researcher asks: if this explanation is correct, what would be the process leading to the outcome of interest? Not every single potential explanation requires a detailed process tracing, however, as some might be quickly proven irrelevant while only a few others will require more detailed investigations.

Debating process tracing

Since the end of the 1990s, the use of process tracing for social science research has become more widespread and increasingly discussed (George and Bennett 2004; Bennett and Elman 2006; Checkel 2008; Vennesson 2008; Collier 2011). Scholars who use the statistical method, for example, consider that the potential value of process tracing is to increase the number of observations within one or a small number of cases and thus make inferences about causal-effect relationships even in small-N studies more significant (King et al. 1994: 226f.). Likewise it was suggested that process tracing could supplement statistical analysis to test theories. Others criticised this narrow conception of process tracing (Tarrow 2004; Collier et al. 2010; Goertz and Mahoney 2012). Case-oriented research and process tracing make scientific contributions in their own terms and should not be regarded as an imperfect epigone of the quantitative logic (George and Bennett 2004; Brady and Collier 2004).

The many faces of process tracing

Like in social science research in general, process tracing accounts in military studies vary along a spectrum from descriptive narration to abstract causal explanations (Bennett and George 2001; Vennesson 2008). An example of a narrative analysis of processes in the military studies field is Arnold Tessmer's study of the Airborne Warning and Control System (AWACS) procurement decision (Tessmer 1988). The author traced the processes within the North Atlantic Alliance (NATO) leading to the decision to collectively purchase AWACS in the late 1970s. By taking into account events before and after the decision Tessmer 'focuses on the process, details, and motivation in a narrow instance of give and take between allied governments with similar but decidedly different interests and values' (Tessmer 1988: xv). Insightful and empirically rich, Tessmer's work did not seek to explicitly test theories. Still he identified the factor – a strong bureaucracy at the collective level – that he deemed critical for the eventual success of AWACS despite the reluctance of some member states to commit to the programme.

In addition to this kind of 'thick description' of a case, process tracing can also contribute to its 'thick analysis' (Bennett and Elman 2006: 472). It can offer both a complex depiction of one or a small number of cases and an analysis of whether a theory's causal mechanisms operate as expected to affect the particular outcome(s) of the case(s). To be sure, description is valuable for gathering evidence on singular events and is an important component of process tracing (Collier 2011). Yet, played to its full strengths, it adds an analytical focus and helps to scrutinise cases in a systematic way with the ultimate aim of making generalisable statements, albeit most likely no universal claims. As such, it does not 'only help us to reveal complexity, but to make sense of it' (Steinberg 2007: 183).

John Nagl's study about the counterinsurgency lessons from Malaya and Vietnam provides an interesting example of an analytical process tracing account.[1] Why is it that the British army in Malaya and the US Army in Vietnam dealt so differently with wars that they had not been prepared for? Focusing on military culture Nagl traced the processes that led to a successful adaptation of military practices in the Malayan case and the failed adaptation of the US Army in Vietnam (Nagl 2005). He shows that one important reason for the outcomes was a different take on lesson learning in each army. Whereas the British army was a 'learning institution' and could quickly adapt to the changed circumstances, the US Army was not (ibid.: xxii). Despite their differences in research interest (procurement decision, military adaptation) and research design (single case study, structured focused comparison) Tessmer and Nagl used the process tracing technique to reconstruct their cases. Nagl's work exemplifies a fuller contribution of process tracing by providing an informing narrative, a sound analytical framework, and a contribution to the theoretical debate about military culture.

A number of related techniques, such as analytic narratives (Bates et al. 1998) and comparative historical analysis (Mahoney and Rueschemeyer 2003), that share some similarities with process tracing have been developed. Furthermore, some interpretivist scholars might go about their research in a similar fashion as positivist case study researchers. There is a disagreement on whether research tools used in interpretive research can be understood as process tracing (Bennett and George 2001; Vennesson 2008) or not (Checkel 2006). Even though many interpretive, or historical, accounts are not concerned with causal analysis in the first place and might not qualify as examples of process tracing, it is a useful procedure to explain but also to understand cases.

Process tracing, within-case analysis and structured focused comparison

Process tracing belongs to case study research, especially within-case analysis (Mahoney 2003; Bennett and Elman 2006: 455). Well-researched single-case studies contribute to the explanation of outcomes, such as Lynn Eden's account of the impact of organisational frames in the US Air Force's neglect of the effects of fire in its damage assessment of atomic blasts (Eden 2004). Process tracing is also useful in small-N comparative study designs, in which more than one case is examined and in which the process tracing technique is combined with a structured focused comparison research design:

> A comparison of two or more cases is 'focused' insofar as the researcher deals selectively with only those aspects of each case that are believed to be relevant to the research objectives and data requirements of the study. Similarly, controlled comparison is 'structured' when the researcher, in designing the study, defines and standardises the data requirements of the case studies. This is accomplished by formulating theoretically relevant general questions to guide the examination of each case.
>
> (George and McKeown 1985: 41)

A theoretically informed research framework such as structured focused comparison allows assessment of two or more cases to generate comparable statements about causal mechanisms in each case and to apply these findings to evaluate theoretical assumptions. Process tracing is one important tool to engage in such a structured focused comparative research.

The utility of process tracing

How can process tracing help social scientists to make sense of a case or a class of events? Even though process tracing does not solely aim at writing good narratives, the descriptive function of process tracing should not be disregarded (Collier 2011). Through descriptive inference based on process tracing the researcher might be able to uncover the causal mechanisms of a unique and outstanding event, such as the terrorist attacks of September 11, 2001, without necessarily aiming at making inferences about the class of phenomena, like the conditions under which terrorist attacks happen. Besides the descriptive value of process tracing it can serve a heuristic function, that is hypothesis generating and theory developing, by 'inductively identify[ing] general causal mechanisms that may be at work in other cases' (Bennett and George 2001: 144).

Moreover, process tracing helps to evaluate theories (Ragin 2000; George and Bennett 2004; Checkel 2006; Mahoney 2012). As a complement of statistical analyses, for example, process tracing can help identify measurement error, spurious correlations or instances of endogeneity (Bennett and Elman 2006: 459). Since correlation does not imply causation, process tracing is one option to assess through observational evidence causal claims that have been made based on statistical operations. The main advantage of process tracing for hypothesis testing is that assumed cause-effect relationships can be verified that otherwise would have required larger cross-case settings (Goertz and Mahoney 2012: 87). Through its focus on within-case causal mechanisms, process tracing can substitute for the lack of cases in small-N studies thus permitting hypothesis testing even in a single case.

Process tracing can also help to uncover factors that have previously been overlooked. During the course of the empirical research, some incidents or conditions might appear important that have not been covered in the theoretical assumptions (Bennett and George 2001: 144). Some scholars further argue that process tracing allows for both theory development and evaluation using the same case(s) (George and McKeown 1985; Bennett and George 2001: 149).

Process tracing in action

The choices for a research design, for the set of sources to consult and ultimately for the conduct of the research is dependent on the particular question the researcher is puzzled by. Process tracing is one technique available to gather evidence to solve the puzzle. The actual use of process tracing is as varied as there are case studies. In what follows we offer some reflections on the application of process tracing based on our own experiences with the procedure. We touch upon the issues of framing the research, data gathering and data analysis.

Framing the research

As an analytical tool, process tracing affects the framing of the research design, the gathering of pieces of data and the analysis (George and Bennett 2004; McNabb 2008: 287ff.). By relying on prior theory-based expectations that guide, at least initially, the empirical work, process tracing differs from research procedures where theorising starts only after the gathering and organising of data.

The conduct of the example study (Wiesner 2013) exemplifies this understanding. An explorative research revealed that despite similar operational requirements, financial resources and rhetorical commitment to the NCW-project the British armed forces were more successful to introduce the concept. The main goal was to explore and understand the reasons for this difference. How did the two military organisations differ in their adoption of NCW, both in terms of process and outcome? Which explanatory factors account for the differences? For these particular research questions, process tracing presented itself as the best choice of method. Had the puzzle been framed differently – for example as an inquiry into the differences in the NCW projects of all 28 NATO countries – a testing of the explanatory power of predefined sets of independent variables under quasi-controlled conditions would have been better adapted, with process tracing serving as a way to examine the internal validity of the argument (Gerring 2007: 172–185).

Prior to the conduct of empirical research on the introduction of NCW two analytical frameworks were developed to guide the case study empirical inquiries. One template concerned the adoption process. Relying on literature on foreign concept adoption (Bennett 1991; Rogers 2003), the typical phases of adoption processes were identified (see Table 9.1). These three phases, knowledge acquirement, utilisation, and implementation and the more fine-grained adoption stages structured the research questions regarding the introduction of NCW such as: when, how, and through which institutional channels did NCW appear? What role did decision-makers play? What differences existed between the original NCW conception and each national version? How were the concept and its introduction discussed within the military organisation and, finally, how (well) did the implementation of the concept proceed? The phases were conceptual categories: they were not seen as normative, nor confused with the actual adoption processes.

Table 9.1 Three phases of the adoption process

Adoption phases	Adoption stages
Knowledge acquirement	From dissemination to awareness
	From awareness to decision to active knowledge acquirement
	Knowledge acquirement
Utilisation	Adaptation
	Legitimising
	Decision-making and decision to adopt
Implementation	Initial stage
	Transitional stage
	Final stage

(Wiesner 2013: 56)

Admittedly, such a linear framework might partially limit the richness of a case study, it might also lead to the omission of otherwise interesting potential factors and sequences of events. However, it helped to reduce the complexity of the cases, which in turn allowed for generalising about the phenomena observed. It is important to note that process tracing can also lead to a refinement or a reordering of these phases.

The examination of the German and the British case of NCW adoption benefited from relying on this analytical framework. The compartmentalisation of the adoption process into its phases and stages enhanced the comparability of the two cases in this structured-focused comparative case study setting. During the research the adoptions phases in both cases were assessed in the form of an analytical narrative. The pre-structuring of the research effort allowed to draw comparative conclusions about the performance of British and German defence in these phases and, hence, also about the qualitative adoption differences between the two cases. These differences are displayed in Table 9.2.

Explaining these patterns was the second aim of the NCW adoption study. Why did the timing (the point in time when the concept was introduced) and the pace of adoption differ in Germany and in the UK? Why were both concept and implementation faithfulness different? To answer these questions, the NCW adoption study was located in a broader discussion of 'effectiveness versus legitimacy'-debate that had inspired thinking about military innovations and diffusion (Goldman 2003). Institutional legitimacy is the social acceptability and credibility that organisations require in order to 'survive and thrive in their social environment' (Scott 2001: 237). Gaining legitimacy can be a motive for foreign concept adoption. Was NCW introduced to increase the effectiveness of the armed forces in military operations? Or did it serve to maintain or increase the institutional legitimacy of the military organisation? To answer these questions, a second analytical framework based on social-institutionalist theory was used.

Table 9.2 NCW adoption patterns in the UK and in Germany (2001–2010)

	UK	Germany
Timing/pace	early/quick	late/slow
Concept faithfulness	low	high
Faithfulness of implementation	moderate to high	low

(Wiesner 2013: 131)

Relying on the existing literature on concept diffusion and adoption, a set of potentially relevant factors was preselected that were likely to have influenced the adoption processes in both cases. To add rigour to the examination those factors were grouped with respect to their level of occurrence (international, national/societal, organisational) and their nature in terms of effectiveness or legitimacy. Finally, the potentially relevant factors were operationalised in a set of questions to be applied to both cases (Wiesner 2013: 66). When the actual conduct of research took place the investigator was equipped with a useful framework to organise and conduct document analysis, interviews and – to a limited extent – direct observation.

In sum, theoretically guided case studies need some idea of social sciences theories or approaches that will be applied, tested or altered in the course of research. For social scientists using process tracing the research agenda might not so much be concerned with understanding a specific case but with patterns and causal processes that were at play not only in the particular case but hypothetically also in others. The use of diverse and independent empirical sources, such as interviews, media reports, documents, as well as when relevant a discerning use of the participants' correspondence, private papers or memoirs, is an important aspect of process tracing. These sources help to identify the arguments or reasons that actors give for their action. In some cases, it might be possible to compare public statements and private deliberations. In others, the researcher can use more spontaneous and unplanned statements to get a more fine-grained knowledge of genuine beliefs. While there is simple recipe to determine that sufficient data has been collected, a researcher can be increasingly confident that it is the case when the gathered evidence becomes repetitive.

Also, explorative research is useful in this research phase. Early evidence sharpens the research question as well as framework and design. Theoretical framing might not be fully completed once the data collection starts. Often the theoretical framework as well as its operationalisation is subject to adjustment once 'real-world' data is coming into play as empirical research progresses.

Data gathering

Qualitative empirical research, especially on topics that have not received much attention, is time consuming. To trace processes scholars may rely on a variety of sources. In the conduct of process tracing, any kind of empirical sources and tool (interviews, archives, statistics, participant observation, etc.) can be put to the task. Official documents, meeting minutes, speech manuscripts, diaries, newspaper articles and articles in professional journals relevant to the case(s) are often valuable, although problematic in their own way, written sources for establishing the process that led to a specific outcome. If process tracing is conducted in a structured and theory-informed way the researcher will specifically look in these written material for the absence or presence of particular process-relevant factors.

If the research puzzle is related to a contemporary case process tracing can benefit from data gathered in interviews (Tansey 2007). Not only can interviews ease the problem of unavailable or inaccessible documentation. Interviews might, moreover, be a valuable source for learning more about actor's motivations, disagreements in decision-making processes and paths not taken.

Although not a standard practice in process tracing, qualitative research on contemporary topics can also benefit from a range of direct observations that can include participant observation. Although access to military organisations or even temporary embedment, especially in foreign armies is hard to negotiate, it is not impossible (Navarro 2013; Ruffa 2013). Embedded research and direct or participant observation have two main advantages within the confines of process tracing. First, direct and participant observation are valuable for making better sense of gathered information especially in cases the researcher is not familiar with (i.e. research including technical issues or in different cultural settings). Second, direct and participant observations bring the researcher closer to the scene. Through closer contacts to political or military actors, the researcher might be able to become aware of, or to obtain, information and documents.

Making sense of the data

Process tracing accounts benefit from the integration of new evidence into the research framework. Moreover, the objectives of data gathering might change in the course of the research. Evidence for rival explanations might appear that need to be addressed or included into the research framework. Social scientific research is a circular process in which the researcher usually goes back and forth between theorising, data collection and analysis. Openness to adjustment can result in a better specification of causal mechanisms and, thus, more reliable research findings.

In the example study it became apparent during a round of interviews conducted with British experts that 'expected cost saving' in the procurement department had been a motive for embracing the networking concept. This factor was unexpected since neither theoretical considerations nor explorative research had suggested budget saving as a potential cause of introducing NCW. As a result, this factor had not been considered in the initial theoretical framework that guided process tracing. Nor had it been explored in the pre-structured interviews with German officials that had preceded the British case study. Cost saving was added to the research framework, and a second round of interviews with German experts was conducted to assess the (potential) impact of this factor which, in the end, did not turn out to have played a decisive role in the German case.

Finally, process tracing accounts do not necessarily need to be organised chronologically but rather with regards to theoretical assumptions (George and McKeown 1985: 53). In the example study empirical evidence was arranged to represent the three adoption phases rather than in their chronological order. Process tracing can, but does not need to result in a narration of a particular event.

Conclusion

In their definition of what makes good process tracing, Bennett and Elman emphasised that, first, process tracing accounts need to be comprehensive and balanced. Second, breaks in the theoretical story need to be avoided. Third, evidence should confirm the hypothesis, and alternative explanation should be ruled out. Finally, they advise the researcher to be attentive to confirmation bias (Bennett and Elman 2006: 459f.). In addition, process tracing provides an opportunity to pay careful attention to 'non-events' or 'negative cases', the process or outcome that did not materialize but could have.

Process tracing is not a magic procedure that miraculously solves the challenge of producing significant generalisations in qualitative case studies. Still, in the field of military studies case-oriented research and especially the technique of process tracing provide a useful way to illuminate specific events, make inferences about cause and effect relations that shaped the cases, uncover causal mechanisms, and finally, even make – with all caution involved – propositions about similar events.

Note

1 It is important to note that our goal here is not to provide a systematic, substantive, assessment of John Nagl's book that would include, for example, a discussion of his case selection or of the empirical elements that he overlooked. We focus instead specifically on the ways in which he uses process tracing to illustrate one possible way to put process tracing to the task in military studies.

References

Bates, R.H., A. Greif, M. Levi, J.-L. Rosenthal and B.R. Weingast (1998). 'Conclusion'. In R.H. Bates, A. Greif, M. Levi, J.-L. Rosenthal and B.R. Weingast (eds), *Analytic Narratives*. Princeton, NJ: Princeton University Press, pp. 231–238.

Bennett, A. and C. Elman (2006). 'Qualitative Research: Recent Developments in Case Study Methods'. *Annual Review of Political Science*, Vol. 9: 455–476.

Bennett, A. and A.L. George (2001). 'Case Studies and Process Tracing in History and Political Science: Similiar Strokes for Different Foci'. In C. Elman and M.F. Elman (eds), *Bridges and Boundaries: Historians, Political Scientists, and the Study of International Relations*. Cambridge, MA: MIT Press, pp. 137–166.

Bennett, C.J. (1991). 'How States Utilize Foreign Evidence'. *Journal of Public Policy*, Vol. 11, No. 1: 31–54.

Brady, H.E. and D. Collier (2004). *Rethinking Social Inquiry: Diverse Tools, Shared Standards*. Lanham, MD: Rowman & Littlefield.

Carreiras, H. and C. Castro (eds) (2013). *Qualitative Methods in Military Studies: Research Experiences and Challenges*. London and New York: Routledge.

Checkel, J.T. (1999). 'Norms, Institutions, and National Identity in Contemporary Europe'. *International Studies Quarterly*, Vol. 43, No. 1: 83–114.

Checkel, J.T. (2006). 'Tracing Causal Mechanisms'. *The International Studies Review*, Vol. 8: 362–370.

Checkel, J.T. (2008). 'Process Tracing'. In A. Klotz and D. Prakash (eds), *Qualitative Methods in International Relations: A Pluralist Guide*. Palgrave: Macmillan, pp. 114–129.

Collier, D. (2011). 'Understanding Process Tracing'. *Political Science and Politics*, Vol. 44, No. 4: 823–830.

Collier, D., H.E. Brady and J. Seawright (2010). 'Sources of Leverage in Causal Inference: Toward an Alternative View of Methodology'. In H.E. Brady and D. Collier (eds), *Rethinking Social Inquiry: Diverse Tools, Shared Standards* (2nd edn). Lanham, MD: Rowman & Littlefield Publishers.

Eden, L. (2004). *Whole World on Fire: Organizations, Knowledge, and Nuclear Weapons Devastation*. New York: Cornell University Press.

Falleti, T. and J.F. Lynch (2009). 'Context and Causal Mechanisms in Political Analysis'. *Comparative Political Studies*, Vol. 42, No. 9: 1143–1166.

Farrell, T. (2002). 'World Culture and the Irish Army, 1922–1942'. In T. Farrell and T. Terriff (eds), *The Sources of Military Change: Culture, Politics, Technology*. Boulder, CO: Lynne Rienner Publishers, pp. 69–90.

George, A.L. and T. McKeown (1985). 'Case Studies and Theories of Organizational Decision Making'. In R. Coulam and R. Smith (eds), *Advances in Information Processing in Organizations*, Vol. 2. London: JAI Press, 21–58.

George, A.L. and A. Bennett (2004). *Case Studies and Theory Development in the Social Sciences* (BCSIA Studies in International Relations). Cambridge, MA, and London: MIT Press.

Gerring, J. (2007). *Case Study Research: Principles and Practices*. Cambridge and New York: Cambridge University Press.

Gerring, J. (2008). 'The Mechanismic Worldview: Thinking inside the Box'. *Journal of Political Science*, Vol. 38: 161–179.

Goertz, G. and J. Mahoney (2012). *A Tale of Two Cultures: Qualitative and Quantitative Research in the Social Sciences*. Princeton, NJ: Princeton University Press.

Goldman, E.O. (2003). 'Receptivity to Revolution: Carrier Air Power in Peace and War'. In E.O. Goldman and L.C. Eliason, L.C. (eds), *The Diffusion of Military Technology and Ideas*. Stanford, CA: Stanford University Press, pp. 267–303.

King, G., R.O. Keohane and S. Verba (1994). *Designing Social Inquiry: Scientific Inference in Qualitative Research*. Princeton, NJ: Princeton University Press.

Mahoney, J. (2003). 'Strategies of Causal Assessment in Comparative Historical Analysis'. In J. Mahoney and D. Rueschemeyer (eds), *Comparative Historical Analysis in the Social Sciences*. Cambridge and New York: Cambridge University Press, pp. 337–372.

Mahoney, J. (2012). 'The Logic of Process Tracing Tests in the Social Sciences'. *Sociological Methods and Research*, Vol. 41, No. 4: 570–597.

Mahoney, J. and D. Rueschemeyer (2003). *Comparative Historical Analysis in the Social Sciences* (Cambridge Studies in Comparative Politics). Cambridge and New York: Cambridge University Press.

McNabb, D.E. (2008). *Research Methods in Public Administration and Nonprofit Management: Quantitative and Qualitative Approaches*. Armonk, NY: M.E. Sharpe.

Nagl, J.A. (2005). *Learning to Eat Soup with a Knife: Counterinsurgency Lessons from Malaya and Vietnam* (paperback edn). Chicago, IL: University of Chicago Press.

Navarro, A. (2013). 'Negotiating Access to an Argentinean Military Institution in Democratic Times: Difficulties and Challenges'. In H. Carreiras and C. Castro (eds), *Qualitative Methods in Military Studies: Research Experiences and Challenges*. London and New York: Routledge, pp. 85–96.

Perecman, E. and S.R. Curran (2006). *A Handbook for Social Science Field Research: Essays and Bibliographic Sources on Research Design and Methods*. Thousand Oaks, CA: Sage Publications.

Ragin, C.C. (2000). *Fuzzy-Set Social Science*. Chicago, IL: University of Chicago Press.

Rogers, E.M. (2003). *Diffusion of Innovations*. New York: Free Press.

Ruffa, C. (2013): 'What Peacekeepers Think and Do: An Exploratory Study of French, Ghanaian, Italian, and South Korean Armies in the United Nations Interim Force in Lebanon'. *Armed Forces & Society*. Online before print, 28 March 2013.

Scott, R.W. (2001). *Institutions and Organizations*. Thousand Oaks, CA: Sage.

Seawright, J. and D. Collier (2004). 'Glossary'. In H.E. Brady and D. Collier (eds), *Rethinking Social Inquiry: Diverse Tools, Shared Standards*. Lanham, MD: Rowman & Littlefield, pp. 273–313.

Steinberg, P.F. (2007). 'Causal Assessment in Small-N Policy Studies'. *Policy Studies Journal*, Vol. 35, No. 2: 181–204.

Tansey, O. (2007). 'Process Tracing and Elite Interviewing: A Case for Non-Probability Sampling'. *PS: Political Science and Politics*, Vol. 40, No. 4: 765–772.

Tarrow, S. (2004). 'Bridging the Quantitative-Qualitative Divide'. In H.E. Brady and D. Collier (eds), *Rethinking Social Inquiry: Diverse Tools, Shared Standards*. Lanham, MD: Rowman & Littlefield, pp. 171–179.

Tessmer, A.L. (1988). *The Politics of Compromise: NATO and AWACS*. Washington, DC: NDU Press.

Vennesson, P. (2008). 'Case Studies and Process Tracing: Theories and Practices'. In D.M. Della Porta and Keating M. (eds), *Approaches and Methodologies in the Social Sciences: A Pluralist Perspective*. Cambridge: Cambridge University Press, pp. 223–239.

Wiesner, I. (2013). *Importing the American Way of War? Network-Centric Warfare in the UK and Germany* (Militär und Sozialwissenschaften). Baden-Baden: Nomos.

10

BEING ONE OF THE GUYS OR THE FLY ON THE WALL?

Participant observation of veteran bikers

René Moelker

René Moelker (2014) *Riding with Veterans.* **Berlin: Springer.**

The aim of this study into veterans who ride motorcycles is to gain knowledge and understanding about the healing effect of riding. What is it that helps veterans cope better with experiences from the past by involving in an activity that in fact is somewhat dangerous, which sometimes is not understood in wider society and which always implies the presence of other bikers. Narratives can illustrate why veterans connect their battle or conflict experiences with riding a motorcycle.

Joop van de Vijver, 87 years old, is the oldest participant on the Veterans Ride to The Hague. During WWII in Indonesia he fought the Japanese. Joop was an orderly in 1942 and thus was supposed to deliver messages by motorcycle. The motorcycle saved his life in the quaintest way. He got into an accident. He drove his bike into a ditch and landed in hospital and whilst he was being treated for his injuries the Japanese lured the rest of his battalion into an ambush. He said 'They have been slaughtered! The Japanese killed my whole platoon. Because of my accident I survived. The others, all of them my own age, they have all been knifed or shot down.'

The objective of the study was to learn from people like Joop van de Vijver how veterans cope and deal with their conflict experiences and to learn about the role the motorcycle played as an instrument of obtaining societal recognition and social support. The researchers compared narratives from American and European veterans in order to learn about the genesis of veteran culture. The findings point to brotherhood and communitas working as a stress release, whilst riding itself has some elements of pilgrimage in it that are healing. The almost holy destination of a ride, often being a place of worship like the Wall in Washington, DC, during Memorial Day or of joyous celebration like Veterans Day in The Hague, makes it worth their while to meet, travel and communicate with each other while the recognition that wider society bestows on the veteran bikers feels like a successful second homecoming.

    Participant observation as a general method proved to work well in order to understand the processes under study. The difficulties experienced were related to obtaining organizational entry, winning trust, and balancing involvement and detachment. In this connection, informed consent and member checks proved to be highly important. Without these research practices the study would have been doomed to fail. Remarkable is the use of unusual artefacts as research instrument, referring to the motorcycle that became integral part of the heuristic strategy.

Introduction: Out of the cold, into the frying pan

It is freaking cold, not freezing, but even when dressed for extreme weather, the wind chill factor and the humidity of the Dutch climate causes the cold to penetrate into the bones. After a ride, merely 65 miles, everything aches, bodies are shivering, hands no longer function well and handling brakes and clutch is getting troublesome. It is getting real dangerous. Why go motorcycling this early in spring? What nutter thought this up? Tension is rising as we reach our destination. It is dark and the last ten miles take the bike along local roads. The last road is narrow, no lampposts, lightning, and not even moonlight on this particular night in the countryside. We are afraid. If they mean us wrong there is no way out, no people to assist us, only our wits to put trust in. Our first visit to a Motorcycle Club (MC), whose members participated in post-conflict situations as military veterans, proves memorable. The participant observers enter a scene that seemingly resembles an episode of the *Sons of Anarchy* series.

    No textbook on research methodology can help us now. The first and only relevant question at this stage is winning trust. Getting the proverbial foot into the door and to continue from that point on. We did have a topic list of questions and an overarching objective to the study. And we did have a predesigned methodology that we coined *kinetic ethnography*, but winning trust was essential to everything that followed. Winning trust could gain us knowledge nobody else could obtain by other means, but it also lured us into the classic problem of participant observation, the problem of involvement and detachment (Elias 2007). Are the researchers 'only a fly on the wall' or do they gain trust by being 'one of the guys'?

    In this chapter the methodology of *kinetic ethnography* is elaborated upon; problems with the balance in involvement and detachment are discussed and the specifics of participant observation like obtaining entry, interviewing, taking (mental) field notes, sense-making and informed consent are dealt with.

Kinetic ethnography and the study of liminality

Paul Willis (2010) defines ethnography in the most clear and simple manner: '"Ethno" is people, "graphy" is writing, so ethnography is writing about people.' But ethnography in itself does not suffice to study groups that are in a transitional phase and can be characterized by high mobility and transformation. Veteran biker groups are defined by closure towards 'normal' citizens and the non-veteran-biker community, i.e. those 'who would not understand'. Outsiders are often and most significantly called 'civilians'. Veteran bikers feel they are different because of past experiences in war zones and the common feeling they share of being rejected by wider society as both a veteran and a biker, and therefore these groups feel vulnerable. Mobility, closure and the vulnerability of these groups, makes it difficult to win trust other than by partly participating in their life style and engage in participant observation using ethnographic methods. Therefore kinetic ethnography, i.e. ethnography on the move, emerged.

Evidently, motorcycling veterans are studied mainly when they are on the move. Earlier on, Michalowski and Dubish (2001) undertook the task of developing kinetic ethnography. They based their work on Turner and Turner's (1978) seminal studies of liminality and pilgrimage, studies where the mobility of the 'respondents' constitutes the most dominant characteristic. The very concept of liminality is inherently motored by kinetics, because it is all about transitory phases and 'spaces in between'. In *Liminality and Communitas*, Turner (1969: 95) defines liminal individuals or groups as:

> neither here nor there; they are betwixt and between the positions assigned and arrayed by law, custom, convention, and ceremony.

In this study liminality will apply to voyaging towards a destination with a sacred character even when the 'sacred' destination in fact has no relationship with religion and sense-making is an immanent enterprise. Within a liminal period different rules apply and the group of travellers develops its own temporal norms and values that can depart from society's accepted civilian norms. In fact the travellers develop a sense of communitas that sets them apart as 'outsiders' from the 'established' (Elias and Scotson 2008). Thus Coleman and Eade (2004: 3) state that sacred journeys are productive of social groupings: 'The Turnerian notion of pilgrimage as a liminoid[1] phenomenon . . . is productive of social encounters without hierarchical constraints.' After the voyage and when reintegration in society is successful the traveller might experience that (s)he has undergone a transformation. Travelling normally broadens the mind, but travelling as a part of an existential journey changes conceptions of meaning and sense-making shedding everyday life in a different light. It also changes the participant observer.

Kinetic ethnography requires that the demarcation line between involvement and detachment be crossed by being liminal yourself, by participation in what goes on. Kinetic ethnography requires the ethnographer to be on the move, and to undertake the journey him/herself. The ethnographer is not necessarily a member, nor a veteran, and that is why detached observation is possible despite the high level of involvement. But it is a subjective process because the ethnographer him/herself is also changed by the experience of journeying. Kinetic ethnography is the only possibility to deploy empathy that is required in order to understanding the meaning that bikers give to their quest.

The rides have a special character. The destination is sacral even if it is secular in origin. A war memorial or battlefield tour as destination certainly is sacral even if it is not at all religious. One of the road trips has 'the Wall', the Vietnam Veterans Memorial, as its destination and Coleman and Eade (2004: 21) refer to this place as 'one of America's most prominent shrines'. Winkelman and Dubisch (2005: XV) named these road trips 'secular pilgrimages'. Preceding Memorial Day, where during 'Rolling Thunder' the veteran bikers are greeted by 900,000 spectators, the *Run for the Wall* forms a cross-nation motorcycle pilgrimage towards this destination in Washington DC. A Dutch – small – nexus to this motorcycle pilgrimage is the road trip heading for Lourdes. Even though it cannot be compared regarding size, the impact and mechanisms at work are the same as the ride to Washington DC. This motorcycle road trip is small but it is embedded in a large international military pilgrimage of mainly disabled veterans who seek healing at the holy places in this city.

These methodological reflections on kinetic ethnography lead to special research tools, i.e. the researcher him/herself, the motorcycle, observation during rides and the campfire interview protocol. But the first task of the researcher is obtaining entry.

Out of the frying pan into the fire

Winning the trust of bikers sometimes was dead easy, and sometimes it felt like entering a snake pit. All veterans share the need to narrate (DeWalt and DeWalt 2011) and to (re)construct a healing identity when the original narrative has been broken (McAdams 1996) by the course of events in war ridden places or by the not always warm welcome upon return from mission. That is why a listening ear is often very welcome, although the interviewer must be wary for the bias that comes along this need to narrate . . . i.e. the fact that reconstructing identities and presenting narratives is not the same as truth telling or factual and objective reporting.

Obtaining entry proved unexpectedly easy when the interviewer in the United States joined the *Run for the Wall*, a ride with Vietnam Vets from Los Angeles to Washington DC. The researcher only needed five minutes to explain the objective of the study, after which he was welcomed by the platoon leader:

> hey guys, listen out, René is going to participate and ask some questions. He came all the way from Holland to write a book on the Run for the Wall.

After this introduction the interviewer put up his tent, camped with the Vets, was invited to the diner hall where the local community in pilgrimage fashion had provided free dinner for 500 bikers. In merely five minutes the interviewer was one of the guys; moreover, the interviewer was ascribed high status, as illustrated by the following quote given by an anonymous biker:

> Hey René . . . can I have a photo taken with you! You came all the way from Holland just to be with us. That is so cool.

By way of contrast, in the Netherlands entering the clubhouse of the Veterans MC did not quite evoke warm feelings of the welcoming kind. Upon introduction, one normally gives the bikers-handshake, but the female co-researcher was not even given a normal handshake, which seemed the summit of impoliteness. Later the bikers explained this was normal, because they were not sure if the female was someone's 'ol' lady'. And you don't exchange pleasantries with another man's 'ol' lady'. So in fact, from their perspective they were being polite, but we missed it being unfamiliar with MC customs!

The interviewers had themselves to blame for starting out on the wrong foot and should have known better. There was a reason for this difficult start. The political situation at that time implied that all MCs were haunted by being affiliated with *Business Clubs*[2] like Hells Angels (HA) and Satudarah (a rivalling Business Club that is supposed to be in contact with HA arch enemies, the Bandidos). Even though the police never produced anything but circumstantial evidence (Dienst Nationale Recherche, 2010), headlines in newspapers shouted 'war is coming' and MC members were severely scrutinized, telephones tapped, and rallies were cancelled on the order of local authorities. Therefore the Veterans MC did not trust the researchers from the 'establishment', the Netherlands Military Academy. But even so, they wanted to hear us out. To our surprise the secretary of the Veterans MC had checked out the research proposal that was published on the academy's website, in the official Academy's Annual Research Plan. His comment was as follows:

Was it The Hague [the MOD] that assigned this study into MCs? Why do you want to know about us? In your research proposal you mention the term 'mal-adaption', what do you mean by that? And besides, what if we allow you to talk to us, what's in it for us?

The secretary was right in being suspicious. The term 'mal-adaption' was derived from stress-theory, and whilst quite common as a theoretical concept, it tapped into the idea that this was yet another stereotyping study into the derailed veteran who after feeling rejected by society turns to crime, madness and violence. Veterans in general dislike this kind of stereotyping, and the secretary was no exception. We had, even before the study started, projected a concept unto our subjects that already was a conclusion, and by his critical question the secretary pointed us to aspects of our study that were presumptuous and demeaning to our subjects. We were allowed access to the field and invited to the international Brothers in Arms Rally but we were more or less on probation.

The answer to the question 'what is in it for us' did finally gain us entry to the field and helped to win trust. The study led to positive publicity and positive image building. We helped organize a Netherlands Veterans Rally with destination The Hague that very much contributed to the positive publicity. Second, collaboration benefited individual bikers who were key actors in the MC. The study brought them into contact with people in high places who not only contributed to emancipation of the group but who also satisfied individual needs for recognition. A number of MC members got in touch with the Prince of Orange as well as shaking hands with the Commander in Chief. The secretary of the MC was awarded the insignia 'Wounded but not Vanquished', a highly valued insignia because it acknowledges his PTSD to be caused by the working conditions in the conflict area, from the hands of the Lieutenant-General of Veterans personally. Without this study he would not have the social network to start the application procedure for acquiring this insignia. Moreover he would perhaps never have thought this was feasible. Motorcycle groups and individuals gained respectability thanks to this study. The researchers nowadays are welcome at biker events.

The campfire interview protocol

When one gets to these destinations, it is impossible to take out a survey form that people can fill in. Bikers don't respond well to quantitative methods and distrust them as they are probably submitted in service of 'the man', i.e. governmental bureaucracy. Imagine some of those ZZ-top bearded guys jotting down their thoughts and answers on a piece of paper complying with official requests by Armed Forces scholars! It wouldn't happen!

Observations and interviews were taken wherever possible. On parking lots (the one at the Pentagon held 1 million roaring bikes), during refuelling, in club houses, in churches, schools, hospitals, memorial sites, biker rallies, camping sites and in private homes. Sometimes tapes held additional noise of thundering engines. The protocol therefore contained questions regarding military life events, motivation and motorcycling. Each question had a deeper motive. For example the question 'how long and why have you been a member of a motorcycle group' was designed to get grip on the Turnerian theoretical concept of 'communitas' and bonding between veterans. The very simple question 'why do you ride motorcycles' was connected to the healing and psychological side of the narrative. We knew from test interviews that these questions would work well. One question in particular, the question what bikers thought of the '1%' insignia, was intended to reveal the meanings attached to symbols and to determine the place of self in the wider symbolic universe. This question proved a core question in our attempt to understand, *Verstehen*, the bikers and therefore it will be elaborated in one of the later sections. The questions were formulated as simple as possible, because we knew in advance we would be working in informal and sometimes noisy surroundings.

Field notes under 'hot' conditions

'In a way, your research journal will become the centre of gravity of your whole project' (Zemliansky 2012). In this journal the researcher can note down interview and research questions, descriptions of artefacts, notes to self, ideal, searchlight hypothesis as well as meta-cognitive reflections. One can make use of electronic recording devices, immediate typing keywords into a computer, or a simple notebook. In special situations one can use whatever one can find to make field notes. If in a bar, write on a coaster. Later the notes can be analysed. Interview protocols can be transcribed and coded. Interviewees can be committed by sending them the protocol and ask them to approve of the text. This procedure, the member check, is very helpful and serves many purposes besides upping the validity of the study, as we will discuss in subsequent sections.

All of the above helps organizing and analysing the data and it sounds pretty straightforward, but alas, it is not. The most difficult thing is when organizational entry is difficult to beget and consent for the interview is not (yet) given. This was the situation we were in whilst trying to gain entry and at the same time interviewing the board members of the Veterans MC. The first acquaintance startled and confused the researchers and the welcome resulted in 'hot' interviewing conditions. Whilst one of the researchers had a hard time defending the rationale of the study and was verbally under fire, the other researcher observed and made mental field notes that she was able to retrieve from memory immediately the next day. In this stressful situation the researchers were fortunate to be working as a duo, otherwise no field notes would have been made. After becoming friends, and gaining trust and entry, the Veterans MC did not object to publication of the findings from this memorable evening.

The balance between involvement and detachment

The ethnographer needs to be involved personally in order to use participant observation, whilst maintaining an adequate balance of involvement and detachment (Elias 2007). According Norbert Elias the balance should be respected because:

> scientists have learned that any direct encroachment upon their work by short-term interests or needs of specific persons or groups is liable to jeopardize the usefulness which their work may have in the end for themselves or for their own group.
>
> (Ibid.: 72)

One needs a detached position in order not to blur observations by one's own Maslovian hierarchy of needs. When one needs something, when interest is at stake, this will taint all observations. Elias himself explains in a very straightforward example:

> a philosopher once said, 'If Paul speaks of Peter he tells us more about Paul than about Peter.' One can say, by way of comment, that in speaking of Peter he is always telling us something about himself as well as about Peter. One would call his approach 'involved' as long as his own characteristics, the characteristics of the perceiver, overshadow those of the perceived. If Paul's propositions begin to tell more about Peter than about himself the balance begins to turn in favour of detachment.
>
> (Ibid.: 69)

In the social sciences it is more difficult to detach oneself, because 'objects' are also 'subjects' (ibid.: 79). In ethnography the problem is even more acute because the researcher uses his body as an instrument, as a research tool; thus the investigators themselves are, as a rule, directly involved in the problems they study. In *kinetic ethnography* the researcher is interested in the preferred cultural items of a group. In the veterans study the motorcycle was both a research tool and the cultural artefact under study, thereby thriving on the homology of the man–machine interface. Homology implies that the production of cultural meaning, identity and behaviours of people is affected by the artefacts they utilize. Thus, biker culture is just as much formed by bikers as by bikes. Paul Willis, who wrote extensively on motorcycle culture (Willis 1978: 189–203; 2010),[3] explains that ethnography depends on bodily engagement:

> When I developed a particular cultural studies approach to human meaning making, I felt I had to be in the situation where I had to use my own body, my own presence, my own sensibility, to understand how other people were making sense of their worlds thru their cultural engagements . . . the whole point of ethnography is that you use the (your) human body as your research instrument. You put yourself in the same situation as those human agents . . . to read from that the similar processes of meaning in other people . . . I stress the materiality of culture.
>
> (Willis 2010)

The homological level is one of three levels of sociocultural analysis that Willis distinguishes.[4] It focuses on the production of meaning by the interaction with material objects, cultural items that are bestowed with meaning. According to Willis:

> the bike itself came into a homological relation with the bike boys in Birmingham, where they argued that a certain kind of masculinity, sense of confidence in the world, and style was reflected in the motorbike, and that over time the boys changed this cultural item the more to reflect their own sense of identity. They took of the straight handlebars that you normally have, so that you would get down low on the bike, to lower wind resistance and you can go faster . . . They put cattle horn handles on the bike that resulted in far more wind resistance, but it gave a distinct style of riding, that helped to hold their identity. They took the baffles out of the exhaust, why? To make the exhaust louder, so that the bike roared and frightened people, rather than having a bike that purred through the grey surroundings of the urban city. All changes to hold their sense of identity. Through the ethnographic method, observing the way they changed the bike in order to express them selves, I argued a distinct motorbike identity and cultural relationship was formed. I think we can take any cultural item, music, car, etcetera, and look at the way it is connected to human activity and human praxis, all these things are in a dialectic about how to develop an identity.
>
> (Willis 2010)

On the one hand, the balance between involvement and detachment is somewhat tilted towards involvement, because it would first of all be difficult to gain organizational entry, but second, if it were not tilted it would not be possible to learn about the process of meaning making. You don't have to be a biker to understand why bikers act like they do. But you do have to put yourself physically in the material situation the group under study is in, and be willing to use your own body as research tool. If you want to practice kinetic ethnography, be ready to be on

Table 10.1 Participant observation type chart (Spradley 1980)

Type of participant observation	*Level of involvement*	*Limitations*
Non-Participatory	No contact with population or field of study	Unable to build rapport or ask questions as new information comes up.
Passive Participation	Researcher is only in the bystander role	Limits ability to establish rapport and immersing oneself in the field.
Moderate Participation	Researcher maintains a balance between 'insider' and 'outsider' roles	This allows a good combination of involvement and necessary detachment to remain objective.
Active Participation	Researcher becomes a member of the group by fully embracing skills and customs for the sake of complete comprehension	This method permits the researcher to become more involved in the population. There is a risk of 'going native' as the researcher strives for an in-depth understanding of the population studied.
Complete Participation	Researcher is completely integrated in population of study beforehand (i.e. he or she is already a member of particular population studied)	There is the risk of losing all levels of objectivity, thus risking what is analysed and presented to the public.

the move just like your respondents are. You need to be 'talking the talk' and 'walking the walk' (DeWalt and Dewalt 2011: 56–60). On the other hand over-involvement can blur observations tremendously. Complete participation, complete integration, is not prerequisite for comprehension of the groups under study. Table 10.1 provides an overview of various types of participant observation, including corresponding limitations.

The study among veteran bikers is an example of rather active participation; touring with the veterans the researcher – with his bike (!) – became virtually part of the group. Claude Weber's ethnographic study (2012) among cadet-officers at the French military academy in Saint-Cyr is an example of passive participation, as this lecturer could never be a member of the group of cadets that he studied. However, over a number of years he attended many meetings, ceremonies and other social events and he developed close ties with the cadets through intensive interviewing and informal talks. This made him a bit of an insider, as through this intensive presence passive participation turned into moderate participation.

Thick description and the '1%' question

The method in use is modelled on Max Weber's heuristic concept of *sinnhaft verstehen* (1985: 427–432) that has culture as its objective and culture all revolves around meaning. Webers' work inspired Geertz (1973: 5) to one of the most quoted definitions of culture.

> Believing, with Max Weber, that man is an animal suspended in webs of significance he himself has spun, I take culture to be those webs, and the analysis of it to be therefore not an experimental science in search of law but an interpretive one in search of meaning.

To grasp meaning one should, according Geertz, apply '*thick description*', wherein:

> lies the object of ethnography: a stratified hierarchy of meaningful structures. (ibid. 7) . . . What we call our data are really our own constructions of other people's constructions of what they and their compatriots are up to . . . we are explicating: and worse, explicating explications.
>
> (Ibid.: 9)

Verstehen or thick description is really a method that we had to use to understand the behaviours and intentions of our motorcycling veterans. Merely objective observation, if observation can be objective, would be thin description. Thus, observing that some bikers wear the '1%' sign, a diamond shaped green-on-white embroidered '1%' is relevant as it describes what people are wearing, but it does not tell us why they are wearing it and what meaning they bestow on it. One of our key questions on the honour code was designed to find out where the veterans stand on the issue of societal integration or alienation. A simple open-ended question like 'what do you think of/feel about the "1%" symbol' triggered a world of significant responses that explained the respondent's place in the social network, his world view, his position towards other groupings and the meaning that he bestowed on this seemingly trivial piece of garment that is only two or three square centimetres but the key to the webs of significance.

The origin of the '1%' patch was disturbance in the town of Hollister (Hayes 2005). A motor race that attracted some 4000 attendants derailed and perhaps 500 people got into a fight. The police nabbed a few of the bikers. About 50 persons needed medical attention. A staged photo of an obviously drunk biker was published in *Life Magazine* and titled 'Cyclist's Holiday: He and Friends Terrorize Town'. According to an urban myth the *American Motorcycle Association* tried to save the day and stated that 99 per cent of bikers are decent and only 1 per cent caused troubles. Nowadays the '1%' patch refers back to this incident, but the meaning given to this patch differs from group to group, from individual to individual.

Some clearly equate the patch with Business Clubs like the Bandidos and the Hells Angels, indicating that this is something to be proud of: 'the one per cent that don't fit and don't care' (Thompson 1967: 4). Hunter S. Thompson, famed for his book *Hell's Angels* (1967), obviously equates the '1%' patch with anti-social behaviours. The respondents we interviewed sometimes did not realize the outlaw connotation of the symbol. Policeman Pete said: 'I have worn the 1% patch on my vest for a while and thought it looked cool, but back then I did not really knew what it meant. When I later got into religion, I immediately have removed the patch'. Policeman Pete felt he had made a mistake stemming from naivety and could not wear the patch for reasons of profession and morality.

But to other bikers, like Jack, member of the Veterans MC, the patch only expresses solidarity with the tradition and history of motorcyclists and to him it signifies the band of brotherhood between bikers. In his worldview the patch is not associated with crime or Outlaw Motorcycle Groups. Here we see a different meaning given to this key symbol in motorcycling.

> What does 1% mean to me? . . . To me, riding my bike is the ultimate feeling of freedom . . . Maybe 1% means the most that you always are and want to be this way. 1% does not stop after Sunday-night. Also my experiences as a soldier in Lebanon had its influence. A half year with my buddies, together one job, all in green; other colors

didn't matter. I watch your back, you watch mine. Even under difficult circumstances you take care of each other. That creates a bond, a brotherhood. Back home it is not easy to re-adapt . . . To the 1%-er, his motorcycle is his life. 1% is not a patch; it's not a Club; it's WHO YOU ARE!

Thick description and kinetic ethnography are thus methodologically joined in order to uncover layers of hidden meaning.

The ethics of involvement and detachment: Informed consent

When entry to the field is obtained and trust is established, the question is under which conditions do groups under study agree to this entry? The follow-up question is how to sustain trust. This is a problem of a general nature that many ethnographers experience.

In his book *Anthropologists at Arms* George Lucas (2009) tries to find a solution to the problem that military Human Terrain Teams experience when they go out information gathering. It is the problem that is inherent to groups that are vulnerable in one way or the other and thus it also applies to the study of motorcycling veterans. If the researcher is involved, and to a degree he or she must be, the group under study will feel it to be an act of betrayal when the results of the study give away information that is harmful to the group.

The reason why the American Anthropological Association is opposed to anthropologists working in Human Terrain Teams is that the information is used for tactical military decisions and political ends of (mostly) Western powers (The Network of Concerned Anthropologists, 2009). There is no problem with critical analysis and solid conclusions, but when the results end up in exploitation of the group, moral frictions arise, trust is violated and the psychological contract broken.

George Lucas (2009) states that informed consent is a way out of this problem. If group members know the observations form part of a study, if the aim of the study is clear, and if the researchers use member checks to verify the quality of interviews the problem of possible harm to groups and feeling that psychological contracts have been broken can be dealt with. The ethical code of the American Anthropological Association states that researchers should obtain:

> in advance the informed consent of persons being studied . . . it is understood that the degree and breadth of informed consent required will depend on the nature of the project . . . Further, it is understood that the informed consent process is dynamic and continuous; the process should be initiated in the project design and continue through implementation by way of dialogue and negotiation with those studied . . . Informed consent does not require . . . a written or signed form. It is the quality of the consent, not the format, that is relevant.
>
> (AAA Code of ethics, quoted in Lucas 2009: 206)

Lucas points at the complexities of informed consent and the study into veterans ran into similar difficulties. Even though the researchers tried to guarantee anonymity to those who wanted their identity protected, the study did affect individuals in their private and professional lives and the researchers not always succeeded in protecting their respondents.

By use of member checks respondents could put forward changes that could enhance their own protection. In the case of the religiously motivated Policeman Pete we used a different name to guarantee anonymity but as a member of a quite particular identifiable group, the

Christian Motorcycle Association, bikers from other groups fitted missing pieces together and discovered his true identity, which raised suspicion against him. But Pete did not stop visiting these rallies trying to bring words of salvation. As a result the Police Force questioned his integrity, probably arguing that he could be liable to corruption, or leak information, if he kept on visiting the scene. Policeman Pete in the end was transferred to a different department not connected to criminal investigations inside the world of the motorcycle Business Clubs.

Bikers could be harmed in many more ways. The Dutch Ministry of Defence does not want its employees to be associated with MCs because of possible infringements to integrity. On the other hand, members of MCs feel incriminated by what they feel are false accusations, allegations, labelling and stereotyping. The study into motorcycling veterans therefore could easily hurt the respondents, especially those who are on active duty. Many fear for their job or chances of promotion. Besides the use of member checks as one method of informed consent and inviting them to the book launch where the results were presented created involvement. Informed consent helped opening up communication with veterans.

Concluding

The balance between involvement and detachment is skewed to the involvement side by the methods that make part of kinetic ethnography. It is necessary to gain entry and to win trust, but there is more to the methodology that causes the skewed balance. The fact that bodies and especially the motorcycle of the researchers are research tools implies that they are physically involved in the situation. Campfire interviews, field notes, thick description and informed consent are methodologies that ethnographers will use to get close to their subjects. This does mean that the researchers run the risk of losing detached observation, and they will have to safeguard themselves from going native. If they succeed in safeguarding themselves from going native they can really understand their subjects well (*Verstehen*). If they fail, they will be lost in involvement.

Notes

1 A transitional ceremony in church would be liminal, whereas going to a rock concert would be liminoid. The difference between the two concepts relates to the religious or non-religious character of the event.
2 International Business Clubs, also known as Outlaw Motorcycle Groups (OMG) are Pagans, Hells Angels, Outlaws MC, and Bandidos. These are 'the big four'.
3 The quotes are taken from an interview that is available on YouTube (see list of references).
4 The levels of sociocultural analyses are the indexical, the homological and the integral (diachronic) (Willis 1978: 189–203).

References

Coleman, S. and Eade, J. (2004) 'Introductions: Reframing Pilgrimage', in J. Coleman and J. Eade (eds), *Reframing Pilgrimage: Cultures in Motion*, London: Routledge.

DeWalt, K.M. and DeWalt, B.R. (2011) *Participant Observation: A Guide for Fieldworkers*, Lanham, MD, and Plymouth: AltaMira Press.

Dienst Nationale Recherche (2010) *Hells Angels en andere 1%-MC's in Nederland*, Driebergen: Korps Landelijke Politiediensten.

Elias, N. (2007) *Involvement and Detachment*, Dublin: University College Dublin Press.

Elias, N. and Scotson, L.J. (2008) *The Established and the Outsiders: A Sociological Enquiry into Community Problems*, Dublin: University College Dublin Press.

Geertz, C. (1973) *The Interpretation of Cultures*, New York: Basic Books.

Hayes, B. (2005) *The Original Wild Ones: Tales of the Boozefighters Motorcycle Club*, St. Paul, MN: Motorbooks.

Lucas, G.R. (2009) *Anthropologists in Arms: The Ethics of Military Anthropology*, Lanham, MD: AltaMira Press.

McAdams, D.P. (1996) 'Personality, Modernity, and the Storied Self: A Contemporary Framework for Studying Persons', *Psychological Inquiry*, 7(4): 295–321.

Michalowski, R. and J. Dubisch (2001) *Run for the Wall: Remembering Vietnam on a Motorcycle Pilgrimage*, New Brunswick, NJ: Rutgers University Press.

Moelker, R. (2014) *Riding with Veterans*, Berlin: Springer [this is an expanded update of Moelker, R. and Schut, M. (2011) *Brothers in Arms, Brothers on Bikes*, Budel: Damon Publishers].

The Network of Concerned Anthropologists (2009) *Counter-Counterinsurgency Manual*, Chicago, IL: Prickly Paradigm Press.

Spradley, J.P. (1980) *Participant Observation*, Orlando, FL: Harcourt College Publishers.

Thompson, H.S. (1967) *Hell's Angels*, Harmondsworth: Penguin.

Turner, V. (1969) *The Ritual Process: Structure and Anti-Structure*, London: Routledge and Kegan Paul.

Turner, V. and Turner, E. (1978) *Image and Pilgrimage in Christian Culture*, New York: Columbia University Press.

Weber, C. (2012) *A genou les hommes, debout les officiers. La socialisation des Saint-Cyriens*, Rennes: Presses Universitaires de Rennes.

Weber, M. (1985) *Gesammelte Aufsätze zur Wissenschaftslehre*, Tübingen: Johannes Winckelmann, 427–432.

Willis, P. (1978) *Profane Culture*, London: Routledge & Kegan Paul.

Willis, P. (2010) *Socio Symbolic Analysis and Homology: Changes in Culture and Society*. Available at www.youtube.com/watch?v=4kimNgCwUCk&feature=related (accessed 22 November 2012).

Winkelman, M. and Dubisch, J. (2005) *Pilgrimage and Healing*, Tucson, AZ: The University of Arizona Press.

Zemliansky, P. (2008) *Methods of Discovery: A Guide to Research Writing*. Available at http://methodsofdiscovery.net/?q=node/19 (accessed 5 December 2012).

11
IN-DEPTH INTERVIEWING

Brenda L. Moore

B.L. Moore (1996; 1998). *To Serve My Country, To Serve My Race: The Story of the Only African American WACs Stationed Overseas during World War II.* **New York: New York University Press.**

To Serve My Country is a qualitative study about women who served in the 6888th Central Postal Directory Battalion (CPDB). The unique factors of being African American, female, and in the United States Army during World War II are discussed throughout the book. The 6888th CPDB was the only unit of African American WACs (women serving in the Army Corps) that was stationed overseas during the war. The battalion was a result of civil rights activists pressuring the War Department to extend the same opportunity to African American WACs to serve overseas that white WACs had. Consisting of more than 800 WACs, the battalion was segregated by race and gender. Members of the 6888th came from all walks of life; some were professionals and others were unskilled. The unit reflected the diversity of African American women in the broader society. The book is about their lives before, during, and after military service. The study illustrates how members of the 6888th actively shaped their lives in an institution that mirrored race and gender biases found in American society during that historical period.

During the time this study was conducted, there was an established body of literature on the service of African American men during World War II. In addition, studies of the contribution of white women to the war effort and the gender inequality they encountered were mounting. However, there was very little documented about the military service of African American women. *To Serve My Country* would help to fill that void.

Moore began the study by reviewing scholarly literature and archival documents on changes in Army policies affecting the enlistment and assignments of racial minorities and women. An Army roster with the names of members of the 6888th surfaced during an extensive review of archival documents. After further investigation, Moore was able to locate a few of the former members. As the study progressed, a snowball sampling design was used to identify additional members. A total of 51 former members of the 6888th were interviewed for this study.

A few of the salient themes include (i) a controversial battalion resulting from a socio-political campaign to allow African American WACs to serve overseas; (ii) a desire on the part of members of the 6888th to meet their citizenship obligations through military service; (iii) unit cohesion; race and gender discrimination members experienced in the United States unified them, giving them the determination to perform beyond expectation; (iv) treated with dignity and respect; all of the respondents claimed that Europeans did not discriminate against them due to their race. Unlike race relations in the United States, all of the women spoke of their interactions with Europeans socially, as guests in their homes as well as socializing in public establishments such as recreational centers and pubs. This information could only be obtained through in-depth interviews.

There are several methodological concerns that accompany the use of in-depth interviewing as a primary source. Two major hurdles the researcher encountered from the outset were: (i) Obtaining information about the battalion, much of which was buried in archival records; and (ii) locating former members of the unit. After information about the battalion was gathered and prospective interviewees had been identified and interviewed, questions about authenticity surfaced. Were respondents able to remember events that occurred some 40 years prior to the interview? How reliable were their memories with regard to specific facts?

Qualitative methods provide valuable tools for analyzing human experiences and perceptions. Unlike quantitative research, those based on qualitative methods allow for full conceptualization of a phenomenon and a more complete understanding of social processes and complex cultural factors. A powerful technique used by qualitative researchers is the *in-depth interview*, which is often the preferred method of data collection for qualitative studies. My objectives for this chapter are to: (i) Show how the in-depth interview differs from other types of interviews used by researchers; (ii) examine the main steps involved in conducting in-depth interviews; (iii) discuss a few limitations with this methodological approach and ways of addressing them; (iv) illustrate how the technique of interviewing has been used extensively in research on military personnel and veterans; particularly narrative, phenomenological, oral history, ethnographic, grounded theory, and case studies; (v) finally, I discuss some factors that make studies of the military institution different from those of other societal institutions.

Categories and types of interviews

Structured, unstructured, or semi-structured

Interviews can be separated into three broad categories: structured, unstructured, or semi-structured. The structured interview is a quantitative method that is usually used in surveys. Such interviews are formal and consist of pre-established, closed-end questions. The questions are standardized and direct with a limited number of possible responses. Each respondent is asked questions in the same sequence and are prompted to give rational, rather than emotional responses. Interviewers are usually neutral and impersonal during structured interviews and are given little or no room to deviate from the pre-established script (Fontana and Frey 2000).

By contrast, unstructured interviews are used in qualitative studies. They are informal and consist of open-ended questions which allow respondents to elaborate on a topic. There are no pre-established questions with pre-set responses; nor is there a preexisting framework.

Unstructured interviews give researchers the flexibility to ask unplanned questions during the interview and to probe respondents for clarification (McCracken 1988; Fontana and Frey 2000).

The semi-structured interview contains both structured and unstructured questions; however it is more flexible than the structured interview but not as amorphous as the unstructured interview. Although there is a general framework of themes to be explored in semi-structured interviews, new questions arise during the interview based on something the respondent says. This was the case with my study of the 6888th. For example, some of the questions asked were as follows:

Let's Talk About Your Experiences with the Six-Triple Eighth

15. Describe the training that the group received to prepare for overseas duty?_____

16. How were you treated by white United States military personnel when you were in England and France during the war?_____

17. How were you treated by African American men in uniform when you were overseas during World War II?_____

18. How were you treated by the British and the French while you were overseas during World War II?_____

19. What social activities were available to members of the 6888th; and did you take advantage of those activities?_____

Each question, illustrated above, allowed the interviewee to expound on the topic in her own words. For the study, several lead questions were asked about respondents' lives before, during, and after military service thereby stimulating discussion and allowing the interviewee to elaborate. It is through this inductive method that I was able to examine themes that emerged from the interview data; rather than imposing a theoretical framework on the data.

One-on-one, telephone, or focus group

The in-depth interview is an unstructured or semi-structured method that may be separated into three types: one-on-one, telephone, or focus group. Each type has its advantages as well as its obstacles. Many researchers, me included, prefer to conduct in-depth interviews by using the face-to-face, one-on-one method. This method requires an interview setting in which interviewees are comfortable talking and sharing their views. Interviews of former members of the 6888th were usually conducted in a quiet area of their homes. During WAC reunions, I interviewed respondents in my hotel suite. These proved to be good venues for one-on-one interviews.

It is not always feasible for the interviewer to travel long distances to conduct one-on-one, face-to-face interviews. Sometimes the process of traveling, obtaining a venue, and conducting in-depth interviews can be cost prohibitive, requiring a fair amount of time and money. When one-on-one, face-to-face interviews are not possible, telephone interviews present a good alternative. Such was the case with my study of the 6888th. There were several women whom I interviewed by telephone, as resources were not available to travel to their homes. Gertrude LaVigne, who lived in Anchorage at the time of my study, is a case in point. I conducted multiple interviews with her by telephone after receiving her informed consent form by mail. All of the women interviewed by telephone consented to being interviewed by mail. They each returned their informed consent to me by mail, along with a telephone number and best time to call them.

A possible challenge associated with the one-on-one interview method may occur if the respondent refuses to speak. Whether the interview is one-on-one, or one conducted by telephone, for it to be successful, respondents have to be articulate and willing to speak (Cresswell 2007). If a respondent is inarticulate, shy, or reticent, then the one-on-one interview may not yield sufficient data. An additional obstacle to the telephone interview is that the interviewer cannot see the non-verbal communication of respondents. This may make it difficult for interviewers to determine how the respondent feels about a question, and whether or not to probe. A researcher's careful attention to the voice tone of respondents during telephone interviews alleviates this problem.

Another alternative to the one-on-one interview is the focus group, where several people are interviewed simultaneously. Although some methodologists assert that the focus group interview is mainly a qualitative method (Madriz 2000), this approach may be used in quantitative or qualitative studies. The interview may be structured, soliciting answers to closed-ended questions. In this case, the focus group interviewer would be formal, requiring interviewees to stay rigidly on a topic. In other cases the focus group may be unstructured, and the interviewer may be flexible, asking open-ended questions and allowing respondents to speak freely. In either case, the focus group interviewer assumes an additional role of group moderator, and is responsible for managing the dynamics of the group (Fontana and Frey 2000).

Methodological steps

There are several steps researchers must take in preparing for an in-depth interview. These steps include: reviewing scholarly literature on the topic, designing an interview protocol and administering a pretest to refine the interview questions (Babbie 2007; Cresswell 2007). Additionally the researcher must identify interviewees, determine the type of interview to conduct (one-on-one, telephone, or focus group), and find a venue for conducting the interview (Babbie 2007; Cresswell 2007; Adler and Clark 2011). A further requirement in the United States is the informed consent form. Investigators must obtain informed consent from interviewees prior to starting the interview; as required by the institutional review board (IRB). All research involving human subjects are required by U.S. law to be reviewed by an IRB, a committee designated by the research institution to approve and monitor the study. The final steps in the methodological process are analyzing and writing. After the data have been collected, then the investigator must analyze it and write-up the findings.

Reviewing previous literature

As a first step, it is helpful to begin by researching existing literature on a selected topic and developing preliminary research questions. When I first decided to conduct a study on African American WACs who served overseas during World War II, I began by examining scholarly literature on African American men who served during that period (Lee 1966; Foner 1974; MacGregor 1981, etc.). There was a considerable amount of literature written about racial segregation in the American armed forces during World War II. There were not as many scholarly studies on women who served in the military during any period. There was only a dearth of information written about African American women's military service. Consequently, it was necessary for me to review several archival sources in order to learn more about the military experiences of women. The U.S. Army special studies of the Women's Army Corps, and other documents at the Center of Military History, were thoroughly examined.

My review of documents at the Military Reference Branch of the National Archives revealed information about the development of a Women's Army Auxiliary Corps (the precursor to the Women's Army Corps) in the United States. A careful investigation of military documents allowed me to learn more about the political circumstances that lead to the development of the 6888th. Further exploration disclosed exactly when each member of the 6888th was enrolled in the Army, the region of the country she entered the military from, and her duty stations. I eventually located a roster with the names of some of the African American women who had served in the battalion.

In addition, other documents from the archives of the National Council of Negro Women (NCNW) verified what so many of my informants had stated during interviews about the role of Mary McLeod Bethune in encouraging them to serve in the military. Several records of the NCNW show Bethune's endorsement of the Women's Army Auxiliary Corps. Other documents revealed that Bethune conferred with the Director of the Corps, Colonel Oveta Hobby, and was assured that African American women who enrolled would be treated fair and equitably, and of the 450 officers, 40 would be African American. The documents also cited Bethune as stating that her endorsement of the WAACs was not an endorsement of its policy of racial segregation; integrating the military was yet another battle.

Refining the research question

During my review of archival documents it became apparent that the experiences of African American women in the military during the World War II era differed dramatically from those of African American men and white women. Yet, there was virtually nothing written in the scholarly literature on the African American women's experience. As observed by other scholars, academic studies about African Americans focused on African American men, and those about women focused on women of European descent (Hull et al. 1982). This was also true of military studies where the voices of African American women had been silent. African American women experienced both racial and sexual oppression in American society. The example study discusses the African American WAC experience during World War II revealing such objective facts as their occupational assignments and their duty stations. But it also discloses subjective information such as how they were received, what military service meant to them, and if they perceived the military to be a turning point in their lives.

Designing a protocol and obtaining IRB approval

As mentioned above, in the United States all universities are designated by the federal government to review and ensure that all research projects involving human subjects comply with federal regulations. The interview protocol and IRB review must be completed before researchers can begin interviewing respondents. Thus, another methodological step is to construct a protocol which is reviewed by an institutional review board (IRB). The IRB is responsible for protecting the rights and the welfare of research subjects. I developed a research protocol consisting of a research proposal and a semi-structured interview schedule, which was submitted it to my university's IRB for approval. After obtaining IRB approval, I was ready to go out into the field.

Included in my protocol was a questionnaire consisting of a semi-structured research design, with both closed-ended and open-ended questions. Closed-ended questions were used to ascertain specific facts, i.e. demographic information and data about each participant's military training, occupational specialty, and assignments. Several open-ended questions were asked in an effort to let respondents speak freely on a specific topic and thereby reveal unexpected insights into their military experiences. Using this general framework, I encouraged participants to speak about their lives before they entered the military. Respondents spoke about what it was like growing up. They spoke about their family life, school, work experiences, and what motivated them to join the military. Interviewees were also encouraged to speak about their experiences in basic training, advanced training, and permanent duty stations. Participants were asked to make comparisons between their occupational assignments and quality of life at their stateside (CONUS) and European (ETO) duty stations. Respondents were also asked about returning home after service and effects that the military had on their post-service lives. Each respondent was encouraged to speak openly about what military service meant to them personally.

Selecting interviewees

Selecting interviewees is yet another step in the process of qualitative research. Interviewees for the example study were selected through a purposeful sampling method. In the early stages of the research process it is necessary for investigators to make initial contact with prospective interviewees. I mailed a letter of introduction to all of the prospective interviewees, specifying the purpose of my study and inviting them to participate. While a couple of women declined to be interviewed, the overall response rate was quite positive.

It is important for the researcher to establish a rapport with respondents, obtaining their trust and confidence early in the interviewing process. During the interview, respondents should be made to feel at ease. Researchers must be attentive listener, allowing respondents to talk freely. It is also imperative that the researcher does not superimpose his/her viewpoint on the interviewee's responses; views of the respondent should be represented authentically. I found my interviewees eager to share their experiences with me, and they were willing to introduce me to other women who had served with the unit. With each interview, the names of one or two additional women were revealed to me. This snowball process continued throughout the entire interviewing period.

Fifty-one women who served with the 6888th were interviewed for this book, 5 officers and 46 enlisted women. These women truly represented the diversity that characterized the unit. Respondents represented the different geographical areas, different socioeconomic backgrounds, and different educational levels of the more than eight hundred women assigned to the battalion.

Determining the type of interview

As mentioned above, investigators of qualitative studies must determine the type of interview they will use; whether they will collect data by telephone, focus group, or individually, face-to-face. For the example study, all three types of interviews were conducted. Some of the women were interviewed by telephone, and others were interviewed in person, and I also met and interviewed small groups of women at two national events held for women veterans. The first event, the Fiftieth Anniversary Convention of the Women's Army Corps, was held at Fort McClellan, Alabama in May 1992. The second was the Black WAAC-WAC Women in the Services Eighth Biennial Reunion held in September of the same year in Orlando, Florida. During these events, hotel suites were used to conduct informal focus group discussions with respondents about their service experiences. All of the in-depth interviews helped me to gain a perspective about serving in an all-black female unit during World War II that I would not have gotten otherwise.

Analyzing and writing-up the findings

The final methodological steps in qualitative research are analyzing the data and writing-up the study. Usually data collected by in-depth interviews are audio-taped and transcribed. This was the case with my study on the 6888th as well. After the data are collected and transcribed, it is necessary for the qualitative researcher to organize the text of transcripts through a process known as coding. Although the specifics of coding vary from researcher to researcher, the goal remains the same regardless of which approach is being used. Through the course of coding, the qualitative investigator moves from a lower to a more abstract level of understanding (Glaser and Strauss 1967; Auerbach and Silverstein, 2003; Strauss and Corbin 1998). There are several steps involved in the coding process. One step is to look for recurring themes that surface throughout the data. These themes will form the bases of theoretical constructs that are elaborated upon in the narrative.

For the *example study*, a grounded theory approach was used in both data collection and analysis. Using this methodological approach allowed me to analyze the data throughout the data collection process. Three levels of coding were used (*open*, *axial*, and *selective*) as illustrated in Strauss and Corbin's (1990) *Basics of Qualitative Research*. In the first level of coding, *open coding*, each line of transcribed data was examined for frequently used words and phrases, and then grouped into categories. During this initial process of analysis, a comparison of words, phrases, and short passages of the text was done. Numerous memoranda were written about the concepts that emerged, taking note of similarities and differences occurring in the text. This was a very lengthy and often tedious process before codes began to cluster around emerging categories.

In the second step of my data analysis, I began to think of the frequently used words and phrases analytically, and to be more theoretically sensitive. In this step, which Strauss and Corbin (1990; 1998) refer to as *axial coding*, preliminary categories and subcategories developed during open coding were connected. Ways that these categories were related to each other began to surface. It was during this process that I was able to give meaning to the events occurring in the lives of members of the 6888th. This process was repeated many times until each category was fully conceptualized (*saturated*) and there was no additional information being learned. At that point, for example, the socio-political conditions under which the 6888th was formed were clearly understood. The involvement of political officials in advocating for an African American WAC unit to serve overseas, and the letter writing campaign on the part of private citizens toward this end had greater meaning as a result of *axial coding*. This coding process also uncovered meaning underlying some of the decisions members of the 6888th made while serving in the United States, while preparing to be deployed overseas, and later when they served in Europe. For example, axial coding gave meaning to such acts on the part of 6888th members as boycotting, refusing to use a water fountain marked "for colored only," refusing to use a recreational facility that was allocated to them in Europe, and performing their work duties beyond what was expected of them by some military officials.

In the final step of my data analysis, *selective coding*, a core category was selected and related all other categories to it. In this final step, relationships between categories were validated. Two salient themes that emerged from the data were: (i) the 6888th CPDB resulted from a social-political struggle for African American women to have the right to serve in all facets of the U.S. Army opened to women during World War II; (ii) the members of the 6888th were eager to serve overseas. During my interviews with respondents almost all of them mentioned that the 6888th was established as a result of a political campaign to allow African American WACs to serve overseas. This claim was verified in archival data, such as the Bethune Museum and Archives, the National Association of Colored People's (NAACP) historical publication, *The Crisis* magazine, and such archival newspapers as the *Amsterdam News*, and the *Pittsburgh Courier*.

In addition, the women expressed their excitement about the opportunity to serve abroad. This enthusiasm stemmed not only for a desire to travel, but from an expressed need to demonstrate to the United States that African Americans were ready, willing, and able to fulfill the obligation of citizenship. Moreover, these women were eager to dispel racial stereotypes and myths that pegged African American women as being biologically incompetent and inferior to white women. A couple of examples of how these themes are represented in the final analysis of the study are illustrated in the following quotes from the book:

> Noel Campbell Mitchell was stationed at Fort Oglethorpe when she received a letter from a good friend informing her of the Army's plans to deploy "Negro" WACs overseas:

> We had joined the Army together and she had been my commanding officer for nine months . . . We hadn't seen each other for over two years but had kept in touch . . . I read the letter and was dumbfounded. Edna said that it was true that colored WACs were to go overseas. The plans were being made at Des Moines and she had been informed that she would be commander of the troops, and if there were any women she wanted as her officers she could ask for them. She said she had thought about me, and if I was interested she would submit my name . . . I was excited because ever since I had heard the rumors I was sure if the opportunity came, I would certainly volunteer.
>
> (Moore 1998: 17)

Similarly, Gladys Carter says that "when the word got out that there was going to be a group [of African American women] to go overseas, everybody wanted to go. I know I wanted to go. I think I would have climbed up a mountain to get on the list" (Moore 1998: 18).

These quotes do not only reveal an historic policy change allowing African American WACs to serve overseas during the war, but they also reflect the women's personal feelings about the change. Almost all of my interviewees revealed that they were excited about the opportunity to serve overseas and were ready to go. A synthesis of the data in the book shows that these women wanted to serve overseas to show that they too were American citizens and were willing to meet the obligation of citizenship by supporting the war effort and serving overseas. What is more, they expected to receive full citizenship rights in the United States after fulfilling their citizenship obligation of military service.

Why and when is it appropriate to use in-depth interviews?

In-depth interviews are best used when explanations are required. For the example study, the in-depth interview allowed me to collect explanatory data about members' military experiences in their own words. Questions requiring subjective answers can only be obtained through the in-depth interviewing method. For example: Who were these women and what were their individual backgrounds? Why did they join the military during a time in American history when they were denied the very rights they were willing to serve for? What were their personal living, working, and social experiences while serving in Europe? How did military service affect their lives when they reentered the civilian world, and later? What can their experiences teach us more broadly about social conflict and social change? These questions can best be answered through in-depth interviews.

Although oral histories were collected for my study on African American WACs, much of the data were obtained from archival documents such as government reports and newspaper articles, and in some cases personal diaries. Studies commonly referred to as *oral histories*, on the other hand, rely almost entirely on the in-depth interview. The purpose of interviewing for oral history is to present an unadulterated view of respondents, without the researcher's interpretation. Oral histories have traditionally been used to give voice to the voiceless, racial minorities in the United States (Tosee and Willams 2007) and women (Gluck and Patai 1991). It is also used to present varied views concerning war. A case in point is Carl Mirra's book, *Soldiers and Citizens*, which is a collection of oral histories of soldiers, veterans, military family members, political policymakers and pundits affiliated with the War in Iraq.

The in-depth interview is also the most appropriate form of data collection in phenomenological research as the primary objective is to learn how subjects perceive an event. For example, Marie Shaw and Mark Hector (2010) researched the experiences of American military members who had been stationed in Iraq and/or Afghanistan since the conflict began in 2003. Using phenomenological method, these researchers interviewed ten military men who had returned from the war zone since 2004. Interviews were necessary for this study as the researchers' objective was to understand the meaning of the experiences of military members stationed in Iraq and Afghanistan. Interview data provided information about whether or not respondents felt they should be deployed to Afghanistan and Iraq. Interviewees also were able to elaborate on the dangers associated with their military assignments and the impact of deployment on their families. Again, these data can only be obtained through in-depth interviews.

Researchers using the grounded theory approach rely greatly on the in-depth interview. In addition to my study of the 6888th CPDB, many scholars use a grounded theory approach in their research on military personnel. Laura Miller (1997) used grounded theory methods to examine resistance strategies used by Army men to target women in their units. To this end, she interviewed soldiers at work sites, during meals, in the field, on military convoys, and on air transport overseas to learn about gender relations in the U.S. Army. Interviews were critical to learn what type of conflict and cooperation occurred between female and male soldiers in the field. Miller also observed how soldiers manage work and family obligations, and what women's experiences were in deployment environments. To obtain this information, it was necessary for Miller to conduct in-depth interviews and ask open-ended questions.

In-depth interviews have also proven to be a valuable method of data collection for case studies. In her case study of Seaside, California, Carol McKibben (2012) interviewed former soldiers and government officials to illustrate the influence Fort Ord had had on fostering democracy in that city. Central to McKibben's argument is that soldiers of all races shared a high regard for authority, law, order, patriotism, and belief in family. McKibben argued persuasively that Seaside became a minority-majority city made up of soldiers who had experienced integration on base and challenged segregation in their civilian community. Studying the impact that the military had on race relations in Seaside, McKibben had to to draw upon the daily experiences of its residents through the use of the in-depth interview.

Finally, ethnographic studies also depend upon in-depth interviews. This is evident in Gold and Friedman's ethnographic study of cadets. These researchers were particularly interested in how cadets cope with stress at the U.S. Military Academy. They conducted informal interviews with upper-class cadets from which they were able to learn about stress associated with leadership roles as well as stress associated with being a new cadet.

In all of these qualitative studies the researcher learns from the perceptions and the experiences of respondents. Each study represents a systematic inquiry concerned with understanding human interactions. Through the use of non-numerical data, patterns of social phenomena are studied in an effort to uncover meaning. By using the in-depth interview, each researcher, in the studies mentioned above, were able to identify issues pertaining to military personnel organically, rather than with pre-defined answers.

A few limitations and ways of addressing them

Although the in-depth interview can be a powerful source of information, it is not without its limitations. An extensive discussion of the limitations of qualitative studies is beyond the scope of this chapter; however, a few are highlighted below. Three major limitations of qualitative research based on the in-depth interview include the lack of reliability, generalizability, and the problem of self-selection. The data collected by interviews are not always reliable and may not yield the same results when duplicated. Among the questions raised about data collected through interviewing are those having to do with the accuracy of respondents' reporting (see Denzin and Lincoln 2000). Is the respondent exaggerating or otherwise embellishing the truth? Does the respondent remember the details of past events?

One of the concerns I had about interviewing members of the 6888th CPDB is that much of the data relied upon their memory of lived experiences many years prior to the interviews. My concern about accuracy was somewhat assuaged by studies that showed the elderly to have accurate memory for events that have occurred in their past. There is some literature that suggests that people's memories actually improve as they get older and reflect upon their lives. Hence, some elderly individuals have been found to recall details about their past with accuracy and clarity (Butler 1964).

Still, other studies show that people tend to have poor recall of *interior events*, such as their motivations, intentions, aspirations and hopes about previous actions (Scott and Garner 2013). It is not that people fail to remember all aspects of their lives. According to Greg Scott and Roberta Garner (2013) *external events* that are memorialized in the "public record" of individuals' social lives are remembered best. Similarly, Barry Schwartz (1999) spoke of *biographical memory* as being a social process understood in terms of our experiences with others. This idea of a collective memory is also found in the work of Eviatar Zerubavel (1996) who claimed that social environments; such as family, profession, ethnicity, race, religion, or the like, affect the way individuals remember the past. These social environments formulate *mnemonic communities* those that shape individual thoughts through the process of socialization. Thus, these scholars argue that much of what people remember is filtered and interpreted through their social environment and is consequently distorted.

In a psychological context, an explanation for distorted memories of interviewees may be found in Dan McAdams' (1993) discussion of the self-narrative; or what he refers to as *personal myth*. McAdams argues that *nuclear episodes* (key events) are those that are special in a person's life story. For McAdams, it is normal for people to tell tales that they compose over the course of their lives in an effort to discover what is true and meaningful. In his words, "In order to live well, with unity and purpose, we compose a heroic narrative of the self that illustrates essential truths about ourselves" (McAdams 1993: 11).

What we can conclude from all of the studies mentioned above is that interviewees are not always able to distinguish between what is real and what is perceived. To the degree that members of the 6888th CPDB shared the experiences of serving overseas in a racially segregated battalion, during World War II, they may be viewed as being a mnemonic community. Surely, their recollections of events were often shaped by their collective memory and interpretation. Although there is no way for an investigator to eliminate all errors found in self-reporting, such errors can be minimized. I addressed the possible issue of inaccurate memory in my study by examining archival documents from multiple sources to verify events. In addition to the research facilities mentioned above, the Schomburg Center for Research in Black Culture, and the Headquarters United States Air Force Historical Research Center at Maxwell Air Force Base are other examples. Additional sources like these helped me to confirm events and times discussed by the interviewees in my study.

Another limitation is that data obtained through the in-depth interviewing method is that it is not generalizable. This is to say that qualitative methods often lack the scope and variation necessary for study results to apply to populations and circumstances outside the original study. Common to qualitative study is the fact that nonprobability sampling is used to obtain respondents, and the sample does not reflect the larger population. There usually is not sufficient data in qualitative studies to make predictions based on probability. Generalizability is generally not an objective of qualitative researchers. This was not the goal for my study on the 6888th as I was not seeking to find statistical trends. My objective was to provide detailed information about a group of women who served in the Army during World War II for the purpose of understanding. However, some qualitative researchers address this issue of generalizability by employing a multi-method strategy thereby capturing both broad as well as individual perspectives. For example, Miller (1997) supplemented her ethnographic data by administering questionnaires to a more representative sample of the Army. This allowed her to obtain precise and detailed information from in-depth interviews as well as observe statistical trends.

A methodological issue closely related to that of generalizability is the problem of selection bias among respondents who volunteer for the study. The perceptions of those who volunteered may have differed from those who did not volunteer for the study. This is an issue associated with all interview data. It is an issue most often found in oral histories, like Mirra's study mentioned above, which depend almost entirely on subjective interviews. Surely, the question of selection bias surfaces in Mirra's as well as other oral history studies. Mirra addresses this issue by interviewing a variety of people, representing diverse perspectives concerning the United States involvement in the Iraq War. He interviewed active-duty military members, family members of soldiers, military veterans, as well as government officials. Many of his interviewees had opposing viewpoints about the Iraq War. By presenting multiple perspectives as to why the United States invaded and occupied Iraq, and the consequences of such action, Mirra was able to present a broad dialogue on the subject and drastically reduce the effects of sample bias.

Problems associated with reliability, generalizability, and selection bias are indeed valid critiques of many qualitative studies, to include that of the 6888th CPDB. However, in spite of these limitations, qualitative studies have been found to produce valuable findings for human research.

What makes studying the military special?

The military differs from other social institutions given its mission of national defense. By necessity, levels of security are high which often pose unique challenges for qualitative researchers. Military personnel sacrifice some of their civil liberties by joining the armed forces and the freedom of speech is one of them. Therefore, in order to interview military personnel, researchers must follow military protocol, seeking permission from the service's public relations office, who in turn will obtain permission from the commanding officer. There is no guarantee that permission to interview active military personnel will be granted.

It is not always possible for researchers to interview desirable subjects. This was the situation with Gold and Friedman's (2000) ethnographic study of cadets at West Point. Although their primary interest was to study how new cadets cope with stress at the United States

Military Academy, they were not permitted to interview new cadets due to military restrictions. Therefore, Gold and Friedman's analysis of new cadet was based on direct observations of such daily activities as mountaineering, drill competitions, weapon exercises, marksmanship, obstacle course maneuvers, and the like. These authors also elicited reflections of upper-class cadets to gain insight on what it is like being a new cadet.

It is not unusual for qualitative researchers studying the active military to acknowledge the highly secured environment and modify their methods accordingly. Miller's (1997) study is a case in point. Interviewing active-duty military members through discussion groups, one-on-one unstructured interviews, participant observation, as well as informal conversations with soldiers, she relied on note-taking rather than audio-tapes. She explained in her methods section that: "Given the military context and the sensitive nature of some of the issues, I relied on written notes rather than tape-recording."

If a researcher is conducting an historical study, as I did in my study of the 6888th, then the challenge is not obtaining permission from the command to conduct the interview, but locating the former military member after so many years of them being separated from service. Military services generally do not collect information on its members after they separate from active-duty. The whereabouts of some former military personnel is easier to trace when they are active in Veteran's organizations, and/or actively participate in reunions that are organized and held by former service-members. These sources were valuable to me when I was trying to locate former members of the 6888th.

Finally, the challenges of collecting data on active military personnel surface when the objective of the researcher is to collect primary data. There are perhaps fewer obstacles for quantitative researchers studying the military as the American armed services are required to publish a wealth of demographic data in annual statistical reports that are public access and invaluable for quantitative analyses. Given the requirement of accountability the U.S. military has to disclose information to the civilian populace through reports submitted to Congress, the General Accounting Office, and the U.S. President, as well as to other public agencies. Volumes of data are reported each fiscal year regarding demographic trends of active-duty personnel, reservists, and members of the National Guard each year. These data are published and available online at the Department of Defense, Office of Personnel Readiness official websites. Still, research involving survey data is further bolstered by qualitative studies which add meaning in a way that quantitative studies alone do not.

References

Adler, E. and Clark, R. (2011). *An Invitation to Social Research*, 4th edn. Belmont, CA: Wadsworth.

Auerbach, C.F. and Silverstein, L. (2003). *Qualitative Data: An Introduction to Coding and Analysis*. New York: New York University Press.

Babbie, E. (2007). *The Practice of Social Research*, 11th edn. Belmont, CA: Wadsworth.

Butler, R.N. (1964). "The Life Review: An Interpretation of Reminiscence in the Aged," in Kastenbaum, R. (ed.), *New Thoughts on Old Age*. New York: Springer, pp. 265–280.

Cresswell, J.W. (2007). *Qualitative Inquiry and Research Design: Choosing Among Five Approaches*. Thousand Oaks, CA: Sage.

Denzin, N.K. and Lincoln, Y.S. (eds) (2000). *Handbook of Qualitative Research*, 4th edn. Thousand Oaks, CA: Sage.

Fontana, A. and Frey, J.H. (2000). "The Interview: From Structured Questions to Negotiated Text," in Denzin, N. and Lincoln, Y. (eds), *Handbook of Qualitative Research*, 2nd edn. Thousand Oaks, CA: Sage, pp. 645–672.

Glaser, B.G. and Strauss, A.L. (1967). *Discovery of Grounded Theory: Strategies for Qualitative Research*. Chicago, IL: Aldine.

Gluck, S, and Patai, D. (eds) (1991). *Women's Words: The Feminist Practice of Oral History*. New York: Routledge.

Gold, M.A. and Friedman, S.B. (2000). "Cadet Basic Training: An Ethnographic Study of Stress and Coping." *Military Medicine*, 165(2): 147–152.

Hull, G.T., Scott, P.B., and Smith, B. (1982). *All the Women Are White, All the Blacks Are Men, but Some of Us Are Brave*. Old Westbury, NY: The Feminist Press.

McAdams, Dan P. (1993). *The Stories We Live By*. New York: NY Guilford Press.

McCracken, G. (1988). *The Long Interview*. Newbury Park, CA: Sage.

Mckibben, C.L. (2012). *Racial Beachhead: Diversity and Democracy in a Military Town*. Stanford, CA: Stanford University Press.

Madriz, E. (2000). "Focus Groups in Feminist Research," in Denzin, N. and Lincoln, Y. (eds), *Handbook of Qualitative Research*, 2nd edn. Thousand Oaks, CA: Sage, pp. 645–672.

Miller, L. (1997). "Not Just Weapons of the Weak: Gender Harassment as a Form of Protest for Army Men." *Social Psychology Quarterly*, 60(1): 32–51.

Mirra, C. (2008). *Soldiers and Citizens: An Oral History of Operation Iraqi Freedom from the Battlefield to the Pentagon*. New York: Palgrave Macmillan.

Moore, B.L. (1996; 1998). *To Serve My Country, To Serve My Race: The Story of the Only African American WACs Stationed Overseas during World War II*. New York: New York University Press.

Schwartz, B. (1999). "Memory and the Practice of Commitment," in Glassner, B. and Hertz, R. (eds), *Qualitative Sociology as Everyday Life*. Thousand Oaks, CA: Sage.

Scott, Gregg and Garner, Roberta (2013) *Doing Qualitative Research: Designs, Methods, and Techniques*. Upper Saddle River, NJ: Pearson.

Shaw, M.E. and Hector, M.A. (2010). "Listening to Military Members Returning from Iraq and/or Afghanistan: A Phenomenological Investigation." *Professional Psychology: Research and Practice*, 41(2): 128–134.

Strauss, A. and Corbin, J. (1990). *Basics of Qualitative Research: Grounded Theory Procedures and Techniques*. Newbury Park, CA: Sage.

Strauss, A. and Corbin, J. (1998). *Basics of Qualitative Research: Techniques and Procedures for Developing Grounded Theory*. Newbury Park, CA: Sage.

Tosee, M. and Williams, C.M. (eds) (2007). *Of Two Spirits: American Indian and African American Oral Histories*. Lawrence, KS: University of Kansas, Hall Center for Humanities.

Zerubavel, Eviatar (1996) "Social Memories: Steps to a Sociology of the Past." *Qualitative Sociology*, 19 (3): 283–299.

12

QUALITATIVE DATA ANALYSIS

Seeing the patterns in the fog of civil–military interaction

Sebastiaan Rietjens

S.J.H. Rietjens (2008) 'Managing civil–military cooperation: Experiences from the Dutch Provincial Reconstruction Team in Afghanistan', *Armed Forces & Society* 34: 173–207.

This study focuses on the cooperation process between civilian actors and the Dutch Provincial Reconstruction Team (PRT) in Baghlan, a northern province of Afghanistan. The problem is that most civil–military cooperation processes are improvisational and *ad hoc*. This leads to inefficient use of limited aid resources, inconsistency between rotations, and conflicting objectives in the (post-)conflict environment. Although there is no single solution to improve civil–military cooperation, the logic of structured cooperation should lead to efficiency gains and greater respect for the comparative advantages of civilian and military actors. The objective of this study is to diagnose civil–military cooperation processes using a model that was earlier developed. In the end this model should enable the development of checklists, an increased understanding of (potential) conflicts in the cooperation process, and procedures to increase the performance of the cooperation.

To meet this objective, the study uses a case study design because of its emphasis on the overall picture (rather than a single element) and the inclusion of contextual conditions. The theoretical framework of the study outlines a model based on theories of interorganizational alliances. This model distinguishes six phases in the cooperation process and within each phase it identifies several key factors. The study subsequently applies the model to eight different cases, each representing a different civil–military cooperation process. These include police training courses with the highway and provincial police corps, removal of explosives and ammunition with the international non-governmental organization Halo Trust and the construction of schools, roads and bridges with the Aga Kahn Foundation.

(continued)

(continued)

A data collection protocol was designed to guide the researcher in carrying out the case studies, organize the data collection, and ensure that the case studies and their results were verifiable. Data collection started with desk study and interviewing of redeployed personnel. Next, the researcher paid a four-week visit to Baghlan. During this visit semi-structured interviews were held with key personnel of the PRT, extensive observations were made and over 60 meetings were held with Afghan actors such as contractors, authorities and police commanders. In addition, many documents were studied, including daily situational reports, project information, meeting minutes and liaison reports.

This abundance of data was then reduced using a coding process. The theoretical model provided a structure. Codes were attached to the phases and key factors that were identified. These codes were then used to analyse the raw data. Subsequently, the researcher displayed the data through matrices. The rows of a matrix contained the phases and key factors, while the columns addressed the different actors that took part in the cooperation process. Having done this for each of the eight cases, the researcher was able to carry out a cross case analysis and compare the cases for similarities and differences. Again a matrix was used to display this. One of the main findings revealed that that cooperation was frequently supply based rather than demand-driven. Activities were selected and prioritized based on the capacity of the military force or humanitarian organization, rather than the needs of the local beneficiaries.

To facilitate the drawing and verifying of conclusions, members of the PRT's civil–military cooperation branch checked the results, personnel of the Dutch Defence Operation Centre reviewed the case study report and the researcher presented his findings at a conference on PRTs in Afghanistan.

Introduction

In recent years studying the interaction between military and civilian actors has become en vogue. There has been a tremendous increase in research focusing on concepts such as provincial reconstruction teams, comprehensive approach, civil–military cooperation and counter insurgency (see e.g. Hynek and Marton 2011; Rietjens and Bollen 2008; Pouligny 2006). Most of the researchers in this field carry out qualitative research. They conduct interviews with military, humanitarian or host nation actors, make detailed observations during field trips or study scores of meeting minutes and project data. Together these data provide a source of well-grounded, rich descriptions and explanations of processes in identifiable local contexts. Using such data enables researchers to unravel the chronological flow and see which events led to which consequences and derive fruitful explanations. In addition, it facilitates understanding of the context within which decisions and actions take place (Myers 2009). And, as Miles and Huberman (1994) argue, good qualitative data are more likely to lead to serendipitous findings and to new integrations.

Despite its great potential many authors have criticized the process of qualitative data analysis. Miles summarized this critique stating that:

> The most serious and central difficulty in the use of qualitative data is that methods of analysis are not well formulated. For quantitative data, there are clear

conventions the researcher can use. But the analyst faced with a bank of qualitative data has very few guidelines for protection against self-delusion, let alone the presentation of unreliable or invalid conclusions to scientific or policy-making audiences. How can we be sure that an 'earthy', 'undeniable', 'serendipitous' finding is not in fact wrong?

(Miles 1979: 590)

There have been many developments in qualitative data analysis since Miles expressed his critique, but researchers have still not come to grips with several main issues. These include the labor-intensiveness of data collection, the overload of data, the possibility of researcher bias, the time demands of processing data, the adequacy of sampling when only a few cases can be managed (for this topic see Ruffa and Soeters 2014, Chapter 19 this volume), the generalization of findings, the credibility of conclusions and their utility in the world of policy and action (Myers 2009; Flick 2009; Miles and Huberman 1994).

This chapter intends to clarify the process of qualitative data analysis and to suggest researchers, in particular those in the field of military and security studies, ways to deal with problems inherent to this research method. To do this, the next section starts by making some remarks on research design and data collection as these precede the actual data analysis. Following Miles and Huberman (1994) the subsequent sections address three steps in the data analysis process. Data reduction, the first step, refers to the process of selecting, focusing, simplifying, abstracting and transforming the data that appear in written-up field notes or transcriptions. The second step concerns data display. This helps researchers to organize and compress information. The third and final step of the data analysis process is drawing and verifying conclusions. The last section of this chapter reflects upon this process and draws conclusions.

Research design and data collection

The decisions that relate to research design can be seen as anticipatory data reduction as they constrain later analysis by ruling out certain variables and relationships and attending to others (Miles and Huberman 1994). They can be conceptual in nature or related to management issues. One of the first conceptual decisions to be made concerns the extent to which the conceptual framework should be made upfront (see e.g. Yin 2009) or should emerge from the field data itself (see e.g. Strauss and Corbin 1998). Many researchers consider civil–military interaction processes to be too complex to be approached with explicit conceptual frames or standard instruments. These researchers are often found within the domains of history (Brocades-Zaalberg 2005) or anthropology (Giustozzi 2009; Verweijen 2013). They prefer a more loosely structured, emergent, inductively grounded approach to gathering data. In this pre-eminently qualitative research approach, a theory or theoretical concept materializes slowly but surely in the course of a research project. Also, the important research questions will come clear only gradually, while instruments, if any, should be derived from the properties of the setting and its actors' views of them.

These 'loosely designed studies make good sense when experienced researchers have plenty of time and are exploring exotic cultures, understudied phenomena or very complex social phenomena' (Miles and Huberman 1994: 17). In the domain of civil–military interaction, Giustozzi's work on the Taliban is a prime example of this (see Maley 2014, Chapter 6 this volume, for an extensive discussion of this study). Spending years in Afghanistan he was able to decode the structure and functioning of the Taliban to a large extent. It is unlikely that he would have succeeded with a detailed framework and instrumentarium that he made up front as this would have narrowed and biased him too much.

When the phenomenon a researcher investigates is better understood, it might, however, be a waste of time to use a loose and inductive design. There is a risk that, despite months of fieldwork, a researcher might only scratch the surface and come up with some clichés. There is merit in entering a research setting looking for questions as well as answers, but it is 'impossible to embark upon research without some idea of what one is looking for and foolish not to make that quest explicit' (Wolcott 1982: 157).

Miles and Huberman (1994) argue that tighter, more deductive research designs are preferable to researchers working with well-delineated constructs. In fact, they remind us that qualitative research can be outright 'confirmatory'. As such it can test or further explicate a conceptualization. Moreover, for beginning researchers tighter designs provide more clarity and focus (Shields and Rangarajan 2013).

Much qualitative research lies between these two extremes (pre-structured versus loose and emergent) and follows an intermediate approach. This is the case when some things are known conceptually about the phenomenon, but not enough to house a theory. Or when the researcher has an idea of the parts of the phenomenon that are not well understood and knows where to look for these things – in which settings, among which actors (Miles and Huberman 1994). Some researchers refer to this intermediate approach as abduction (Richardson and Kramer 2006). Introduced by the American philosopher Charles Sanders Peirce (1955), this concept stresses that practical scientific programs cannot be based on either pure deduction or pure induction. As such abduction is the inferential process that starts with an initial puzzling fact and finally leads to a theoretical hypothesis, which can explain it.

The example study on civil–military cooperation in Afghanistan presents a clear example of an intermediate approach. Bollen and Beeres (2002: 22) state 'by no means does civil-military cooperation constitute an exception with regard to other interorganizational alliances'. However, as a result of structural fundamental differences between the military and their civilian counterparts, alliances are bound to be fragile. Taken on their own, interdependencies generate too few safeguards to shield the collaborators from hidden agendas, self-interest, or from their partners' opportunistic behaviour. Rietjens (2008) therefore decided to use the rich body of knowledge on interorganizational alliances as a foundation to develop a conceptual framework for civil–military cooperation processes. Having applied the conceptual framework to cooperation processes in case studies as diverse as Kosovo, Iraq and the Kabul area, the conceptual framework became more constrained. It, however, left significant space to integrate the influences of new cultures and less known actors. This was when the framework was applied to civil–military cooperation in northern Afghanistan.

In addition to the conceptual framework, several other issues are important in the design phase (Miles and Huberman 1994). First, the research questions must be formulated. These may precede or follow the development of a conceptual framework and represent the elements of the empirical domain that the researcher wants to explore. Defining the case is a second design issue. Researchers often struggle with what exactly constitutes their case. Cases can be defined in various ways such as the nature and size of the unit of analysis; a case might be located spatially or it can be defined temporally. In the example study the case was defined as the cooperation process between the Dutch Provincial Reconstruction Team and at least one civilian actor in the Afghan province Baghlan during the period February and July 2005.

Selecting cases is closely linked to defining the case. There are several methods that enable the researcher to select cases. These methods include a random selection, selection based on practical reasons and selection on homogeneous or heterogeneous (in)dependent variables. Ruffa and Soeters (2014, Chapter 19 this volume) treat these methods in more detail.

The next design issue is the choice of instrumentation. This may mean little more than some shorthanded devices for observing and recording events. However, even when performing an open-ended interview some technical choices have to be made including deciding between taking notes or taping an interview (see e.g. Yin 2009). Additional issues that are relevant in the design phase include linking qualitative and quantitative data (Bryman 2008); selecting computer software to support the work (Flick 2009); and making agreements with the people being studied (Fine et al. 2000).

Having completed the research design, data collection is usually the next step in the qualitative research process. Although there are many different taxonomies on collecting data, researchers typically rely on four methods for data collection: (a) participating in the setting, (b) observing directly, (c) interviewing in depth, and (d) analysing documents and material (Marshall and Rossman 2006). An extensive treatment of these and other methods can be found in the many (hand)books on doing qualitative research (e.g. Marshall and Rossman 2006; Bernard and Ryan 2010). For now it suffices to say that most of the researchers studying civil–military interaction end up with a great amount of data, varying for example in size, form, content, background and reliability. In the example study the researcher obtained much data through interviews and observations. Moreover, he was given 19 gigabytes of data files. The number of files ran in the ten thousands and included operational orders, situation reports, minute notes, key leader engagement plans and photographs. The files were hardly structured and contained many different formats. To make sense of such an abundance of data turned out to be a challenging task. The next sections deal with this process of data reduction, data display and drawing and verifying conclusions, together labelled data analysis.

Data reduction

Coding is the process that qualitative researchers use to reduce and focus the great amount of raw data. A coding process moves in a stepwise fashion progressively from unsorted data to the development of more refined categories and concepts (Hahn 2008). Although qualitative researchers use many different types of coding, three main types can be identified: open coding, axial coding and selective coding. The main goal of open coding is to break down and understand data and to attach and develop categories and put them into an order in the course of time (Flick 2009). The result of open coding is often a list of the codes and categories that the researcher has attached to the text. In this context categories are seen as a collection of codes that have some sort of commonality. Following Dewey (1938), Shields and Rangarajan (2013) compare categories with the sorting of similar items into bins. Constructing the categories involves finding understandable and explicable uniformities between the coded items within the bin. Shields and Rangarajan (2013) use the example of a kitchen mess to illustrate this. The coded items that share certain commonalities are placed in the same bin. For example items such as knives, forks and spoons are brought together in the bin/category *eating utensils*. Figure 12.1 presents an example of an open coded text from the example study. The text illustrates a gate meeting between military of the Dutch PRT and a representative of the non-governmental organization Halo Trust. On the right side the codes and categories to which they belong are included.

Gate Meeting Military Observer and Liaison Team (MOLT) 1
May 9, 2005
District KHINJAN

Participants:*
- Lieutenant DENDERS (MOLT 1 representative)
- Warrant officer RIEBEEK (EOD advisor)
- Warrant officer JANSEN (CIMIC advisor)
- DR. KHAN (Representative of Halo Trust)

There was a short meeting with the representative of
HALOTRUST, DR. KHAN. Before clearing the ammunition
depots it is necessary to repair the bunker on the
KARKAR barracks.   *Code 45: Ammunition*
According to Dr. KHAN, Mr. SAFI has approximately   *removal (category:*
20 truckloads of ammunition behind LIMAK. Each   *partnership implementation)*
day four truck loads can be transported to the KARKAR barracks.
This means that this operation takes 5 days. MOLT 1 will,
together with warrant officer RIEBEEK, map the other locations
of the ammunition depots. Subsequently, agreements will be made
with SAFI and/or DELA about transporting the ammunition to
the road or to a place that the truck of HALOTRUST can reach.
The transportation costs are 1000 Afghani for each 7 kilograms
of cargo. The number of kilograms to be transported have
to be estimates. MOLT 1 will request SAFI on Wednesday
(mission KHINJAN) to transport the less   *Code 33: Agreement*
accessible ammunition to the road. The PRT is   *(category: partnership*
willing to pay the transportation costs.   *design)*

Figure 12.1 Example of an open coded text from the example study

*The names of the participants are fictitious for confidentiality reasons

After identifying a number of substantive categories, the next step is to refine and differentiate the categories resulting from open coding. Strauss and Corbin (1998) suggest doing a more formal coding for identifying and classifying links between these categories. They label this axial coding. When qualitative researchers code axially, they intend to answer questions such as why, where, when, how and with what results and in doing so they uncover relationships among categories.

Axial coding is sometimes criticized as forcing a structure on the data instead of discovering what emerges. For this reason Glaser (1978) suggested a list of basic codes as a step following open coding. He grouped these into coding families that can be used as tools for advancing an understanding of the material. Table 12.1 illustrates these coding families. The right column includes civil–military interaction examples.

The third main type of coding, selective coding, is the process of integrating and refining categories (Strauss and Corbin 1998). Here the researcher looks for further examples and evidence for relevant categories. Selective coding allocates specificities to the theory and enables the researcher to make use of explanatory statements such as 'under these conditions', 'then' and 'when this set of events occur' (Strauss and Corbin 1998). Finally, the theory is formulated in greater detail and again checked against the data. The procedure of interpreting

Table 12.1 Coding families applied to examples of civil–military interaction (adapted from Glaser 1978: 75–82; Flick 2009: 315)

Coding families	Concepts	Examples
Six Cs family	Causes, contexts, contingencies, consequences, covariances, conditions	Causes of civil–military interaction, operational context
Process family	Stages, phases, phasings, transitions, passages, careers, chains, sequences	Different phases in the civil–military interaction process such as partner selection or transfer
Degree family	Extent, level, intensity, range, amount, continuum, statistical average, standard deviation	Intensity of interaction
Type family	Types, classes, genres, prototypes, styles, kinds	Types of interaction (e.g. de-confliction or joint activities)
Strategy family	Strategies, tactics, techniques, mechanisms, management	Strategies for dealing with civil–military interaction
Interactive family	Interaction, mutual effects, interdependence, reciprocity, asymmetries, rituals	Dealing with asymmetric resources (e.g. the large numbers of military personnel versus low numbers of civilians)
Identity self-family	Identity, self-image, self-concept, self-evaluation, social worth, transformations of self	Different actor perspectives on interaction (e.g. local perspective versus military perspective)
Cutting point family	Boundary, critical juncture, cutting point, turning point, tolerance levels, point of no return	New level in the interaction e.g. due to increased resource allocation
Cultural family	Social norms, social values, social beliefs	Different social values between civil and military partners
Consensus family	Contracts, agreements, definitions of the situation, uniformity, conformity, conflict	Making of agreements between military and civilian actors

data, like the integration of additional material, ends at the point where saturation has been reached. This means that further coding or enrichment of categories no longer provides or promises new knowledge (Flick 2009). Yin (2009) refers to this as analytical saturation, which he contrasts with statistical generalization. Statistical generalization refers to inferences made about a population based on empirical data collected about a sample from that population. Analytical generalization uses a previously developed theory as a template to compare the empirical results.

Turning to the example study, a comparison of eight different processes enabled the researcher to carry out selective coding and to reach analytical saturation. It turned out that all civil–military cooperation processes went through six successive phases: (1) decision to cooperate, (2) partner selection, (3) design, (4) implementation, (5) transfer of tasks and responsibilities, and (6) evaluation. Moreover, the analysis showed that at strategic and operational levels, there was often no clear priority setting, demarcation of the activities, and formulation of end-states, making it difficult to determine when the objectives of the military force were met and redeployment could begin. NATO's doctrine proved to be unsuitable to facilitate this.

Data display

Data display is the next step in the data analysis process. Its goal is to systematically present information in a visual format. This should assist researchers to further organize and compress their information. For many qualitative researchers, however, the typical mode of display takes the form of extended, unreduced text, usually in the form of written-up field notes. Often this is a weak and cumbersome form of display (Miles and Huberman 1994) and hard on analysts because it is dispersed over many pages and is not easy to see as a whole. Moreover, displaying text in such a way makes it difficult to look at two or three variables at once.

This type of display does not fit Cleveland's (1985) definition of a good display, namely that it enables the researcher to absorb large amounts of information quickly. According to Miles and Huberman (1994) good displays can take various different forms, but generally fall into two major families: matrices and networks. A matrix is essentially the crossing of two lists, set up as rows and columns. Miles and Huberman (1994) distinguish a variety of different matrices. These include time-ordered matrices to display time-linked data and role-ordered matrices that sort data in rows and columns that have been gathered from or about a certain set of "role occupants" with data that reflect their views.

Within the realm of civil–military interaction data matrices are often used. The matrix that De Coning and Friis (2011) developed is a well-known example. It maps four levels of coherence (intra-agency coherence, whole of government coherence, inter-agency coherence, and international-local coherence) against six types of relationships varying from 'actors are united' to 'actors compete'. The matrix provides the reader with a great, easy to read overview as well as with conceptual strength, which enables understanding of the different civil–military relationships.

In the example study the researcher also made use of data matrices. For each of the eight civil–military partnerships studied the researcher drew a matrix. The rows of these matrices contained the phases and key factors, while the columns addressed the different actors that took part in the cooperation process. To facilitate comparison of these eight different civil–military partnerships again a matrix was used. In this matrix the rows contained the partnerships, while the columns included the different steps in the cooperation process. An excerpt of this matrix containing two civil–military partnerships is presented in Table 12.2.

Networks make up the second major family of displays. A network is a collection of nodes or points connected with lines and is generally helpful when a study focuses on more than a few variables at a time. A well-known type of network display includes context charts. These charts map in graphic form the interrelationships among the roles and actors that make up the context of individual behaviour. Also causal networks are very common. These network displays contain the most important independent and dependent variables and the relationships among them.

In their research on cultural understanding Rentsch et al. (2009) effectively use the network display to illustrate the attributes that are relevant to a soldier for understanding a foreign culture. Rentsch et al. (2009) extracted information and experiences from US Army soldiers who had deployed to many different countries. As a result they were able to determine what cultural attributes the soldiers considered most important, based on their experience. Figure 12.2 presents this network display. Items with the greatest number of links in this network are the most central concepts, as reflected in responses from their sample.

Table 12.2 Data matrix displaying the characteristics of the civil–military partnerships in Baghlan province (Rietjens 2008)

Partnerships	Main Characteristics of Partnerships					
	Step 1: Decision to Cooperate (Motive NL PRT)	Step 2: Partner Selection	Step 3: Partnership Design	Step 4: Partnership Implementation (Main Activities)	Step 5: Transfer of Tasks and Responsibilities	Step 6: Partnership Evaluation
Construction of microhydropower plants	Limited implementing capacity of NL PRT; increase local capacity	Contractor selection is based on added value for NL PRT, complementary resources, personal fit, and prior reputation. District governors are considered a given partner of the cooperation	Detailed written contracts between NL PRT and the contractor and between NL PRT and two (out of three) district governors	Assessment: NL PRT Construction power plant: Constructor Construction and financing transformation house, electrical wires and transmission: District governors and local population Financing power plants: NL PRT	Microhydropower plants were constructed, but responsibilities of the district governors were by far not fulfilled. It was not clear how the electricity was to be divided into the community	No evaluation
Police training courses	Contribution to SSR program	Police forces are considered a given partner of the cooperation	Detailed written contract between NL PRT and the police commanders	Preparing trainings program: NL PRT Selection trainees: Police commanders Training: NL PRT Delivery of truncheons: Trainees Financing: NL PRT	Little follow-up to train the trainers program since graduated trainees were not granted time to function as instructor and were not provided with sufficient means to do so	No evaluation

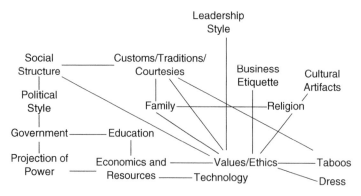

Figure 12.2 Network display of core cultural attributes (Rentsch et al. 2009)

Drawing and verifying conclusions

Having displayed the data, the final step of the analysis process is drawing and verifying conclusions. Many different tactics can be discerned to generate meaning and draw conclusions from a particular configuration of data in a display. An often used tactic is *noting patterns or themes* (Ryan and Bernard 2000). This can be very productive when the number of cases and/or the data overload is severe. The tactic seems rather easy to apply but it is important to see added evidence of the same pattern ('recurring regularities', as Guba (1978) puts is) and to remain open to unexpected findings when they appear (see also Yin's (2009) 'pattern matching'). Tactics that are closely linked to *noting patterns or themes* and that are rather concrete and descriptive include *seeing plausibility, clustering, making metaphors* and *counting* (Miles and Huberman 1994). With regard to counting Miles and Huberman state that counting tends to get ignored in qualitative research. There are, however, good reasons to do counting in a qualitative study. First, looking at distributions rapidly enables the researcher to notice the general drift of the data and to see the outliers. Second, counting can facilitate the verification of a hunch or hypothesis. And third, it can protect the researcher against biases.

A tactic that is more explanatory in nature is *building a logical chain of evidence*. This tactic develops a complex chain of events over a certain time period. The events are staged in repeated cause–effect patterns, whereby a dependent variable (event) at an earlier stage becomes the independent variable (causal event) for the next stage (Yin 2009). In Chapter 9 of this volume Vennesson and Wiesner analyse the concept of process tracing and deal with the issue of chains of evidence more in depth.

When a researcher has drawn conclusions it is necessary to verify whether they are valid, repeatable and right. There are numerous examples of qualitative studies that tell a wonderful and powerful story but do not match the data and are in fact wrong. Tactics for testing or confirming findings are extensively treated in qualitative research handbooks (e.g. Flick 2009; Myers 2009; Miles and Huberman 1994). Some examples of these tactics include:

- checking for representativeness: the extent to which a sub sample can be taken as representative of a wider set;
- checking for researcher effects: the influence a researcher has on its surroundings and vice versa can lead to biased observations and inferences;
- triangulation: the rationale of using multiple sources of evidence; types of triangulation include: (1) data source triangulation (multiple data sources), (2) investigator triangulation

(multiple investigators), (3) theoretical triangulation (multiple theoretical viewpoints), and (4) methodological triangulation (multiple methods) (Stake 1995);
* getting feedback from informants: local informants can act as judges, evaluating the major findings of a study; this is often referred to as a member check (see e.g. Lewis-Beck et al. 2004).

Having applied several tactics to draw and verify conclusions, how can a researcher know whether or not his finally emerging findings are good? There is great debate on what determines the quality of conclusions. Many researchers argue that it is not really possible to specify criteria for good qualitative work (see for example Schwandt 1996) and some even claim that qualitative researchers are always striving to 'not get it all wrong' (Wolcott 1990, 126). Miles and Huberman (1994) argue that it is worth striving for shared quality standards. They outline five commonly agreed upon issues that determine the goodness of a study:

* Objectivity/confirmability of qualitative work: the question here is whether the conclusions depend on the subjects and conditions of the inquiry rather than on the inquirer.
* Reliability/dependability/auditability: the underlying problem is to what extent the study is consistent, reasonably stable over time and across researchers and methods.
* Internal validity/credibility/authenticity: the questions raised here include whether the findings of the study make sense and are credible to the readers and to the people that have been studied.
* External validity/transferability/fittingness: this issue addresses the generalization of the findings: to what extent are they transferable to other contexts?
* Utilization/application/action orientation: even if findings are valid and transferable, the question remains what the study does for its participants (both researchers and researched) and customers. This issue closely links to ethical questions such as who benefits from the study and who may be harmed.

For researchers focusing on civil–military interaction these issues are very much applicable as many of their studies are set in foreign cultures and include actors that are unfamiliar to them. Moreover, in several studies local informants run a safety risk when they are openly seen with an outside researcher. Paying full attention to these quality issues can assist the researcher in unravelling these complex civil–military relationships and determining the boundaries within which conclusions are valid.

Conclusion and reflection

Most qualitative researchers that study civil–military interaction are confronted with an enormous amount of data varying from interview notes to internal memoranda to field observations. This chapter has attempted to guide these researchers, as well as those working in adjacent fields, in working with these data and coming to good conclusions. The process of qualitative data analysis starts with the research design and data collection as this is in fact anticipatory data reduction. Subsequently three phases are discerned: (1) data reduction, (2) data display and (3) drawing and verifying conclusions. Albeit no guarantee for success, addressing each of these phases significantly increases a researcher's ability to see the patterns in the fog of civil–military interaction.

Despite the many tactics and procedures that were addressed in this chapter, several limitations and open ends remain. A first limitation is inherent to the nature of qualitative research.

The general critique of this type of research is that it is too subjective, difficult to replicate, that it faces problems of generalizability and lacks transparency (e.g. Bryman 2008). Meticulously applying the tactics and procedures of the data analysis process does help to counter this critique but offers no guarantee that quality criteria such as objectivity and generalizability are being met.

A second limitation is related to data reduction. During this phase there is a potential for endless coding and comparisons. A researcher could apply open coding to all passages of a text and further elaborate all the categories (Flick 2009). The method provides few hints about what criteria the end of coding should be based on. The criterion of analytical saturation leaves it to the theory developed and therefore ultimately to the researcher to make this decision. Another commonly mentioned limitation related to data reduction is that by taking parts of text out of the context within which they appeared, the social setting can be lost.

A next limitation that some researchers face deals with using their creative capacity. If one applies the phased approach of qualitative data analysis in a very mechanistic way it can destroy creativity. While analysing patterns or developing data matrices are important, they may not create something new. Creating, however, is aimed at finding something new whether it is a descriptive category, hypothesis, or finding (Shields and Rangarajan 2013).

A last limitation that is addressed here concerns the quality and quantity of data with which many researchers are confronted. Data might be classified and therefore prohibited to use. An enormous quantity of data could make coding and displaying all the data an impossible a task. The emergence of computer-aided qualitative data analysis software (CAQDAS) can assist the researcher addressing this issue (see Bryman 2008). Programs such as NVivo or Atlas can take over many tasks of the researcher including allocating chunks of text to a code and linking them together (Friese 2012). However, as promising as these developments may sound, the qualitative analyst must still interpret his or her data and in the end analysis and interpretation remains the work of humans.

References

Bernard, H.R. and Ryan, G.W. (2010) *Analyzing Qualitative Data: Systematic Approaches*, Thousand Oaks, CA: Sage Publications.
Bollen, M.T.I.B. and Beeres, R. (2002) 'On the Conditions for CIMIC during Humanitarian Operations', in M.T.I.B. Bollen, R.V. Janssens, H.F.M. Kirkels and J.M.M.L. Soeters (eds) *NL Arms: Civil-Military Cooperation: A Marriage of Reason*, 19–30, Breda: Royal Netherlands Military Academy.
Brocades-Zaalberg, T. (2005) *Soldiers and Civil Power: Supporting or Substituting Civil Authorities in Peace Support Operations during the 1990s*, Amsterdam: University of Amsterdam.
Bryman, A. (2008) *Social Research Methods*, Oxford: Oxford University Press.
Cleveland, W.S. (1985) *The Elements of Graphing Data*, Belmont, CA: Wadsworth.
De Coning, C. and Friis, K. (2011) 'Coherence and Coordination: The limits of the comprehensive approach', *Journal of International Peacekeeping*, 15: 243–272.
Dewey, J. (1938) *Logic: The Theory of Inquiry*, New York: Henry Holt and Company.
Fine, M., Weis, L., Weseen, S. and Wong, L. (2000) 'FOR WHOM: Qualitative research, representations and social responsibilities', in N. Denizen and Y.S. Lincoln (eds) *The Sage Handbook of Qualitative Research*, 107–131, Thousand Oaks, CA: Sage Publications.
Flick, U. (2009) *An Introduction in Qualitative Research*, 4th edn, Thousand Oaks, CA: Sage Publications.
Friese, S. (2012) *Qualitative Data Analysis with Atlas*, Thousand Oaks, CA: Sage Publications.
Giustozzi, A. (ed.) (2009) *Decoding the New Taliban*, New York: Columbia University Press.
Glaser, B.G. (1978) *Theoretical Sensitivity*, Mill Valley, CA: University of California Press.
Guba, E.G. (1978) *Toward a Methodology of Naturalistic Inquiry in Educational Evaluation*, Los Angeles, CA: UCLA Center for the Study of Evaluation.
Hahn, C. (2008) *Doing Qualitative Research Using Your Computer: A Practical Guide*, Thousand Oaks, CA: Sage Publications.

Hynek, N. and Marton, P. (eds) (2011) *NATO's Provincial Reconstruction in a Comparative Perspective*, London: Routledge.

Lewis-Beck, M.S., Bryman, A. and Liao, T.F. (2004) *The SAGE Encyclopedia of Social Science Research Methods*, Thousand Oaks, CA: Sage Publications.

Maley, W. (2014) 'Studying Host-National in Afganistan', in J.M.M.L. Soeters, P.M. Shields and S.J.H. Rietjens (eds) *Routledge Handbook of Research Methods in Military Studies*, London: Routledge.

Marshall, C. and Rossman, G.B. (2006) *Designing Qualitative Research*, Thousand Oaks, CA: Sage Publications.

Miles, M.B. (1979) 'Qualitative Data as an Attractive Nuisance: The problem of analysis', *Administrative Science Quarterly*, 24: 590–601.

Miles, M.B. and Huberman, A.M. (1994) *Qualitative Data Analysis*, 2nd edn, Thousand Oaks, CA: Sage Publications.

Myers, M.D. (2009) *Qualitative Research in Business and Management*, London: Sage Publications.

Peirce, C.S. (1955) *Philosophical Writings of Peirce* (ed. J. Buchler), New York: Dover Publications, Inc.

Pouligny, B. (2006) *Peace Operations Seen from Below*, Bloomfield, CT: Kumarian Press Inc.

Rentsch, J.R., Mot, I. and Abbe, A. (2009) *Identifying the Core Content and Structure of a Schema for Cultural Understanding*, Arlington, VA: United States Army Research Institute for the Behavioral and Social Sciences.

Richardson, R. and Kramer, E.H. (2006) 'Abduction as the Type of Inference that Characterizes the Development of a Grounded Theory,' *Qualitative Research* 6: 497–513.

Rietjens, S.J.H. (2008) 'Managing Civil-Military Cooperation: Experiences from the Dutch Provincial Reconstruction Team in Afghanistan', *Armed Forces & Society* 34: 173–207.

Rietjens, S.J.H. and Bollen, M.T.I.B. (2008) *Managing Civil-Military Cooperation: A 24/7 Joint Effort for Stability*, Aldershot: Ashgate Publishers.

Ruffa, R. and Soeters, J. (2014) 'Cross National Research in the Military: Comparing operational styles in peace missions', in J. Soeters, P.M. Shields and S. Rietjens (eds) *Routledge Handbook of Research Methods in Military Studies*, London: Routledge.

Ryan, G.W. and Bernard, H.R. (2000) 'Data Management and Analysis Methods,' in N. Denzin and Y.S. Lincoln (eds) *Handbook of Qualitative Research*, 769–802, Thousand Oaks, CA: Sage Publications.

Schwandt, T.A. (1996) 'Farewell to Criteriology', *Qualitative Inquiry*, 2: 58–72.

Shields, P.M. and Rangarajan, N. (2013) *A Playbook for Research Methods: Integrating Conceptual Frameworks and Project Management*, Stillwater, OK: New Forums Press.

Stake, R.E. (1995) *The Art of Case Study Research*, London: Sage Publications.

Strauss, A.L. and Corbin, J. (1998) *Basics of Qualitative Research*, 2nd edn, London: Sage Publications.

Verweijen, J. (2013) 'Military Business and the Business of the Military in the Kivus', *Review of African Political Economy*, 40: 67–82.

Wolcott, H.F. (1982) 'Differing Styles of On-Site Research, or "If It Isn't Ethnography, What Is It?"', *The Review Journal of Philosophy and Social Science*, 7: 154–169.

Wolcott, H. (1990) 'On Seeking – and Rejecting – Validity in Qualitative Research', in E. Eisner and A. Peshkin (eds) *Qualitative Inquiry in Education: The Continuing Debate*, 121–152, New York: Teachers College Press.

Yin, R.K. (2009) *Case Study Research: Design and Methods*, 4th edn, Thousand Oaks, CA: Sage Publications.

13

VISUAL COMMUNICATION RESEARCH AND WAR

Michael Griffin

M. Griffin and J. Lee (1995) "Picturing the Gulf War: Constructing images of war in *Time, Newsweek*, and *U.S. News and World Report*", *Journalism and Mass Communication Quarterly* 72(4): 813–825.

"Picturing the Gulf War" attempts to account for the visual representation of war as a potentially independent and influential component of news coverage of military conflicts. The research was a direct response to media reporting of the 1991 Gulf War, which widely purported to provide ongoing, "live" pictorial coverage of the conflict. During and after the war a great deal of impressionistic commentary presumed that visual images were the driving force in news reporting on the war. Indeed, it was described as a "living room war" for readers and audiences. Yet, no systematic research actually charted the nature, frequency and role of published or broadcast war visuals. The tendency to treat pictures as direct and uncomplicated reflections of reality with instinctively presumed effects, together with the difficulties of quantifying and measuring analogic visual material, effectively forestalled more systematic analysis.

Griffin and Lee surveyed historical collections of war photography, literature on previous wartime photojournalism, and news coverage of the buildup to the Gulf War to construct a classification system for the analysis of visual representations during the six weeks of open warfare, January–March 1991. Concerned more with patterns of visual representation than the uniqueness of individual images, yet conscious of the difficulty of parsing and counting discrete units in analogic pictorial material, the authors strove to create analytical categories that would simultaneously account for manifest content and forms of visualization. This involved identifying historically established pictorial genres and techniques of visualization in war photography, and utilizing written information on the event contexts of published images. This specifically pictorial content analysis was designed to distinguish such differences as: individual portraits of soldiers vs. pictures of groups of soldiers, file photographs of troops taken outside of combat theaters vs. pictures of troops engaged in combat within war zones, pictures from arms catalogs and defense industry publications vs. photographs of aircraft, missiles, artillery or tanks in actual combat situations, and images that position the viewer within civilian contexts affected by the war vs. those that assume the perspectives of advancing or defending military personnel.

The authors sorted the entire population of 1,104 visual images published in the newsweeklies *Time, Newsweek*, and *U.S. News and World Report* for the duration and immediate aftermath of "Operation Desert Storm," issues dated January 21 through March 18, 1991. Beginning with 41 image categories to account for a potentially wide range of pictorial type and visual content, they found that only 6 categories comprised more than half, and 12 categories more than 76 percent, of all published images. Results showed that the pictorial record of the war in US news weeklies was much narrower in scope and content than might have been expected, and that it coalesced around a small number of themes and news narratives concerning the war, including the massing and mobilization of US troops and armaments in the Gulf region, "cataloguing the arsenal," whose categories comprised 37 percent of all images, and photos of political and military leaders, predominantly pictures of George H.W. Bush, Saddam Hussein, and several US generals. Only 3 percent of the published pictures showed events from actual combat zones.

A significant finding of the study is that many types of visual images presumably associated with war photography – images of ongoing combat, military and civilian casualties, material destruction, the lived experience of soldiers – appeared rarely or not at all in newsmagazine illustrations. This highlights both the inadequacy of thinking of pictures as independent records and the importance of *absence* as a significant factor in studies of representation.

The study is noteworthy for its attempt to develop more systematic methods of specifically visual content analysis, and to move from a traditional descriptive-interpretive focus on individual pictures and picture-makers to an analysis of patterns of visual representation across media. The study has become a common reference point for subsequent research on the visual portrayal of military conflicts in the former Yugoslavia, Afghanistan, Iraq, and the Israel-Hezbollah war in Lebanon.

Introduction

Visual communication studies are concerned with the specific ways in which visual images, as well as design relationships between visual elements, communicate ideas and emotions. The functions of visual images in communication are still largely unspecified by empirical research. There is some evidence that humans process the simulated visual cues of photography and motion pictures in ways that mimic the processing of natural visual stimuli. There is also counter evidence that apprehending particular types of visual portrayal, such as pictures that use techniques of linear perspective to suggest depth in a two-dimensional picture plane, depends upon exposure to the representational conventions of a specific culture. A long-standing paradigmatic question for visual research has been the degree to which the apprehension of pictures is natural or culturally learned, how much visual images simply reflect the surfaces of the world around us or how much they depend upon a knowledge of cultural systems of signification or *visual languages* (Messaris 1994).

In the illustrative study the authors grapple with the contradictory notions that photographic technologies can deliver a direct experience of warfare, but that the images of conflict we most likely see represent only a limited and conventional view of war (Griffin and Lee 1995). The tendency to equate images with direct experience involves the degree to which images operate on a more immediate and affective level than language, at times prompting more spontaneous and visceral responses from viewers. This is why visual media, and especially virtual 3D technology can be useful for simulation training. Some research has also shown improvement in subjects ability to recall the detail of stories when accounts are accompanied by visuals (Graber 1990). Other research suggests that images primarily serve to "prime" existing psychological schemata, encouraging rapid closure around preconceived attitudes and beliefs (Domke et al. 2002). This chapter addresses some of the salient concerns and methodological challenges facing visual communication scholars attempting to study visual representation of war. A comprehensive treatment of the myriad perceptual, psychological, cultural, social and political factors shaping the use and function of visual images in our surveillance and understanding of the world remains beyond the scope of this brief essay. Instead the chapter will focus on a few key issues in the study of media images of war.

Visual communication research is inherently concerned with both the ontological and epistemological qualities of visual images: what is the status of visual images as a form of human symbolic communication and what can we know or learn from visuals, especially as opposed to verbal information? These questions often revolve around the tendency to confuse visual images with the things they purport to represent, what is sometimes referred to as the "reflection hypothesis" or "reflective approach" (Hall 1997). Because military conflict is inherently political and emotionally charged, studying images of war foregrounds key aspects of visual research: the concern with distinguishing the abstract and symbolic nature and functions of images from their potential as descriptive records of places and events, and identifying the inevitably rhetorical nature of image selection, construction and juxtaposition.

Because every picture and every visual presentation is the result of a series of choices about where to direct attention, how to approach a subject, how to frame and compose a shot, and how to order and structure chains of images and text, studies of visual communication pose theoretical and methodological challenges at four levels. The first involves the relationship between images and their subject matter – what could be called the mediating process between image-maker (photographer, filmmaker) and subject. This is directly relevant to the uncertain status of pictures as records and/or evidentiary data. The second involves the many layers of institutional filtering through which visual images are produced, selected, ordered, distributed and potentially reproduced for viewer/audiences. Even a cursory look at a photojournalist's contact sheets (the full set of thumbnail photos from which individual images are selected for printing), or the raw video footage from which a broadcast or online news report is culled, reveals that the images presented to us are inevitably only fragments of a much larger universe of visual experience. The third involves the difficulty in deciphering viewer perceptions, as distinct from the image-objects they encounter. And the fourth concerns the difficulty and complexity of visual analysis and interpretation itself, which has proved a continuing problem for mass media studies and communications research. A particular methodological challenge in this regard has been the difficulty of systematically distinguishing and quantifying visual characteristics and relationships in what are largely analogic and unified visual fields.

In wartime contexts additional factors frequently affect visual representations and their circulation and these must also be considered in analyses of conflict imagery. Such potential complications include the difficult and high-risk conditions for the production of media images; the regulation of access to conflict zones by governments, military organizations, or political groups; the censorship restrictions (both external and self-imposed) that often constrict the circulation of images; the competing institutional interests involved in government-media relations and media marketing; the allegiances and world views (embedded ideology) of those organizations and individuals involved in image making and distribution; the cultivated expectations and demands of audiences and media markets during wartime; and the frequent competition of rival wartime propaganda interests, whether nationalist or counter-nationalist.

In other words, the production of media images, and therefore their study and analysis, are affected by all of the same social, political, economic and institutional factors that shape journalism and historical documentation in general. But because the realm of the visual carries an assumption of immediate apprehension and impact, and therefore the power to influence public opinion, special attention is often devoted to filtering and controlling the output of images from war zones.

Photo technologies have also played a crucial role in military surveillance and targeting, producing millions of items of visual information over hundreds of conflicts. In addition, as early as World War I soldiers began to carry personal cameras, producing copious records of daily military life. Yet those images of war that have been publicly circulated, the pictures that potentially influence public perceptions of what war looks like, represent only those pictures culled through multiple layers of filtering and compression. As Taylor (1991) documents in his book *War Photography: Realism in the British Press*, millions of wartime photographs from World War I, World War II and other twentieth-century conflicts are preserved in British national archives, but those pictures featured in the British press have focused heavily on stereotypes of family life and patriotism at home. Taylor writes:

> These stereotypes enable a national history to be seen and learned. This history is not solely conserved as "heritage": it is actively produced, turned into fiction and presented as the thing itself. It is simulated in replicas, or re-enactments, and massively represented in photographic realism.
>
> (1991: 165)

In public representations of Britain's wars, Taylor notes, "The disturbing effects of shocking photographs remained a hypothetical question because there was none to be seen" (1991: 112).

The emotional emphasis of picture making encourages the search for the emotional moments of war. Historical, geographical and political specificity is abandoned for icons of nationalist fervor and heroism, or more universal human experiences of suffering and sacrifice. This tendency to reduce images of war to iconic rhetorical statements has produced a legendary tradition of war photography but has diminished the value of wartime imagery as social and historical information (Griffin 1999). What we can potentially learn about war through the study of pictures remains an open question in social research, for visual imagery has been systematically analyzed only in the technical fields of military engineering, surveillance and tactics.

Why study images of war?

The fact that media images of warfare and military conflict often contain highly charged content, content thick with the potential for impending violence, destruction, or death, which is moreover connected to feelings of solidarity, nationalism, partisanship, or antagonism towards a defined enemy, means that wartime images are likely to have a strong attraction for viewers and more likely than routine news images to provoke strong emotions. This makes the production and publication of wartime images a high stakes enterprise. Images with such emotional potential, also seem to have greater potential to influence public perceptions, and affect levels of public support for government policies and military actions.

Two levels of analysis are relevant when studying images of war: (1) the individual picture or film sequence with its potential psychological impact on viewers, and (2) patterns of visual representation across sustained photographic, film or news production. Individual images often draw attention for their dramatic capacity to evoke a powerful sense of a particular event or incident, yet may tell us little about the sustained picturing of war, or our enduring representations of nation, social identity and conflict. The powerful impact of any one image may owe precisely to its rarity, its disruption of the routine flow of media imagery and consequent thwarting of expectations. Sustained patterns of visual representation, on the other hand, suggest a continuing process of image production and cultural representation, revealing underlying social influences on picture production and diffusion. So an important task for visual analysis is to detect and describe the range and types of images characteristic of fictional and non-fictional portrayals of war, and to attempt to explain the influences of history, culture and media practice on the range and types of pictorial material presented to the public.

Analyzing Persian Gulf War images

The example study found that pictorial coverage of the war converged around a narrow range of picture types, dominated by images of U.S. military deployment and "backstage" preparation (Griffin and Lee 1995). The US government and military, like other governments throughout history, tried to regulate and manage the images of the war circulated to the public. In the case of the Gulf War various media outlets were given access to the war zone through a "pool system" in which journalists assigned to travel with military units shared information with pools of fellow reporters. This system resulted in photo coverage of the war that was dominated by a category we named "cataloguing the arsenal." These were pictures of various U.S. military weaponry – missiles, rockets, fighter jets, artillery, "smart bombs," tanks and other armored vehicles – often created and filed during the period of military mobilization prior to the war itself, and sometimes reproduced from arms catalogs and weapons industry brochures. The second most frequent category of published pictures comprised photographs of "U.S. troops" in various stages of deployment and preparation but not in combat. Together, these two categories of imagery accounted for 37 percent of all pictures published in the U.S. newsmagazines.

By contrast, types of imagery that we would expect to be prominent in news coverage of the war – military casualties, damage and destruction from bombing or shelling, wartime effects on civilian life in Iraq, Kuwait, Saudi Arabia, or the U.S., pictures of Iraqi troops or Iraqi prisoners of war – were largely absent from the pictorial coverage.[1] Surprising at the time, 97 percent of the newsmagazine images were made in non-combat situations, providing empirical support for anecdotal impressions that the media had presented a sanitized view of the war. A photograph such as "American Soldier Grieving for Comrade" by David Turnley (www.corbisimages.com/stock-photo/rights-managed/TL001241/american-soldier-grieving-for-comrade) won photojournalism prizes months after the conclusion of the Gulf War for its presentation of a powerfully gripping instance of wartime suffering and empathy, but such a photo was a rare exception amid the routine images published weekly from the Gulf. While a tradition of humanistic photography is often associated with the work of twentieth-century magazine photojournalism and documentary film – evoking "universal human emotions," in "decisive moments," with "powerful individual vision," according to the founders of Magnum photo agency – in contemporary practice the individual image cannot be separated from the flow of texts and presentational contexts in which audiences encounter them (Rose 2012).

The Gulf War study taught this lesson well. Picture captions, acknowledgements and other textual information provided crucial analytical information. The research unit of analysis was almost never the picture alone, but rather the image-text. It quickly became clear that methods of analysis needed to account for contextual information to distinguish between photos of American tanks in the Kuwaiti desert and pictures of similar tanks in the Mojave Desert of

California. The entire history of visual communication, in fiction, non-fiction, and propaganda, is filled with decontextualized uses of imagery to create strategic juxtapositions and manipulated impressions. Precisely because of the realism and emotional connection promised by visual images, identifying the sources and contexts of images are as important as analyzing their content and presentational form.

The challenge of accounting for both the iconic and the routine in images of war

It is a methodological challenge to attempt to account for the culturally resonant and enduring characteristics of individual images and at the same time chart the quotidian landscape of war representation within any given cultural/historical context or media system. The humanistic tradition of twentieth-century photography emphasizes the power of single images and has created for each war certain icons in the public record and imagination (Hariman and Lucaites 2007). The desire to establish such iconic images is explicitly recognized by journalists themselves, as when, in the early days of the 2003 invasion of Iraq, a CBS news reader exclaimed, "the search is on for the one great image that will define the battle of Iraq" (quoted in Hariman and Lucaites 2007: 291). To evaluate the cultural resonance and impact of individual images requires the interpretive analysis of historical, cultural and rhetorical studies (Zellizer 2004). But most of the research in visual communication studies concerns patterns of cultural and professional practice in media production. In this regard, a growing body of research has appeared since the 1991 Gulf War that attempts to systematically gauge the range and foci of war-related visual representations.

Methods of visual analysis in communication studies

Manifest content analysis

To understand why we get the steady diet of war images that we do, and why many other types of revealing and informative images remain unseen, we need to view war images as the result of institutionalized media production that is influenced by business interests, government management, and political persuasion. The most common approach to tracking this image production involves traditional methods of content analysis: counting the frequency with which particular features of visual portrayal appear in mediated accounts of world events. The strength of this method is its consistency and reliability. Observers can consistently agree on the presence or absence of discrete visual features – the appearance of an identifiable figure, perhaps, or the inclusion within the pictorial frame of a particular social role, character type, object, shape, color, or symbol. Such discretely identifiable features can be counted to document the frequency of their occurrence. The key methodological issues in content analysis are: (1) the conceptualization and definition of coding categories – do content categories account for factors that validly index research concerns and questions (construct validity)? and (2) inter-coder reliability – to what degree do different independent coders agree in their identification of pertinent features of content? If different coders independently and consistently identify a pertinent feature of pictorial display, then one can claim the occurrence of that feature with a certain degree of confidence.

However, methods of manifest content analysis are limited in their capacity to describe or index many potentially significant components of visual representation, especially those involving complex or interrelated characteristics of the visual field. These might involve technical

aspects of visual presentation, such as framing and composition, camera distance, angle or movement, lighting effects, color filtering, or other special effects – factors that fundamentally shape
the portrayal of pictured subject matter, but in ways that only technically trained experts may
easily recognize. They might involve cultural conventions of portrayal and symbolism (i.e.
iconography), the recognition of which requires training in fields such as anthropology or art
history; or displays of social space, posture or behavior readily apparent only to those trained to
study kinesics and social communication. It may simply be that the interrelationship of multiple
elements within an analogic pictorial field is too complex to disentangle and classify in terms of
separate, discrete elements.

In the simplest example, one could count the frequency with which particular recogniz-
able figures, such as Afghani soldiers, appear in a specified universe of wartime news images.
However, the mere frequency of their appearance in news images would reveal nothing about
the ways in which they are pictured, whether they are shown in a way that suggests professionalism and competence, or hesitance and discomfort, whether they are shown working collectively
with fellow soldiers or individually in isolation, whether patrolling Afghani villages in a cooperative and protective manner, or confronting civilians as authoritarian figures (perhaps from a
low camera angle?). In other words, a sufficient visual analysis may well require much more than
an analysis of manifest content alone.

Iconographic/semiotic analysis

The fields of art history and film studies have contributed valuable models of analysis for visual
scholars. In art history the practice of iconography and iconology has heavily influenced visual
analysis since the early decades of the twentieth century (Panofsky 1939). Iconography refers
to the "mapping" of patterns of symbols and motifs within specific cultural systems of image
making and visual representation. A prime example is the mapping of the system for representing religious figures and saints in European Christian art. For those conversant with this
medieval and renaissance system of visual communication the identities of particular figures
represented in painting, printmaking, sculpture or stained glass is readily apparent. St. Jerome
can be recognized by his portrayal with books and scrolls of scripture in Hebrew and Greek
(which he is diligently translating to Latin), and by the frequent placement of a lion at his feet.
St. Peter routinely wears a tunic and robe of specific colors, the "keys to heaven" hanging at
his waist. Similarly, military history paintings in the European tradition portray military leaders
with unmistakable signs of their identity in dress, emblems and gesture – Alexander the Great,
Julius Caesar, George Washington, Napoleon, the Duke of Wellington – and places them in
the composition of the frame in a manner that clearly distinguishes them from lower ranking
figures. Indeed, the study of iconography has shown us that the world of visual representation is
dominated by a finite set of pictorial genres, limited styles of depiction, and specific practices of
visual symbolism. To think that patterns of visual representation will simply be driven by patterns of content is to remain ignorant of the history of picture making.

However, identifying significant visual motifs, visual figures of speech (especially metonyms and
metaphors) and/or "visual quotations" may require an advanced level of knowledge and experience
in art history, cinema studies, the history of graphic design, or related cultural systems of expression.
For example, many news photographs of the sick or injured, including fallen or wounded soldiers,
frame the victim in the arms of a comrade or loved one in a pose that mimics traditional Christian
Pieta paintings and sculptures. In fact, several World Press Photo and Pulitzer Prize winning photographs over the years have made use of long-standing conventions of portrayal drawn from religious art. Recognizing the recurrence of such representational conventions may require iconological

training and the ability to conduct historical and contextual analyses that reveal patterns of expressive form as well as content. Similarly, the recognition of "visual quotes" (Masters et al. 1991), or conventionalized "video packages" in television news, necessitates a familiarity with news production practices, current public affairs, and the history of representational forms.

Semiotic analysis is likewise grounded in the cultural analysis of signs and symbols, but emphasizes to an even greater extent the operation of individual images within a structure and grammar of cultural systems of representation and meaning. With its roots in structural linguistics, semiotics treats the visual as language-like, with images acting like words, phrases, or units of language within a larger discourse of representation. Like studies of iconography, this moves the study of visual imagery away from the idea of a one-to-one correspondence between pictures and things and toward the study of images as units within syntactical chains of image/concepts and meaning. A news photograph of a U.S. tank rumbling along a highway past groups of people walking along the side of the road coalesces meanings from the relationship of this photograph to other pictures of tanks and armored vehicles identified as part of a U.S. expeditionary force headed across the southern part of Iraq toward the capital of Baghdad. Such photos joined numerous news images during the Iraq invasion that repeated the visual motif of troops and armored vehicles crossing the desert, accompanied by captions, headlines and news text narrating the story of the "Road to Baghdad," "Halfway to Baghdad," "Closing In," and the fall of Saddam – with the headline "Free" superimposed over photographs of US Marines toppling the statue of Saddam Hussein in Firdos Square.[2] A semiotic analysis of this photograph will recognize the syntactical and narrative context linking this individual image to other images, visual motifs, and preexisting cultural patterns of representation.

Framing analysis

A related and overlapping approach originating in research on social perceptions, public opinion research and political communication is *framing analysis*. The term *framing* itself comes from the original idea that the picture frame shapes the composition of an image and determines the point of view of the spectator. As Burgin writes in *Thinking Photography*, "the frame" of the photograph organizes the objects depicted within "into a coherence," emphasizing to the viewer that this way of seeing the subject is "important" (1982: 146). The frame determines what will be included within the limits of the picture, and perhaps even more importantly what will be left out. In his provocative book on combat journalism Knightly writes, "although in most cases the camera does not lie directly, it can lie brilliantly by omission" (2004: 14). The social anthropologist Erving Goffman, in his seminal work on gendered displays in advertising, showed how the graphic space of the picture frame has routinely been used to establish particular visual hierarchies among figures and other elements in advertising images, strongly supporting traditional notions of gendered social behavior and relationships (1979).

Interestingly, the concept of framing was adapted from its concrete application to pictures and developed by social scientists as a metaphor for the delimiting, organizing, and emphasizing of political ideas and social issues in news, rhetoric, and political communication, before once again being applied in visual framing analysis to the specific role of visual images in shaping social and political discourse. Tuchman first adopted the metaphor for news analysis, comparing news frames to window frames, limiting "what may be seen" (1978: 209). Soon after, Gitlin elaborated the notion of "media frames." He wrote, "Media frames are persistent patterns of cognition, interpretation and presentation, of selection, emphasis, and exclusion, by which symbol-handlers routinely organize discourse whether verbal or visual" (1980: 7). Entman (1993) revisited the concept in his analyses of the specific role of "news frames" in the control and projection of dominant issues and political discourse, defining framing as the selection of certain aspects of reality to "make them more salient in a communicating text in such as way as to promote a particular problem definition, causal interpretation, moral evaluation, and/or treatment recommendation" (1993: 52). Messaris and Abraham point to the special power of visual images as seemingly natural reflections of the world to frame and strengthen "the commonsensical claims of ideology" (2001: 220), a notion Griffin applies to the analysis of war images from Afghanistan and Iraq (Griffin 2004).

Similarly, Parry (2010) demonstrates how news photographs from the 2006 Israel-Lebanon war published in two newspapers effectively framed the conflict differently, producing a different impression of the scale and severity of destruction, and of culpability on each side. Parry's work provides a new model for comprehensive visual analysis through her elaboration of multiple levels of coding that include analysis of compositional elements, editorial selection, placement and verbal framing of photographs. But Parry warns, "There is a danger of becoming too removed from the original images via over-fragmentation of the photographic details" in analysis, losing a sense of a photograph's "emotional pull" or overall "significance" (2010: 82). She recommends, "Findings for detailed content and framing analysis (should) therefore be supplemented with more qualitative 'stylistic' methods of analysis" (2010: 82).

Conclusion

Studies of visual images that wish to account for more complex combinations of visual features, and still preserve a sense of the unique qualities and significance of the original photographs, are most likely to augment visual content analysis with in-depth formalist, iconographic, semiotic, and stylistic analyses of individual shots or frames. Parry's attempt to include analyses of gaze, camera angle, picture sourcing and scaling, and image/text relationships provides an encouraging direction for future research. Growing attention to the uniquely visual aspects of late twentieth-century media has also prompted scholars to begin to think about patterns of visualization as a basis for comparing media representation in different types of media, on different platforms, and at different points in time in different cultures and nations (Müller and Griffin 2012). Schwalbe et al. (2008), and Keith et al. (2010) have begun to identify patterns of framing and master narratives in war imagery across different media platforms. Keith et al. (2010) point to the methodological challenges of quantitative content analysis of war images across print, broadcast and online media, but argue for the importance of meeting these challenges because multi-platform exposure "is consistent with many news consumers' experiences with war coverage" (2010: 94).

The number of scholars attempting to combine multiple levels of visual analysis in research on media images of war continues to grow. Examples include research on the shifting status and presentation of the Abu Ghraib photos as they moved back and forth from the Internet to television to news magazines (Andén-Papadopoulos 2008; Griffin 2011), and work on visual commemorations of the 9/11 attacks (Grittmann and Ammann 2009). Such studies have attempted to design methods of *visual* content analysis that integrate closer attention to specifically visual elements and characteristics (iconographic analyses, attention to visual form and style), with procedures for tracking patterns and frequencies of specific features over representative media samples. Combining methods of analysis from different disciplines may lead to more comprehensive analyses of visual representations in the future.

Meanwhile, applying systematic social research methods to the analysis of visual images will remain a challenge. And the visual representation of human conflict will continue to represent a politically charged and inevitably controversial arena of media practice. Partly this is because visual images themselves are often the source of conflict and not just reflections of it. The

Muhammad cartoon crisis, for example, sparked by the publication of 12 cartoons in the Danish newspaper *Jyllands Posten* in September 2005, joined the Abu Ghraib photographs from the year before as potent instruments of foreign conflict, disseminating "enemy images" through global channels, and setting an agenda for global tensions that pitched the "West" against "the Muslim world" (Müller et al. 2009: 37). Other examples have followed, in the form of cell-phone pictures and online videos as well photographs and cartoons. An increasingly wired world may make visual images and conflict increasingly indivisible.

Notes

1 Regarding a similar absences of images of casualties in TV news coverage see Sean Aday (2005) The Real War Will Never Get on Television: An Analysis of Casualty Imagery in American Television Coverage of the Iraq War.
2 www.google.com/imgres?imgurl=http://graphics7.nytimes.com/images/2003/04/09/international/09cnd-free.slide1.jpg&imgrefurl=http://www.network54.com/Search/view/221692/1049984474/Re%253A%2BWar%2Bon%2BIraq,%2Bpart%2BII.?term%3Dwarehouse%2B%26page%3D2154&h=427&w=650&sz=72&tbnid=Am2d1h-4kykSKM:&tbnh=90&tbnw=137&zoom=1&usg=__G2DM9Iw_G7xalPDgwJCIC1OtE-U=&docid=0UkuqlaLGJ6w9M&itg=1&sa=X&ei=bzqmUsL3NoreqAGEsICYBQ&ved=0CHQQ9QEwCg.

References

Aday, S. (2005). The Real War Will Never Get on Television: An Analysis of Casualty Imagery in American Television Coverage of the Iraq War. In P. Seib (ed.), *Media and Conflict in the Twenty-First Century*, pp. 141–156. New York: Palgrave Macmillan.

Andén-Papadopoulos, K. (2008). The Abu Ghraib Torture Photographs. *Journalism* 9(1): 5–30.

Burgin, V. (1982). *Thinking Photography*. London: Macmillan.

Domke, D., Perlmutter, D., and Spratt, M. (2002). The Primes of Our Times? An Examination of the "Power" of Visual Images. *Journalism: Theory, Practice & Criticism* 3(2): 131–159.

Entman, R.B. (1993). Framing: Toward Clarification of a Fractured Paradigm. *Journal of Communication* 43: 51–58.

Gitlin, T. (1980). *The Whole World Is Watching*. Berkeley, CA: University of California Press.

Goffman, E. (1979). *Gender Advertisements*. New York: HarperCollins Publishers.

Graber, D.A. (1990). Seeing Is Remembering: How Visuals Contribute to Learning from Television News. *Journal of Communication* 40: 134–155.

Griffin, M. (1999). The Great War Photographs: Constructing Myths of History and Photojournalism. In B. Brennen and H. Hardt (eds), *Picturing the Past: Media, History, and Photography*, pp. 122–157. Urbana, IL: University of Illinois Press.

Griffin, M. (2004). Picturing America's "War against Terrorism" in Iraq and Afghanistan: Photographic Motifs as News Frames. *Journalism: Theory, Practice & Criticism* 5(4): 381–402.

Griffin, M. (2010). Media Images of War. *Media, War & Conflict* 3(1): 7–41.

Griffin, M. (2011). Ereignis und Phantom: Das wechselhafte öffentliche Leben der Fotografien von Abu Ghraib. *AugenBlick: Marburger Hefte zur Medienwissenschaft* 48/49, February.

Griffin, M. and Lee, J.S. (1995). Picturing the Gulf War: Constructing Images of War in *Time, Newsweek*, and *U.S. News and World Report. Journalism and Mass Communication Quarterly* 72 (4): 813–825.

Grittmann, E. and Ammann, I. (2009). Die Methode der quantitativen Bildtypenanalyse. Zur Routinisierung der Bildberichterstattung am Beispiel von 9/11 in der journalistischen Erinnerungskultur. [The Method of Quantitative Image Type Analysis. On routines in visual press coverage. The example of 9/11 in journalistic remembrance]. In Petersen, T. and Schwender, C. (eds), *Visuelle Stereotype*. [Visual Stereotypes], pp. 141–158. Köln: Von Halem.

Hall, S. (1997). *Representation: Cultural Representations and Signifying Practices*. London: Sage Publications in association with The Open University.

Hariman, R. and Lucaites, J.L. (2007). *No Caption Needed: Iconic Photographs, Public Culture, and Liberal Democracy*. Chicago, IL: University of Chicago Press.

Keith, S, Schwalbe, C.B., and Silcock, B.W. (2010). Comparing War Images across Media Platforms: Methodological Challenges for Content Analysis. *Media, War & Conflict* 3(1): 87–98.

Knightly, P. (2004). *The First Casualty: The War Correspondent as Hero, Propagandist and Myth-Maker from the Crimea to Iraq*. Baltimore, MD: The Johns Hopkins University Press.

Magnum Photos Website (www.magnumphotos.com/).

Masters, R.D., Frey, S., and Bente, G. (1991). Dominance and Attention: Images of Leaders in German, French, and American TV News. *Polity*, 23(3): 373–394.

Messaris, P. (1994). *Visual Literacy: Image, Mind, and Reality*. Boulder, CO: Westview Press.

Messaris, P. and Abraham, L. (2001). The Role of Images in Framing News Stories. In S. Reese et al. (eds), *Framing Public Life*, pp. 215–226. Mahwah, NJ: Lawrence Erlbaum.

Müller, M.G. and Griffin, M. (2012). Visual Comparison: Comparative Approaches in Visual Communication Research. In F. Esser and T. Hanitzsch (eds). *Handbook of Comparative Communication Research*, 94–118. New York: Routledge.

Müller, M.G., Özcan, A., and Seizov, O. (2009). Dangerous Depictions: A Visual Case Study of Contemporary Cartoon Controversies. *Popular Communication* 7(1), 28–39.

Panofsky, E. (1939). *Studies in Iconology*. Oxford: Oxford University Press/Westview Press, 1972.

Parry, K. (2010). A Visual Framing Analysis of British Press Photography during the 2006 Israel–Lebanon Conflict. *Media, War & Conflict* 3(1): 67–85.

Rose, G. (2012). *Visual Methodologies: An Introduction to Researching with Visual Materials*, 3rd edn. London: Sage.

Schwalbe, C.B., Silcock, B.W., and Keith, S. (2008). Visual Framing of the Early Weeks of the U.S.-Led Invasion of Iraq: Applying the Master War Narrative to Electronic and Print Images. *Journal of Broadcasting and Electronic Media* 52(3): 448–465.

Taylor, J. (1991) *War Photography: Realism in the British Press*. London: Routledge.

Tuchman, Gaye (1978) *Making News: A Study in the Construction of Reality*. New York: Free Press.

Zelizer, B. (2004). When War Is Reduced to a Photograph. In S. Allen and B. Zelizer (eds), *Reporting War: Journalism in Wartime*, pp. 114–135. London: Routledge.

14

RESEARCHING 'THE MOST DANGEROUS OF ALL SOURCES'

Egodocuments

Esmeralda Kleinreesink

S. Hynes (1997) *The Soldiers' Tale: Bearing Witness to Modern War*. New York: Penguin.

In *The Soldiers' Tale*, Samuel Hynes examines English-language journals, memoirs, novels and letters of mainly middle-class men, the literary civilian-soldiers who fought in the two World Wars and in Vietnam. Reviewers often praise the book for its clarity and jargon-free style. It merges autobiography, history and literature to describe and analyse the themes of war: fear, comradeship, courage, cowardice, confusion and the will to survive.

As all egodocument researchers, Hynes faced three methodological challenges – scoping, collecting and analysis. In the prologue of this book, which does not have a separate methodology chapter, Hynes explicitly describes his scoping choices, but leaves solutions to other challenges of collection and analysis implicit.

Hynes begins his scoping process by focusing on understanding what it is like to be 'there, where the actual killing was done' (xvi). Therefore, he concentrates on the combatants and excludes the memoirs of generals and other senior officers. Hynes maintains there is no reason to include these officers' writings because they 'don't do the fighting, or live with their troops, or get themselves shot at' (xv). Hynes focuses on the twentieth century 'because their wars are still our wars . . . and also because this has been the century of personal narratives of war' (xiii). He chooses to examine World War I, World War II and Vietnam, because they seem to him crucial points of change in our century's 'war story' (xiv). These three conflicts are the wars 'that have been most remembered and most recorded' (xiv).

He does not explain how he collected the books, only that he chose books and reports 'with a voice that is stubbornly distinct' (xv), indicating that he dismissed books that were poor reads, thereby delimiting the selection.

(continued)

(continued)

Although he also does not explicitly account for his method of analysis, the method he chooses is clear. *The Soldiers' Tale* is a typical qualitative study in that extensive quotes from the books researched support the main argument. The work is multidisciplinary, using theories to support his arguments from fields ranging from psychology and sociology to history.

He concludes with a paradox: the war egodocuments are true, but not historically truthful; they are neither travel writing nor autobiography, nor history (16). War is an almost alien, indescribable experience, and what the egodocument describes is not usually what happened, because memoirs are 'filtered reality, what memory preserves' (23).

Hynes shows that each war generates its own stories and myths. In the First World War, the notion of a romantic war in which the British soldier could become a hero disappeared in the trenches, although it remained in the air war where aces were still heroes. World War I is a war of disillusionment. '[A] generation of innocent young men . . . went off to war to make the world safe for democracy. They were slaughtered in stupid battles planned by stupid generals. Those who survived were shocked, disillusioned and embittered by their war experiences' (101).

However, that did not stop the young men in the Second World War from enthusiastically enlisting. Hynes concludes that the seduction of war lures each new generation. 'Every generation, it seems, must learn its own lessons from its own war, because every war is different and is fought by different ignorant young men' (111). Significantly, this was a new war, with another myth, that of the Good War. The men remained frustrated by the ways in which it was fought, 'but they did not regret their service' (173).

The next large war, Vietnam, was not a Good War, but a Bad War. The US fought the war 'for political reasons, and wrong ones' (178). It was to the US what World War I was to Britain: 'a war of national disillusionment that changed the way a generation thought about its country, its leaders and war itself' (179).

In the epilogue, Hynes concludes that storytelling is a primal need. It helps to order a disordered experience and thereby give it meaning, and for the listener to give a human face and voice to war.

Although the results presented in this seminal study are interesting and convincing, the study suffers from a lack of methodological foundations and methodological guidance, problems common to qualitative studies.

Sometimes it is hard to study the military. In her article 'Studying the Military Comparatively', Deschaux-Baume concludes that the military is a fairly inaccessible social field for outsiders. The military limits access to internal documents, senior officers may have internalised censorship and participant observation is 'far from being welcome and facilitated' (Deschaux-Beaume 2013: 138). However, there is a rich source of data on the military available to any researcher: military egodocuments.

This chapter delves more deeply into military egodocuments to discover what they have to offer the military researcher and what kind of challenges they bring. It starts by looking at what egodocuments are, then it focuses on their advantages and drawbacks and how they can be studied. The chapter concludes with the three main challenges that studying egodocuments brings: scoping, collecting and analysis.

Egodocuments

The term 'egodocument' refers to 'a text in which an author writes about his or her own acts, thoughts and feelings' (Dekker 2002: 14). Until the middle of the twentieth century, egodocuments as source were regarded by historians as 'extremely unreliable' and 'simply useless' (Dekker 2002: 21). Dutch historian Romein even dubbed them 'the most dangerous of all sources' (Romein in Dekker 2002: 19).

However, with a changing, postmodern orientation, research emphasis has shifted to the social construction of facts instead of the facts themselves. French autobiography researcher Lejeune stresses that autobiographies should not be seen as sources of historical information, but 'rather as primary social *facts* in their own right' (Lejeune 1989: xx). Based on memory research, Krassnitzer concludes that it is not a personal truth that can be read in autobiographies, but an experience of how social collectives ('Erinnerungskollektive') interpret and remember events (Krassnitzer 2006: 214). This is what makes egodocument research so interesting. These works are not just personal stories, but manifestations of (military) culture.

Egodocuments are broadly divided into three categories based on the intended public (Epkenhans et al. 2006: xiii) (see Figure 14.1).

First, egodocuments are written for personal use. For example, writers use diaries to order and reconstruct thought, feelings and memories (Baggerman 2010: 65). These private documents are usually not intended for wider distribution. For this reason, diaries can be purchased with a lock on the cover to protect them from being read by others. Second, egodocuments can be produced for a limited distribution. Traditionally, military personnel communicated with the home front using letters. These days they do the same using emails. These email exchanges are egodocuments intended for one or more persons to read, but are not expected to be widely distributed outside the limited circle of friends and family. Finally egodocuments may be written for the public. Internet blogs and books are examples of egodocuments aimed at a broad public.

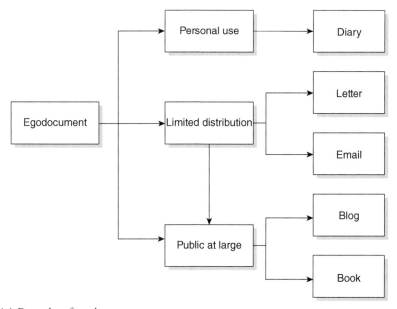

Figure 14.1 Examples of egodocuments

The kind of egodocument does not dictate its eventual audience. Some diaries were kept with the purpose of being published in book form, such as the Anne Frank diary (Frank 2007; 1952) and Internet blogs can be screened so that only invited people can see the content of the blogs, thereby making them of limited distribution.

Hynes, the author of this chapter's illustrative study, *The Soldiers' Tale*, uses different kinds of egodocuments for his research. The majority of the personal narratives he uses are memoirs. Still, he also includes journals, diaries and letters (Hynes 1997: xiv).

Why study egodocuments?

Egodocuments are such rich data sources that their content is applicable to military researchers of every conceivable background. A medical researcher uses military egodocuments to study post-traumatic stress disorder and smoking in military personnel (Robinson 2012), a sociologist uses them to study military strategy (King 2010), and a historian reads egodocuments to look at changing ideas about the relationship between body and mind (Harari 2008).

Aside from their rich content, egodocuments are attractive to all sorts of military researchers, from all sorts of methodological backgrounds. According to H. Russell Bernard, '[p]ositivists can tag text and can study regularities across the tags . . . interpretivists can study meaning' (Bernard 1996: 9). Working with unobtrusive methods, or what Bernard calls 'found texts' such as egodocuments, eliminates researcher influence on the text compared to 'created texts' such as interviews.

That brings us to one of the disadvantages of studying egodocuments. Because there is no direct contact between the author of the text and the researcher, a detailed probing of the narrative is impossible (Woodward 2008: 380). Of course, content analysis could be complemented by other research methods such as interviews, but getting in touch with book authors and publishing houses is often challenging. In my study of Afghanistan memoirs published between 2001 and 2010 (Kleinreesink 2014), I found that many soldier-authors failed to disclose their age in their books. After repeated contact attempts, a substantial portion of them did not respond to my enquiry. Unfortunately the age variable in my data base was missing a value in 17 per cent of the cases.

Another drawback, which was mentioned earlier, is the uncertain historical truth of egodocuments. As Hynes notes, '[a]s history they are unsatisfactory: restricted, biased, afflicted by emotion, and full of errors' (Hynes 1997: 15). Bias and emotion are not the only psychological reasons that affect the content of egodocuments. In the *The Great War and Modern Memory*, Fussell concludes that in letters and postcards home World War I soldiers wrote only about socially desirable subjects in an effort to spare the recipient's feelings (Fussell 1975: 182).

Social desirability is not the only cause of this self-censorship. Self-censorship also results from an organisational constraint that in Western countries is specific to the military: official censorship. In order to preserve operational security, some egodocuments are checked by the military before distribution. In both World Wars the military routinely censored letters written by its personnel to the home front (Fussell 1975: 182). Although currently letters home or blogs are no longer actively censored, they are bound by operational security rules. As a result, the military still check books written by military personnel before publication for security breaches.

A final drawback to mention is that the representativeness of these authors is unclear. Can they be considered a proxy of the average soldier, or are military authors a separate breed? As most studies into military egodocuments only look at specific groups (Vernon 2005: 3) using them to draw conclusions about the military in general is tricky at best.

What to study in egodocuments?

Having discussed the advantages and disadvantages of studying egodocuments in general, let's now look at three main text elements of egodocuments (see Figure 14.2). There are paratext, text, and the words that make up the text.

The first element to be considered for study is paratext. The term 'paratext' (Genette 1997) refers to all those elements that surround a text. These elements include book covers, forewords and acknowledgments in the narrow sense to book reviews and interviews with the author in the broader sense. Paratext is most useful for studying the relationship between authors and their publics. For example, in the preface of a memoir the author makes the motivation for writing it explicit, and the book cover establishes what kind of audience is sought. Book reviews, or the absence of reviews, give an indication of the book's impact.

Images present a special case of paratext. Military egodocuments (memoirs, blogs or emails) are often accompanied by photographs. Ninety-four per cent of contemporary Afghanistan memoirs have photographs or other images such as maps. On average, 25 pages (10 per cent) of the books comprise images (Kleinreesink 2014). However, so far, hardly any research has been conducted into military images. Most of this research deals with images *of* the military (e.g. Griffin 2010) whereas it would be equally interesting to look at images *by* the military: images they find important to show others or to remember.

Second, characteristics of the 'text' like its main themes or the plot are subjects of investigation. Classical military egodocument studies such as Hynes' *The Soldiers' Tale*, and Fussell's *The Great War and Modern Memory* delve more deeply into common, often universal, themes that military authors write about, such as fear, comradeship, honour and disillusionment. These universal military themes are good and recognisable starting points for comparative studies between, for instance, countries or time periods.

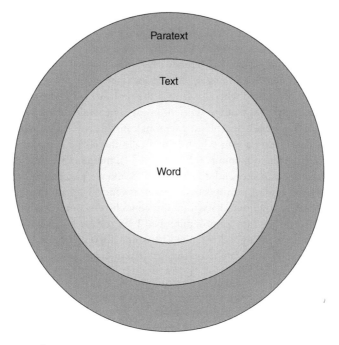

Figure 14.2 Three text elements

Plot is another global text element. Most Western stories are told and written in the form of an Aristotelian plot. This means a narrative in which the hero of the story makes a journey. During this journey, which has a limited time frame, he overcomes obstacles, and in the process possibly changes the world and himself (Aristotle 2004: VII 51a6). There are many theories that can be used to study plot structure. These theories range from plotting the positive or negative value of the story in time (Gergen and Gergen 1988), to Friedman's highly structured and detailed, but easy to use 14 basic plot types (Friedman 1955).

Third, at a deeper level, the words that make up the text can also be studied. With the advent of digital documents and improved optical character recognition software, it has become possible to study texts on the level of words. Qualitative data analysis software, such as ATLAS.ti and NVivo, have standard word frequency query options available, which can be used to identify important themes or concepts. Specialised word counting software exists (LIWC, which stands for Linguistic Inquiry and Word Count) that makes it possible to study emotional, cognitive, and structural word usage in texts from a psychological point of view (Pennebaker and Seagal 1999).

Three challenges

Now that it is clear what egodocuments are and what can be studied in them, it is time to delve more deeply into the characteristic challenges that come with studying egodocuments. Three challenges will be explored: scoping, collecting and analysis.

Challenge 1: Scoping

The first challenge is how to do scoping. This refers to defining what is and what is not part of the study. Scoping will be particularly challenging for the egodocument researcher as a plethora of material is available. The first choice to make is the time period researched. Should the researcher look at historical egodocuments or contemporary ones? This chapter's illustrative author, Hynes, chose egodocuments from three different wars for his research: both World Wars and Vietnam and explicitly excluded Korea because it 'came and went without glory, and left no mark on American imaginations' (Hynes 1997: xiii).

A second aspect of time is the timing of the egodocuments themselves. Three distinct types of narratives can be distinguished when looking at the time factor (see Figure 14.3).

The first are those narratives that are written on the spot while the writer is still in theatre. Examples include diaries, emails and blogs. Memoirs can also be written while the war is still going on, or immediately after a war, which Hynes calls immediate memoirs (Hynes 1997: 4). Finally, there are retrospective memoirs (Hynes 1997: 4), memoirs written long after the war ends. Each type has its advantages and disadvantages. Some are easier to collect (see challenge two). Some are easier to read. A retrospective memoir is generally of another quality than a blog written on the spot. A handwritten diary found in an archive is not as comfortable a read as a diary that has been reworked into a book published by a regular publisher. Hynes specifically selected documents that were a good read, and he is not the only one as 'most critics instinctively gravitate to the study of literary masterworks' (Eakin 1989: xx).

Figure 14.3 Three types of narratives

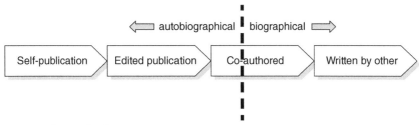

Figure 14.4 Autobiographical continuum

The next choice is whether to study all egodocuments available, or only look at texts from authors with a certain background. A common limitation is to include only narratives by those who have fought, which is what Hynes does. For contemporary pieces, this would be extremely limiting due to the current tooth-to-tail ratio of the military. While at one time front-line combatants made up the majority of personnel, in current militaries supporters comprise the majority of the organisation (Vernon 2005: 3). Another common limitation in research is looking at specific minority groups, such as African Americans, or women, to such an extent that Vernon points out that 'personal narratives by male noncombatant military persons – white males especially – are easily the most neglected of all military life writings in Anglo American criticism' (Vernon 2005: 3).

Another often-used scoping mechanism is choosing country or language specific texts, as multi-language research is quite rare. Hynes for example limits his research to combatants who write in English both from Great Britain and the US. These kinds of scoping decisions have to do with the researcher's language skills and preferences, which are always a good starting point for any research.

If books are the preferred medium, one of the classical dilemmas (Lejeune 1989: 3) the researcher has to deal with is where the autobiography ends and the biography starts. Books are seldom only written by the author himself or herself, instead there is an (auto)biographical continuum ranging from entirely self-written to written by others (see Figure 14.4).

Self-publishers (publishing companies that publish books at the risk and cost of the author) generally contribute little to nothing to the content of the book. At most they edit the manuscript for mistakes after payment by the author. Regular publishers (who publish books at their own risk and cost), in contrast, have an editing process that normally includes changes in style and content. Further, regular publishers often have general content requirements for their writers which take into account their target audience. Sometimes regular publishers even offer an inexperienced author a co-author, which is generally an experienced writer or journalist. This is where the change from autobiography into a biography happens. As the *Encyclopedia of Life Writing* puts it, 'the most perplexing texts in terms of authenticity are collaborative autobiographies, because of their virtually oxymoronic nature . . . collaborative autobiography disrupts the single identity of author cum narrator cum subject that is the constituting feature of the genre' (Couser 2001: 72). A co-author who thoroughly adapts the texts of the original author might still be seen as producing an autobiography, a co-author who interviews the original author and does the writing herself, produces in effect a biography.

Challenge 2: Collecting the documents

When the research scope has been established, the documents that fall under this scope have to be collected, and that can be difficult and time consuming. The kind of document dictates, to a certain extent, the collection method. In the next section, five different types of egodocuments (emails, letters, diaries, blogs and books) are discussed, including the form in which they could be collected.

The first three document types, emails, letters and diaries, are mainly intended for personal use and limited distribution. That means that in order to get hold of these documents, the researcher often has to ask people to share them. Researcher's can use their own network of military personnel to contact authors of these egodocuments. That existing network can then be extended by snowballing. In snowballing, the researcher asks person A to provide introductions to two or more people who might also be willing to share their egodocuments. Another way of getting in touch with former military personnel is by placing advertisements asking for egodocuments in military media such as veterans' magazines and military blogs. Advertising can be inexpensive, because many military magazines offer announcement opportunities for free.

For those researchers interested in historical letters or diaries, there is also a third option: the archives. In many European countries, egodocument cataloguing projects have been set up that identify egodocuments available in public archives, libraries and museums. These projects are often followed by publication series in which the most interesting texts are published. For an overview of these projects, see Dekker (2002: 28–30). Military personnel are excellent contributors to public archives. The Dutch project revealed that between 1500 and 1900 the most prolific authors of archived egodocuments were clergymen and military personnel (Blaak in Baggerman 2010: 68–69).

For limited access Internet egodocuments, the same personal approach to getting access to the sites may be necessary as for emails, letters and diaries. However, since many blogs and websites exist in the public domain, finding these may be easier. Holding on to them is more difficult, though. They disappear quickly, so in order to work with them, an appropriate archival strategy has to be chosen. Possible strategies vary from printing them out to using specialised web archiving software.

The disadvantage for the four types of documents mentioned above is that they are always part of a sample of the total number of documents available, but that the size of the total is unknown, and therefore the sampling bias is unknown. Books, however, offer the opportunity to capture the entire population because they are less numerous if rightly scoped, and because their existence is documented in various ways. Woodward and Jenkings, for example, study all 150+ British military memoirs from 1980 to present (Woodward and Jenkings 2012: 351), my own research deals with all 54 Afghanistan memoirs published between 2001 and 2010 in the US, the UK, Canada, Germany and the Netherlands. Even though theoretically it is possible to collect all of them, it takes much time and effort.

Several techniques can be used to reach saturation. A classical starting point for finding books is the library. Specialised national military libraries are most helpful in this, as these libraries often have the most extensive collections of military books. Internet book sites make snowball sampling possible. Starting with one relevant book, these sites offer suggestions for similar books ('Customers Who Bought This Item Also Bought . . .'), which can lead to similar books, and so on. All in all, this quickly leads to a good overview of available books in the Internet site's geographical market. And, finally, memoir researchers also browse (secondhand) bookshops to find books.

For example, in order to find all Afghanistan memoirs published between 2001 and 2010 for my research, I started by looking in military library catalogues. Next, I solicited reading lists from military historical societies. In addition I employed Internet lists on military memoirs, such as the almost 300 Listmania! lists from Amazon.com that come up when searching on the word combination Afghanistan + war, and browsed book review pages of veterans' magazines. All the books that showed up in these searches were then fed into the main book websites of the countries researched, such as Amazon.co.uk for the UK and Bol.com for the Netherlands, to start the snowballing process. This process took place over several months, but left me feeling that the chances of having missed a book were very low.

Depending on the research method chosen (see challenge three below) it might be interesting to look at the digital availability of the texts. The advantage of working with blogs and websites is that they are by nature digitally available. Books also exist in digital form, but my experience is that acquiring a digital copy in a format that can be used in analysis software can be difficult. Not all publishers, especially not the larger ones, will provide a digital copy for research. And digitalizing them yourself, by scanning them on a copying machine with OCR (object character recognition) is tedious. Commercially available OCR techniques still require manual text correction.

Challenge 3: Analysis

As discussed in the section 'Why study egodocuments?' working with texts is extremely versatile, and makes it possible to do all different types of research. Therefore, one of the challenges it brings is the choice of research method. The first choice is whether the research will be multidisciplinary or not. Hynes is a literature professor, but his book combines literature, psychology, sociology and history with apparent ease.

The second choice is whether to use qualitative or quantitative analysis. The traditional approach for studying texts is the qualitative approach that Hynes chose. He looks at the main themes that come up while reading and analysing the egodocuments and substantiates his findings with fitting quotes from the texts. Exactly what analytic method he uses remains unclear, but there are several possible methods. Next, three often-used techniques are discussed: the historical method, grounded theory and content analysis.

The historical method mainly takes place in the mind of the historian/scientist. Carr, quoting writer L. Paul, describes it in this book *What Is History?* as 'rummaging in the ragbag of observed "facts", selects, pieces and patterns the *relevant* observed facts together, rejecting the *irrelevant*, until it has sewn together a logical and rational quilt of "knowledge"' (Carr 1975: 104). This loosely describes Hynes' method.

In the sixties, Strauss and Glaser devised a general methodology called *grounded theory* 'for developing theory that is grounded in data systematically gathered and analysed' (Strauss and Corbin 1994: 273). It substantiated the rummaging-the-ragbag-method with an inductive process, whereby the researcher continues to switch between data collection and analysis, helped by coding techniques. Currently, grounded theory may be the most common qualitative research method used by researchers (Morse 2009: 13).

Also, scholars developed other approaches for qualitative data analysis. Miles and Huberman have collected all sorts of techniques for qualitative analysis in their source book (Miles and Huberman 1994), as did Krippendorff for an approach aimed at analysing text in the context of its use called *content analysis* (Krippendorff 2004). What they all share is that formal coding techniques aid the analysis. In this process the researcher assigns codes to parts of the text that are deemed interesting. Computer-aided qualitative data analysis software programs (CAQDAS) have been developed that support these practices, such as ATLAS.ti and NVivo. These programs do not analyse the data themselves, but support the researcher during the analysis phase.

I used grounded theory in my research when analysing writing motives. Instead of starting with a preconceived theory on writing motivation, I started by writing down every relevant quotation from each book analysed. These quotations were then fed into ATLAS.ti and given a code that I made up on the fly, a process called open coding. This resulted in almost 60 different codes. These codes were then clustered and related to each other by theoretical coding (Strauss and Corbin 1994: 277). This procedure resulted in five main categories and a theory that explains why soldier-authors say they write books.

Studying egodocuments does not have to stop at qualitative methods, however, concludes H. Russell Bernard in his article *Qualitative Data, Quantitative Analysis*, because '[c]oding turns qualitative data (texts) into quantitative data (codes)' (Bernard 1996: 10). The coding makes it possible to search for patterns. CAQDAS programs usually offer the possibility to export the results into SPSS format, thereby providing the opportunity to perform statistical analyses on the data. I used this option to note whether a specific book/author did or did not mention specific writing motives. The coding of motives was done in ATLAS.ti but the resulting dichotomous results (the book mentions this motive: yes/no) were exported into SPSS.

It is also possible to code variables directly into SPSS, as I did in my Afghanistan research to answer questions related to the authors and their plots. I considered each book a separate case (a row in SPSS) for which variables (columns in SPSS) were noted down. Coding the books was done by indicating the variables in SPSS such as nationality, age, whether the author is a reservist or a professional, or whether it was published by a traditional publisher or via self-publishing. Combining these results (and the dichotomous writing motives that were imported from ATLAS.ti) by means of, for instance, a crosstabs analysis, or a t-test shows whether the combination is statistically significantly different. In this way, the research shows for example that independent of country, a professional soldier is almost eight times more likely to get published by a traditional publisher than a reservist.

When there are only a small number of egodocuments in the research, however, only a limited range of statistical analyses is possible. In these cases, Ragin's Qualitative Comparative Analysis (QCA), a method of Boolean analysis can be used to look for patterns (Ragin 2008). Several freeware programs are available to support QCA, such as Ragin's own *fs/QCA*.

Some researchers, such as Scott et al. in their study of post-deployment stress and growth of US soldiers, do not choose between qualitative and quantitative method. Instead, they consciously use a mixed methods approach combining the two methodologies 'to achieve a product that is more than the sum of its parts' (Scott et al. 2011: 275). So even in the choice of method, egodocuments offer a wide range of possibilities.

Conclusion

Egodocuments present an incredibly rich source of data with great research opportunities for any researcher, regardless of their discipline or methodological background. Given the density of the information contained in these works, it is surprising that military researchers do not use it more often. Egodocuments are an important source for studies that aim to understand the person behind the soldier. These documents provide deep insight into the people who write them, the culture they live and work in, and the discourses in which they take part. These insights go much deeper than surveys or interviews can provide. Norwegian autobiography researcher Marianne Gullestad even concludes to her surprise that '[m]any of the written texts offer the reader a rapport and an intimacy of a kind that an anthropological fieldworker develops only after a long period of time with a few people' (Gullestad 1996: 36). Studying auto-narratives is a great way to gain more insights into operations and the well-being of the people who carry them out. They also offer an attractive and easy starting place for researchers interested in doing cross-cultural research. And as military researcher Abel Esterhuyse concludes in his historiographical overview on the South African counterinsurgency, sometimes egodocuments are the only available source (Esterhuyse 2012: 355).

In short, egodocument research is definitely worth considering for any military researcher.

References

Aristotle (2004; ca 330 BC) *Poetica*, Amsterdam: Athenaeum-Polak and Van Gennep.

Baggerman, A. (2010) 'Travellers in Time: Nineteenth-century Autobiographers and Their Fight Against Forgetting', in Bardet, J.P., Arnoul, E. and Ruggiu, F.J. (eds) *Les écrits du for privé en Europe, du Moyen Âge à l'époque contemporaine. Enquêtes, Analyses, Publications*, Pessac: Presses Universitaires de Bordeaux.

Bernard, H.R. (1996) 'Qualitative Data, Quantitative Analysis', *Field Methods*, 8: 9–11.

Carr, E.H. (1975) *'What Is History?' The George Macaulay Trevelyan Lectures Delivered in the University of Cambridge, January – March 1961*, London: Penguin.

Couser, G.T. (2001) 'Authenticity', in Jolly, M. (ed.) *Encyclopedia of Life Writing*, London: Fitzroy Dearborn Publishers.

Dekker, R. (2002) 'Jacques Presser's Heritage: Egodocuments in the Study of History', *Memoria y Civilización*, 5: 13–37.

Deschaux-Beaume, D. (2013) 'Studying the Military Comparatively', in Carreiras, H. and Castro, C. (eds) *Qualitative Methods in Military Studies*, New York: Routledge.

Eakin, P.J. (1989) 'Foreword', in Lejeune, P., *On Autobiography*, Minneapolis, MN: The University of Minnesota Press.

Epkenhans, M., Förster, S. and Hagemann, K. (2006) 'Einführung: Biographien und Selbstzeugnisse in der Militärgeschichte – Möglichkeiten und Grenzen [Preface: Biographies and Egodocuments in Military History – Possibilities and Limits]', in Epkenhans, M., Förster, S. and Hagemann, K. (eds) *Militärische Erinnerungskultur. Soldaten im Spiegel von Biographien, Memoiren und Selbstzeugnissen*, Paderborn: Ferdinand Schöningh.

Esterhuyse, A. (2012) 'South African Counterinsurgency: A historiographical overview', in Rich, P.B. and Duyvesteyn, I. (eds) *The Routledge Handbook of Insurgency and Counterinsurgency*, New York: Routledge.

Frank, A. (2007; 1952) *The Diary of a Young Girl: The Definitive Edition*, London: Penguin.

Friedman, N. (1955) 'Forms of the Plot', *The Journal of General Education*, 8: 241–253.

Fussell, P. (2000) *The Great War and Modern Memory*, New York: Oxford University Press.

Genette, G. (1997) *Paratexts: Thresholds of Interpretation*, Cambridge: Cambridge University Press.

Gergen, K.J. and Gergen, M.M. (1988) 'Narrative and the Self as Relationship', *Advances in Experimental Social Psychology*, 21: 17–56.

Griffin, M. (2010) 'Media Images of War', *Media, War & Conflict*, 3: 7–41.

Gullestad, M. (1996) *Everyday Life Philosophers: Modernity, Morality, and Autobiography in Norway*, Oslo: Scandinavian University Press.

Harari, Y.N. (2008) *The Ultimate Experience: Battlefield Revelations and the Making of Modern War Culture, 1450–2000*, Basingstoke: Palgrave Macmillan.

Hynes, S. (1997) *The Soldiers' Tale: Bearing Witness to Modern War*, New York: Penguin.

King, A. (2010). 'Understanding the Helmand Campaign: British Military Operations in Afghanistan', *International Affairs*, 86(2), 311–332.

Kleinreesink, L.H.E. (2014) 'On Military Memoirs: Soldier-Authors on Afghanistan: A Mixed-Method Study into Military Autobiographies from the UK, Canada, Germany and the Netherlands', unpublished thesis, Erasmus University Rotterdam/Netherlands Defence Academy.

Krassnitzer, P. (2006) 'Historische Forschung zwischen "importierten Erinnerungen" und Quellenamnesie. Zur Aussagekraft autobiographischer Quellen am Beispiel der Weltkriegserinnerung im nationalsozialistischen Milieu [Historical Research between "False Memory" and Source Amnesia. About the Evidence Power of Autobiographical Sources such as World War II Memories in a Nazi Environment]', in Epkenhans, M., Förster, S. and Hagemann, K. (eds) *Militärische Erinnerungskultur. Soldaten im Spiegel von Biographien, Memoiren und Selbstzeugnissen*, Paderborn: Ferdinand Schöningh.

Krippendorff, K. (2004) *Content Analysis: An Introduction to its Methodology*, 2nd edn, Thousand Oaks, CA: Sage.

Lejeune, P. (1989) *On Autobiography*, Minneapolis, MN: The University of Minnesota Press.

Miles, M.B. and Huberman, A.M. (1994) *Qualitative Data Analysis: An Expanded Sourcebook*, 2nd edn, Thousand Oaks, CA: Sage Publications.

Morse, J.M. (2009) 'Tussles, Tensions, and Resolutions', in Morse, J.M., Stern, P.N., Corbin, J., Bowers, B., Charmaz, K. and Clarke, A. (eds) *Developing Grounded Theory: The Second Generation*, Walnut Creek, CA: Left Coast Press.

Pennebaker, J.W. and Seagal, J. (1999) 'Forming a Story: The Health Benefits of Narrative', *Journal of Clinical Psychology*, 55: 1243–1254.

Ragin, C.C. (2008) *Redesigning Social Inquiry: Fuzzy Sets and Beyond*, Chicago, IL: University of Chicago Press.

Robinson, L. (2012) 'Explanations of Post-Traumatic Stress Disorder in Falklands Memoirs: The Fragmented Self and the Collective Body', *Journal of War and Culture Studies*, 5(1): 91–104.

Scott, W.J., McCone, D.R., Sayegh, L., Looney, J.D. and Jackson, R.J. (2011) 'Mixed Methods in a Post-Deployment Study of U.S. Army National Guard Soldiers', *Journal of Workplace Behavioral Health*, 26: 275–295.

Strauss, A. and Corbin, J. (1994) 'Grounded Theory Methodology', in Denzin, N.K. and Lincoln, Y.S. (eds) *Handbook of Qualitative Research*, Thousand Oaks, CA: Sage Publications.

Vernon, A. (ed.) (2005) *Arms and the Self: War, the Military, and Autobiographical Writing*. Kent, OH: The Kent State University Press.

Woodward, R. (2008) 'Not for Queen and Country or Any of That Shit . . . ': Reflections on Citizenship and Military Participation in Contemporary British Soldier Narratives', in Cowen, D. and Gilbert, E. (eds) *War, Citizenship, Territory*, New York: Routledge.

Woodward, R. and Jenkings, K.N. (2012) 'Military Memoirs, their Covers and the Reproduction of Public Narratives of War', *Journal of War and Culture Studies*, 5: 349–369.

15

SCRUTINIZING THE INTERNET IN SEARCH OF "HOMEGROWN" TERRORISM

Risa Brooks

R. Brooks (2011) "Muslim homegrown terrorism in the United States: How serious is the threat?" *International Security,* **36(2): 7–47.**

This article evaluates the claim that homegrown Islamist terrorism is a growing threat in the United States. The "threat" of homegrown terrorism is defined as an increase in the number of deaths within the United States perpetrated by American citizens or residents inspired by Islamic militant jihadist ideologies, but acting independently from established terrorist organizations. The author identifies three conditions that could produce a growing threat of this kind. These include (1) an increased incidence of the number of American Muslims initiating terrorist plots in the United States; (2) an increase in the efficacy and skill of aspiring militants, such that even if more plots are not initiated, more Americans will be harmed by those that are attempted; (3) an increase in the ability of militants to hide or conceal their terrorist activities, such that the activities of aspiring terrorists are less likely to be detected and foiled by arrests, resulting in a greater number of successfully executed attacks. Evidence in support of any of these conditions suggests the threat of homegrown terrorism is indeed growing.

Online research is a principal method employed by the author. The article uses the Internet to search for resources to analyze the empirical record of terrorism in the United States. The diversity and accessibility of sources online is a principal advantage. The author also uses the Internet as a means for assessing conventional views and definitions of homegrown terrorism. This is facilitated by examining a wide sample of materials to identify trends in the reporting and descriptions of homegrown terrorism. Specifically, relying on Internet resources offered several benefits to the author's research.

(continued)

(continued)

First, through online research, the author was able to access court records and, especially affidavits by federal and local law enforcement officials involved in terrorism investigations. These revealed the expanded efforts and novel methods employed in monitoring and investigating terrorist activity in the United States. These records detail use of "informants" who monitor local communities and supply information to law enforcement. There was also evidence of extensive efforts by officials to covertly assist suspected militants in the advancement of their plans, in order to develop legal cases against them, in a process known as "sting operations." The use of such operations raised questions about whether the plots would have been pursued by militants without law enforcement influence.

Second, Internet research allowed for the investigation of factual details about when and how suspected militants first formulated and began to implement their plots. This research revealed that recent spikes in terrorist-related arrests are the result of a clustering of arrests of individuals who had become engaged in militancy at different times in the past. This finding suggests, contrary to conventional wisdom, that a spike in terrorism arrests is not evidence of a growing trend in the amount of terrorist activity occurring in the United States.

Third, the use of online research helped the study confirm the accuracy of data, such as about the number of terrorism related arrests in the United States. Online research allowed for cross-checking of information by making available different studies and data bases that use variable criteria or coding rules for identifying terrorist activity.

Fourth, online research provided a means for integrating factual details from diverse news and official sources to learn operational details about plots. This helped the author establish the pervasiveness of mistakes and errors in operational security perpetrated by the militants. These errors provide evidence of the limited capabilities of homegrown terrorists in the United States.

Fifth, online research revealed biases in how terrorism is reported, and drew attention to the different definitions of homegrown terrorism used by analysts. It highlighted the editorial approaches of media outlets in their reporting on acts of suspected terrorism. Recognizing such biases was crucial to the author's efforts to provide a more comprehensive view of domestic terrorism in the United States. A comprehensive survey reveals that Muslim originated terrorist activity has not been the sole or even primary source of threat in recent years. These characteristics of reporting on terrorist activity help explain the common mischaracterization of the homegrown terrorism threat.

The Internet represents a vast and evolving resource for researchers, with enormous potential to link scholars and analysts to primary and secondary information on an array of phenomena. Relying on the Internet as a tool or method for research, however, can expose scholarship to weaknesses and biased results if key problems and methodological issues are not explicitly recognized.

Both the promise and pitfalls of online research are illustrated by the effort to employ the Internet to study the incidence and nature of homegrown terrorism in the United States. Homegrown terrorism is defined as terrorism committed by American citizens or residents who are inspired by the propaganda of a militant jihadist group, but who operate independently from the organization (see e.g. Bjelopera and Randol 2010). The discussion that follows describes how online research can be a useful method for analyzing terrorism. The analysis also illuminates broader methodological issues that can arise in online research on military or security related issues.

As a method, online research involves employing a set of tools or strategies for searching the Internet in order to locate relevant and desired factual, analytical or opinion-laden information. A principal advantage of online research is the speed with which a researcher can access information from diverse sources. The web lacks inherent structure or administration, however, so that how and whether that information is accessed depends on the tools a researcher employs to search the Internet.

Search engines and directories structure how online information is conveyed to the user. The results yielded from a search reflect an imposed order and hierarchy that is otherwise absent on the web. How the hierarchy of results is determined and then displayed depends on the nature of the search engine chosen by a user. Searches are mediated by the algorithms and indexing of the search engine employed, or of the methodology of the directory that a researcher consults. The results of any given search reflect those rules and methods (Comer 2011).

To the extent it is possible, a working understanding of the methodology employed by search engines can increase the efficiency of using the Internet. This background information can help individuals anticipate what kinds of information and results are most likely to be captured by the search engines they use. The best search results come from using multiple search engines, and employing targeted terms and search techniques. Also valuable is learning how to access the vast amounts of materials not captured by the spiders that compile indexes from which search results are built, which is known as the invisible web. Generally, researchers using the Internet will benefit from a basic understanding of how the web works, and of the search engine services and directories on which they rely.

Benefits of online research

There are several ways that online research can benefit researchers.[1] By focusing on the specific example of researching homegrown terrorism, these advantages of online research are illustrated.[2]

First, the Internet expands the volume of open-source, or publicly available, information accessible about militant groups and their violent activities, which represents a critical resource to terrorism analysts. This information comes in the form of quantitative data located in large databases made available online, through free or paid access. Alternatively, it can come from coverage and analyses of events related to terrorist-related activities, from news media, social media, blogs, private think-tank reports and collections, and court and government documents accessed online.

Second, it can provide primary source information about militant groups' recruitment and operational activities. Researchers can study the militants' ideological doctrine through open-source reporting and by accessing propaganda available on extremist web sites. This includes audio and video files, training manuals, pamphlets and writings, and copies of speeches. They can monitor the debate and discussion that may occur on websites or in other online forums. This may reveal themes or narratives in the group's doctrine or guiding beliefs.[3]

Visiting militant groups' websites and monitoring communications is also a valuable intelligence tool for members of law enforcement or the intelligence community. Militants may use the Internet to facilitate their violent activities in a variety of areas, including training through the supply of instructional materials; planning by using the Internet to facilitate communications or undertake surveillance; recruitment and incitement with online propaganda; and fundraising and financing. Authorities therefore can use the Internet to enhance knowledge about the organization and operational methods of terrorist groups and individuals by studying these activities online. Researchers can also gain insight into these aspects of militant groups' operations and organization by visiting relevant websites. Accessing these sites, however, can be difficult for lay people because many groups may restrict access to cyber forums, such as Internet chat groups, or employ platforms such as password protected websites.

Third, for researchers interested in learning about the scope and nature of terrorist-related activity, the Internet can provide a means of tracking or verifying under-reported events. Terrorist plots that are serious, or are executed successfully, will receive a great deal of media coverage. Assessing the nature and degree of terrorist activity in a country, and hence the quality of the threat it poses, however, requires that researchers also examine plots that do not result in actual attacks or injuries.

This subset of attacks includes, for example, those that fail due to a mistake in planning or in fabricating a weapon. It includes plots that are abandoned before execution, and those that end in the militants' arrest as the result of law enforcement's detection of a plot. By incorporating details about plots that are foiled or fail, researchers have a clearer picture of the actual operational skills of the pool of terrorists in a country. The analysis also reveals the ways in which law enforcement involvement can influence the development of a terrorist plot. Only focusing on plots that are executed and result in deaths could lead to a distorted understanding of who is engaging in home-grown terrorist activity, and risks overstating the efficacy and skill of the pool of aspiring militants (Dahl 2011). Online research can therefore provide an important methodological advantage to studies by allowing researchers to incorporate "non-events" into their studies of terrorist activity.

Fourth, Internet research can allow researchers to establish the accuracy of particular details and accounts of events that are otherwise difficult to confirm. Through triangulation of information and reporting available from different sites, researchers can confirm details about cases and events that are otherwise only available to intelligence and law enforcement authorities. Drawing from the Internet, for example, can help researchers parse otherwise scarcely reported operational details of attempted attacks or terrorist-related activities. When different sources report similar details, it provides some confidence in the accuracy of the information. Similarly, when a detail is reported in one source, but is not consistent with other accounts, it can alert the reader to potential factual errors.

This requires that the sites are consulting independent sources and are not relying on each other to confirm details. If apparently independent reports turn out to refer back to the same source, it can promote a circuitous, self-reinforcing chain of evidence that artificially lends credibility to a story. In particular, researchers should make sure factual details cited in online resources do not link back to the same source. This issue is also discussed below.

Fifth, the Internet provides novel methods for evaluating popular attitudes, reactions or beliefs about terrorist groups and activities within a larger public or subset of the population. This is afforded by the possibility of deploying online surveys and engaging in online interviews. There are many logistical and cost-saving benefits, as well as the possibility of reaching otherwise difficult to access populations. Researchers, however, should consider that there may be potential sources of bias in a sample or results that come with relying on Internet surveys over onsite methods (see Hooley et al. 2012). This can originate in the way that respondents react to Internet surveys, or differences in who is likely to respond to online solicitations, versus those contacted via other mediums. Generally, researchers should be attentive to issues of recruitment and how the use of online versus onsite methods may affect their research if relying on the Internet means some subgroups of the population are less apt to participate, and therefore that a population relevant to the study is systematically underrepresented in the sample (see Hooley et al. 2012: 66; Hamilton and Bowers 2006; Salmons 2009).

The emergence of reputable online companies and commercial entities that can be hired by researchers to conduct surveys, online interviews, and carry out experiments on their behalf has expanded the use of these methods in some academic disciplines. These online companies facilitate research about political and social phenomena in foreign countries, in particular, where in the past language differences and logistical costs would pose obstacles to the researcher. In addition to evaluating the credentials of the site, analysts with funding who aim to employ such entities should look carefully at how the population to be sampled is compiled by the organization. This will help ensure that demographic or political differences in the sampled population that are important for the researcher's study are actually controlled in the random sample provided by the polling organization. For example, a survey of attitudes about terrorist groups active in a foreign country, such as Iraq or Lebanon, would likely need to control for the religious or ethnic differences of respondents, by providing a sample that encompasses individuals from different sects. These differences may not be captured in a random sample of individuals that varies primarily in age, education or other demographic variables.

Information about attitudes can also be developed through ethnographic methods, such as by observing virtual communities and reading participant contributions in opinion oriented forums, such as chat rooms, comments pages and the like. Scholars or analysts may read through participant contributions in order to gauge attitudes or reactions and get a sense of how consumers of the information and visitors to online sites understand and evaluate different events or phenomena. While, as I explain below, one must be careful not to assume these expressed views are representative of the patterns of opinion within a larger audience, they can reveal important themes or narratives, and illuminate more extreme or particular interpretations and reactions.

Potential methodological problems of online research

Clearly, there are benefits to online research. There are also problems that such methods can generate.

Definitional issues in online searches

One set of issues relates to how researchers choose the key words employed in searches. A problem occurs if the terms are likely to be used selectively by those authoring and supplying material on websites. This can occur if a term, like "terrorism," has political implications, or implies normative judgments about the validity of an act or actor. As a result, the term may not be applied consistently and its use in a story may correspond with the biases or perspective of those reporting an event (Silke 2004).

The terms used in keyword searches can also generate biased results because the terms themselves have no widely shared meaning, and are used arbitrarily to describe events. Consider the use of the term "homegrown." As stated above, homegrown terrorism is often used in reference to Islamist militants who are citizens of the United States (or Europe) and operate independently from organized militant groups. In this usage, analysts associate the word "homegrown" primarily with Islamist fundamentalist, or jihadist ideologies, thereby employing the term to designate acts of terrorism perpetrated by individuals inspired by that particular ideology. Analysts may conversely use the term "domestic" terrorism for acts inspired by other secular or religious-based ideologies, such as individuals pursuing extremist left- or right-wing causes. Hence, members of the Hutaree militia who were prosecuted in 2010 for an alleged terrorist plot involving the murder of a police officer and a follow-on attack on his funeral may be referred to as "domestic" rather than "homegrown" terrorists.

Other scholars, however, use the term homegrown to refer to all self-starters operating independently from large organizations, regardless of the particular ideology that inspires him. They may refer to the 2011 shooting in Norway by Anders Breivik as an act of homegrown terrorism, despite the fact that he espoused right-wing ideology.

A third possible distinction involves discriminating terrorism that might be perpetrated by Muslims from that perpetrated by Islamist fundamentalists. Some analysts, for example, include in their studies of homegrown terrorism all Muslims perpetrating acts that could meet the criteria of terrorism, not just individuals inspired by a particular ideological doctrine associated with militant jihadism. Hence, the October 2002 Beltway or "D.C. Sniper" is included in these data bases, because the chief perpetrator, John Allen Mohammed, was a Muslim. He is rarely included in other data on homegrown terrorism because although he was a Muslim, his shootings were thought to be motivated by personal grievances, and not by jihadist ideology.

The importance of definitions can also be illustrated by considering the term "terrorism" in greater detail. The difficulty involved in deriving a shared definition of terrorism is well-known. Less appreciated is how that definitional problem can skew search results and, consequently, efforts to assess the nature and intensity of terrorist-related activity in a country, like the United States. These problems require vigilance in any terrorism related research online. Consider a researcher that is examining incidents of terrorist violence in the United States and using the following working definition: terrorism is violence aimed at individuals who are not implicated in the offending policies (civilians) to generate fear in a broader audience, in an effort to advance the militants' political goals. All of these are common elements in definitions of terrorism.

An online search of U.S. news reports in which the word "terrorist" is used would, however, yield incomplete results because of the reluctance of some editors, reporters, and government officials to apply the term consistently regardless of the alleged perpetrator's political viewpoint. For example, researchers might observe reluctance by some news outlets to use the term "terrorist" to describe those perpetrating violence for the sake of anti-government ideologies, in order to avoid the repercussions of being seen as questioning or delegitimizing causes sometimes associated with the political right in the United States. Hence, the 2010 attack by the long time anti-tax activist Joseph Stack on an I.R.S. building in Austin, Texas, which was accompanied by a detailed manifesto, often will not appear in searches of terrorist activity in the United States. Alternatively, it will appear relatively low in search results, because the term terrorism is not used in descriptions of his violent act. Fortunately, in that case, the researcher may stumble upon articles detailing the details of the attack, and correct his or her data so that the incident is included, in accordance with the aforementioned definition of terrorism.

More problematic are the cases that are not detected because the individual reporting or supplying information about the events chose to selectively avoid (consciously or not) the term terrorism in describing acts committed by one subsection of the population, regardless of whether or not those acts qualify as terrorism according to objective analytical criteria. Add to this the deeper problem that news organizations lack the economic incentive to invest the same resources monitoring and covering terrorist acts that originate in non-jihadist militants, compared with those that resonate with post 9–11 apprehensions about violence originating from Muslim fundamentalists. The result is that searches of terrorist attacks or acts in the United States will yield a biased sample in which Islamist oriented attacks may appear to occur in greater incidence or proportion to those perpetrated by others. In short, the use of different definitions of "homegrown terrorism" yields different quantitative and qualitative data, which affects assessments of the magnitude and nature of the problem. If right- and left-wing terrorists as well as Islamist extremists are included in the definition of homegrown terrorism employed in a researcher's online sources, quite a different picture emerges of the nature of the threat than a study based on sources that defines homegrown terrorism as a strictly Islamist phenomenon.

One lesson for researchers in this regard is that search terms that could potentially have varied interpretations or definitions must be parsed into constituent concepts, or the researcher must look closely at the definition of the term that informs the selection of cases or events in the source from which he or she is deriving data. Researchers may want to avoid terminology that is loaded, or ambiguous, and identify more concrete or fundamental aspects of the phenomenon studied and employ terms derived in that manner. While these dangers are not exclusive to online research, the variety of reports and data sources available from a simple keyword search can disarm the researcher and reduce the impulse to critically analyze those resources. Unlike a report that a researcher might solicit from a known scholar after learning of its content, a researcher may have little background on the methodology or definitions employed in online reports or databases and must remain vigilant in attending to these critical details.

Selection bias

A second set of lessons stems from the methodological bias that can be introduced into research when analysts rely on online sources. One can consider this a kind of "selection bias." The information found by a researcher is presumed to represent an unbiased subset of the knowledge available on a topic. In actuality, however, the information available is only partial and incomplete.

To see how information may be biased in this manner, a first step is to consider who has access to the Internet and what information they may and may not make available online. While it may seem limitless, the Internet does not capture the universe of information available on any given issue. It does not even capture a representative subset. Consider that, whether participating in an online discussion forum, or uploading reports, supplying information online requires investment in time and money, however nominal, by the person or entity involved. Therefore, that supply is inherently selective and partial. Information may be supplied by organizations and individuals who often have an editorial perspective, or a political, commercial or social motivation to provide it. In short, what is put online reflects the perspectives or interests of those able and willing to make available the information. This may seem a straightforward observation, but it has profound implications for those employing the Internet in their research.

For example, an individual researching the incidence of terrorism may be drawn to government reports and official data. Yet, information may be selectively provided by the government institution in question. Some data may be omitted in a document or resource online, or in the case of state censorship, as a result of the sensitivities of the authorities to the public availability of such information (Langford 2000). All of these factors affect the baseline pool of data available online. In the case of subject matter like terrorism, they can influence the information obtained through online research.

In general, analysts should regularly reflect on what is being offered online, and why. One set of issues relates to government interference. In the case of a government release of a report on terrorism, why has some information been made available and what might not be released? Is there an opaque agenda designed to influence assessments and understandings of terrorist activity occurring in the country? What data might the state have that is not being publicly offered? What are the boundaries of online monitoring or censorship in the state and how might that affect what opinions appear, or do not appear? In short researchers should be mindful of bias that comes from government selectivity, controls, or other forms of censorship.

Another factor that could influence what is available online is the commercial interests or organizational goals of those producing content on websites. Given the spread of online advertising and other commercial activities, what information is made available on websites could be influenced by economic pressures and forces. Given the non-hierarchical nature of the web, which suggests that information will flow unhindered by the interventions and control of large institutions, users may neglect that those using the web must fund their activities and therefore may be influenced by commercial motives as well. This could shape reporting on issues and what is made available online by these websites. Analysts should in general bear in mind the interests and motives of institutions, both public and private, in supplying information on their websites, or in blocking or concealing other information.

Sample bias

Internet research can also be vulnerable to the methodological problem of sample bias. Consider the problems that can occur in efforts to monitor social media or opinion oriented websites or discussion forums. Analysts may look at chat rooms, discussion boards, listservs, blogs, and a variety of social networking sites, such as Twitter feeds and Facebook pages, to gauge popular reactions or opinions about an issue or event. A researcher may, for example, try to gauge sympathy for terrorism or how acts of terrorism are being received and interpreted in a local setting or community. In the case of social media or discussion forums, the ability of individuals or a subset of the population to access the Internet, technological and financial barriers to entry and the varying motivations to participate in online commentary and communications may affect who is participating in online discussions. If who is online is not a representative sample of the population of interest, then inferences about the attitudes exhibited in those online contributions will reflect that sample bias.

Consequently, analysts should consider who has access to the Internet and how the demographic or political backgrounds of those who are active online might affect what opinions are represented – and not represented. The absence of a set of opinions should not be taken as evidence that those opinions are not held in the wider population. Rather, the absence of such evidence may simply mean that subset of a population lacked the will or capacity to participate in online discussions or share their opinions online.

A related issue, especially relevant for researching the attitudes of participants in online forums, is the relationship between the online community and actual real-world lives of members of that community. Are the assessments about attitudes and behaviors toward extremist causes and terrorist activity gleaned through ethnographic research of online communities correlated with professed attitudes and observed behaviors offline? Put simply, is what people say online related to what they think and do offline, and therefore, can reliable inferences be drawn from observing online communities? Similarly, scholars should consider the significance of studying individuals that interact as a virtual "community" versus in-person social relationships. For example, scholars have debated whether the social bonds that emerge online in militant networks have the same resilience and depth as in-person social networks (Sageman 2008). In assessing sympathy for terrorism or propensity for extremism, the impact of the Internet as a medium on the content and expression of attitudes should be considered.[4]

In general, as scholars or analysts contemplate relying on online resources as a research method, they should consider how sample or selection bias can influence or skew their findings. The sheer volume of material available online generates the image that the Internet is a comprehensive and neutral source of information. Online information, however, is not inherently value neutral, representative or universal in its supply. How information becomes available, and who makes it available, can shape the results of Internet searches, introducing potential sources of bias.

Misinformation

An additional concern about online research relates to the validity of the information researchers find online. Information may not just be skewed by selection or sample bias. It may be factually wrong or incomplete. This can be result of error or lack of experience among those supplying the information, or the deliberate efforts to manipulate content on websites.

Concerns about the veracity of information and data in research certainly are not exclusive to online sources. Yet, information online may be more vulnerable to inaccuracies, omissions and distortions (Vedder 2001). For those with interest and access to the web and a desire to contribute to public debate and discussion, the technological barriers to entry have fallen considerably. In the past, information about defense or military related topics, or terrorist activity, would often originate in print and broadcast media reports, government institutions and academic researchers. When information is reported by established institutions, assuming adherence to conventional standards of evidence in academic scholarship and journalism, it would be sourced and vetted. The advent of individuals and small groups providing news and commentary means that those standards or conventions of validating information may not be accepted or followed. Hence, with the supply of more information from more diverse sources, the relative reliability of the information has fallen.

Also relevant is the phenomenon of "citizen journalism." This refers to the opportunity for individuals with smartphones, or computers to act as de facto freelance journalists, supplying information to established news sources, to websites of their choice, or communicating it themselves via social media. This "democratization" of journalism has clear advantages in that it means more diverse and varied information may be available to the public. But it also means that information is circulating with few checks on its reliability.

Add to this the speed with which information spreads, and inaccuracies that might in the past have been detected before being introduced to the public, can be widely circulated and, through their very ubiquity, gain credibility. Misinformation, like accurate information, spreads quickly online. Such a phenomenon occurred in the aftermath of the May 2013 Boston Marathon bombings in Massachusetts, when an individual was identified by an onlooker as a potential perpetrator of the bombings. His picture was taken and then circulated widely on the web. Only subsequently did it become clear that the individual in question had nothing to do with plotting the attack.

Also relevant, is how stories and facts reported online often come to be seen as valid and reliable. Consider the algorithms employed by search engines and the indexes created from which search results are built. Well-known search engines rely on algorithms that order the results of searches according to what amounts to the popularity of websites; how many times the site is visited may affect where it appears in the hierarchy of results. Search engines may use links to webpages from other webpages in indexing, such that "popular" pages can move up the hierarchy of search results.

A source that, in turn, appears on the first page of search results may in turn seem to be more legitimate or credible than one buried in subsequent pages. Consequently, a website may appear credible because it is frequently accessed, independent of its actual accuracy and consistency with real events. In other words, the more people who visit a site, the more popular it becomes, and the more accepted and therefore reliable it may appear. Search engines, however, do little to evaluate the actual credibility or reliability of website content.

In general, the frequency that a report or fact appears online should not be taken as evidence of its accuracy. For example, a particular fact or event may be reported in stories on apparently unrelated websites. A reader may conclude that the widespread coverage means the information reported is accurate. Researchers, however, should always consider tracking back to original sources. At the least, it is useful to click through the links provided on a website to other sites to find where the relevant information originated. A danger is that each seemingly independent story may in fact all reference the same source. This does not mean the information is incorrect, but it does suggest it has not been as widely validated as its appearance in stories on multiple sites suggests. Rather, the spread of the report reflects the non-hierarchical and unfettered flow of information online.

Researchers seeking to assess the accuracy of information provided on websites can examine a number of features of those sites. This evaluation can also reveal biases or editorial perspectives that could affect the content or presentation of information. A first step is to assess the identity and credentials of the author or organization that produced the website. Online sites can be evaluated in a manner similar to that of conventional print sources. A researcher may look at who funds the organization supporting the website, examine its mission statement and principal audience, and investigate the background and experience of the authors whose work appears on the site. Other steps involve looking at the text and linked reports. One should assess the evidence provided in support of an author's claims, and whether attributions to source material are appropriate and common; the most reliable sources will include references, citations and the like.

Other steps relevant to ascertaining the validity of online sources include looking for contact information of the authors or organizations publishing or sponsoring a site to see if it is provided. Generally, more reputable sources will provide a means for contacting those sponsoring the site, or publishing material that appears on it. The reliability of a website also depends on how current is the information, and whether it is frequently updated. Researchers should also look at the server hosting the site to see if it is reputable and consider the domain (e.g. ".edu"; ".gov"; ".com"). Looking to see what links connect the site to other sites is also useful in assessing the reliability and biases of a website.

Many of these steps are intuitive, and most Internet users will be accustomed to detecting sites that seem suspect. Yet, for those aiming to use online research in support of their work, it is worthwhile to be systematic in evaluating websites. In addition to the suggestions cited above, many government institutions and libraries also publish comprehensive guides for evaluating Internet resources.

Propaganda and the strategic use of the Internet

Mistakes and errors represent one potential source of misinformation. In these instances, the intent of those supplying the inaccurate information is not necessarily to deliberately mislead. Another set of problems, however, that could affect online research stems from efforts by individuals or institutions to deliberately mislead or provide false information online. This can come in the form of fabricating or embellishing information and stories on websites or in the form of a more concerted propaganda campaign aimed at influencing a particular audience.

The Internet, in fact, represents a tremendous resource to governments, organizations and individuals seeking to influence a designated target audience (Shah 2005). It provides opportunities to alter or control information and shape popular reactions and opinion. The motivation for such efforts can be political or commercial. For example, companies may deploy paid workers to surf the web and offer favorable reviews and contribute positive commentary about their products or services. Government authorities may covertly participate in cyber forums, or otherwise provide selective information targeted to shape debate on an issue of concern. For these reasons, it is essential to consider how the Internet can be used as a tool or instrument of influence by individuals and institutions. This will safeguard against researchers unwittingly reporting and using incomplete, skewed or false information and data.

Research on terrorism and militant groups once again illustrates these concerns. Assume a Western government is monitoring and covertly participating in discussion in Internet chatroom forums on militant jihadist websites. That government in turn is aiming to undermine the organization and supplies stories and commentaries by its own agents posing as visitors to the sites. In an effort to sow divisions and provoke factionalism, for example, government employees might pose as participants who offer divisive opinions or information intended to strike discord in the organization. An outsider that monitors that website can come away with the impression that the fissure is real or originating within the movement's leadership. But it may be artificial and may not reflect any actual debate occurring in the group. Although not the intended audience, the researcher nonetheless will have an inaccurate understanding of the dynamics within the organization he or she is studying.

Similarly, a researcher seeking to analyze counterinsurgency operations in a country could experience related problems. With the emphasis in counterinsurgency doctrine on grassroots appeals to local populations, a government seeking to advance its goals could conceivably have incentives to control information or influence reporting about local military events or economic development efforts. While these tactics of shaping reporting and public information are certainly nothing new to the practices of military organizations, the Internet provides new and creative opportunities to disseminate stories and means for disguising their sources and authenticity. A researcher interested in how economic development efforts are proceeding or being received locally in a conflict zone might, consequently, be misled by positive reports disseminated as part of a larger public relations effort.

In summary, the Internet provides an opportunity for government entities to influence targeted audiences, by shaping information online, or through subterfuge and participation on relevant websites. Those with commercial interests, or those motivated by other political and social motivations, may also try and influence what does and does not appear online. For this reason, researchers need to be cautious and stay mindful that the information they might find on sites may be the result of third parties' efforts to manipulate data or otherwise to use the Internet to their advantage.

Conclusion

The Internet represents a vast and unharnessed resource and opportunity for researchers. Yet, even as scholars and analysts exploit these opportunities, it is essential that they remain mindful of potential pitfalls and dangers of using the Internet as a resource and method in their research. These include problems related to selection bias, sample bias, misinformation and propaganda, and problems with definitional and concept uniformity. Some of these issues are similar in kind to conventional research methods, but may be rendered more acute in online research, while others are problems that originate in the nature of the Internet itself. Regardless, just as researchers invest time and resources in learning to employ conventional methodologies in their research, they are wise to educate themselves about both the opportunities and potential risks of online research.

Notes

1 I focus here on the benefits and methodological considerations related to online research. The Internet is also an important resource for researchers in their efforts to enhance collaboration, share information, disseminate and market their research to academic and other audiences. See for example, "Social Media: A Guide for Researchers," Research Information Network, February 2011. Available at www.rin.ac.uk/our-work/communicating-and-disseminating-research/social-media-guide-researchers
2 For general overviews of online research across different disciplines see Johns et al. (2003), Hooley et al. (2012) and Hewson et al. (2003).

3 For an example of an online resource that focuses on monitoring jihadist websites see the SITE Intelligence Group, which provides, among other products, a subscription service for governments and corporations. Available at http://news.siteintelgroup.com/services.
4 For discussion of issues that arise in online ethnographic research see Hooley et al. (2012: pp. 73–89), Kozinets (2009) and Garcia et al. (2009).

References

Bjelopera, J.P. and M.A. Randol (2010). *American Jihadist Terrorism: Combating a Complex Threat*. Washington, D.C.: Congressional Research Service, Library of Congress.
Comer, D.E. (2011). *Computer Networks and Internets*. Upper Saddle River, NJ: Pearson Higher Education.
Dahl, E. (2011). "The Plots That Failed: Intelligence Lessons Learned from Unsuccessful Terrorist Attacks against the United States." *Studies in Conflict and Terrorism*, Vol. 34, No. 8: 621–648.
Garcia, A.C., A.I. Standlee, J.H. Bechkoff and Y. Cui (2009). "Ethnographic Approaches to the Internet and Computer-Mediated Communication." *Journal of Contemporary Ethnography*, Vol. 38, No. 1: 52–84.
Hamilton, R.J. and B.J. Bowers (2006). "Internet Recruitment and E-Mail Interviews in Qualitative Studies." *Qualitative Health Research*, Vol. 16, No. 6: 821–835.
Hewson, Y.C., P. Laurent and C. Vogel (2003). *Internet Research Methods*. London: Sage.
Hooley, T., J. Marriott and J. Wellens (2012). *What Is Online Research?* New York: Bloomsbury.
Johns, M., S.L. Chen and J. Hall (eds) (2003). *Online Social Research: Methods, Issues and Ethics*. New York: Peter Lang.
Kozinets, R.V. (2009). *Netnography: Doing Ethnographic Research Online*. Thousand Oaks, CA: Sage.
Langford, D. (2000). *Internet Ethics*. New York: St. Martin's Press.
Sageman, M. (2008). *Leaderless Jihad: Terror Networks in the Twenty-First Century*. Philadelphia, PA: University of Pennsylvania Press.
Salmons, J. (2009). *Online Interviews in Real Time*. London: Sage Publications.
Shah, A. (2005). "War, Propaganda and the Media." *Global Issues*, March 31, 2005. Available at http://www.globalissues.org/article/157/war-propaganda-and-the-media.
Silke, A. (ed.) (2004). *Research on Terrorism: Trends, Achievements and Failures*. London: Frank Cass.
Vedder, A. (2001). *Ethics and the Internet*. Oxford: Intersentia.

PART III

Quantitative methods

16

SURVEY RESEARCH IN MILITARY SETTINGS

James Griffith

J. Griffith (1995) 'The Army Reserve soldier in Operation Desert Storm: Perceptions of being prepared for mobilization, deployment, and combat,' *Armed Forces & Society* 21: 195–215.

In the mid-1970s, the Total Force policy shifted the active components' combat support and service support to the reserve components. This policy made it necessary to mobilize and to deploy reserve component forces in the event of a large-scale war. During the Persian Gulf War, 228,000 reservists were called up, of which 139,207 were Army Reservists. The war, then, provided a test of the Total Force policy: Were the Army reserve components ready for immediate mobilization and deployment in support of combat missions?

The study obtained survey responses from panels of deployed (N = 259) and nondeployed (N = 576) Army Reserve junior-ranking enlisted soldiers, before and after Operation Desert Storm (ODS). Soldiers were part of a stratified-random, proportional sample of Army Reservists, constructed to adequately represent responses of all deployed and nondeployed soldiers before and after ODS. Survey data were subsequently weighted to represent the responses of all reservists.

Perceptions of equipment and unit leadership preparation showed significant moderate and positive relationships to perceptions that the soldier and the unit were prepared to fight. Favorable spouse and employer attitudes toward reserve service (as reported by the soldier) were significantly and positively related to the soldier's stated intent to stay in the Army Reserve, and negatively related to problems caused by extended mobilization and deployment periods. Soldiers' perceptions of how well their unit leadership was prepared and how well weekend drill prepared them for war were significantly and positively related to reporting for mobilization and staying in the Army Reserve. In contrast, both before and after Operation Desert Storm, large percentages of deployed and nondeployed soldiers reported problems in unit leadership, preparation in individual job and common soldier skills, and weekend drill personnel utilization.

Surveys in the military: Then and now

One of the first dedicated survey efforts was that of Sam Stouffer and his colleagues during World War II (Stouffer et al. 1949) – often considered a classic study of military life supported by data largely obtained through systematic surveys of soldiers. Stouffer and other, now familiar names in psychology surveyed over a half million American soldiers on topics, such as racial integration, officer leadership, unit morale, perceived individual and unit readiness, and others. Survey findings were the basis of several personnel policies, including decisions regarding which units were best suited to land during the D-Day invasion (Converse 2009). Since then, surveys have evolved and become commonplace both in the public and in the military sectors (Kraut 1996). Results of surveys serve to inform leaders and policymakers for a variety of purposes, such as obtaining accurate information regarding need and preferences, evaluating use and effectiveness of programs, and determining what and how to improve organizations (Edwards et al. 1997). This chapter serves as a broad overview of the survey process applied to policy issues of concern to the military. The content of this chapter is structured to respond to key questions, which correspond to essential steps of the survey process.

What is a survey?

A survey may be defined as a *standard method of collecting* information on individuals through the *questioning* of identified *samples of individuals* (Rossi et al. 1983). This definition points to several important elements of a survey – the why, the what, the who, the how and the when, which are used to construct this chapter. "The why" asks, What is the purpose of the survey and potential uses? What is the problem being investigated? "The what" asks, Given the purpose of the survey, what are the relevant domains to represent in the survey and to develop specific survey items? To what extent does the research literature help elaborate on the issue of interest, suggesting specific content and/or a cause map to develop content and to suggest an analysis design? "The who" asks, What is the target population to be surveyed? Who should provide responses to help elaborate on the problem for which the survey is designed? How will potential respondents be chosen? What sampling methods will be considered? "The how and when" asks, What method of data collection and respondent follow-up will be used? What method is most appropriate given the topic, sampling method, and population considered – paper-and-pencil survey questionnaires, telephone survey, web-based survey, and in-person survey? After having conducted the survey, pertinent questions are: What is to be done with the survey responses? How will the results be structured for presentation to sponsors of the survey?

The why, which defines the what: Content domains for the survey

Key to determining what will be gathered in the survey is describing the purpose of the survey. First, the generic purpose of the survey might be described – whether for purposes of providing a point estimate (e.g. what are soldiers' attitudes toward allowing homosexuals to serve openly in the U.S. military?), monitoring estimates over time for trends (e.g. what are mental health problems of deployed soldiers from year to year?), or evaluating organizational policies and programs (e.g. to what extent do suicide prevention programs impart knowledge and attitude change among soldiers?). Second, specifying the purpose of the survey in very concrete terms is useful. Let us illustrate this beginning step of survey purpose with the illustrative study.

The primary purpose of this survey was to examine U.S. Army Reserve soldiers' readiness to be mobilized and to be deployed. Readiness had to be defined in terms of responses to survey questions. Previously published studies (Reference Note 5 in the illustrative study – Gal 1986; Gal and Manning 1987; Griffith 1988; Hauser 1980; Kellett 1982; Segal and Harris 1993) suggested three broad human dimensions relating to soldier perceptions of combat readiness: (1) the quality of unit leadership; (2) the condition of and soldier familiarity with individual weapons and major weapon systems; and (3) non-problematic family and domestic life. These broad content domains then had to be described in greater detail in order to develop specific survey items and questions.

Methods for identifying what to ask

There are *several methods for developing explicit survey content* for these domains (Edwards et al. 1997), specifically: past surveys, published literature, official documents, interviews of key informants, and focus groups. For the illustrative study, *past Army surveys* were examined for defining and then developing survey items relating to mobilization readiness and then organized by general content domains, such as, leadership, individual and unit training, equipment availability, functionality, and familiarity, etc. Automated *literature searches* (e.g. EBSCO) resulted in more defined content to represent on survey of the illustrative study, including: weekend drill mobilization preparation (e.g. effective use of drill time, spend little time on unnecessary things, train as a team, train soldiers in individual job and common soldier skills); unit leadership mobilization preparation (e.g. trust and confidence in unit officers/NCOs, leaders treat me as a person, apply discipline fairly, care about soldiers, provide good supervision, train as a team, promote teamwork and cooperation), etc. *Official documents*, such as memoranda, policy letters, program descriptions, etc., can be used to gain background on the problem for which the survey will gather data. In the illustrative study, the survey team examined memos and policy letters that described the nature and extent of the problem and probable causes, incentive programs to get youth to join and to remain in reserve military service, etc. Developed survey content included reasons for enlistment and reasons for re-enlistment and the role of the various incentive programs in their decision processes (e.g. knowledge and use of incentives).

Another source for identifying survey content is *interviewing of key informants* on the topic being investigated. These interviews are a good source for broad specification of the topic and related content, or "the cause map" – a pictorial or conceptual understanding of antecedents, intervening variables, and consequences pertinent to the key content domain for which survey data is wanted. To prepare for these interviews, the survey team should prepare a statement regarding the purpose of the survey and broad questions relating to the survey topic, for example, How prepared are reservists to be mobilized and deployed to combat areas? Subsequent questions should cascade to greater specificity, for example, what are areas reservists are most and least prepared? During the interview, the survey team should use probes to embellish areas and seek potential antecedents, for example: "Tell me more about this . . . " and "Why do you think this is the case . . . ?" In the illustrative study, interviews were conducted with key personnel, such as the retention and readiness staff at the Continental U.S. Army Commands and several major U.S. Army Reserve Commands. Another form of interviewing is the *focus group*. In this method, participants – usually comprised of 6 to 12 people of the population to be surveyed – are asked questions for purposes of group discussion (O'Brien 1993). First, a few broad questions are asked followed by probes and participants' elaboration. Responses lead to identifying major themes and subthemes, in addition to possible specific survey questions, items, and response options. For the illustrative study, several focus groups were conducted at several major Army headquarters. Two survey team members facilitated the discussion of 10–15 junior-ranking enlisted (privates through sergeants) for one and a half hours concerning reserve military service: reasons for joining and leaving; readiness for mobilization and deployment; quality of unit training; availability, quality and familiarity with weapons; quality of unit leadership; and the role of civilian employment and family life in reserve military service. The survey team took notes, identifying content for each domain, and later, developed as survey items organized by identified content domains.

Generating specific items

Specific survey content should be developed by domains identified in the review of previous questionnaires, literature, focus groups, and other initial activities. At most, there should be a dozen or so content domains for the survey. Depending on the specificity desired, content should be developed for each domain. Theories, models, and organizing frameworks identified are useful in developing explicit survey content, as well as suggesting an analysis plan. Ajzen and Fishbein's (1980) theory of reasoned behavior, for example, served as an organizing perspective for several large-scale military surveys, including the Army Communications Objectives Measurement Study (Rhoads and Elig 1988), which assessed the effectiveness of various marketing and advertising strategies to recruit soldiers for the U.S. Army's all-volunteer force. Survey content inquiring about information from respondents take two general forms: *questions* and *statements*. Examples of each are found in Table 16.1

Questions ask for either one or multiple responses, respectively: What was your age at your last birthday? Or, what are the reasons you joined reserve military service? Response options can take two general forms: *open-ended*, which allow the respondent to write in text; and *closed-ended*, which provide predefined response options for the respondent. While the former allows more spontaneity and at times more comprehensiveness, such responses also entail coding – that is, developing a scheme to organize responses into general categories and assign numbers to the responses for analysis. The latter, closed-ended response options, while limiting respondents' answers, provides easy data recording of responses and is preferred, in particular, for surveys of small budgets. Closed-ended responses can take many forms (as displayed in the table). Of particular note is whether response options indicate from positive to negative versus much quantity to none (see Table 16.2). These descriptors can then be arranged as a Likert-type response scale. Response options include both descriptors and the corresponding numerical assignments (ordinally scaled, e.g. from low to high or high to low). Likert-type scales have anywhere between 3 to 7 responses options, though, generally, the variance sufficient for analyses provided by few point response options (usually minimally, three) is similar to that provided by more response options (Dawes 2007; Garland 1991). Other scales for attitudinal assessment are discussed in Oskamp and Schultz (2005), namely, Bogardus Social Distance Scale, Thurstone's Equal-appearing Interval Scale, Guttman's Scalogram.

These response scales are then used to respond to specific questions or statements contained in the survey instrument. Simple "one-line" questions or statements for respondents are preferred, as it takes less effort for respondents to read and answer. Insofar as possible, the survey team should develop questions and statements of similar format, for example, a series of statements that require the same response options. This format, again, makes it easy for the respondent to read and respond. Table 16.3 outlines common problems in crafting survey items.

Some questions or statements may require more than one response, such as reasons for joining reserve military service. Responses to such items may represent either independent responses, i.e. coding each response as yes versus no, or dependent responses requiring representation of various combinations. The first situation is considered mutually exclusive responses, either yes

Table 16.1 Examples of survey questions and statements

Questions

What is your military status? MARK ONE:

___M-day soldier, only "part-time"
___Full-time soldier on temporary funding
___Technician, e.g. ADSW
___Full-time AGR soldier
___Other

In the last year, have you been deployed to any one of the following locations?

MARK ALL THAT APPLY:

___Iraq
___Afghanistan
___Kuwait
___Other location

Statements

For each statement, place a checkmark to the right of each statement indicating your response.

Survey statement	Strongly agree	Agree	Disagree	Strongly disagree
There is a lot of teamwork and cooperation among members in my unit				
When things don't get done, members of my unit pull together				
Soldiers in my unit stick together to accomplish the mission				

Table 16.2 Common descriptors for response options

Types of response	Example descriptors assigned to numerical ratings on Likert-type scale	Ratings represent
Agreement	Strong agree, agree, disagree, strongly disagree	Positive versus negative
Satisfaction	Very satisfied, satisfied, dissatisfied, very dissatisfied	Balanced
Quality	Very good, good, average, poor, very poor	Positive versus negative
Expectations	Much better than expected, better than expected, as expected, worse than expected, much worse than expected	Positive versus negative
Effectiveness	Very effective, effective, ineffective, very ineffective	Positive versus negative
Likelihood	Very likely, likely, unlikely, very unlikely	Positive versus negative
Frequency	Always, often, seldom/rarely, never	More to less
Extent	To great extent, to some extent, to small extent, to no extent	More to less
Importance	Very important, somewhat important, slightly important, not all important	More to less

Table 16.3 Common problems in crafting survey items and helpful hints

Common problem	Example of problem	Helpful hint
Use of double-barreled items	I am in the military to serve my country and feel an obligation to others	Be sure to keep survey item to one referent
Use of complex language, not appropriate for population being surveyed	My military services are a deterrent to the global spread of totalitarian regimes	Keep language simple and appropriate for population being surveyed
Being vague regarding referent behavior and related factors	Are you satisfied with military service?	Be specific regarding referent behavior and related factors
Use of leading questions	Most people feel that serving in the military is. Do you agree?	Avoid questions which introduce bias in response
Use of double negatives	I do not like the idea of not receiving bonuses	Do not use two negative in survey item

or no, to each item. The second situation is when responses are not mutually exclusive and can take various combinations, usually making coding and analysis more difficult. That is, there can be any number of various combinations of responses that will have to be coded as unique responses. Additionally, response options that often pose difficulties for the respondent and survey team are: Don't Know, Not applicable, Neutral, and Other. Don't knows and/or Not applicable are often seen as reflecting a neutral position in an attitude assessment, as responding "neutral." Don't know and Not applicable responses may, however, reflect a non-attitude, or not even responding to the response scale or item. For these ambiguities, survey research studies suggest omitting a middle response category for attitude assessment.

Determining reliability and validity

Survey items nearly always serve to measure a variable or construct, and thus, respondents' answers to such items must show some degree of reliability and validity. A common method of reliability assessment is examining the consistency in responses to survey items which are thought to assess the corresponding construct. The SPSS Reliability routine can determine internal response consistency – either by way of Cronbach alpha or item-total correlations or both (see Pedhazur and Schmelkin 1991). Factor analysis (Gorsuch 1983) can also determine the extent to which a set of survey items assess the same underlying construct. In confirmatory factor analysis, the researcher has substantial justification for the arrangement of survey items in relation to facets of the underlying construct. The researcher specifies which of the survey items correlate with which facets of the underlying construct. For example, commitment is often thought of as having facets of normative, affective, and continuance (Meyer and Allen 1991). Survey items presumed to assess these facets would be tested simultaneously using confirmatory factor analysis (see SPSS add-on module called AMOS; Arbuckle 2009). If the researcher is less certain about the way in which items arrange themselves in relation to underlying factors, then alternatively exploratory factor analysis can be used (see SPSS Data Reduction, Factor Analysis). Sometimes, it is appropriate to conduct cognitive labs on a limited number of respondents to discern whether the content of questions is understood as intended. An example method is "read aloud," where the investigator reads the questionnaire item to the respondent (Jobe and Mingay 1990). The respondent then repeats back his (her) understanding of what has been said. The investigator can then tell the extent to which the meaning of an item has been conveyed.

A more complicated measurement issue is one of validity, whether survey items obtain data on what they purport to assess. Face and content validity are, perhaps, the easiest to demonstrate. Survey items have face validity if they look like they measure what they are supposed to measure. For example, survey items that ask about various experiences of immediate leaders would seem to assess leadership. Content validity refers to the extent to which a measure represents all facets of a given construct. Thus, measures of leadership would have to include various aspects identified in the literature – from theories and/or empirical findings. Several other methods to establish validity of measures include concurrent, predictive, and discriminant. For an introduction to these topics, see Oskamp and Schultz (2005).

Arrangement of survey items

After survey questions and statements have been drafted along with respective response options, the content needs to be arranged in a survey questionnaire. Items of similar content should be grouped together, again, for ease of the respondent's understanding and responding. More simple, less threatening content should be placed at the beginning of the questionnaire and more complex, obtrusive content to the end of the questionnaire. In this way, the respondent's trust and confidence is built as they go through the questionnaire, and thus, are more likely to respond to more personal questions later, such as age, income, etc. The survey team should be mindful of common problems encountered in respondent's responses. Respondents often answer survey content without regard to content, for example, check all items as "agree." Presenting survey content as alternating positive and negative content prevents this problem (called a "balanced format"). Respondents also may respond according to what they believe the survey team wants then to say, called "response acquiescence." Finally, respondents may wish to present themselves in the best light and answer accordingly; this is called social desirability. Each of these problems results in responses that are not genuine, and thus, threatens the validity of the measurement and should be avoided. It is advisable to examine the responses of the first 100 or so questionnaires to determine whether such problems exist for remedial action.

The who

"The who" asks the questions, What is the target population to be surveyed? Stated alternatively, who should provide responses to help clarify the problem for which the survey is designed? And subsequently, how will potential respondents be chosen? What sampling methods will be considered? Ideally, everyone in the target population would be surveyed. But, due level of effort constraints – both staff and money, this is rarely feasible. This would entail providing a survey instrument to everyone with subsequent follow-up to ensure every respondent responds. It is more realistic to survey a smaller subset of the target audience with repeated follow-up to ensure high completion rates. And indeed, regardless of the population's size, a carefully chosen sample of a subset numbering 1,500 achieves a reasonable degree of precision for estimates (i.e. the population percentage is expected to plus or minus 3 percent of the sample estimate). Sampling requires knowing eligible individuals in the entire population followed by systematic selection of respondents for the sample (Fowler 2009). Before beginning, several terms are important to understand when sampling: universe or population, sampling frame, sample, precision, and error.

The *universe* or *population* is a term used when referring to all possible respondents. For example, a survey of U.S. Army soldiers would be all soldiers currently serving in the U.S. Army. The *sampling frame* refers to a listing of all possible respondents and is useful in selecting a smaller subset for purposes of surveying them. Such lists often do not include every eligible individual in the population, though nearly everyone. For example, in the earlier example study, not every soldier serving in the U.S. Army may be found on a personnel list, due to being newly accessed.

The smaller subset from the sampling frame is called the *sample*. The number of members chosen from the population determines the precision and error associated with any estimate derived from the survey data. Small sample sizes (up to about 500) generate estimates having more error and less precision. For example, the "true" population percent associated with a sample percent (derived from a sample of 500) would be between plus or minus 5 percent of the sample percent. Error and precision are important when wanting to detect differences between groups (men versus women, junior-ranking enlisted versus others, those treated or not). A convenient way to calculate approximate error associated with a given sample percent is:

$\sqrt{(\text{p} \star \text{q} / \text{N})} \star 1.96 \star 100 = +/-$ band within which the population parameter is likely to fall in 95 out of 100 random samples.

Let p = 0.5 (where maximum variability occurs for a proportion); q = 1 − p; and N = sample size.

1.96 is the z-value associated with 95% confidence interval, and the multiplier of 100 converts the proportions into percentages.

In determining the sample size, the survey research team should ensure enough precision is achieved to show differences between groups (demographically or programmatically defined) exceed expected error. Power analysis is used to calculate sufficient sample sizes to allow for this. (For more detail, see chapter 6, "Determining Sample Size," in Rea and Parker 1992.) Sampling design also reflects policy interests. For example, there may be interest in knowing certain characteristics of low-frequency groups in the population. Thus, such groups would have to be over-sampled or over-represented in the sample in order to yield a reasonably reliable estimate on survey responses, and when combined with all respondents would have to be weighted "downward" to represent their occurrence in the population.

There are several ways to determine who is included. A major concern in survey research is implementing a design that obtains results from a smaller subset of the population (called a sample), which represents, to some degree of confidence, population results sample. Broadly, sampling occurs as two approaches: *probabilistic* and *non-probabilistic*. The non-probabilistic approach is problematic in that it is not possible to determine whether the sampled respondents actually represent the larger population. It is more likely the probabilistic approach will achieve this, that is, a representative sample that resembles the population in key background characteristics, especially those characteristic correlated with the topic of interest. This is *external validity* or the extent to which results obtained from a sample describe those obtained from the entire population.

To achieve such results, the sample must be a probabilistic sample (simple random, stratified-random, and systematic, etc.) Key statistical methods also rely on probabilistic sampling, such as error band associated with statistics derived from the sample of respondents and inferential statistics used to determine whether associations among survey variables occur by chance (i.e. sampling and measurement errors) or represent true observed associations. Probabilistic surveys require some way to enumerate all potential members of the population. That is, lists of potential respondents are available and/or members are nested in some way to sample from the "nestings" to achieve randomness, such as households or telephones. The *non-probabilistic* approach to sampling is also called opportunistic sampling. While some criteria for inclusion in the sample may have been applied, not everyone has been enumerated and assigned a chance of being selected as a respondent. Both probabilistic and non-probabilistic approaches occur in several forms, as described below.

Probabilistic sampling methods

To collect a *simple random sample*, each individual of the target population is assigned a number. A set of random numbers is then generated and the individuals having those numbers are included in the sample. To perform *systematic sampling*, individuals in the target population must first be arranged in some ordering scheme. Individuals are then selected at regular intervals through that ordered list. A random start on the list is determined and then every *n*th individual is chosen for the sample. This method assumes that there are no biases in the arrangement of cases on the list (called periodicity). For example, choosing every *n*th house along a street might result in taking too many corner households, which typically have bigger lots and more expensive houses. In *stratified-random sampling*, respondent characteristics important to the survey estimates are considered, such as rank, gender, etc. Population members are then arranged into cells corresponding to these characteristics, called strata. Members are sampled randomly from the various cells (private–junior sergeant men, privates to sergeant women, senior sergeant men, senior sergeant women, etc.) Members can be sampled proportional to their occurrence in the population (proportional probability sampling) or not (disproportional probability sampling). Disproportional probability sampling would be appropriate if reliable estimates are needed for a low-frequency group, such as senior sergeant who are women. This then would provide more reliable estimates from the survey (estimate with smaller error band). If, however, overall estimates for the population are desired, strata from which members were disproportionally sampled would have weights applied. Weights are derived as a ratio of rate of occurrence in population/rate of occurrence in the sample. The weights are used to multiply the cases having the sampling characteristics, e.g. senior sergeants who are women.

Cluster sampling is used when it is either impossible or impractical to compile an exhaustive list of individuals who comprise the target population. Sometimes lists of members of a population are not readily available. But, where the members typically occur or "reside" is known. That is, population members are known to "cluster" or to gather in geographically defined groups, such as by their unit membership (e.g. people reside in households, census tracts, cities, etc.). With cluster sampling, it is best when the clusters are internally heterogeneous on the characteristics being studied, so as not to bias results on any particular respondent characteristic. Also, smaller numbers in clusters are desired. The larger the number of respondents per cluster, the greater the within-group variance making the sampling method less efficient.

Because military personnel situate themselves as intact groups, obtaining a representative sample is generally accomplished through cluster sampling where soldiers within each randomly selected unit or cluster would be surveyed. A recent example of cluster sampling was employed by Schaubroeck et al. (2012) where brigades were chosen from combat divisions, battalions from brigades, companies from battalions, platoons from companies, and finally, squads from platoons. Soldiers in sampled squads then completed surveys. Another recent examples are the Army's Mental Health Advisory Team Surveys (MHAT 2008) where units (squads and platoons) were randomly selected from larger organizational clusters, such as brigades and battalions. Clustering can reduce travel and administrative costs of the survey by not having to travel to all units deployed throughout Afghanistan and surveying only a few in each unit (as in simple random sampling of soldiers).

Non-probabilistic sampling methods

Non-probabilistic sampling occurs in several types; convenient, purposive, and quota. A *convenience sampling* is a matter of taking whoever is eligible to complete the survey. Volunteers would constitute a convenience sample. In *quota sampling*, respondents are taken from the population in some pre-specified numbers so as to achieve some heterogeneity in the sample. However, the selection of respondents is not random. A *purposive sample* is having chosen a non–representative subset of a larger population for a very specific need or purpose.

Sampling in the illustrative study

The illustrative study (presented earlier) used a fairly complicated sampling design, which required several professional statisticians to develop, review, and apply final weights to the sample. The sample was a stratified-random, disproportional sampling. The study reported survey data gathered in 1991 and in 1992. Previously, the survey had been conducted annually starting in 1988. A list of reserve soldiers was obtained from the Army's personnel system (called the Standard Installation Division Personnel Reporting System). Each year, the sample numbered about 31,000 reservists who were randomly selected from strata defined by background characteristics, such as rank, gender, and race. Selected respondents represented were members of about 3,300 reserve units across the U.S. In the first three years of the survey, annual samples were cross-sectional. In the fourth year of the survey, the First Gulf War broke out. Senior Army leaders were interested in the level of preparedness of reservists for the war, in addition to their experiences and how these related to their intentions to remain in reserve military service. Given this policy interest, the annual cross-sectional sample was augmented by reservists who had been deployed or not, to allow for comparisons between the two groups concerning readiness, deployment experiences, and retention intentions. This sampling also provided panels of reservists from the previous year to the current year, which had been deployed or not. The panels provided survey responses on the same soldiers before and after mobilization and deployment. To accomplish the augmented sampling, reservists were stratified by whether they had been deployed or not. Deployed reservists were over-sampled to ensure adequate numbers for point estimates and analyses. Both deployed and nondeployed reservists were stratified into several groups: nonmedical personnel and medical personnel (including physicians, licensed nurses, and practical nurses). Many medical personnel deployed in support of the First Gulf War. There was thus interest in examining medical personnel's intention to stay or leave reserve military service upon return. Both nonmedical and medical personnel were then stratified by rank, gender, and minority status due to the policy interests in junior-ranking, women, and minority soldiers.

The how and when of survey data collection

"The how and the when" asks, What method of data collection and respondent follow-up will be used? What method is most appropriate given the topic, sampling method, and population considered? There are three primary modalities for gathering survey data: paper-and-pencil surveys (either group or individually administered), through personal interaction (individually in personal interview or over the telephone), and via the Internet (Groves et al. 2009).

Paper-and-pencil surveys take the form of hard-copy material on which the respondent records their answers, administered either in group settings or mailed individually to prospective respondents. Group administration requires survey staff to travel to the site of administration. This practice can achieve a high completion rate due to the presence of the survey team, unit leadership, and others in the unit, in addition to command allocation of specific time. The flexible individually administered surveys allow the respondent to complete the survey but usually on their own time. Unfortunately these surveys are less likely to be completed. Mail surveys often have long delay times between delivery and eventual return of the completed questionnaires. Individually administered surveys often require substantial follow-up to get respondents to complete the survey questionnaires. Follow-ups should usually occur one week to ten days after initial contact. Two to three follow-ups may be required to achieve an acceptable completion rate (usually strive to obtain 70 percent or higher). While the absence of interviewers during data collection avoids interviewer bias, there is little opportunity to clarify ambiguous survey questions and items.

Telephone interviewing is another modality of gathering survey responses (Dillman 2006). Telephone surveys more often occur as computer-assisted telephone interviewing (called CATI), where interviewers read screens from a pre-programmed survey instrument and enter respondent's answers directly into the computer program. Such telephone surveys are usually fairly expensive involving a large staff who call from telephone call centers. A less expensive method is the interactive voice response system, which involves pre-recording of the survey questions and responses, and the respondent answers questions by saying the response or touching a key pad on the telephone. There are several advantages to telephone surveys. Interviewers can actively encourage sampled individuals to participate in the survey, leading to higher response rates. By answering questions respondents have about the meaning of questions and response options, interviewers can clarify and increase comprehension. Disadvantages of telephone surveys include: time and expense in training interviewers, development of the computer-assisted survey screens, and potential for interviewer influence on respondents' answers.

A modality growing in popularity is the *web-based survey* (Bethlehem and Biffignandi 2012; Vehovar and Lozar 2008). Such surveys are initiated by informing prospective respondent (via email or mail) of a web site where he (she) is to go to complete a survey. Web surveys are relatively inexpensive once set-up. There are several advantages of web-based surveys. The data collection period is shortened because respondents are typically notified electronically (via email) and their responses are recorded instantaneously as they respond. Web-based data collection is less intrusive, allowing sensitive questions to be asked and minimizing interviewer influences on respondents' answers. Web-based surveys also allow for – complex skip patterns, implemented unbeknownst to the respondent, pop-up instructions to help clarify questions and response options, and lists of answer choices as drop downs. Distinct disadvantage of web-based surveys are the availability of Internet-connected computers as well as respondents' abilities to use computers and navigate the Internet.

In-person interviews are the final form of data collection described. Here, interviewers are recruited and trained. Interviewers also undergo extensive training in the survey content – questions and response options, and how to record responses uniformly across respondents. Interviewers then go to where the prospective respondent is physically located to conduct the interview. Nowadays, interviewers generally use personal computers, which display questions on successive screens (called computer-assisted personal interview or CAPI). The interviewer reads them to the respondent, and then enters the respondent's answers, questions and response options. The interviewer record respondents' answers which are then uploaded regularly uploaded to mainframe computers housing all respondents' answers. A major advantage of the personal interview is personal contact with respondents, which results in high cooperation and the lowest refusal rates. The interview also allows for longer, more complex questions and responses. Disadvantages include the high costs of interviewers personally contacting selected respondents, the longer data collection period, and the potential for interview influence on respondents' answers.

Whatever the modality, the importance of achieving a high response cannot be over-emphasized. While mail surveys and Internet surveys are less expensive, usually require much follow-up to achieve acceptable response rate. More person-contact methods – telephone or in-person interviews – achieve higher response rates. The survey team should develop a plan for follow-up whatever the modality of data collection. The planning includes a method to track and trace survey questionnaires to determine whether the respondent responded and for those who have not to follow-up with reminders. Knowing who responded and did not also allows for adjustments to the data set once data collection is closed. For example, having basic demographic characteristics for responders and nonresponders allows for the possibility of weight adjustments, i.e. for those respondents of specific characteristics who under-responded, the respondents who did answer might be weighted upward to represent them proportional to their occurrence in the sample.

Data collection method in the illustrative study

In the illustrative study, the survey sample consisted of about 31,000 reservists scattered across the U.S. Telephone numbers were not readily available, and if they were, the cost associated with telephone survey would be prohibitive, though likely to achieve a high response rate. In-person interviewing was also cost prohibitive – travel costs for survey staff visiting many locations and spending lengthy time periods collecting data. Mailing questionnaires to respondents was less expensive. Questionnaires were designed and printed as optical scannable forms, with identification codes. Each respondent was then matched to a code. In that way, responding and nonresponding reservists could be tracked for follow-up. It further facilitated the weighting of data set to more equitably represent under-responding reservist. Several reminders were sent out during the months of data collection. In follow-ups, nonresponding reservists were sent replacement questionnaire forms. Slightly over 41 percent of the sample completed and returned questionnaires. Another important aspect of data collection, especially before ending data collection, is examining the extent to which groups within the sample responded at similar rates. If not, then there may be problems in non-representativeness of the survey responses. In the case study, completion rates were compared across the sampling strata (gender, rank, and deployments status) and the percentage of personnel in each stratum in the initial sample was compared to the percentage that completed surveys. The percentage of personnel initially sampled who completed surveys by geographic location of the unit, U.S. commands, regional commands, and states, were compared. No systematic difference between the percentages of personnel who had been initially sampled and who had then completed surveys among the various geographic and individual characteristics were observed. If systematic differences are observed between respondents and non-respondents in known characteristics for each group, such as age, rank, gender, race, etc., then weights can derived to "weight up" under-responding groups and "weight down" over-responding groups. One method for weighting is the percentage represented doing population divided by the percentage in the sample. For example, if women represent 20 percent of the population, yet in the probability sample, only 15 percent respond, each responding woman would get a weight of 1.33.

The reporting

After the survey is conducted, pertinent questions are: What is to be done survey to the responses? Specifically, what is the design for the analysis and what results will the design yield? How will the results be structured for presentation to sponsors? How should the purpose and questions to be answered by the survey results, or how should the research questions, structure the analysis and presentation of findings?

Broadly, results can be presented as simply descriptive, comparative or associative (see chapters 8 and 9, Rea and Parker 1992). Descriptive presentations involve survey results presented for one group, e.g. the responding sample. Comparative presentation involves presentation of survey results for two or more groups. These groups are usually defined by the survey purpose, e.g. comparison of deployed versus nondeployed on readiness survey items. Finally, associative presentation involves relating survey results to important outcomes of interest. For example, regression analyses might be conducted in which perceptions of preparedness, deployment experiences, etc. are regressed on intentions to stay or leave reserve military service. Non-scientific audiences, likely policymakers sponsoring the survey, typically understand presentation of percentages better than presentation of means and other forms of descriptive statistics. In each presentation, it is important to report the appropriate confidence level of the finding or error associated with finding. For descriptive presentations, this is usually an error band or interval of confidence.

The illustrative study used all three approaches to analysis and reporting. Descriptively, percentages of soldiers in the sample who represented various categories in demographic subpopulations were presented. Descriptive analyses also included more complex scaling methods, such as exploratory factor analysis. Items representing various content of readiness (e.g. equipment, unit leadership, training, and family) underwent exploratory factor analysis to examine the extent to which all items could be summarily used to describe dimensions of readiness. The arrangement of items (i.e. items that correlated most with each factor) was used to derive summated, averaged scale scores for equipment, unit leadership, training, and family. Comparatively, responses of deployed soldiers to readiness items were compared before deployment (1990) and after deployment (1991). Similarly, responses of nondeployed soldiers to the same items were compared between 1990 and 1991, noting how these differed to the deployed soldiers' responses overtime. Finally, associative analyses included simple correlations and multiple regression analyses in which associations between the readiness scale scores and several outcomes were examined, such as perceived self-preparation for combat, unit preparation for combat, willingness to report for duty were activated, and intention to remaining remain in reserve military service.

Other important elements of reporting include details on sampling, data sources and analytic approaches. Description of the sampling design should include what the method was and how it was accomplished, and the number of eligible respondents and the number who completed. Summary statistics (percentages) of background characteristics of soldiers in the responding sample are compared to those of the population to provide a sense of respondent sample representativeness. Data source should be described, including the survey questionnaire and how it was developed, pretested, and how variables were constructed, in particular, scale score through factor analysis and reliability of ratings given to items comprising constructed variables or scales; and the use of any ancillary data sets. The analytic approach or design should be described, including the rationale and the steps taken in the analysis – both corresponding o the survey purpose and research questions.

Summary

Surveys are ever-present and expanding in their use in society. So too, the military has increasingly used surveys to gather information from soldiers – their backgrounds, experiences, and attitudes – for purposes of informing the development and implementation of policies. To this end, the present chapter provides an overview of the survey research method. The survey process is described in response to several key questions – the why (survey purpose), the what (survey questionnaire content), the who (selection of potential respondents), the how and when (data collection method), and finally, how best to summarize and present survey data. To show more concretely how these steps occur, an illustrative study was used throughout.

References

Ajzen, I. and Fishbein, M. (1980) *Understanding Attitudes and Predicting Social Behavior*, Englewood Cliffs, NJ: Prentice-Hall.

Arbuckle, J.L. (2009) *Amos 18 User's Guide*, Chicago, IL: SPSS, Inc.

Bethlehem, J. and Biffignandi, S. (2012) *Handbook of Web Surveys*, Wiley handbooks in survey methodology, Hoboken, NJ: Wiley.

Converse, J. (2009) *Survey Research in the United States: Roots and Emergence 1890–1960*, New Brunswick, NJ: Transaction.

Dawes, J. (2007) "Do Data Characteristics Change According to the Number of Scale Points Used? An experiment using 5-point, 7-point and 10-point scales" *International Journal of Market Research*, 50: 61–77.

Dillman, D.A. (2006) *Mail and Internet Surveys: The Tailored Design Method*, 2nd edn, Hoboken, NJ: Wiley.

Edwards, J.E., Thomas, M.D., Rosenfeld, P. and Booth-Kewley, S. (1997) *How to Conduct Organizational Surveys: A Step-by-Step Guide*, Thousand Oaks, CA: Sage.

Fowler, F.J. (2009) "Sampling," in *Survey Research Methods*, 4th edn, Thousand Oaks, CA: Sage, 19–47.

Gal, R. (1986) "Unit Morale: From a theoretical puzzle to an empirical illustration – an Israeli example," *Journal of Applied Social Psychology*, 16: 549–564.

Gal, R. and Manning, F.J. (1987) "Morale and Its Components: A cross-national comparison," *Journal of Applied Social Psychology*, 7: 369–391.

Garland, R. (1991) "The Mid-Point on a Rating Scale: Is it desirable?" *Marketing Bulletin*, 2: 70.

Gorsuch, R.L. (1983) *Factor Analysis*, Hillsdale, NJ: Erlbaum.

Griffith, J. (1988) "The Measurement of Group Cohesion in U.S. Army Units," *Basic and Applied Social Psychology*, 9: 149–171.

Griffith, J. (1995) "The Army Reserve Soldier in Operation Desert Storm: Perceptions of being prepared for mobilization, deployment, and combat," *Armed Forces & Society*, 21: 195–215.

Groves, R.M., Fowler, F.J., Couper, M.P., Lepkowski, J.M., Singer, E. and Tourangeau, R. (2009) *Survey Methodology*, Hoboken, NJ: Wiley.

Hauser, W.L. (1980) "The Will to Fight," in S. Sarkasian (ed.) *Combat Effectiveness: Cohesion, Stress and the Volunteer Military*, Beverly Hills, CA: Sage.

Jobe, J.B. and Mingay, D.J. (1990) "Cognitive Laboratory Approach to Designing Questionnaires for Surveys of the Elderly," *Public Health Reports*, 105: 518–524.

Kraut, A.I. (1996) "An Overview of Organizational Surveys," in A. Kraut (ed.) *Organizational Surveys: Tools for Assessment and Change*, 1–14, San Francisco, CA: Jossey-Bass.

Mental Health Advisory Team (MHAT) V (2008) *Operation Iraqi Freedom 06–08*, Office of the Army Surgeon General and U.S. Army Medical Command, Washington, D.C.

Meyer, J.P. and Allen, N.J. (1991) "A Three-Component Conceptualization of Organizational Commitment: Some methodological considerations," *Human Resource Management Review*, 1: 61–98.

O'Brien, K. (1993) "Improving Survey Questionnaires through Focus Groups," in D.L. Morgan (ed.) *Successful Focus Groups: Advancing the State of the Art*, 105–117, Newbury Park, CA: Sage.

Oskamp, S. and Schultz, P.W. (2005) *Attitudes and Opinions*, 3rd edn, Hillsdale, NJ: Erlbaum.

Pedhazur, E.J. and Schmelkin, L.P. (1991) *Measurement, Design, and Analysis: An Integrated Approach*, Hillsdale, NJ: Erlbaum.

Rea, L.M. and Parker, R.A. (1992) *Designing and Conducting Survey Research: A Comprehensive Guide*, San Francisco, CA: Jossey-Bass.

Rhoads, M.D. and Elig, T. (1988) *The Army Communications Objectives Measurement System (ACOMS): Survey Methods*, Arlington, VA: U.S. Army Research Institute for the Behavioral and Social Sciences.

Rossi, P.H., Wright, J.D. and Anderson, A.B. (1983) "Sample Surveys: History, current practice, and future prospects," in P.H. Rossi, J.D. Wright and A.B. Anderson (eds) *Handbook of Survey Research*, 1–20, Orlando, FL: Academic.

Schaubroeck, J.M., Hannah, S.T., Avolio, B.J., Kozlowski, S.W.J., Lord, R.G., Trevino, L.K., Dimotakis, N. and Peng, A.C. (2012) "Embedding Ethical Leadership within and across Organizational Levels," *Academy of Management Journal*, 55: 1053–1078.

Segal, M.W. and Harris, J. (1993) "What We Know about Army Families," Technical Report No. DAALO03–86-D-0001, U.S. Army Research Institute for the Behavioral and Social Sciences, Alexandria, VA.

Stouffer, S.A., Suchman, E.A., DeVinney, L.C., Star, S.A. and Williams, Jr., R.M. (1949) *The American Soldier: Adjustment during Army Life*, Vol. 1 in *Studies in Social Psychology in World War II*, Princeton, NJ: Princeton University Press.

Vehovar, V. and Lozar, M.K. (2008) "Overview: Online surveys," in N. Fielding, R.M. Lee, and G. Blank (eds) *The SAGE Handbook of Online Research Methods*, 177–194, Thousand Oaks, CA: Sage.

17

LONGITUDINAL DESIGN IN USING SURVEYS IN MILITARY RESEARCH

Common challenges and techniques

Jing Han and Manon Andres

J. Han, L.J. Xiao, and J. Han (2011) 'The adjustment of new recruits to military life in the Chinese Army: The longitudinal predictive power of MMPI-2,' *Journal of Career Assessment* **19(4): 392–404.**

The purpose of this study is to investigate the validity of the Minnesota Multiphasic Personality Inventory–2 (MMPI-2) as a screening tool for selecting candidates with the potential for adjusting to Chinese army life and for detecting recruits with psychological problems. The unique military environment and the intense training often lead to young recruit's maladjustment, and results in serious consequences such as reducing a troop's training quality as well as its combat effectiveness. One of the critical practices for ensuring the successful adjustment of military recruits is screening recruits with psychological assessment tools such as MMPI-2. These tests identify recruits with psychological problems or mental illness and then prevent them from entering the military in the first place. MMPI-2 is the most widely used and researched multi-scale psychopathology measurement tool in the world. In the early 1990s, MMPI-2 was also introduced and adopted as a personnel selection tool for duty in special operations within the Chinese military. However, there has been no empirical evidence about the validity of MMPI-2 in predicting the adjustment of Chinese military recruits. Because of this, it is unclear if MMPI-2 should even be used as a selection tool to ensure the quality of the military personnel, if its use cannot predict long-term success.

In order to contribute to a better understanding of the validity of MMPI-2 in predicting new recruit's adjustment in military life, the authors conducted a longitudinal study in the Chinese People's Liberation Army in Gansu Province. The authors obtained approval for the study from the brigade commander and assistance from the new recruits' training company commanders. Measures were obtained at four points in time. All 326 new recruits participated in the first round survey and completed the survey of MMPI-2. Using the new recruits' roster, authors randomly grouped these 326 participants into 10 teams of approximately 30 soldiers each. The authors distributed surveys

---

within each team and used the standardized instructions to all the participative teams. The authors tracked the same respondents and asked them to finish the measurement of the army life adjustment survey three more times, at the 3rd, the 9th, and 15th month. Because there was a conflict between data collection and the respondents' military duties, there was an attrition problem. Specifically, 192 of the original 326 soldiers who had participated in round one of the survey completed the final survey. Of these 192 respondents, 100 provided complete and usable responses across all four measurement-periods, resulting in a final response rate of 30.7 percent.

The authors adopted the latent growth modeling (LGM) approach to examine the longitudinal predictive power of MMPI-2 on the initial level of adjustment, as well as on the subsequent change rate of a new recruit's adjustment. The results showed that latent mean changes were positive for both interpersonal adjustment and training adjustment, indicating that, on average, these two forms of adjustment improved incrementally over time. In addition, MMPI-2 scores were negatively related to interpersonal adjustment at the initial stages as well as with the linear rate of change in interpersonal adjustment. Similarly, MMPI-2 had a significant negative relationship with training adjustment at initial stages as well as with the linear rate of change in training adjustment. Based on these findings, the authors concluded that mental health was a good indicator of adjustment that should be considered during the selection of military personnel. Recruits deemed mentally healthy based on the MMPI-2 would have fewer problems during the subsequent training process as compared to those who had poorer mental health.

The use of longitudinal design is gaining currency in military research (e.g. Gray et al. 2004; Milliken et al. 2007; Smith et al. 2011). The purpose of longitudinal (sometimes also referred to as cohort, panel, or time series) studies is to assess changes that occur in knowledge, opinions, actions, or perceptions in study samples over the course of time and the factors that influence the change. As such, it is a prospective way of studying phenomena: looking forward instead of looking back.

The illustrative study raises several interesting issues we plan to discuss throughout this chapter:

1 How to determine the time intervals between the measurement points?
2 How to maintain study participation over time and deal with attrition problems?
3 How to deal with sensitivity and privacy issues in military research?
4 How to match data across time?
5 How to analyze the longitudinal data?

Longitudinal design: What, how and why

Definition and types of longitudinal research

The longitudinal research design involves collecting data (e.g. through an experiment, survey, or archive) from a sample drawn from a specified population at two or more points in time; this is distinct from cross-sectional designs consisting of measurements at a single occasion. Three main types of longitudinal design can be distinguished: panel, cohort, and times series designs.

In the longitudinal panel survey, a representative sample of respondents (a panel) is surveyed repeatedly, over time. A researcher could, for example, select a group of university alumni and survey them at different points in time and ask them similar questions, for instance, to assess (individual) changes in their habits. Cohort studies track a specific subpopulation over time of individuals who share a predetermined event or characteristic (e.g. individuals who were born or married in the same year). A researcher could, for example, select a group of university alumni who graduated in a certain year and monitor them at regular intervals for a specified amount of time. Whereas panel and cohort studies sample individuals, times series designs examine aggregated organizational data over time. In time series designs, the same variables are studied at different points in time (e.g. monthly or annually), usually with the aim of examining trends and explaining variability over time. For instance, these studies can address annual military expenditures or rates of domestic violence or alcohol use in certain areas at various points in time.

Usually the purpose of longitudinal studies is to examine causalities among variables, and explain or predict changes, developments, and dynamics over time. Researchers need to tailor the research design to the research purpose and questions.

Different aims and designs

If the purpose is to examine specific behavioral or attitudinal changes across time, researchers usually trace the same respondents and measure the targeted behaviors or attitudes repeatedly. The illustrative study tracked the same 326 new recruits in the Chinese military and measured their military life adjustment three times in order to have a dynamic view of adjustment changes over time. A longitudinal study conducted in the Netherlands, which followed military personnel and their spouses along the cycles of deployment to an operation abroad (e.g. Andres et al. 2012a/b), is another example. Survey data were collected at three points in time: before, during and after the deployment separating the partners. One of the main aims of this study was to assess changes over time, for instance with respect to couples' relationship satisfaction.

If the research objective is to assess the power of independent variables (X) in predicting changes in a dependent variable (Y), one possible design is to measure the independent and dependent variables separately at different times. As described in the illustrative study, the researchers aimed to examine the predictive power of MMPI-2 on new recruits' adjustment to military life and therefore distributed a four-wave survey. In the first round, respondents filled out the surveys that contained the measurement of the independent variable: MMPI-2. Then, researchers tracked the same respondents across multiple follow-up measurements and asked them to fill out the forms measuring the dependent variable, which was adjustment to military life.

Another strategy is to repeatedly assess the same variables, which was done in the aforementioned Dutch study, in order to control for earlier scores on the variables (see also Britt and Dawson 2005). For instance, relationship satisfaction before the deployment was considered to be an important predictor of relationship satisfaction afterwards. That is, if couples are less satisfied or already experience relationship problems before the separation, they are likely to experience the same or worse afterwards. Applying this design allows the researchers to examine what best predicts relationship satisfaction after deployment, controlling for the effects of earlier relationship satisfaction. Moreover, this design allows for the examination of relationships between the variables within (cross-sectional) and across time frames (longitudinal). For instance, it is interesting to assess the specific stressors and levels of distress in each phase of the deployment, in addition to the prediction of distress over time.

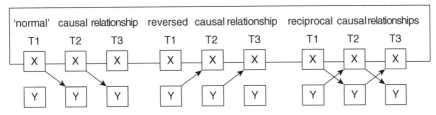

Figure 17.1 Three types of causal relationships

In general, if the research question is about testing the causal relationship between two constructs, one can collect data from the same respondents or independent samples drawn from the same population at two or more points in time (see Lang et al. 2011; Schuman et al. 1985). Between-wave changes in the independent variables (X) should be mirrored by between-wave changes in the dependent variable (Y). Four criteria must be met to interpret an effect as a causal effect.

Four criteria to interpret an effect as a causal effect (De Lange et al. 2003)

- The independent and dependent variables that attempt to measure the underlying theoretical concepts in the hypotheses correlate significantly.
- The independent variable precedes the dependent variable in time.
- The effect is not due to third variables.
- There is a plausible theoretical argument for the effect of X on Y.

Examining the nature, magnitude and (causal) direction of relationships between constructs is an important part of longitudinal research. Various kinds of causal relationships can be distinguished, including the "normal" causal relationships (i.e. hypothesized cause and effect; X causes Y), reversed causal relationships (i.e. effects opposite to the hypothesized cause and effects; Y causes X), and reciprocal causal relationships (X and Y mutually influence each other over time) (Figure 17.1) (De Lange et al. 2003; Zapf et al. 1996). The study among Dutch military personnel (Andres, Moelker and Soeters, 2012b) demonstrated, for instance, that work-family interference was significantly correlated with turnover intentions, within and across time frames. Although turnover intentions have usually been regarded as an outcome of work-family interference, the data showed that this relation can not be viewed as unidirectional. That is, taking other relevant variables into account, the variables mutually influenced each other over time. The authors provide a plausible theoretical reasoning for this – related to employees who think about leaving the job being more vulnerable to experiencing work–family conflict – but also urge for more empirical evidence and refining theory.

Advantages and disadvantages of longitudinal designs

A number of advantages are associated with longitudinal design. The greatest advantage is that one can identify individual variations in growth and test causal hypotheses with longitudinal data. As illustrated earlier, one can examine whether prior levels of an independent variable can predict changes over time in a dependent variable. One can also examine whether changes over time in an independent variable correspond to changes in a dependent variable over the same period of time. The illustrative study adopted the longitudinal design with the purpose to test the predictive power of MMPI-2 on the new recruits' adjustment changes over time. They found that new recruits' low scores of MMPI-2 (meaning the new recruits have little mental health problems) during the soldiers' first week in the military training camps predicted an increasing adjustment towards military life assessed the 3rd, the 9th, and 15th month after the new soldiers' formal incorporation into the military companies. Another advantage of longitudinal design in the illustrative study is that it helps reduce the common method bias (i.e. variance that is attributable to the measurement method rather than the constructs the measures represent; see Podsakoff et al. 2003) caused by both self-report measures of MMPI-2 and adjustment. The correlation between MMPI-2 and adjustment can be simply a reflection of response bias, that is one's tendency to keep consistent in one's responses at one particular time of measurement, rather than the genuine correlation between the two constructs. Therefore, using longitudinal design and separating the measurement times of MMPI-2 and adjustment can reduce the effect of such response bias. Additional advantages of the longitudinal design include, yet are not limited to (1) no reliance on self-reported retrospective data, (2) the flexibility of adding new variables after the first data collection, and (3) the accumulation of a large number of variables.

Despite the advantages, longitudinal studies also have disadvantages. First, longitudinal studies are more time-consuming and costly than cross-sectional studies because of the personnel costs, the techniques needed to maintain contact with respondents over time, the costs of incentives, and the need for detailed documentation of data. Second, respondents tend appear consistent in their responses across studies, especially in longitudinal surveys. Therefore, respondents may be reluctant to report any opinions or behaviors that appear inconsistent with what they had reported during earlier studies, which may mask the genuine changes over time. Or, the other way around, participation in the initial study may sensitize respondents to the issues under investigation. As a result, respondents may give special attention to these issues, which may influence their responses in the follow-up study.

Challenges and techniques

Besides the above-mentioned advantages and disadvantages, there are many challenges researchers encounter during the process of conducting longitudinal studies in military settings. We summarize the common challenges and provide some general techniques and tips to solve these problems.

How to determine the time intervals between the measurement points?

Longitudinal design fundamentally involves collecting data at multiple times, so first researchers must decide the number and time points of the measurements. The length of longitudinal research projects range between several days or weeks to many years. How the measurement occasions are defined can affect the efficiency of the study. The longer the period in which the study takes place, the more likely it is that some external changes occur possibly affecting the data collected. Individuals may also change over the course of data collection procedures. Therefore, the passage of time may cause changes in hypotheses or even research questions. It is assumed that at least three measurement occasions allow for an accurate estimate of change, but the more measurement occasions, the more accurate the estimation of change over time (Mroczek 2007; Ployhart and Vandenberg 2010).

Collins (2006) argues that theory informs about the appropriate time lag between measurements. For instance, different time points may be determined if change is assumed to be recurrent or to happen at specific moments. Additionally, a thorough literature search of previous studies will provide a reliable guideline in selecting time intervals. In practice, researchers need to choose time intervals according to their research purposes and in accordance with practical constraints such as costs, respondent burden, recall difficulties, and the frequency of transitions of interest.

In the illustrative study, measures were obtained at four points in time. The first measurement of MMPI-2 was conducted during the soldiers' first week in the military training camps, when they were acquiring basic military knowledge and skills. The researchers selected this period of time to measure MMPI-2 because one of the research goals was to test the predictive power of MMPI-2 on new recruits' adjustment of military life. As said, they then tracked the same respondents and asked them to finish the measurement of the army life adjustment survey three more times, at the 3rd, the 9th and 15th month after the new soldiers' formal incorporation into the military companies. The time intervals were selected based on prior literature of newcomers' adjustment, which gave a better view of the dynamic changes of new recruits' adjustment to military life. Moreover, equal spacing among time intervals has been suggested to be either optimal or close to optimal for all situations considered (Morrison 1970).[1]

In the Dutch study, military personnel and their families were followed along the cycles of deployment to the operation abroad. The researchers aimed at collecting data at each stage of the deployment, that is, the preparation phase, the actual separation, and the reintegration phase. This was done in order to examine the specific challenges and experiences in each stage of the deployment as well as to assess changes in experiences, attitudes, and perceptions over time. The specific times of measurement were chosen on the basis of a literature review. For instance, literature suggests that service members' reintegration into family life after their return may be a turbulent time and that family functioning generally stabilizes within three months after the reunion. Therefore, the researchers chose to perform the final measurement three months after the return. The time intervals between the data waves were equally spaced and were four or five months, depending on the length of the deployment to the mission abroad (which varied between four and six months).

How to maintain study participation over time and deal with attrition problems?

Perhaps every researcher in longitudinal study has to cope with the problem of participants' attrition. The main causes of attrition are losing track of participants and refusal to continue to participate for various reasons, such as research fatigue. Particularly in military settings, keeping track of respondents over time is challenging as military personnel acquire other positions, move to other bases, or are sent abroad on a regular basis. Moreover, given the specific conditions in which they engage (e.g. challenging situations that require all their time and effort) and the amount of research attention already paid to military personnel, they may feel reticent about study participation or just may be research-tired. However, participant retention is crucial to the success of the study; high attrition rates threaten the internal validity and generalization of the study results. Therefore, researchers should include procedures to maintain participants' cooperation throughout the study.

Although attrition cannot be avoided, researchers can employ various techniques to keep track of respondents and to keep participants motivated and engaged with the study. In this way researchers can maximize retention and minimize non-response. Such techniques include for instance sending a reminder letter or postcard (Welch et al. 2009); having personal contact between the data collections to obtain up-to-date address information and maintain interest in the study; keeping participants informed about the nature, purpose and progress of the study and sharing preliminary descriptive results (e.g. through websites, newsletters, or information packages); and providing incentives for participation (see for instance Hunt and White 1998 for a detailed discussion on tracking and retaining participants in longitudinal studies). Incentives that are valued by the respondents, such as a small cash award, a voucher or gift card, have been shown to have a positive effect on the response rate (Armstrong 1975).

In addition to encouraging participation and expressing appreciation for cooperation in the study, it is important that researchers foster participants' perceptions of the importance of the study. Moreover, researchers should disclose fully and clearly why participants' responses are valued and how the data will be used. Laurie et al. (1999) have delineated several important points, including quality control at all stages of the longitudinal study, a specified number of follow-up visits, telephone contact, and clarity of survey content. In addition, researchers can use a repeated cross-sectional design, revolving panel design, or multiple cohort panel design to prevent or reduce the problem of participant attrition (see Menard 2002 for details).

In the illustrative study conducted in the Chinese military, the researchers used their military contact and obtained approval for the study from the brigade commander and assistance from the new recruits' training company commanders. We explained to the respondents that the test was used for research purposes only. This top-down approach of getting access to the sample ensured the response rate to a certain extent; however, the attrition problem still existed because there was a conflict between data collection and the respondents' military duties.

Obtaining detailed information about the reasons for non-response helps understanding participant loss. Furthermore, non-response analysis is needed to assess whether those who dropped out along data collection procedures differ significantly from those who completed all measurements. Non-response analyses include: examining whether demographic characteristics differ at baseline and in follow-up data waves to see if non-response is selective; assessing whether respondents and drop-outs significantly differ on their scores on the study-variables at baseline; and examining whether the relations between the study-variables differ for respondents and drop-outs at baseline. It is important to realize that these non-response analyses are not solutions to the non-response problem, but rather means of attempting to reduce its biasing effect on the survey estimates. Detailed technical aspects of these analyses are beyond the goal of this chapter (see Kalton 1983).

How to deal with sensitivity and privacy issues in military research?

Confidentiality and anonymity are two distinct and very important concepts, which need to be considered by researchers in designing and managing the research project. The privacy of the study participants should be protected in any research, though it may require extra attention in longitudinal designs. Respondents are more likely to drop out or refuse to participate if they do not perceive their information to be held in confidence. For instance, in studies that aim at examining changes over time, the researcher needs to link or match individual data collected at multiple points in time. Usually, a code is used to be able to do this (we discuss this in more detail in the next section). Hence, in some cases one cannot claim that the research design is strictly anonymous. If a study is completely anonymous, it is impossible for the researcher to link the data to an individual. Similarly, if face-to-face or telephone interviews are conducted, the researcher knows who provided the data.

Thus, researchers should ensure confidentiality and inform research participants about the procedures of data collection and the use of data. It is wise to receive both individual informed consent and institutional approval when conducting a study in military settings.

Researchers should also explain and make sure that personal information of the participants, such as names and home addresses – necessary for the researcher to collect data of the same respondents at multiple points in time – are kept in a safe place, which is only accessible to the researcher and that the information will be destroyed once the research will have been completed. Moreover, in the dissemination of the study results, researchers should make sure that data or information cannot be traced to individuals on the basis of demographic characteristics. In military settings, this means being careful when presenting results while providing for instance information about gender, rank, and unit. When the number of individuals who meet that profile is very small (e.g. one female general in unit X), readers of the research report may easily identify the person who provided that particular information.

In the illustrative study, the researchers randomly grouped 326 new recruits into 10 teams. Surveys were distributed in each team with the standardized instructions. Participants were explained that the test was used for research purposes only and that the results would be interpreted at the aggregated level. The researchers emphasized that individual responses were kept confidential, so that respondents would have less evaluation apprehension and provide answers as candidly as possible.

In addition to the aforementioned ethical issues on anonymity and confidentiality, some research projects deal with sensitive topics. These topics may be central to the research objectives, but are perceived by participants as private or may produce some kind of risk or conflict (Lee 1993). Demonstrative of this issue is the study conducted among families of military personnel (e.g. Andres et al. 2012 a/b). Family issues such as the quality of family relationships are typically perceived to be private and personal. Hence, family members were approached with prudence and the researchers emphasized that participation in this study was voluntary and that one was free (not) to answer any question. Participants were reassured confidentiality in the introduction of the questionnaire and again when introducing the sensitive topics.

Sensitive questions should not be asked at the beginning of questionnaires; it is better to include these near the end. Respondents should be drawn into the process with easy and comfortable questions and become committed to complete the questionnaire. When research includes sensitive topics, researchers should be conscious of the methodological issues. For instance, participants may react differently to sensitive topics: they may be reluctant to answer the questions honestly if they are afraid of possible negative consequences, or they may be reluctant to answer sensitive questions at all.

How to match data across time?

One important goal of longitudinal research is to examine dynamics, changes and developments in behaviors or attitudes over time. Therefore, researchers may need to match data collected at multiple points in time. Several techniques can be applied to do this. Using identification codes (i.e. giving respondents a numerical designation) is a commonly used procedure in longitudinal research (Lee 1993). In the illustrative study, researchers got the roster of all the new recruits in a Chinese military garrison. They assigned a unique code to each new recruit, and pre-typed the code on the questionnaire before distributing the survey. This unique code was kept the same and used in the follow-up surveys in order to keep track of each participant and match their responses. Similar procedures were used in the Dutch study among military personnel and their families. The codes in this study were constructed by the researcher and only known by her. By using an invented code, rather than soldiers' registration numbers for instance, there were no chances that answers could be traced back to identifiable individuals by anyone other than the researcher. The codes solely allowed the researcher to re-contact respondents on subsequent data waves to send follow-up surveys and to link the data collected during the different data waves. The link between the codes and the personal information of the respondents was kept in a separate and secure place, accessible only to the researcher, and destroyed once the data collection was completed. The purpose of the identification codes was expounded in the accompanying letter.

Another strategy is to let the participants generate their own unique code (e.g. Yurek et al. 2008). They need to receive clear and specific instructions in order to make sure that the code will be unique for each participant and the same at each data wave. Usually, the code is a combination of personal information (letters and numbers/dates; see Yurek et al. 2008 for an example). Although errors and omissions can occur, this strategy is more anonymous, as the researcher is unable to link the data to an individual, though is able to link the data across time points.

How to analyze the longitudinal data?

Longitudinal studies usually generate large amounts of data and various techniques can be applied to analyze the data (e.g. Singer and Willett 2003), depending on the research questions to be answered, the assumptions of the statistical tests, and the presence of missing data. In longitudinal research, missing data is quite common. Respondents may drop out in the course of data collection or, for instance in the case of sensitive topics, may leave certain questions unanswered. Researchers should decide how to deal with missing data. Various approaches exist: there is not one best method (see for instance Menard 2002 for a detailed description; Collins 2006). Furthermore, if necessary or preferred, weight variables could be used to mitigate under-representation of certain groups of people (Ruspini, 2000), such as service members in certain ranks.

Exploratory quantitative data analyses may focus on assessing means and standard deviations to see if the scores on the variables significantly differ at different points in time. Furthermore, exploratory analyses usually include analyses of correlations to assess (a) cross-sectional correlations between the different variables at each data wave, (b) correlations between the same variables at different data waves (i.e. stabilities or autocorrelations), and (c) longitudinal or cross-lagged correlations between the different variables at different data waves. Subsequently, hierarchical regression analyses can be performed to examine cross-sectional and longitudinal predictors of (change in) the dependent variable. Control variables must be included in the first step. In the next steps, one can include the dependent variable at Time 1, the independent variables at Time 1, and the independent variables at Time 2; to examine whether changes in the dependent variable are related to changes in the independent variable (Zapf et al. 1996). In order to assess or rule out reverse causation, that is, whether Y may also influence X, one can perform the same procedure, treating the independent as the dependent variable and the dependent as the independent variable.

Researchers should be aware that when they measure the same individuals repeatedly, the observations are not independent. The repeated observations in longitudinal studies are usually (positively) correlated. The sequential nature of the measures also indicates that certain types of correlation structures may arise. Therefore, longitudinal data often requires more sophisticated statistical techniques to address the issues of linear dependence and autocorrelation of variables (see Singer and Willett 2003 for a review). Structural equation modeling (SEM) techniques are popular to analyze longitudinal data in order to control for the measurement errors across measurement occasions (Chan and Schmitt 2000; Lang et al. 2011). A popular method for the analysis of longitudinal data is Hierarchical Linear Modeling (HLM, see Porter and Umbach, 2001). In the Chinese illustrative study, researchers adopted the latent growth modeling (LGM) approach to examine the longitudinal predictive power of MMPI-2 on new recruits' adjustment. There are a number of advantages to using LGM for modeling individual differences in change trajectories such as initial status and change functions (see Chan and Schmitt 2000 for a detailed review).

Conclusion

Conducting longitudinal research is a complex and time-consuming process. It has several advantages over cross-sectional designs. However, being aware of the purpose of longitudinal research and the advantages and disadvantages, researchers should consciously consider which design is necessary for meeting their objectives, and how to tackle potential problems associated with their research design.

Although we mainly focused on quantitative longitudinal research, longitudinal research designs can also be qualitative. Depending on the study objectives, researchers can choose for either a quantitative or qualitative approach, or a combination of the two. Where longitudinal quantitative research designs usually aim at measuring the extent of change and what factors are related to the change, a longitudinal qualitative research design can provide a deeper understanding of why change occurs and how the factors or mechanisms that produce change operate (Molloy et al. 2002). Just as in cross-sectional designs, a mixed-method longitudinal design can be a powerful mix, and provide complementary insights.

Note

1 There are different opinions regarding the necessity of ensuring equal spacing in measurement occasions (see Mitchell and James, 2001). We suggest it is more important that measurement occasions occur with enough frequency to be able to detect the hypothesized changes.

References

Andres, M., Moelker, R. and Soeters, J. (2012a) "A longitudinal study of partners of deployed personnel from the Netherlands' Armed Forces," *Military Psychology*, 24(3): 270–288.

Andres, M., Moelker, R. and Soeters, J. (2012b) "The work-family interface and turnover intentions over the course of project-oriented assignments abroad," *International Journal of Project Management*, 30(7): 752–759.

Armstrong, J.S. (1975) "Monetary incentives in mail surveys," *Public Opinion Quarterly*, 39(1): 111–116.

Britt, T.W. and Dawson, C.R. (2005) "Predicting work-family conflict from workload, job attitudes, group attributes, and health: A longitudinal study," *Military Psychology*, 17(3): 203–227.

Chan, D. and Schmitt, N. (2000) "Inter-individual differences in intra-individual changes in proactivity during organizational entry: A latent growth modeling approach to understanding newcomer adaptation," *Journal of Applied Psychology*, 85(2): 190–210.

Collins, L.M. (2006) "Analysis of longitudinal data: The integration of theoretical model, temporal design, and statistical model," *Annual Review of Psychology*, 57: 505–528.

De Lange, A.H., Taris, T.W., Kompier, M.A.J., Houtman, I.L.D. and Bongers, P.M. (2003) "'The very best of the millennium'": Longitudinal research and the demand-control-(support) model," *Journal of Occupational Health Psychology*, 8(4): 282–305.

Gray, M.J., Bolton, E.E. and Litz, B.T. (2004) "A longitudinal analysis of PTSD symptom course: Delayed-onset PTSD in Somalia Peacekeepers," *Journal of Consulting and Clinical Psychology*, 72(5): 909–913.

Han, J., Xiao, L.J. and Han, J. (2011) "The adjustment of new recruits to military life in the Chinese Army: The longitudinal predictive power of MMPI 2," *Journal of Career Assessment*, 19(4): 392–404.

Hunt, J.R. and White, E. (1998) "Retaining and tracking cohort study members," *Epidemiologic Reviews*, 20(1): 57–70.

Kalton, G. (1983) *Compensating for Missing Survey Data*, Ann Arbor, MI: Survey Research Center, University of Michigan.

Lang, J., Bliese, P.D., Lang, J.W.B. and Adler, A.B. (2011) "Work gets unfair for the depressed: Cross-lagged relations between organizational justice perceptions and depressive symptoms," *Journal of Applied Psychology*, 96(3): 602–618.

Laurie, H., Smith, R. and Scott, L. (1999) "Strategies for reducing nonresponse in a longitudinal panel survey," *Journal of Official Statistics*, 15(2): 269–282.

Lee, R.M. (1993) *Doing Research on Sensitive Topics*, London: Sage Publications.

Menard, S.W. (2002) *Longitudinal Research: Quantitative Applications in the Social Sciences* (2nd edn), Thousand Oaks, CA: Sage.

Milliken, C.S., Auchterlonie, J.L and Hoge, C.W. (2007) "Longitudinal assessment of mental health problems among active and reserve component soldiers returning from the Iraq war," *Journal of American Medical Association*, 298(18): 2141–2148.

Mitchell, T.R. and James, L.R. (2001) "Building better theory: Time and the specification of when things happen.' *Academy of Management Review*, 26(4): 530–547.

Molloy, D., Woodfield, K. and Bacon, J. (2002) "Longitudinal qualitative research approaches in evaluation studies," Working paper number 7, London: Department of Work and Pensions. Available at: http://research.dwp.gov.uk/asd/asd5/WP7.pdf (accessed January 22, 2013).

Morrison, D.F. (1970) "The optimal spacing of repeated measurements," *Biometrics*, 26(2): 281–290.

Mroczek, D.K. (2007) "The analysis of longitudinal data in personality research," in R.W. Robins, R.C. Fraley and R.F. Krueger (eds) *Handbook of Research Methods in Personality Psychology*, New York: Guilford Press, 543–556.

Ployhart, R.E. and Vandenberg, R.J. (2010) "Longitudinal research: The theory, design, and analysis of change," *Journal of Management*, 36(1): 94–120.

Podsakoff, P.M., MacKenzie, S.B., Lee, J.Y. and Podsakoff, N.P. (2003) "Common method biases in behavioural research: A critical review of the literature and recommended remedies," *Journal of Applied Psychology*, 88(5): 879–903.

Porter, S.R. and Umbach, P.D. (2001) "Analyzing faculty workload data using multilevel modeling," *Research in Higher Education*, 42(2): 171–196.

Ruspini, E. (2000) "Longitudinal research in the social sciences," *Social Research Update*, 20, Guildford: University of Surrey. Available at: http://sru.soc.surrey.ac.uk/SRU28.html (accessed January 14, 2013).

Schuman, H., Steeh, C. and Bobo, L. (1985) *Racial Attitudes in America: Trends and Interpretations*, Cambridge, MA: Harvard University Press.

Singer, J.D. and Willett, J.B. (2003) *Applied Longitudinal Data Analysis: Modeling Change and Event Occurrence*, London: Oxford University Press.

Smith, T., Jacobson, I., Hooper, T., LeardMann, C., Boyko, E., Smith, B., Gackstetter, G., Wells, T., Amoroso, P., Gray, G., Riddle, J., Ryan, M., and Ryan, M. (2011) "Health impact of US military service in a large population-based military cohort: Findings of the Millennium Cohort Study, 2001–2008," *BMC Public Health*, 11(1): 69.

Welch, K.E., LeardMann, C.A., Jacobson, I.G., Speigle, S.J., Smith, B., Smith, T.C., Ryan, M.A. (2009) "Postcards encourage participant updates," *Epidemiology*, 20(2): 313–314.

Yurek, L.A., Vasey, J. and Sullivan Havens, D. (2008) "The use of self-generated identification codes in longitudinal research," *Evaluation Review*, 32(5): 435–452.

Zapf, D., Dormann, C. and Frese, M. (1996) "Longitudinal studies in organizational stress research: A review of the literature with reference to methodological issues," *Journal of Occupational Health Psychology*, 1(2): 145–169.

18

MULTILEVEL ANALYSIS

The examination of hierarchical data in military research

Irina Goldenberg and Joseph Soeters

J.M. Schaubroeck, S.T. Hannah, B.J. Avolio, S.W.J. Kozlowski, R.G. Lord, L.K. Trevino, N. Dimotakis and A.C. Peng (2012) 'Embedding ethical leadership within and across organizational levels,' *Academy of Management Journal* 55(5): 1053–1078.

Like most organizations the military is made up of hierarchical layers. Starting at the bottom layer, the organization consists of individual soldiers, teams or squads, platoons, companies, battalions, brigades and sometimes divisions. One level is nested into another, together constituting the military organization.

Most organizational research, including military research, focuses on what is happening among samples of employees belonging to organizational units at the same level, which in this case translates into soldiers belonging to squads or platoons. Horizontal or within-unit research, however, disregards influences on individual behaviour that stem from other – 'higher' – organizational levels. To get a better understanding of what is happening in complex organizations one needs to study cross-level linkages in addition to within-level influences.

The study by Schaubroeck and associates examines the impact of ethical leadership and culture in the US Army, at the squad, platoon and company level, on the ethical behaviour of soldiers in those squads, platoons and companies. On the basis of theoretical and practical insights, it was assumed that ethical leadership and culture not only impact soldiers' behaviour within the same hierarchical layer, but also across layers, directly through trickle-down or bypassing effects, indirectly through higher-level leadership on lower-level ethical culture, or by moderating the within-level relations.

Soldier's ethical behaviour was measured via the perceived frequency of transgressions against non-combatants (e.g. mistreatment of bystanders or causing unnecessary damage) and against the Army (e.g. stealing), as well as with respect to peer exemplary behaviour and moral efficacy. Ethical leadership was measured by means of perceptions of the leader's style of discussing ethical issues

(continued)

(continued)

and setting examples, whereas ethical culture was measured by scoring on standard practices, for instance issuing penalties, in the squad, platoon or company. To assess these variables, soldiers in the respective squads rated squad ethical leadership and culture, the squad leaders rated the platoon leadership and culture, whereas platoon leaders and sergeants rated the ethical leadership and culture of their company.

The data were collected in a cross-sectional survey of 2,048 US soldiers engaged in combat operations in Iraq in 2009. The questionnaire data was aggregated and combined with multiple other ratings into statistical information on 172 squads (consisting of the scores of at least 4 members), 78 platoons (consisting of at least 2 squads) and 40 companies (consisting of on average 4 platoons). These data were used for elaborate multilevel model testing.

The results largely confirmed the hypotheses. In particular, the analyses demonstrated that ethical leadership and culture show strong horizontal, within-level effects (i.e. soldiers within the same squads have more similar scores compared to soldiers from different squads). This is the well-known immediate supervisor effect. In addition, the data revealed important direct vertical effects of leadership at one level on the adjacent lower-level leadership, which is the cascade- or trickle-down effect. There were strong indirect effects as well, indicating that ethical leadership at the company level exhibits significant effects on lower levels, including effects on ethical culture at both the platoon and squad levels. Another important finding was that ethical leadership at a lower level had a stronger positive influence on ethical culture at that level when the leader at the next higher level was reported to exhibit a high level of ethical leadership. This was a notable moderating effect of ethical leadership at higher levels. Apparently, leadership at the higher levels can facilitate or reinforce lower-level leadership, whether in a positive or in a detrimental direction.

This large-scale, complex study underlines the importance of the combined impact of ethical leadership and culture within and across hierarchical levels, i.e. throughout the whole military organization. Clearly, the 'final proof' could not been given, as this would have required a longitudinal, experimental design that would have been replicated a number of times in different contexts. Yet, the findings of this study are unequivocal. Their practical implications are clearly evident and can be instructed in courses and training programmes in military organizations all over the world.

In many research applications such as our ethical leadership illustrative study, data is hierarchically structured and consists of lower-level observations nested within higher levels. Multilevel models are developed for analysing these hierarchically structured data. Consider Figure 18.1: soldiers are *nested* in squads, squads are nested in platoons, which are nested in companies or more generally in larger military environments (Army, Navy, Air Force). In such cases there is often a significant relationship not only between individual-level variables and the outcome or construct of interest, but also between group level variables and these outcomes, as well as between the individual and group level variables themselves. As in our illustrative study, this suggests that understanding the effects of both the individual and group level or contextual variables, as well as how they work together, is important to understanding the phenomenon under study (Rousseau 1985; George and James 1994; Hox 2010).

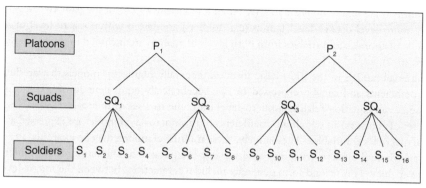

Figure 18.1 Hierarchical structuring of military organizations

Accordingly, multilevel data analysis is becoming increasingly popular in many fields and disciplines, including military research, because it allows researchers to take into account how individual-level processes or outcomes operate within different levels of analysis, such as organizations, geographical locations, time frames, or other higher-level units. For example, soldiers' organizational commitment may be predicted by perceptions of organizational support and satisfaction with leadership at the individual-level of analysis, leadership style at the unit level of analysis, and organizational culture at the service/environment (Army, Navy, Air Force) level of analysis. Further, it is then also possible to model both within-level interactions among predictors (e.g. between individuals' perceptions of organizational support and individuals' satisfaction with leadership), as well as cross-level interactions (e.g. between unit leadership style and organizational culture), as shown in the ethical leadership illustrative study.

Quantitative and qualitative applications

The term multilevel data analysis or multilevel modelling refers to a set of related approaches for analysing quantitative data measured at two or more levels of analysis. Although quantitative analyses are predominant in this field of research, qualitative multilayer studies are recognized as important. In his famous study about the accidental shootdown of US Black Hawks over Northern Iraq, Snook (2000) was not satisfied with either individual-level accounts (why did the F-15 pilots misidentify the Black Hawks?), the group level account (why did the AWACS fail to intervene?) or organization-level account (why wasn't the Army aviation detachment integrated into task force operations?). Instead of just listing the separate layer-explanations, which are interesting and important themselves, Snook developed a theory that explains the mishap in terms of cross-level mechanisms. His 'practical drift' theory emphasizes the slow, steady uncoupling of practice from written procedures, occurring throughout the whole organization and leading to this tragic event in the military that is less exceptional than one would perhaps expect.

Despite this impressive multilevel qualitative study, multilevel research is predominantly developed and applied to quantitative research. Multilevel models are called by various names such as hierarchical models, mixed models, cluster models, growth curve models, contextual models, and random coefficient models. These models extend traditional linear models to take into account situations in which individual-level data is clustered or nested into a higher-order structure. The lowest-level measurements are often said to be *micro-level*, and all higher-level measurements are said to be *macro level* (Kreft and de Leeuw 1999). In the basic two-level linear model, micro-level data or level 1 units (e.g. soldiers) are nested within macro level or level 2 units (e.g. platoons), and variables from both levels of analysis are included in the mode l (Bliese and Jex 2002).

Multilevel models in the most basic form are generally regression models that are linear in their coefficients and can be expressed in two algebraically equivalent forms. They may be expressed as an equation relating a micro-level outcome to a set of micro-level variables along with a set of equations in which the coefficients of this micro-level model are expressed as functions of macro level variables. Alternatively, these multilevel models may be expressed in a single equation where the micro-level outcome variable is expressed as a function of both micro and macro variables. This second form generally includes interactions between the micro-level and macro level variables, or cross-level interactions, to be discussed below (DiPrete and Forristal 1994).

Several terms related to variable level are important to note in the consideration of multilevel data analysis (Chan 2006). *Global variables* are those that are measured at their natural level (Hox 2010). For example, soldier years of service and gender are global variables at the individual-level, and platoon size is a global variable at the group level. It is of note that variables measured at a given level may be "moved" to a higher level through *aggregation*, which entails grouping lower-level units to form a smaller number of higher-level units. For example, soldiers' morale scores may be aggregated by computing a mean morale score to form unit morale scores. Such new variables aggregated to a higher level from a lower level are referred to as *analytical variables*. Similarly, variables can be moved from a higher level to a lower level through *disaggregation*, which entails decomposing variables at a higher level into a larger number of lower units. For example, in the disaggregation of platoon size to the soldier level, each soldier within a platoon is assigned the same value for platoon size. This creation of a new variable resulting from disaggregation provides information on the higher-level context (platoon) to the lower-level units (soldiers), and thus such variables disaggregated to a lower level from a higher level are referred to as *contextual variables* (Chan 2006). However, it is important to note that creation of such variables should be done judiciously with significant concern for construct validity. A detailed framework specifying functional relationships between constructs at different levels that may be used for the composition of such variables is discussed in Chan (1998).

Relations between the levels of analysis

Traditional methods of data analysis, such as ordinary least squares (OLS) regression models, that attempt to include both individual and contextual-level variables are not well-suited to understand these multilevel effects. In particular, the clustering of individual-level observations within these higher-level or contextual units violates the assumption of independent errors, which leads to biases in both the parameter estimates and standard errors (Bliese et al. 2002). Of course, individual-level observations within the same group are not truly independent because there is some underlying similarity resulting from the group membership that leads to dependence among the observations and the errors within these group level units (Fullerton et al. 2007).

A significant advantage of multilevel modelling then is that independence of observations is not required, and in actuality, independence is often violated at each level of analysis (Tabachnick and Fidell 2007). For example, recruits within Army combat training sessions are likely to influence each other or be influenced by their instructors, and are therefore likely to be more similar than recruits in other Army combat training sessions. Similarly, recruits within

Army training schools are likely to be more similar than recruits in different training schools. In addition, there may be interaction across levels of the hierarchy (or cross-level interactions, as in our illustrative study and as discussed below). For example, student characteristics within Army training sessions may interact with the approaches of instructors at the session level. As such, ignoring the hierarchical or nested nature of the data and analysing it as if it was on the same level can lead to both interpretational and statistical errors (Chan 2006; Dansereau et al. 2006; Snijders and Bosker 1999).

One of the main types of interpretive error is the *ecological fallacy*, also referred to as *the Robinson effect*, whereby relationships at the group level are thought to imply relationships at the individual-level (Hox 2010). For example if data on military services (e.g. Army, Navy, Air Force) is used to make inferences about individuals (e.g. soldiers, sailors, airmen or air-women). Failing to acknowledge the within-group variability that is present in the data can distort the relationships under examination (Heck and Thomas 2009). The ecological fallacy may be either positive or negative. A positive ecological fallacy occurs when a relationship at the group level (e.g. military families in communities where Military Family Resource Centres (MFRCs) provide a greater number of services are healthier) is used to make conclusions about the same relationship at the individual-level (e.g. military families that use MFRC services more frequently are healthier). A negative ecological fallacy occurs when a lack of relationship at a group level (e.g. there is no relationship between the proportion of soldiers in a unit that suffer from posttraumatic stress disorder and units' rates of attrition) translate into conclusions about a relationship at the individual-level (e.g. there is no relationship between posttraumatic stress disorder and attrition from the military). In this case the group is erroneously used as the unit of analysis, which results in a lower n (based on the number of groups instead of the number of individuals within each group). Statistically, this type of analysis leads to increased standard errors and reduced statistical power, and therefore a greater likelihood of committing Type II error, or erroneously failing to observe an effect when it actually exists (Chan 2006).

The other main type of interpretative error that may result from ignoring the hierarchical nature of data is the *atomistic fallacy*, sometimes referred to as the *individualistic fallacy*, whereby conclusions about group level variables are inferred based on data collected at an individual-level. For example, soldiers who have been deployed more frequently have a stronger warrior (versus peacekeeper) identity, therefore leadership in platoons that deploy more often place greater emphasis on the warrior identity. Statistically, Type I error (i.e. erroneously concluding that an effect exists when in fact it does not) is inflated if analyses performed at the lower level are used to make inferences at the group level because analyses are based on too many degrees of freedom that are not actually independent, and standard errors are therefore erroneously reduced resulting in an overestimation of the precision of the parameters of interest (Heck and Thomas 2009).

Intra-class correlations

As discussed, in hierarchically nested data it is often assumed that individuals or first-level units within the same group or second-level unit are more similar to each other than individuals in different second-level units. This homogeneity or similarity of individuals within groups can be measured by calculating the *intra-class correlation* (Bliese et al. 2002). Computing these intra-class correlations at the squad, platoon and company level was a major first step in the data analysis of the illustrative study on the impact of ethical leadership and culture. The range of these correlations indicated that the data at the various levels were suitable for aggregation to the adjacent, higher levels (Schaubroek et al. 2012: 1063–1064).

A high intra-class correlation indicates that individuals within groups are homogeneous or that the groups are very different from each other. In general, a low intra-class correlation indicates that the groups are only slightly different from each other. An intra-class correlation of zero means that no group differences exist on the variable of interest, and that individuals within the same group are as different from one another on this variable as individuals across groups. Thus, if the intra-class correlation is zero, clustering the data has no consequence for the relationship between the variables of interest and can be ignored in further analyses. Conversely, if there is a substantial intra-class correlation, modelling the intra-class correlation is appropriate in that it takes the nested structure of the data into account, and will lead to a better understanding of the phenomenon of interest (Kreft and de Leeuw 1999).

Since the intra-class correlation can also be thought of as a measure of the degree of dependence of individual units (Bliese 2000), the existence of an intra-class correlation indicates that the assumption of independent observations applicable in traditional data-analytic techniques is violated. The more individuals share in terms of common experiences due to closeness in space or time, the more similar or dependent they are likely to be. Further, taking into account the existence of intra-class correlations is important in that these correlations change the error variance in traditional statistical analysis techniques, as alluded to above. Under the assumption of independence of observations, error variance represents the effect of all omitted variables and measurement errors. As such, in traditional analyses omitted variables are assumed to have a random, rather than a structural effect, which, as discussed in this chapter, is often not the case if the data is hierarchical or nested in nature (Kreft and de Leeuw 1999). Of note, intra-class correlation coefficients are often used in decisions regarding aggregation of data (for greater detail refer to Bliese 2000 and Kozlowski and Klein 2000).

Cross-level interactions

Cross-level interactions or influences, as the name implies, entail interaction effects between different levels of analysis, such as interactions between individual-level predictors and group level predictors. When such interactions are present, the effects of the individual-level variable on the outcome is said to be *moderated* by the group level variable. As an extension, the relationship between two individual-level variables on the outcome may be moderated by a group level variable (i.e. the nature of the relationship between the individual-level variables may be different in different groups). For example, research on the effects of deployment on retention of military personnel has yielded mixed results. To clarify these mixed results, it has been suggested that the type of deployment (at the group level) may moderate this relationship, such that deployment may increase retention for individuals deployed in less hostile or peacekeeping operations, whereas deployment may lead to decreased retention in those deployed in more hostile operations (Fricker et al. 2003; Wisecarver et al. 2006). In the ethical leadership illustrative study one could see a larger impact of ethical leadership on ethical culture in the same unit if the higher-level leadership was ethical as well, and a more limited impact if the higher-level leadership was not very ethically oriented. These types of interaction effects can only be tested using models that take the nested structure of the data into account, and specify the estimation of these cross-level interaction effects.

Hierarchical linear modelling (HML)

The two major types of established multilevel data-analytic techniques are multilevel linear hierarchical models (HLM) and multilevel latent variable models. Understanding HLM models requires basic knowledge of multiple regression. Further, understanding multilevel latent variable models requires basic knowledge of latent variable (i.e. covariance structures) analyses (Chan 2006). A detailed discussion of multilevel data-analytic techniques is beyond the scope of this chapter. However, HLM will be presented briefly in this chapter since these represent the most common class of multilevel approaches used in multilevel research (Hox 2000). HLM was also the analytic technique used in the illustrative study by Schaubroeck et al. (2012) on the impact of ethical leadership and culture within and across different levels.

HLM is an extremely useful and popular approach to multilevel data analysis. It allows for the identification and partitioning of the different sources of variance in the outcome variable, and further, provides a means for modelling these different sources of variance using multiple predictors at different levels of analysis. Moreover, HLM provides a powerful tool for assessing both cross-level main effects and cross-level interactions.

As such, HLM is usually used to assess the influence of both individual and group level predictors on an individual-level outcome, as well as the moderating effects of group level variables on the relationships between individual-level variables (Gavin and Hoffman 2002).

More specifically, multilevel modelling deals with potential group effects, and the potential dependence among individual-level observations within groups by allowing intercepts (means) and slopes (the criterion-predictor relationships) to vary between groups. For example, the relationship between recruits' training scores (the criterion) and recruits' aptitude scores (the predictor) is allowed to vary between training schools. This variability is modelled by treating the group intercepts and slopes as criterion variables in the next level of analysis. For example, in the next level of analysis, differences in means and slopes within training schools may be predicted by instructors' leadership between the training schools.

Conceptually, HLM can be thought of as a two-level approach where the Level 1 analysis consists of regressing the outcome (e.g. training scores) onto the criterion (e.g. aptitude scores) separately for each group or training school. The regression equations estimated for each group generate intercept and slope terms summarizing the relationship between training scores and aptitude for each group or training school, and it is not assumed that this relationship is consistent across training schools. The Level 2 analysis in HLM would then assess the degree to which these intercepts and slopes can be predicted by training school. Thus, in this HLM model the main effect of aptitude would be estimated in the Level 1 part of the model, the main effect of training school would be estimated in the Level 2 part of the model through regressing the intercept terms onto training schools, and the cross-level interaction between aptitude and training school would be assessed in the Level 2 model by regressing the slope terms onto training school (Castro 2002; Gavin and Hofmann 2002). Significant cross-level interactions indicate that group level variables moderate the relationship between two individual-level variables (e.g. the aptitude scores-training scores relationship is moderated by training school) because the value of the Level 1 relationship (i.e. the value of the Level 1 regression slope) differs or depends on the value of the Level 2 or group level variable. As with traditional single-level Ordinary Least Squares regression analysis, a main effect should be interpreted with caution when there is the potential for moderation of the relationship (Gavin and Hofmann 2002).

Although the earliest applications of multilevel data analysis focused on two levels in relation to a continuous outcome, this basic model has been extended in a number of ways to include three or more levels of analysis and a variety of different types of outcomes. The researcher should consider the features of the particular data and the overall goals of the research in the selection of the specific multilevel data-analytic approach (Heck and Thomas 2004).

Longitudinal studies: Growth curve analysis

Cross-sectional multilevel models examine individual data nested within higher-level units. In longitudinal analyses, multilevel models examine patterns of repeated measures nested within individuals. Although the lowest level of data in most analyses is usually an individual, in longitudinal designs the lowest level of data is repeated measurements of individuals, with these measurements said to be nested within individuals. Thus, in longitudinal analyses, instead of analysing inter-individual differences in the context of different groups, the primary focus is usually on analysing intra-individual changes over time (Bliese et al. 2007; Han and Andres 2014, Chapter 17 this volume). In such cases, the intra-class correlation measures the degree to which behaviour of the same individual is more similar to his/her previous behaviour in comparison to the behaviour of other people (Kreft and de Leeuw 1999).

Because there are separate analyses of each case over time, individual differences in *growth curves* may be evaluated (Heck and Thomas 2009). For example, do military children differ in their adaptation over the course of their military parent's deployment (e.g. through the pre-deployment, deployment, and post-deployment phases)? If so, are there variables, such as support from other family members or military family services, which predict these differences?

Considerations in multilevel modelling

The role of theoretical guidance and the choice of predictors

Given that a main purpose of multilevel data analysis is to consider predictors at different levels of analysis, the correlations among predictors at all levels of analysis are considered together and adjusted for each other. As a result, it becomes more likely that none of the regression coefficients associated with these predictors will be statistically significant. Thus, it is of key importance to select the right number and combination of predictors to maximize the utility of the analysis in explaining the phenomenon of interest. In particular, it is suggested that only a very small number of predictors be selected, and further, that these predictors are relatively uncorrelated with each other (Tabachnick and Fidell 2007). Of course, strong theoretical and conceptual rationale should be used in the selection of predictors, and will be helpful in selecting a limited number that optimizes explanation of the phenomenon of interest.

Only the most theoretically relevant predictors are included in the model to begin with. Following this, predictors may be added in order of importance, and those that do not improve prediction of the phenomenon of interest are dropped from the analysis (unless they add meaningfully to cross-level interactions) (Raudenbush and Bryk 2001). If there are a large number of potential predictors, they may first be screened using simple modelling techniques, such as linear regression, to eliminate those that do not contribute to explanation of the phenomenon of interest from the start. Further, if the sample is large enough, it is suggested that these exploratory type analyses be cross-validated by using half of the sample to build the model, and the other half of the sample for cross-validation. This will attenuate the degree to which these exploratory model-building techniques are influenced by chance (Tabachnick and Fidell 2007).

Statistical assumptions and sample size

The statistical assumptions and limitations that pertain to traditional data analyses techniques generally apply to multilevel data-analytic techniques as well (Castro 2002). As such, preliminary data cleaning and analyses needs to assess conformity with distributional assumptions as well as outliers.

Ideally, it is recommended that screening of lower-level predictors should be conducted within each higher-level unit. However, this may be impractical, especially when the number of higher-level units is large. In such cases, the lower-level units may be combined over the higher-level units. Likewise, second-level predictors should be examined within third-level predictors if possible, or they may be aggregated across the third-level predictors (Tabachnick and Fidell 2007).

By their nature, multilevel models are generally more complex than traditional models, because they entail calculating a greater number of equations at various levels of analysis. As discussed, in addition to the effects of interest within each level, effects of parameters, including the intercepts and slopes, are also of interest at each level. As such, these types of models generally necessitate larger sample sizes at each level to counteract the instability inherent in such models (Chan 2006). The illustrative study was based on a sample of 2,048 soldiers which was necessary in order to build multilevel models that will then consist of much fewer cases at each subsequent level, such as squads, then platoons and finally companies.

As in most analyses, power increases with increased sample sizes, larger effect sizes, and smaller standard errors. However, there are some more complex issues related to power in these types of analyses that pertain to having effects at different levels of analysis. For example, it has been shown that power grows with the size of the intra-class correlation (i.e. the difference between groups relative the differences within groups, as discussed above), particularly for tests of higher-level effects and cross-level interactions. In general, it has been demonstrated that power is greater with a greater number of groups (or second-level units) and fewer cases per group (first-level units) than the other way around, but that power increases with greater sample size at both levels (Tabachnick and Fidell 2007).

Limitations and cautionary notes

Although multilevel data analysis provides sophisticated methods for analysing complex phenomenon and considering the influence of predictors at different levels of analysis, it is important to recognize the trade-offs between using these types of models as compared to more traditional approaches. One particularly important point for consideration is that although multilevel models may yield more realistic explanations of real-life phenomena, these types of models are generally more complex, and thus may not always be the best approach. Of note, multilevel data analysis usually results in more complex statistical models that are generally more difficult to interpret than simpler models.

Further, the results of complex models are usually more difficult to replicate across samples and across different studies. This is because complex models are more sensitive to changes in what is a more complex system, which may entail a greater number of explanatory variables, measured at multiple levels of the hierarchy, and may include multiple cross-level interactions among variables of different levels, which leads to instability in parameter estimates across models that differ in minor ways (Kreft and de Leeuw 1999). At the least, these types of models are not generally recommended for exploratory data analysis or extensive modifications to increase model-fit (Kreft and de Leeuw 1999).

In addition, it is important to pay attention to the number of higher-level units and not to confuse the number of higher-level units with the total study sample size or the total number of lower-level observations. Although the statistical power of the tests of significance of lower-level estimates is dependent on the total lower-level sample size, the statistical power of estimates for the higher-level estimates and cross-level interactions is based on the number of higher-level units. Because HLM and other multilevel techniques assume large sample sizes it is important to ensure a sufficient number of groups in order to properly test and interpret the effects of multilevel analyses (Castro 2002; Chan 2006).

Finally, although multilevel models are very flexible and allow for the testing of a variety of hypotheses concerning variables and relationships at multiple levels, as well as various cross-level relationships, this flexibility also makes such models more vulnerable to misuse resulting in misleading or erroneous inferences (Chan 2006), such as the ecological fallacy and atomistic fallacy discussed above.

Conclusion

Military research is replete with phenomena that are multilevel, or hierarchical, in nature. As such, military researchers are interested in understanding individuals (or other micro-level units) within their social or organizational contexts. Individuals within higher-level groups or contexts often share common properties or characteristics or are subject to common experiences. Similarly, properties of groups or contexts may also be influenced by the individuals within them. It is clear that multilevel analysis is not only a useful, but in fact is often an essential approach for military research, enabling researchers to understand the phenomena under investigation more accurately and more completely.

References

Bliese, P.D. (2000) 'Within-group agreement, non-independence, and reliability: Implications for data aggregation and analysis', in K.J. Klein and S.W. Kozlowski (eds), *Multilevel Theory, Research, and Methods in Organizations* (pp. 349–381), San Francisco, CA: Jossey-Bass.

Bliese, P.D., Chan, D. and Ployhart, R.E. (2007) 'Multilevel methods: Future directions in measurement, longitudinal analyses, and nonnormal outcomes', *Organizational Research Methods*, 10(4): 551–563.

Bliese, P.D., Halverson, R.R. and Schriesheim, C.A. (2002) 'Benchmarking multilevel methods in leadership: The articles, the model, and the data set', *The Leadership Quarterly*, 13(1): 3–14.

Bliese, P.D. and Jex, S.M. (2002) 'Incorporating a multilevel perspective into occupational stress research: Theoretical, methodological, and practical implications', *Journal of Occupational Health Psychology*, 7(3): 265–276.

Castro, S.L. (2002) 'Data analytic methods for the analysis of multilevel questions: A comparison of intraclass correlation coefficients, $r_{wg(j)}$, hierarchical linear modeling, within- and between-analysis, and random group sampling', *The Leadership Quarterly*, 13(1): 69–93.

Chan, D. (1998) 'Functional relations among constructs in the same content domain at different levels of analysis: A typology of composition models', *Journal of Applied Psychology*, 83(2): 234–246.

Chan, D. (2006) 'Multilevel research', in F.T.L. Leong and J.T. Austin (eds), *The Psychology Research Handbook* (2nd edn) (pp. 401–418), Thousand Oaks, CA: Sage.

Dansereau, F., Cho, J. and Yammarino, F.J. (2006) 'Avoiding the "Fallacy of the Wrong Level": A within and between analysis (WABA) approach', *Group and Organization Management*, 31(5): 536–577.

DiPrete, T.A. and Forristal, J.D. (1994) 'Multilevel models: Methods and substance', *Annual Review of Sociology*, 20, 331–357.

Fullerton, A.S., Wallace, M. and Stern, M.J. (2010) 'Multilevel models', in K.T. Leicht and J.C. Jenkins (eds), *Handbook of Politics: State and Society in Global Perspective*, Handbooks of Sociology and Social Research (pp. 589–604), Springer Science + Business Media.

Fricker, R.D., Hosek, J. and Totten, M.E. (2003) 'How does deployment affect retention of military personnel?' RAND Corporation (research brief).

Gavin, M.B. and Hofmann, D.A. (2002) 'Using hierarchical linear modeling to investigate the moderating influence of leadership climate', *The Leadership Quarterly*, 13(1): 15–33.

George, J.M. and James, L.R. (1994) 'Levels issues in theory development', *Academy of Management Review*, 19(4): 636–640.

Han, J. and Anders, M. (2014) 'Studying Longitudinal Influences on the adjustment of new recruits in the Chinese military', in J.M.M.L. Soeters, P.M. Shields and S.J.H. Rietjens (eds) *Routledge Handbook of Research Methods in Military Studies*, London: Routledge.

Heck, R.H. and Thomas, S.L. (2009) *An Introduction to Multilevel Modeling Techniques* (2nd edn), Routledge: New York.

Hox, J.J. (2000) 'Multilevel analyses of grouped and longitudinal data', in T.D. Little, K.U. Schnaubel, and J. Baumert (eds), *Modeling Longitudinal and Multilevel Data: Practical Issues, Applied Approaches, and Specific Examples* (pp. 15–32), London: Laurence Erlbaum.

Hox, J.J. (2010) *Multilevel Analysis: Techniques and Applications*, Routledge: New York.

Kozlowski, S.W.J., and Klein, K.J. (2000) 'A multilevel approach to theory and research in organizations: Contextual, temporal, and emergent processes', in K.J. Klein and S.W.J. Kozlowski (eds), *Multilevel Theory, Research and Methods in Organizations: Foundations, Extensions, and New Directions* (pp. 3–90), San Francisco: Jossey-Bass.

Kreft, I. and de Leeuw, J. (1998) *Introducing Multilevel Modeling*, London: Sage.

Raudenbush. S. and Bryk, A.S. (2001) *Hierarchical* (2nd edn), Newbury Park, CA: Sage.

Rousseau, D.M. (1985) 'Issues of level in organizational research: Multi-level and cross-level perspectives', *Research in Organizational Behavior*, 7: 1–37.

Schaubroeck, J.M., Hannah, S.T., Avolio, B.J., Kozlowski, S.W.J., Lord, R.G., Trevino, L.K., Dimotakis, N. and Peng, A.C. (2012) 'Embedding ethical leadership within and across organizational levels', *Academy of Management Journal*, 55(5): 1053–1078.

Snijders, T.A.B. and Bosker, R.J. (2011) *Multilevel Analysis: An Introduction to Basic and Advanced Multilevel Modeling* (2nd edn), London: Sage.

Snook, S.A. (2000) *Friendly Fire: The Accidental Shootdown of U.S. Black Hawks over Northern Iraq*. Princeton, NJ: Princeton University Press.

Tabachnick, B.G. and Fidell, L.S. (2007) *Using Multivariate Statistics* (5th edn), Toronto, ON: Pearson.

Wisecarver, M.M., Cracraft, M. and Heffner, T.S. (2006) *Deployment Consequences: A Review of the Literature and Integration of the Findings in a Model of Retention*. U.S. Army Research Institute for the Behavioural and Social Sciences.

19

CROSS-NATIONAL RESEARCH IN THE MILITARY

Comparing operational styles

Chiara Ruffa and Joseph Soeters

C. Ruffa (2014) 'What peacekeepers think and do: An exploratory study of French, Ghanaian, Italian and South Korean Armies in the United Nations Mission in Lebanon,' *Armed Forces & Society* 40(2): 199–225.

'What peacekeepers think and do' is about how and why different national armies display recurring and systematic variation in the way they behave in operation. Ruffa focuses on how four different national contingents behave during their daily military activities in a peace operation, the United Nations Interim Force in Lebanon, launched after the Israeli–Hezbollah war in 2006. The author argues that variation in different armies' daily military activities (e.g. force protection, civil–military coordination and operational activities) is consistent with the way these armies perceive the operational environment they face. She also shows that the way this environment is 'constructed' is consistent with the previous experience of these armies in the country of operation.

Methodologically, the paper is based on in-depth empirical research comparing carefully selected cases. This selection follows the logic of controlled comparison. The selection is based on two criteria. First, armies had to be deployed under similar circumstances, i.e. similar levels of operational difficulty, with an identical mandate and in more or less the same areas. Second, the contingents had to be sufficiently different from each other in order to be able to expect variations. This resulted in the selection of four national contingents: two Western (French and Italian) and two non-Western contingents (Ghanaian and Korean).

While the four contingents had a more or less similar number of troops, they had different levels of material capabilities: the Ghanaian contingent is from a relatively poor African army, the Korean is rich and extremely well-equipped, while the French and Italian units shared high-level and almost identical characteristics in equipment and vehicles. In addition to this, the four national armies had different previous experiences with the mission in Lebanon and peacekeeping in general.

The data collection in this study was quite eclectic, because it brought together interpretivist research strategies, based on in-depth interviews and participant observation, and data collection through the distribution of questionnaires among a selected stratified sample across ranks. The

---

process of getting access to the field was authorized by national authorities in each of these four armies and this formal permission allowed for several months of proximity with soldiers of the four contingents in the field.

Ruffa, a female civilian researcher, gained full access to the field but of course her own identity and language skills may have influenced the actual findings in ways that can hardly be controlled. Her data analysis was based on triangulation and plurality of sources. Throughout the paper she made use of her interview transcripts, observations and the results of questionnaires.

The study has three main findings. First, the French, Italian, Ghanaian and Korean contingents differed consistently and remarkably in their daily military activities. While the Ghanaian and Italian units prioritized humanitarian activities, the French and Korean contingents emphasized the importance of patrolling and displayed relatively high degrees of force protection. Second, these variations are consistent with the way in which each of these four armies understands the context they are embedded in. The Ghanaian and Italian contingents had a relatively low threat perception, they did not identify an enemy and they had a restrictive interpretation of the use of force. The French and Korean contingents had a different way of perceiving the situation: they understood the mission as having a high threat level and a real enemy. Third, this finding is consistent with the previous experiences of these armies in the country of operation. The French soldiers linked the perceived operational environment to the overall traumatic experience they had in Lebanon during the Multinational Force in 1984–1985. The South Korean military seemed to link it to their lack of experience, UNIFIL II being their first peacekeeping operation. By contrast, Italian soldiers had a good memory of Lebanon because during the Multinational Force they had close to no casualties and the Ghanaian military attached a good memory to the country seemingly because of its long-lasting presence within UNIFIL.

Introduction

Cross-national research applied to the military seems to be a relatively new phenomenon. However, it is not very new in the social and behavioural sciences in general. In many cases nations have existed for centuries and nation-related languages and economies, laws and regulations, traditions and everyday practices, policies and national ambitions had comparable time to become distinct from one another. The crisis in the Eurozone reflects this differentiation despite optimistic hopes that the internationalization of production and trade would smooth these differences easily. Apparently, such cross-national differences are fairly stubborn, even if they are subtle and perhaps not always so easy to discern.

In the social and behavioural sciences international variation in psychological characteristics (e.g. learning styles), organizational structures (e.g. hierarchies and formalization), and political cultures and general societal values (e.g. cosmopolitanism) have attracted quite some scholarly attention, leading to flourishing and established branches of research (e.g. Almond and Verba 1963; Hofstede 2001; Chokar et al. 2007). The complexity of comparative social research has even led to the emergence of specialized methodological concerns and considerations, as displayed in Przeworski and Teune (1970), Lijphart (1971), van de Vijver and Leung (1997) and Davidov et al. (2011). The majority of these studies are of a sophisticated quantitative nature, but more recently qualitative studies have been published as well, for instance in the *International Journal of Cross Cultural Management*.

As said, in military studies attention for such international differences has not been a truly established practice, perhaps because the armed forces – national phenomena *par excellence* – predominantly attract national scholarly attention. The 'one-nation, one-case' approach seems dominant in military studies, particularly in military history. However, due to the growing need for national armed forces to engage in supranational strategies and to cooperate internationally, cross-national and comparative military studies have started to appear in gradually increasing numbers. Sometimes, they are of a more historical nature, such as Kier's study (1997) on doctrine development in France and the UK between the two World Wars or the famous study by John Nagl (2002) about the UK operations in Malaya and the American operations in Vietnam (see also Lieb 2012). Sometimes, they present a set of country-descriptions of specific characteristics – policies, transformations, strategies, input features or adaptation during action – of national armed forces (e.g. Kuhlman and Callaghan 2000; Moskos et al. 2000; Caforio 2000; Farrell et al. 2013).

However, there is a growing urge to delve deeper in the operational side of national militaries working together in operation, whether in the same areas of operation or in the same mission (e.g. Soeters and Manigart 2008; Soeters and Tresch 2010). That is because the idea has emerged that national armed forces may also differ in the way they approach conflictual situations and the way in which they interpret the same mandate; studying these operational variations may help to better understand how to prevent, contain and solve violent conflicts (Soeters 2013b). Carefully comparing operational actions and styles – sometimes in a sort of quasi-experimental way – may even lead to knowledge about cause-and-effect mechanisms and evidence-based practices, which is highly needed in military studies. Like for example Morjé Howard (2008) did to compare successes and failures of 10 UN-missions.

In this chapter we focus on a number of methodological issues related to the study of operational styles of national militaries in the field. Conducting operations is the military's unique asset. The comparison of 'peacetime' defence policies, human resource practices, army structures, rules and regulations is not that different from methodological practices in comparative administrative, political, organization and economic studies. Hence, our main focus here is the military in operation.

Purpose: Description, theory development and theory testing

Comparing armies in action can be either purely descriptive or theory oriented. A description may provide information on armies that were not studied before or on which we mainly have anecdotal evidence. Once variation in operational styles has been assessed empirically, one can opt for different kinds of research design. In general, there are two options (e.g. George and Bennett 2005). First, one could contrast or complement existing knowledge about the characteristics of certain armies. Comparing operational styles across armies can be used to develop new theories and tease out new hypotheses. For instance, if a scholar detects consistent and systematic variations across armies deployed in the same peace operation under similar conditions, (s)he can formulate a hypothesis to explain these variations, retrieving omitted variables and proposing new ones. Second, one can test already existing hypotheses to new cases. One can compare different operational styles with a theory-testing purpose, for instance to understand which operational style is the most effective in a particular situation or to understand whether culture accounts for variations in operational styles.

In general, one can aim to (1) describe different national operational styles, (2) to identify and study those 'operational styles' as a dependent or intervening variable (for instance, when a scholar looks at the determinants of cross-national differences in operational styles) or (3) as an independent variable (i.e. how different operational styles influence the outcome of the mission, or the specific effectiveness of an army). Obviously all these academic ambitions can have extensive practical implications if they lead to more knowledge about how to prevent, contain and solve violent conflicts by military means in conjunction with other instruments.

When soldiers are deployed in operations, they put into practice their logics and repertoires of action, resulting from their societies' context and their organization's traditions, mission, 'worldviews', leadership styles and training procedures. In their day-to-day military activities in operation, the military unveils the core characteristics of their organizations. As such, comparing armies during the same mission almost seems like a sort of laboratory for a researcher. It provides the opportunity to collect evidence on the military's everyday practices, resulting from the organizational memory, culture, leadership, adaptation, reactions to the existing operational environment and traditions of civil-military relations in their home societies. As organizational scholars would put it: military practices are path-dependent. In addition to this, comparing armies in operation allows the researcher to control for other determinants of their behaviour, such as the role of equipment and other material resources, the 'difficulty' of the area of operation and the content and scope of the mandate. The possibility to control for other determinants is related to the research design.

Research design and case selection[1]

The research design heavily depends on the kind of research purpose one has in mind. The case selection is the gist of the matter here. This specific methodological issue goes back to the origins of experimentation as developed by John Stuart Mill about 175 years ago (e.g. Lijphart 1971; Moses and Knutsen 2007). This method is based on careful comparisons of different situations. These situations may differ in time: before, during and after an event or intervention. Or, by comparing different groups: in its simplest form comparing a group without a certain characteristic, such as an intervention, and a control group without that particular characteristic. Of course most experimental research designs are more sophisticated than that. The experimentation method has become the dominant research strategy in the natural and life sciences. New drugs, medical treatments or food products will not be allowed to be sold on the market before they have been extensively tested in series of experiments.

In the social, organization and administrative sciences time-related conditions or different groups conditions, however, cannot be manipulated the way this happens in research laboratories. In recent years, however, in fields like political science and economics, experimental designs have emerged as a new trend, that while opening promising research avenues also pose tremendous feasibility and ethical issues (Fotini et al. 2013). Hence, in these disciplines the best seems to strive for so-called *quasi-experimental research* (Campbell and Stanley 1963). As said, the comparative method is related to the (quasi)-experimental logic. In order to come to the development and even testing of hypothetical causal inferences, there are basically two research designs (Przeworski and Teune 1970: 31–46). One can chose to compare cases that are most similar (see Table 19.1), or just the opposite, cases that are most dissimilar (see Table 19.2).

In the first research set-up all cases are similar with respect to the variables X2 to X5, whereas there is comparable variation in X1 and Y (see Table 19.1). As a consequence, X1 may be seen as a relevant factor to explain the differences in the dependent variable Y. This is based on the idea of *verification*, ideally leading to causal inferences.

In Table 19.2 a research design is displayed consisting of five cases that differ with respect to the variables X2 to X5, whereas the variables X1 and Y show similar scores, which means that they co-vary in an identical manner. By consequence, X1 and Y are – perhaps even causally – interrelated. This set-up is based on the idea of *falsification*: variables that are not relevant may be excluded as explanatory factors. Because the number of cases in this type of

Table 19.1 Most-similar comparative research design with five cases and six variables

	Case 1	Case 2	Case 3	Case 4	Case 5
Variable X1	0	0	0	+	+
Variable X2	0	0	0	0	0
Variable X3	0	0	0	0	0
Variable X4	+	+	+	+	+
Variable X5	+	+	+	+	+
Dependent Y	0	0	0	+	+

Table 19.2 Most-different comparative research design with five cases and six variables

	Case 1	Case 2	Case 3	Case 4	Case 5
Variable X1	+	+	0	+	+
Variable X2	+	+	+	0	0
Variable X3	0	+	+	+	0
Variable X4	0	0	0	+	+
Variable X5	+	0	+	0	+
Dependent Y	+	+	0	+	+

research is usually limited – this is so-called *small N-research* – and because the determination of effects is difficult, new techniques for data analysis have been developed making use of Boolean algebra (Ragin 1989).

Clearly, Ruffa (2013) used the most similar approach in her analysis of the four national contingents in Lebanon. Quite a number of variables (period of time, mission, mandate, task assignment, areas of deployment, operational environment) were similar, whereas the perception of the situation based on previous experiences and the operational approaches of the contingents were different. Hence, the hypothesis concerning the relation between these two latter characteristics emerged. What is more, the hypothesis was substantiated by the nature of her data based on a research design that was much tighter than one usually sees in military studies.

Normally, scholars in military studies so far have not been very explicit on these methodological issues. Nagl's famous study (2002) compares the UK actions to combat communist uprising in Malaya with the US war against Northern Vietnam and their communist allies. In this study the set-up is less tight than in Ruffa's study, because at least the time period was not the same (1940s/1950s compared to 1960/1970s), nor was the status of the two Western countries (colonial power for centuries versus a new, invading power). Hence, the relation between national operational style and effectiveness may perhaps not be as strong as suggested. Soeters (2013a) compared the UK approach vis-à-vis the upheaval in Northern Ireland in the early 1970s with the Netherlands' approach towards Moluccan activists' violent actions in the same years. Here, many variables were similar: both conflicts emerged within the own national borders in Western Europe in exactly the same period of time; in both cases the opponents were ordinary civilians and in both conflicts the violence and upheaval had a historical, colonial connection; finally, in both cases a third country (Ireland, Indonesia) played a role in the background, even though this was not active or manifest. The political and military approaches, however, were rather different and so were the outcomes in terms of casualties and duration of the conflicts.

Of course, every conflict situation is unique, which means that many variables cannot be controlled the way this can be done in an experimental setting. Hence, the resulting analysis cannot go much further than suggesting a correlation between operational styles and effectiveness in conflict prevention, containment and solution. The proof can only be found by conducting more studies to provide converging evidence. Clearly, one comparative case analysis is not enough, but it is better than the 'one-nation, one-case' research design that has been so favourite in military studies so far. Still, comparing may present trade-offs in terms of how deep one can go.

Plurality of strategies of data collection

The literature on operational styles is pluralistic in its strategies of data collection, in both the quantitative and qualitative traditions. Data collection ranges from participant observation, the distribution of surveys among soldiers, the use of secondary sources such as policy documents and process tracing to conducting focus groups interviews and content analysis of blog written by individual soldiers. In fact, it may contain the use of a number of methods at the same time, making it an example of mixed-methods research (Tashakkori and Teddlie 2010). An immersion in the field, like Ruffa did, is recommendable but it is not necessary per se. Sometimes the security situation or personal reasons do not allow an immersion in the field and this is perfectly valid. In case an immersion is not possible, valid alternatives are post-operation data collection or ways of reaching soldiers remotely, for instance through email exchanges and chatting while soldiers are still in the field. Ruffa used it with a couple of soldiers she remained in contact with once she had left Southern Lebanon for follow-up questions.

Participant observation is a classical and fruitful research practice, which is, however, time-consuming and demanding. The researcher's time in the 'field' may range from minimally one week, which could be referred to as 'blitz fieldwork' (Soeters and Manigart 2008), to several months. In a military study this would be in a military base or a compound in an area of deployment; in a comparative study of national operational styles this would require a stay in several camps or compounds. In the Lebanon study, Ruffa was embedded with the national contingents discontinuously between June 2007 and June 2009. This included a period of four weeks of embeddedness with each of the four contingents under study plus a period of six months distributing semi-structured questionnaires and conducting individual qualitative interviews with experts, representatives of NGOs working in the area and conversations with several local families. When doing participant observation, Ruffa was in the UN bases at Tibnin (Italian), At-Tiri (French), Tyre (Korean) and Al-Rmeisch (Ghanaian).

The researcher's presence in operation makes it possible to interact with soldiers of different ranks in the base. Observation is a powerful strategy of data collection because it allows for a comprehensive assessment of both ordinary routines and exceptional events. The researcher is exposed to a number of formal and informal conversations relevant for cross-cultural comparisons. At the same time, observation requires great caution because the researcher can influence and be influenced by the people around, in ways he/she can be unaware of. Observation needs to be prepared as much as other strategies of data collection through self-reflection and a clear outline of elements to look for. In comparative studies observation practices should ideally be similar across contingents, which makes the data collection even more complex. It is recommended for the researcher to keep a fieldwork observation diary, in which all interesting or noticeable things are noted down throughout the period of stay inside the base and the accompanying operational activities.

Questionnaires are another way to detect variations across national contingents. Questionnaires can be fully structured or semi-structured. The former are easier to code and analyse quantitatively, allowing for structured comparisons across the national contingents under study. Semi-structured questionnaires provide each soldier the possibility to elaborate on the answers and express her or himself more freely and creatively. However, some respondents are likely to refrain from responding in an elaborate manner in semi-structured questionnaires, simply because that implies too much work for them.

Ideally, the researcher administers identical questionnaires to all units involved in the study. This may be problematic with military institutions for what are often called 'security reasons'. The researcher in this situation should be open to compromise by offering guarantees in exchange. For instance, when Ruffa designed her questionnaires, the French military was dissatisfied with a question that asked about 'victory'. The other contingents had no problems with this particular question. Nonetheless, for reasons of data equivalence this question was deleted from all questionnaires, but Ruffa was authorized to introduce it as a question in the interviews.

In-depth qualitative interviews are a good way to gain access to insights and accounts about soldiers' operational experiences. In general, guaranteeing anonymity is a good way to make respondents feel comfortable, confident and willing to talk. This holds particularly true when soldiers come from a country with conflictual civil-military relations. In-depth interviews allow soldiers to elaborate on stories and account as much as they like and sometimes this becomes a good way for them to talk about their problems and experiences in operation. In-depth interviewing permits the researcher to develop a sort of narrative approach (Boje 2011) to the research question, which can only add to the quality of the cross-national case comparison. These different strategies of data collection shall ideally be used in a fruitful mix. Data supported by different strategies of data collection make them much stronger and convincing. In cross-national comparisons, it is additionally prerequisite that the researcher uses the mix of these strategies across the cases as *consistently* as possible. This also implies the application of the same methods and instruments to categories of respondents and interviewees that are *functionally equivalent* (comparing soldiers with soldiers, officers with officers, engineering NGOs with engineering NGOs, etc.). Otherwise the comparative character of the findings across the cases may become essentially flawed.

Methodological peculiarities in cross-national comparative research

Anecdotal evidence

While it may seem common knowledge that different armies behave differently, the research literature on operational styles tries to provide systematic evidence of these variations. Even if the literature on operational styles has grown over the past years, systematic evidence of differences between national armed forces is still lacking. There are quite a number of occasional observations, but they lead to anecdotal evidence at best. For instance, Rory Stewart's account of a year among British and Italian troops in Basra in Iraq, in 2003/2004, provides highly interesting observations about these national contingents' actions and their impact in the area (Stewart 2007: 402). His conclusions, however, are based on first-hand experiences, not on thorough comparative research. And this impressionistic account also changed overtime: while he had a negative impression of the Italian army at first, this impression reversed after a few months. On the one hand, an observer's assessment of a national operational style needs time to form. On the other, effects of an operational style may need months before one is able to empirically measure them.

To ascertain national operational styles researchers need to identify variations in operational styles that are recurring and systematic. This means that specific differences in behaviour are shared by different units on the ground, by different soldiers across ranks and assessed through triangulation of evidence. If possible, this should be assessed through a combination of methods, both quantitative and qualitative, as said before (e.g. Tashakkori and Teddlie 2010). In mere quantitative research, statistical procedures and modelling procedures exist to ascertain if variation between (national) cases is larger than the variation within (national) cases, permitting further cross-national analyses (e.g. Davidov et al. 2011).

Level of analysis

What is the appropriate level of analysis for studying (national) operational styles? The smallest unit of analysis is probably the platoon level. But it makes sense to study operational styles at that level only as – *and if it is* – representative of the national contingent's actions. The level of individual persons (soldiers, officers) is rarely the preferred level of analysis because in cross-comparative case-research one is interested in organizations and their missions, not in the actions of individual respondents per se. Nonetheless, the aggregation of individuals' scores (actions, responses, attitudes) can lead to analyses at higher levels, such as platoons or the whole national contingent. In quantitative studies this is referred to as *multilevel analysis*, as is perfectly illustrated in a large study among US Army soldiers and their units in Afghanistan (Schaubroeck et al. 2012; see also Chapter 18 in this volume). The level of the national contingent in multinational operations is probably the most meaningful one to compare national operational styles, given that it is usually the national unit that is deployed in a well-defined area of operation. However, comparative research among various (national) HQs may be illustrative as well. Besides, the data collection does not need to be limited to ground forces; national navies in action in multinational sea operations (e.g. when bordering vessels or arresting pirates) may be compared meaningfully too.

Language issues

Interviewing soldiers in their mother tongue is fundamental to enabling them to express themselves freely with all the nuances and complexities that come along with in-depth conversations. Relying on English as the general bridging language will often prove to be inadequate, because it will lead to biased selections of respondents/interviewees – to those who master that language – or to an insufficient quality of information exchange. The researcher shall therefore be proficient in as many of the languages used as possible. If a team of researchers collects the data, it would be wise to have an adequate and relevant distribution of language skills among the various team members. When distributing questionnaires in languages one does not master it is wise to first have a translation into that particular language, and then have a back-translation into the original language again as well as circulating the questionnaires among native speakers with a wide array of expertise and different levels of education. If differences between the two translations emerge, the researcher(s) and the translator(s) will need to discuss these and agree about possible solutions.

If relevant language skills are lacking or insufficient, the use of interpreters cannot be avoided. Priority should be given to the ability to grasp complexity, phrases and expression of the interviewees. Whether this is done by the researcher or by a translator depends on the language skills of the researcher. The use of interpreters may have limits (van Dijk et al. 2010), because one will often be unsure about how to interpret and trust the translator's work. However, at times the use of interpreters is the only realistic solution as it was for Ruffa when studying the South Korean army. Devoting time and effort to the study of a language is not always a viable option.

Reliability and validity

Research standards for quantitative data are generally quite transparent. In cross-national studies they rely on the consistent use of identical – preferably internationally validated – instruments across functionally equivalent samples. In qualitative studies such standards have not been as self-evident so far. Qualitative methodologies have been applauded for their in-depth validity, but have often been problematic in terms of their reproducibility and *credibility*. Lincoln and Guba (1985) have developed a set of indicators to check for the quality of qualitative data. One of them, credibility, seems particularly relevant in cross-national military research. If a researcher wants to make correct inferences, it is important to rely on data whose transcription has been checked by the interviewees themselves (so-called *member-checks*). But even more importantly, the researcher needs to discuss the general observations and conclusions with all the stakeholders to make sure that the study has produced credible results. Generally, identifying divergent views and counter-evidence will make the conclusions more balanced and in fact probably stronger. Additionally, recent debates in the political science have suggested how it might be good to provide further information on how evidence was inferred from the body of data, through for instance, annotated references and quotations (Moravcsik 2010).

The cross-cultural researcher's profile

Since it is difficult for scholars to have a profound understanding of languages, codes and cultures of two or more nationalities it is important that the researcher reflects on the potential challenges to his or her objectivity. In cross-national research subjectivity and *ethnocentrism* of the researcher(s) are almost unavoidable phenomena that endanger the quality of the research. We would argue that a scholar can rarely be perfectly objective but he/she should at least strive for this. Also, it is very important that a researcher, before going to fieldwork, reflects on what might be his/her attitudes, values and beliefs that might shape preconceived ideas about what happens in the field.

In addition to this, there is also a set of beliefs and ideas about how the researcher is perceived that might influence how he/she behaves despite him or herself. For instance, being a female or a male researcher might influence the way he/she is perceived by interviewees in the various national cases. In some national cases a female scholar may be seen as perfectly natural, in others perhaps not. The same problem may occur with respect to the fact that the researcher is a civilian or a military and whether he/she has some kind of military background. In some national cases a civilian without any military background may not be taken seriously, whereas in other national cases this would pose no problem at all and even be an advantage.

As said, it is important that the researcher has the opportunity to be embedded with troops for some period of time. This does not only allow the researcher to access a range of data unavailable from home, but it also permits the researcher to bond with the troops and being accepted when the researcher is with the troops in a 'totalising experience' (Wacquant 2004; White 2003). Doing research in composite teams involving researchers with diverse skills and expertise is another way to minimize cross-cultural misunderstandings and refine the understanding of cross-national variations.

Conclusions and warnings

Conducting research into national operational styles by comparing cases of military action by different national contingents in fairly similar circumstances is important because it may provide insight and evidence with respect to how things work in the field. If there is variance in the important variables, it may even get close to quasi-experimental studies that may lead to what looks like causal inferences. For sure, the military needs such inferences: the precise impact of military operations in preventing, containing and solving violent conflicts still seems a conundrum. However, one should be cautious in doing so. There are a number of pitfalls and caveats.

Comparing military actions by national contingents in an appropriate manner requires a careful research design, in which some of the research variables are identical and others are not. Besides, cross-national research needs highly qualified researchers who know how to apply similar instruments of data collection in different languages to equivalent samples in a manner that excludes preconceived ideas and ethnocentrism as much as possible. Even then, some historians and other ideographically oriented scholars – not all of them though (e.g. Mahoney and Rueschemeyer 2003) – would argue that every situation is unique and that every comparison is futile. This is a position we do not take. In the general social and political sciences, there are many examples of comparative studies that have produced important insights and findings.

However, one should be careful while generalizing findings from one study to a population in general. If the conduct of the Italian contingent in UNIFIL has been rather peaceful, this does not mean the Italian armed forces never display a warrior ethos, or never have. These would be unwarranted generalizations. Neither would this imply that each and every Italian soldier deployed to Lebanon is truly peaceful. The latter inference would be a so-called fallacy of the wrong level: applying a central tendency found at a collective level to all individual people belonging to that collectivity. This fallacy is often made in cross-national comparisons due to ethnocentric biases of the researcher(s) or selective interpretations by the readers of their work.

In addition to this, the cross-cultural researcher should be aware of the fact that comparing may be perceived as sensitive as it may imply considerations about different levels of effectiveness of different national contingents. The researcher needs to be careful with such considerations without shying away from the discovery of empirical realities that may be problematic. At the same time, we would also like to encourage organizations, like NATO, to commission these kinds of these studies because understanding which armies are best at doing certain things is the most appropriate strategies to enhance the likelihood of success in future operations.

In general, one cannot develop a proper understanding of particular national operational styles from one comparative study only. Obviously, one needs more studies, possibly leading to convergent evidence as to the existence of such national operational styles, but then only as central tendencies, not as determinative, never changing 'truths' (Soeters 2013b). What is more, such convergent evidence may also relate to insights about what is effective military action in particular conflictual situations. A careful comparison of the various national contingents' actions in the different Afghan provinces over the last ten years may lead to findings that illuminate our comprehension of the use and impact of different manifestations of military action. Since so many people suffered from these actions, it is morally imperative to conduct such studies.

Note

1 This section and the conclusions draw heavily on a previous publication, written in Dutch: A.F.M. Bertrand, P. de Jong, A.F.A. Korsten and J.M.L.M. Soeters, Methodische problemen bij internationaal-vergelijkend onderzoek. In: A.F.A. Korsten, A.F.M. Bertrand, P. de Jong and J.M.L.M. Soeters (1995), *Internationaal-vergelijkend onderzoek.* Vuga: Den Haag, pp. 85–102. Moses & and Knutsen (2007) provide a

similar overview of research designs, going back more specifically to John Stuart Mills original work. This chapter is also very much indebted to insights provided by Hofstede (2001).

References

Almond, Gabriel A. and Sidney Verba (1963). *The Civic Culture: Political Attitudes and Democracy in Five Nations*. Princeton, NJ: Princeton University Press.

Boje, David (ed.) (2011). *Storytelling and the Future of Organizations: An Antenarrative Handbook*. New York and London: Routledge.

Caforio, Guiseppe (2000). *The European Officer: A Comparative View on Selection and Education*. Pisa: Edizione ETS.

Campbell, Donald T. and Julian C. Stanley (1963). *Experimental and Quasi-Experimental Research Designs for Research*, Boston, MA: Houghton Mifflin.

Chokar, Jagdeep S., Felix C. Brodbeck and Robert J. House (2007). *Culture and Leadership across the World: The GLOBE Book on In-Depth Studies of 25 Societies*. Mahwah, NJ, and London: Lawrence Erlbaum.

Davidov, Eldad, Peter Schmidt, and Jaak Billiet (eds) (2011). *Cross-Cultural Analysis: Methods and Applications*. New York: Routledge.

Farrell, Theo, Frans Osinga and James A. Russell (eds) (2013). *Military Adaptation in Afghanistan*. Palo Alto, CA: Stanford University Press.

Fotini, Christia, Andrew Beath and Ruben Enikolopov (2013) 'Empowering Women through Development Aid: Evidence from a Field Experiment in Afghanistan', *American Political Science Review* 107(3): 540–557.

George, Alexander L. and Andrew Bennett (2005). *Case Studies and Theory Development in the Social Sciences*. Cambridge, MA: Belfer Center for Sciences and International Affairs.

Hofstede, Geert (2001). *Culture's Consequences: Comparing Values, Behaviors, Institutions, and Organizations across Nations* (2nd edn). Thousand Oaks: Sage.

Kier, Elizabeth (1997). *Imagining War: French and British Military Doctrine between the Wars*. Princeton, NJ: Princeton University Press.

Lieb, Peter (2012). 'Suppressing insurgencies in comparison: The Germans in Ukrain, 1918, and the British in Mesopotamia, 1920'. *Small Wars and Insurgencies* 23(4–5): 627–647.

Lijphart, Arend (1971). 'Comparative politics and the comparative method'. *American Political Science Review* 65(3): 682–693.

Lincoln, Yvonna S. and Egon G. Guba (1985). *Naturalistic Inquiry*. Newbury Park, CA: Sage.

Mahoney, James and Dietrich Rueschemeyer (eds) (2003). *Comparative Historical Analysis in the Social Sciences*. New York: Cambridge University Press.

Moravcsik, Andrew (2010). 'Active citation: A precondition for replicable qualitative research'. *PS: Political Science and Politics* 43(1): 29–35.

Morjé Howard, Lise (2008). *UN Peacekeeping in Civil Wars*. Cambridge and New York: Cambridge University Press.

Moses, Jonathan W. and Torbjon L. Knutsen (2007). *Ways of Knowing: Competing Methodologies in Social and Political Research*. Basingstoke and New York: Palgrave Macmillan.

Moskos, Charles C., John A. Williams and David R. Segal (eds) (2000). *The Post-Modern Military: Armed Forces after the Cold War*. New York: Cambridge University Press.

Nagl, John A. (2002). *Learning to Eat Soup with a Knife: Counter-Insurgency Lessons from Malaya and Vietnam*. Chicago and London: Chicago University Press.

Przeworski, A. and Henri Teune (1970). *The Logic of Comparative Social Inquiry*. New York: Wiley.

Ragin, Charles (1989). 'The logic of the comparative method and the algebra of logic'. *Journal of Quantitative Anthropology* 1(1): 373–398.

Ruffa, Chiara (2014). 'What peacekeepers think and do? An exploratory study of French, Ghanaian, Italian and South Korean Armies in the United Nations Mission in Lebanon'. *Armed Forces & Society* 40(2): 199–225.

Schaubroeck, John M., Sean T. Hannah, Bruce J. Avolio, Steve W. Kozlowski, Robert G. Lord, Linda K. Treviño, Nikolaos Dimotakis and Ann C. Peng (2012). 'Embedding ethical leadership within and across organization levels'. *Academy of Management Journal* 55(5): 1053–1078.

Soeters, Joseph (2013a). Odysseus prevails over Achilles. A warrior model suited to post-9/11 conflicts. In: James Burk (ed.), *How 9/11 Changed Our Ways of War*. Palo Alto, CA: Stanford University Press, pp. 89–115.

Soeters, J. (2013b). 'Do distinct (national) operational styles of conflict resolution exist?' *Journal of Strategic Studies* 36(6): 898–906.

Soeters, Joseph and Philip Manigart (eds) (2008). *Military Cooperation in Multinational Peace Operations: Managing Cultural Diversity and Crisis Response*. London and New York: Routledge.

Soeters, Joseph and Tibor Szvircsev Tresch (2010). 'Towards cultural integration in multinational peace operations'. *Defence Studies* 10(1–2): 272–287.

Stewart, Rory (2007). *The Prince of the Marshes: And Other Occupational Hazards of a Year in Iraq*. Orlando, FL: Harcourt Inc.

Tashakkori, A. and Ch. Teddlie (eds) (2010). *The Sage Handbook of Mixed Methods in Social and Behavioral Research* (2nd edn). Thousand Oaks, CA: Sage.

Van Dijk, Andrea, Joseph Soeters, and Richard de Ridder (2010). 'Smooth translation? A research note on the cooperation between Dutch service personnel and local interpreters in Afghanistan'. *Armed Forces & Society* 36(5): 917–925.

Vijver, Fons van de and K. Leung (1997). *Methods and Data Analysis for Cross-Cultural Research*. Newbury Park, CA: Sage.

Wacquant, Loic (2004). *Body and Soul*. Oxford: Oxford University Press.

White, William F. (2003). *Street Corner Society the Social Structure of an Italian Slum*. Chicago, IL: University of Chicago.

20
EXPERIMENTAL METHODS IN MILITARY AND VETERAN STUDIES

Jeremy M. Teigen

R.S. Erikson, and L. Stoker (2011) "Caught in the draft: The effects of Vietnam draft lottery status on political attitudes," *American Political Science Review* **105: 221–237.**

Few governmental policies touch the lives of citizens more vividly than conscription. Compulsory induction into a country's military means that individuals face the possibility of being taken out of their community or country, placed within a new hierarchy with different rules and norms than civilian life, possibly placed into dangerous combat duty, and must remain for an extended period of time, often more than a year. Only incarceration and taxation are in the same league as conscription in terms of how citizens' fates can be controlled by a government, even in democratic regimes. Does the possibility of being conscripted during a war influence citizens' attitudes about government? Foreign policy? Political preferences? Erikson and Stoker's article "Caught in the Draft," published in 2011 in the leading political science journal *American Political Science Review*, examines these questions using an experimental methodology. They exploit the natural conditions of the draft in the United States in 1969 during the Vietnam War to understand how vulnerability to conscription as a young adult influenced later-life political attitudes.

By using the randomly assigned draft lottery numbers as a proxy for the vulnerability to conscription for a group of men during an unpopular war, Erikson and Stoker's work uses experimental methodology to reveal the causal influence of war and conscription on citizen' political attitudes. Field experiments such as this take advantage of arbitrary, or in this case, random assignments of cases to different conditions and leverage the differences between groups to infer causation. Because an exogenous and random individual attribute, one's birth date, determined the likelihood of being inducted into a wartime military, scholars can exploit these conditions toward understand how draft eligibility influences attitudes (see chapter for details on how the randomization occurred). While the randomization of young men toward their likelihood of military induction provided the causal inferential power, the authors' data comprised a national panel study of individuals who were all approximately 22 years old. Hence, the authors were able to investigate the political legacy of conscription's effects by using birth dates to mark vulnerability to military service in early and later life among the same men.

Their findings indicate that military induction policy influences citizens' political attitudes. For young men more susceptible to conscription into the US Army, their views toward the war were more negative. Even decades later, men who drew "unlucky" draft lottery numbers were more likely to see the Vietnam War as a mistake than those with less vulnerability to military service. Erikson and Stoker also found that these men's political preferences were transformed by their relative likelihood of conscription. In the 1972 presidential election, when this cohort was 25 years old, and their draft eligibility was no longer in question, men with high vulnerability to the draft were substantially more likely to vote for the Democratic Party nominee, George McGovern, than they were for Republican Richard Nixon, even when controlling for known correlates of voter preferences.

In the scholarly area of military studies, the opportunities for field experiments and other experimental methodologies are not massive but they are probably underutilized. While complications due to preemptive enlistment and other concerns require attention, conscription provides researchers with potential field experiment data if those that serve are randomly selected. If military service is randomly distributed among citizens, then differences between veterans and nonveterans provide an experimental window into the later-life effects of military service.

The essence of the experimental method is simple: divide individuals into different groups assigned randomly and, leaving one aside as a control group, expose the remaining groups to varying degrees or types of stimuli, measure outcomes among all groups, and infer that any intergroup outcome differences stem from the stimuli differences. Because of the random assignment of subjects to groups, potentially conflating influences that may be correlated with the hypothesized causal relationship are minimized. The method is tantamount to the way that pharmaceutical research tests for the influence of potential drugs in its most elemental form, with the control group standing in for the placebo group. The design of the study has the ability to control subjects' exposure to different treatments, the independent variable. After the groups' subjects are exposed to the stimuli (or in the case of the control group, straightaway), a measure of the dependent variable takes place, the attitude or behavior that the researcher theorized would change. Because the randomness in group assignment negates the role of confounding influences and the fact that the causal phenomenon of interest is the only thing different between the groups, any differences within the dependent variable between groups can therefore be explained by the experimental conditions the researcher set forth, so long as the approach and execution followed appropriate experimental protocols. To express the difference between experimental and observational studies in the most reductionist terms, the former assigns values of the independent variable to subjects while the latter measures those values as they occur naturally.

Experimentation has become mainstream in political science recently, but its use to understand causal relations is not new. The logic of experimentation is at the heart of scientific inquiry and a central tool in making predictions and enhancing generalizable knowledge. John Stuart Mill's contributions to science are difficult to overstate as his nineteenth-century writings formalized conceptions of scientific causation (see also Ruffa and Soeters 2014, Chapter 19 in this volume). Experimentation, the process of suppressing extraneous factors while varying a factor of interest, is naturally congruent with Mill's method of difference (1848). The design that an analyst can use with an experiment to understand causal linkages can vary. The number of conditions can range from two to any number that befits the theoretical needs of the researcher. Further, the use of pretests and posttests has further implications for ameliorating concerns about an experiment's validity. Campbell and Stanley's authoritative work described these various ways to design stimulus groups within experiments and compares them with an eye toward minimizing validity issues (1963).

Types of experimental studies

Experimental studies generally come in one of two settings, the more controlled laboratory-style research and the more realistic field experiments. "Laboratory studies" accentuate control by bringing subjects into a space designed specifically for exposure to the experimental stimuli. The conditions need not be an actual laboratory of course, as studies frequently utilize classrooms, shopping malls, conference halls, or other venues that are appropriate and tailored for their study. Consider some recent studies that exemplify this type of research. Boettcher and Cobb (2006) used college undergraduates who had volunteered to join a psychological study subject pool for their research on Americans' sensitivity to casualties during war. They administered paper surveys to the students in routine educational settings, and found that the way that mock newspaper articles framed war casualties influenced support for the Iraq War. Schott and his collaborators conducted an important study to understand citizens' feelings toward war after sustaining casualties (2011). Using student subjects and other recruited adults in an experimental laboratory setting and exposing them to different hypothetical situations, they investigated attitudes toward casualties during war and whether people might tolerate higher casualties after having already sustained war deaths. They found that citizens' support for war actually increases after war deaths to avoid a sense of wasting earlier casualties. Attempting to understand how a political candidate's military experience influenced voters, a different study recruited adult subjects to view doctored election campaign advertising by candidates with military service to investigate how typical voters perceive candidates' military biography (Teigen 2013).

In those studies, each resembled some version of what Campbell and Stanley (1963: 8) call a "pretest-posttest control group design." With this design, subjects are randomly allocated to at least two groups: a control group and one or more treatment groups that will be exposed to the stimuli representing the variable of interest. A pretest is administered to all groups' members that includes some measure of the variable of interest. Then, the treatment groups are exposed to the experimental stimuli while the control group is not. Lastly, a posttest measures the variable of interest again. If the values differ between the control group and the treatment group, then the random allocation of subjects ensures that the only reasonable conclusion to explain the difference is the stimuli. Figure 20.1 depicts this experimental design with pretests and posttests and randomization.

A growing subset of the laboratory-style experiments embeds experimental designs within telephone surveys that query many subjects in representative samples of the population. These types of study do not take place in a laboratory at all; they more resemble a typical attitudinal survey conducted over the phone. They work by randomizing the subjects in the respondent pool and assigning them to the different stimuli groups. The groups can receive different background information, different priming, different batteries of questions, and conclude with a common set of questions regarding the dependent variable. In their research on Americans' perceptions of war casualties, Gelpi, Feaver and Reifler (2009) collected their experimental data

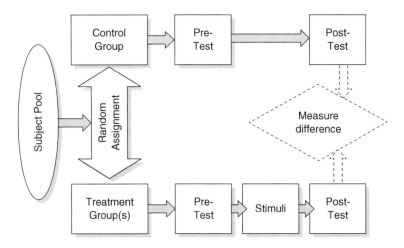

Figure 20.1 Pretest-posttest control group experimental design

Adopted from *Experimental and Quasi-Experimental Designs for Research* (Campbell and Stanley 1963).

using a "large-n" (a study that includes a large number of subjects, typically over 1,000) sample of the population. The subjects in their study were randomly placed into different groups who were presented with different hypothetical American security dilemmas. To generalize the findings from their book, their multi-method study provides evidence suggesting that Americans are more averse to military failure than to casualties.

With laboratory type research, the mechanism that exposes the experimental subjects to the different stimuli must be as standardized as possible. An experiment is thought to have high internal validity if it is internally consistent. The questionnaire or survey instrument, the tone with which the instructions are given to subjects, recruiting protocols, consent forms, et cetera, must be identical across groups. Only the factor that is intended to vary across the groups should differ. The point of the exercise is to attribute any difference in values of the dependent variable to the causal factor introduced to the non-control group(s), ergo every care must be taken by the researchers to homogenize everything else about the experimental conditions.

Beyond the laboratory-style experiments that use subjects who are recruited or surveyed with tightly controlled stimuli designs or in large surveys, the other type of experimentation in the social sciences is field experimentation, sometimes referred to as natural experiments and quasi-experiments. These studies exploit conditions in the real world that either closely resemble random or arbitrary subject selection into different groups to create a natural experiment, or are quasi-experiments that take advantage of nonrandom group selection that is methodologically useful because of the group contrasts. The subjects live and react to the forces that the research identifies post hoc as variables of interest, so the research lacks the artificiality of the laboratory setting. Researchers refer to the ability to extrapolate findings from an experiment to the real world as external validity, and field experiments enjoy higher external validity than their laboratory counterparts (Gerber 2011). On the downside, researchers with these designs are constrained in the questions they can research because they lack control over the parameters and application of the stimuli.

Scholars have taken advantage of conscription policies for experimentation in the area of military and veteran studies. When demand for manpower was at its highest during the

United States' involvement in the Vietnam War, young men's chances of being compulsorily drafted into the armed forces were based upon their birth dates starting in 1969. The 366 days of the year were randomly selected to create an order to draft young men as needed. The government's purpose in conducting this draft lottery system, using arbitrary attributes of the eligible men such as the month and day of their birth was presumably to make the system fair. For a researcher, because the men were randomly ordered into groups with higher and lower likelihood of being inducted, men born between 1944 and 1950 inadvertently comprise a rich study pool to measure the effects of draft eligibility through natural experimentation. One such study by Erikson and Stoker is highlighted as this chapter's illustrative study. The dataset from which the study measures political attitudes had the further benefit of being a longitudinal study, so political attitudes prior to the draft were measured, which serves a pretest akin to the experimental design depicted in Figure 20.1. Their important work studies how an individual's early-life vulnerability to the 1969 draft shaped later-life attitudes toward war, political ideology, and even their voting behavior in subsequent presidential elections.

Earlier studies have also exploited the draft lottery system as a natural experiment. One study ruled out draft vulnerability as an explanation for higher self-reported alcohol consumption among military veterans with the lottery data (Goldberg et al. 1991), and other studies have used the same lottery data to examine the implications of military service on later-life earnings (e.g. Angrist 1990). In essence, these studies exploit the government's induction policy to remove confounding explanatory reasons, such as self-selection or socioeconomic origins, and allow them to isolate and ascribe causal explanations to data patterns in the real world. It is important to note the difficulty in conducting a pretest prior to the stimuli. While not fatal to the inferential power of such an experiment, studies with pretests exhibit more validity. Figure 20.2 visually demonstrates the process of a simple version of this experimental design without a pretest, which Campbell and Stanley refer to as "posttest-only control group design" (1963: 25). Goldberg et al.'s study on drinking (1991), for example, uses this experimental design by comparing those with high draft eligibility versus those with low likelihood of conscription on alcohol consumption measured years later.

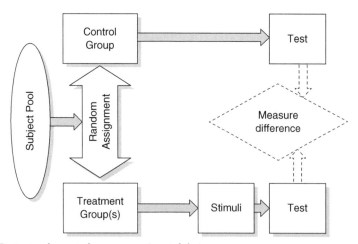

Figure 20.2 Posttest-only control group experimental design

Adopted from *Experimental and Quasi-Experimental Designs for Research* (Campbell and Stanley 1963).

Subject selection

The selection of subjects depends on the nature of the research question. The relatively small number of experimental studies in the field of military and veteran studies have generally used civilians or civilian military veterans as subjects because the research questions they posed related to attitudes about the military, foreign policy, war casualties, and other topics. Some of these studies have sought to understand how citizens within a democracy feel about military institutions, governments, policy, or wars, and with this aim, the subject pool need not be members of the military. Sometimes, researchers select specialized or unique subject pools to match with their study's design. Kleykamp's (2009) study on whether past military service makes a job candidate more attractive to potential employers sent manipulated résumés to real, advertised job listings to compare responses, making the hiring employers the subjects of the study.

While some question the use of samples of convenience when conducting experimental research, college students can serve as appropriate experimental subjects if the study seeks to generalize knowledge about how typical members of the public would react to given stimuli. An observational study hoping to infer something about attitudes or behavior in a nation's electorate requires a representative sample of the public, typically achieved through the random sampling methods used by polling outfits, and these samples need to exceed approximately 1,000 to keep the margin of error at or under about 3 percent. An experimental study does not need a representative sample of the public, nor does it demand a large sample akin to a national survey. It only needs to be large enough to obtain sufficient statistical power, depending on in part, the level of significance sought (Stephano 2003). The inferential power of an experiment stems from the random assignment of subjects to groups and the controlled stimuli, not necessarily from the size or representativeness of the subject pool itself.

Rationale

The key reason behind employing experimental methods is to gain leverage on causal relationships. Observational studies provide scholars with an estimate of the existence and strength of relationships between variables or concepts and may give great insight toward possible causal relationships. However, these studies cannot account for all the possible reasons behind why some cases exhibit one value of the dependent variable while others cases vary. Imagine a tongue-in-cheek hypothetical study that found, through a well-conducted survey of service members, compelling evidence that members of a nation's navy preferred life at sea while those in that same nation's army preferred to keep their boots on terra firma. If the researchers of such a study hoped to conclude that something related to serving in one branch or the other influenced their attitudes toward nautical or terrestrial life, the observational methodology only hints at causation. While the research would be valid if it concluded nothing beyond "those in the navy prefer x, while those in the army prefer y," the epistemological aim for many social scientists is to establish and understand causal explanations. One could not conclude that service in the navy is what engendered the preference for life on the high seas. Self-selection biases might also explain the difference, meaning those with a priori preferences for life at sea seek out a career in the navy. Social desirability might also explain the difference: those in the army's ranks may perceive a "correct" response to the survey question. Beyond those, many other conflating forces might be muddying the waters of why members of one branch feel one way or the other even if the two variables correspond in a strong pattern.

While the correlation between branch of service among military members versus their preference for living ashore or at sea may be vivid and obvious in the data, observational studies indicate relations and inform our scholarly understanding of the phenomena but cannot rule out other causal paths that might explain variation of the dependent variable. To observe and measure people, countries, or military institutions is to see how they are, and can reveal how different phenomena interrelate, but making conclusions about causal relationships based on those observational studies alone is methodologically problematic. Even when observational studies control for known correlates of their independent variable, by their nature, no observational study can possible "control for" as many possible causal explanations as an experimental design.

A more realistic example might entail the analytic problems with understanding the causal mechanisms behind why different individuals with different racial and ethnic identities in the armed forces perceive different level of satisfaction with their job in the military. Much has been written about race and identity in the U.S. armed forces on important topics such as racial integration, the all-volunteer force, noncitizens' service, and other matters. One recent article used cross-sectional survey data from men and women in the ranks of the U.S. military to demonstrate differences between gender, race, and ethnic groups in regard to views about job satisfaction and happiness in the ranks (Lundquist 2008). Using appropriate multivariate models to quantitatively estimate the relationship between race, ethnic, and gender variables and self-assessed job satisfaction, Lundquist concluded that minority groups enjoy higher levels of satisfaction in their military roles than minority groups in civilian occupational roles. This finding, she asserts, stems from the meritocratic nature of military hierarchies that lacks many of the structural inequalities found in civilian life.

To be sure, her conclusion is plausible, empirically based, and accords with other persuasive and previous research in this scholarly domain (Moskos and Butler 1996). However, it is difficult to infer causation from the relationship that the regression tables indicate exists. Is the ostensibly meritocratic structure of promotions and recruiting in the military the reason behind elevated levels of minority job satisfaction? Certainly, job satisfaction depends on the military's structure in some fashion, but an observational study such as this one, while valuable and informative, only suggests at the causal role of structure on attitudes. The study comprises control variables in the quantitative models, and the cross-sectional data quality and size are about as good as one can expect given the difficult-to-sample nature of military members (Dempsey 2009). Self-selection biases that likely influence who serves and who does not in the all-volunteer era are challenging to contend with analytically. Lundquist's observational study does not control for a priori attitudes because the data design cannot allow it, and large, representative panel studies are costly endeavors. Even if the study could control for previously held attitudes, it would still not be able to claim that the military's structure is the sole cause of the racial differences because racial, ethnic, and gender identities are likely correlated substantively with a host of other attitudes and social phenomena that are not 'in the model,' and hence are possibly biasing inferences about the causal role of the specified independent variables.

As a complement to observational studies, experiments help understand the causal relationships because they manipulate values of an independent variable, a postulated causal path, and then assess how those differences influence variation within the dependent variable. Experiments in political science have increased substantially, starting in the 1980s and beyond (Druckman et al. 2006), and while experiments do not befit all studies of the military, veterans, and civil–military relations, recent experimental studies within the field show that there is room for increased use of the method.

Drawbacks and limitations of experimental research

Considering again the problems of observational research highlighted with the superficial example of the army and navy service members, I pointed out that observational studies cannot nail down the causal explanation while experimental methodologies have that ability. In order to design an experimental study that would provide an explanation of cause, we could consider the following: the observational study lacked the ability to pinpoint cause due to the potentially confounding influences of unseen correlates, such as self-selection. We cannot state that service in the navy engenders a preference for life at sea even if the observational data correlate strongly because we cannot rule out alternative explanations, such as the fact that people with a priori nautical preferences choose the navy over the army. So, to remedy this analytic shortcoming by piloting an experimental approach, the solution is theoretically simple. To eliminate the potentially biased results, we only need to randomize the subjects' entry paths into the military by contacting the government in question and directing them to change their recruitment and induction policies. Rather than recruit to further defense and security needs, the government should instead allow social scientists to direct manpower decisions for the purposes of conducting research. This outcome is obviously not only unlikely but is rather politically and ethically dubious.

Experimental approaches to conduct social scientific research are circumscribed by limits that proscribe their use in several contexts. An early empirical study refuting claims that experience in the armed forces increased authoritarian attitudes among its members actually concluded by lamenting the impossibility of using an experiment in their context while explaining its difficulty: ' . . . ideally one should have had a true experiment in which equated groups were assigned by lot to various military and civilian life experiences and their attitudes compared after an appropriate period of time. But such an experiment not only is unfeasible but would not even then be ideal, as the experimental assignment would inevitably be obvious to the participants and as such would be so special a source of resentment and self-consciousness as to preclude generalization to the normal' (Campbell and McCormack 1957: 489). The drawbacks and limitations of experimentation generally stem from two sources: problems with external validity and shortcomings stemming from practical and ethical limits. These limits, which vex experimental researchers across the social sciences, are also constraining to those studying military topics and veterans.

The ability for an experiment to yield findings that pertain to the real world is referred to as external validity. Experimental designs gain their analytic advantages from controlling the environment in which subjects encounter the stimuli, but this control also contributes to the main weakness of experimental methodologies: the setting in which the experiment takes place where "results" are measured may be too far removed from how ordinary subjects in the real world encounter stimuli and react to it. Several of the experimental research examples cited above, as well as others, illustrate how citizens in a democracy react to battle casualties while a nation is at war. They employed experiments where arbitrary subjects were exposed to hypothetical wars or conflicts, often with conditional statements about casualties. Part of Gartner's (2008) study on how Americans' perceive casualties and casualty trends uses an experimental design with manipulated casualty rates in a hypothetical conflict. As the author concedes, it is challenging to infer that the findings from an artificial setting extend to explaining how people will react to real casualties, stating "[t]he concern is about external validity, that the scenarios represent artificial tests that lack real world applicability" (Gartner 2008: 105). His work is similar to Gelpi, Feaver, and Reifler's (2009) book, not only in its subject of war and perceptions of casualties, but also in the way that it uses multiple methodologies to hedge against the analytic shortcomings of any one of them.

Another criticism of experimental methods on external validity grounds is the unrepresentativeness of the usual subject in experimental studies: college undergraduates. Their availability and willingness to participate in studies have made students a staple of experimental research in the social sciences. Random assignment of test subjects to the experiment's various conditions washes away potentially confounding attributes that subjects bring with them. However, if the pool of possible subjects differs substantially from the population, representativeness concerns arise. College students represent a "narrow data base" and they differ in important ways from the population and those distinctions might have implications for the inferences drawn from experiments that employ them (Sears 1986: 515). They are younger and enjoy more cognitive skills than average, but their attitudes have often not coalesced and they have an underdeveloped sense of self and are more likely to comply with authority figures. They also consume news media in different ways than older adults. The degree to which college sophomore data are biased in this way may not always be a problem for experiments in military studies and potential biases hinge on the questions asked. In terms of the topic that has heretofore been most commonly investigated in military studies with experiments, war casualty sensitivity, potential bias from college sophomore data may arise from the fact that conscription or selective service may seem more salient for that age group.

Other threats to external validity for experiments in military studies are common to most laboratory or classroom style experimentation. The execution of the experimental research design may create effects itself that may erroneously appear as effects from the hypothesized independent variables. Unintended artifacts of the testing conditions, forms, question wording, research assistant demeanor, or other peculiarities may introduce results that will quietly bias the results that appear in the data. So-called "observer effects" may also introduce exaggerated or understated findings, referring to the possible tendency of experimental subjects to change their attitudes or behavior because of their awareness of the observation. For these issues, endemic to laboratory experimentation, the best remedy is to scrutinize the experiment's setting and protocols seeking to homogenize the experience across all groups.

Beyond practical limits to the subject and nature of experimentation in military and veteran studies, there are also ethical limits. In order to conduct human subject research, colleges and universities since the 1960s have developed ethics panels and institutional review boards to approve research on human subjects based upon an evaluation of the risks to subjects versus the potential for generalizable knowledge gained by such a study. The need for such protection of human subjects has its roots in concerns over biomedical research, and implementing these protections for evaluating work in political science, especially with interviewing and field work, has not been without problems (Schrag 2010). Experimentation as it has manifested in military and veteran studies presents little risk of harm to human subjects beyond the use of deception and the presentation of hypothetical casualties in a fictional scenario. It is the norm for studies to acquire subjects' consent for conducting research, frequently in written form. Deception in social scientific experiments, ruses that researchers employ to obfuscate the nature of the experiment's protocol and intent, generally involve minimal risk to subjects and these risks are minimized by conducting a debriefing after the experiment's stimuli and measurements have concluded.

Conclusion

To summarize, experimental methods are not a rival to observational studies, they are a complement to help scholars better establish causation. Using experiments successfully entails carefully balancing the concerns of internal and external validity. With gains in controlling the stimuli and context for experimental subjects come commensurate declines in the real world generalizability of a study. The most successful examples of research here rely not solely upon experiments to draw conclusions but rather employ multiple methodologies to gain traction on understanding causes and effects (e.g. Erikson and Stoker 2011; Gelpi et al. 2009). In the realm of military studies, investigating how citizens react to and feel about war casualties has been the most ripe area for experimentation, but that does not preclude innovations in other areas of studying civil-military relations, staffing, leadership, veterans, or other topics. New data sources have emerged that allow for relatively low-cost experimentation using internet opportunities, such as the Cooperative Congressional Election Study. Experiments are not a panacea for all scholars or questions in military and veteran studies, but their increased use and acceptance in political science means that we should look for opportunities to employ them to better understand phenomena within our field.

References

Angrist, J.D. (1990) "Lifetime Earnings and the Vietnam Era Draft Lottery: Evidence from social security administrative records," *American Economic Review* 80: 313–336.

Boettcher, W.A.I. and Cobb, M.D. (2006) "Echoes of Vietnam? Casualty framing and public perceptions of success and failure in Iraq," *The Journal of Conflict Resolution* 50: 831–854.

Campbell, D.T. and McCormack, T.H. (1957) "Military Experience and Attitudes toward Authority," *American Journal of Sociology* 62: 482–490.

Campbell, D.T. and Stanley, J.C. (1963) *Experimental and Quasi-Experimental Designs for Research*, Chicago, IL: Rand McNally & Co.

Dempsey, J.K. (2009) *Our Army: Soldiers, Politics, and American Civil-Military Relations*, Princeton, NJ: Princeton University Press.

Druckman, J.N., Green, D.P., Kuklinski, J.H. and Lupia, A. (2006) "The Growth and Development of Experimental Research in Political Science," *The American Political Science Review* 100: 627–635.

Erikson, R.S. and Stoker, L. (2011) "Caught in the Draft: The effects of Vietnam draft lottery status on political attitudes," *American Political Science Review* 105: 221–237.

Gartner, S.S. (2008) "The Multiple Effects of Casualties on Public Support for War: An experimental approach," *The American Political Science Review* 102: 95–106.

Gelpi, C., Feaver, P. and Reifler, J.A. (2009) *Paying the Human Costs of War: American Public Opinion and Casualties in Military Conflicts*, Princeton, NJ: Princeton University Press.

Gerber, A. (2011) "Field Experiments in Political Science," in J.N. Druckman, D.P. Green, J.H. Kuklinski and A. Lupia (eds) *Cambridge Handbook of Experimental Political Science*, New York: Cambridge University Press.

Goldberg, J., Richards, M.S., Anderson, R.J. and Rodin, M.B. (1991) "Alcohol Consumption in Men Exposed to the Military Draft Lottery: A natural experiment," *Journal of Substance Abuse* 3: 307–313.

Kleykamp, M. (2009) "A Great Place to Start? The effect of prior military service on hiring," *Armed Forces & Society* 35: 266–285.

Lundquist, J.H. (2008) "Ethnic and Gender Satisfaction in the Military: The effect of a meritocratic institution," *American Sociological Review* 73: 477–496.

Mill, J.S. (1848) *A System of Logic, Ratiocinative and Inductive: Being a Connected View of the Principles of Evidence and the Methods of Scientific Investigation (1843)*, New York: Harper & Brothers.

Moskos, C.C. and Butler, J.S. (1996) *All That We Can Be: Black Leadership and Racial Integration the Army Way*, New York: Basic Books.

Ruffa, R. and Soeters, J. (2014) "Cross National Research in the Military: Comparing operational styles in peace missions,' in J. Soeters, P.M. Shields and S. Rietjens (eds) *Routledge Handbook of Research Methods in Military Studies*, London: Routledge.

Schott, J.P., Scherer, L.D. and Lambert, A.J. (2011) "Casualties of War and Sunk Costs: Implications for attitude change and persuasion," *Journal of Experimental Social Psychology* 47: 1134–1145.

Schrag, Z.M. (2010) *Ethical Imperialism: Institutional Review Boards and the Social Sciences, 1965–2009*, Baltimore, MD: Johns Hopkins University Press.

Sears, D.O. (1986) "College Sophomores in the Laboratory: Influences of a narrow database on social psychology's view of human nature," *Journal of Personality and Social Psychology* 51: 515–530.

Stephano, J.D. (2003) "How Much Power Is Enough? Against the development of an arbitrary convention for statistical power calculations," *Functional Ecology* 17: 707–709.

Teigen, J.M. (2013) "Military Experience in Elections and Perceptions of Issue Competence: An experimental study with television ads," *Armed Forces & Society* 39: 415–433.

21

THE EMPIRICAL ANALYSIS OF CONFLICTS, USING DATABASES

Min Ye and Uk Heo

J. Oneal, B. Russett, and M. Berbaum (2003) "Causes of peace: Democracy, interdependence, and international organizations, 1885–1992," *International Studies Quarterly* 47: 371–393.

"Causes of peace" is an empirical analysis of the Kantian peace theory. According to Kant, international peace depends on three factors: republican constitutions or democracy, economic interdependence through trade, and common membership of international organizations. The theoretical logic behind this argument is as follows. Democracies tend not to fight each other because democratic norms discourage using force to solve disputes and democratic government structures make the decision to go to war against another democracy difficult. Trading goods and services results in interdependence between trade partners and waging a war against an important trade partner significantly affects citizens' everyday life. Common international organization membership provides government officials with opportunities to develop personal networks with other government representatives. Thus, as the number of common international organization membership increases, the two countries are likely to have stronger personal networks among government officials, which makes a war less likely.

Due to the potential simultaneity bias between conflict and trade, the authors developed two empirical models to test the Kantian peace theory: conflict and trade equations. The dependent variable of the conflict equation is fatal militarized interstate disputes. Since militarized interstate dispute data include pairs of nations that never threatened or used force against each other, they used the fatal disputes, which are a corrected version of militarized interstate disputes. Independent variables of the conflict equation include democracy, trade, joint inter-governmental organization (IGO) memberships, national capability ratio, alliance, territorial contiguity, distance, minor powers, and fatal disputes in the past seven years. The trade equation's independent variables are democracy, joint memberships of IGOs, alliance, gross domestic product (GDP), population, trade amount in the previous ten years, fatal disputes in the past two years, territorial contiguity and distance.

Using the Correlates of War (COW) data for 1885–1992, the authors conducted a statistical analysis and found that democracy, economic interdependence, and common IGO memberships significantly reduce conflicts. They also found that democratic countries trade with other democracies more than non-democracies, and the number of joint IGO membership were commensurate with trade amount. In contrast to previous findings, alliance did not have significant effects on conflicts.

The contribution of this study is threefold: first, the authors developed an integrated model based on extant literature. Incorporating all the theoretical tenets included in realism and liberalism, the authors proposed an empirical model that can be widely used in conflict studies. Many conflict studies published after this work employed similar model specifications. Second, both realists (power ratio, distance, and contiguity) and liberal arguments (trade interdependence, democratic peace, and common IGO memberships) were empirically supported. Third, this study included distributed-lags modeling to incorporate the accumulated effects of certain variables over time. By doing so, the authors analyzed a certain variable's combined effects of past and present on the dependent variable. Considering history often plays a significant role in conflict onset and trade relationship, this approach is theoretically meaningful and methodologically innovative. Thus, it suggests a new direction to conflict studies.

Introduction

Important theoretical contributions need empirical confirmation. Since the scientific revolution in political science in the 1960s, empirical analysis using quantitative data – also known as data-based analysis, large-N analysis or, more generally, quantitative research, or scientific study – has been one of the most prevailing approaches in the discipline. In *American Political Science Review*, the most prestigious journal in political science, the proportion of articles that employ empirical analysis with quantitative data sets has dramatically increased from less than a quarter in the 1960s to about a half in the 1980s (King 1991). In the subfield of international relations, approximately 45 percent of the articles published in the leading journals between 1990 and 1999 used quantitative data and methods (Zinnes 2002). In the meantime, great improvements have been made in both methods and data collection. As a result, students today have a rich repertoire of rigorous methods and databases, covering a wide range of significant issues in conflict studies. For instance, the Inter-university Consortium for Political and Social Research (ICPSR) has archived a total of 60 data sets under the subject of "Conflict, Aggression, Violence, and Wars."

In this chapter, we provide a comprehensive review of conflict studies that used quantitative datasets. Since the validity of empirical analysis heavily relies on the proper method and the quality of data, the focus of this study is on methodological innovation and advances in data collection. To this end, we analyzed the articles published in *Journal of Conflict Resolution* (*JCR*) for 1957–2009. There are two reasons for us to do this. First, *JCR* is generally considered one of the best journals in studying international conflicts. Another reason is that *JCR* well represents theoretical, empirical, and methodological advancement in conflict studies.

Empirical analysis in conflict studies: Then and now

Of the 1,120 conflict studies published in *JCR* between 1957 and 2009, 704, or 63 percent, are empirical analyses using some sort of data. Figure 21.1 illustrates the overall growth of empirical studies in *JCR*. Our analysis suggests three major stages in the development of empirical analysis of conflicts, as marked in the figure. At the beginning, less than 20 percent of the articles

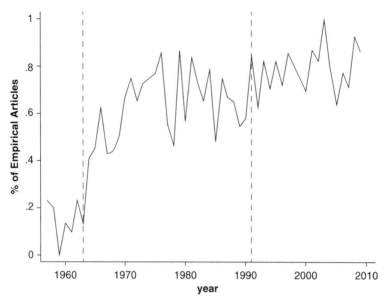

Figure 21.1 The growth of empirical analysis of conflicts with data sets

published in *JCR* used empirical data and methods. Most empirical data used in these studies were from governments, international organizations, businesses, or borrowed from other disciplines of social sciences. Most of these data were processed with basic descriptive statistical methods, such as percentages and cross tabulations. The most sophisticated inferential statistical method adopted in these studies was bivariate correlation. This is not surprising considering the lack of methodological skills among political scientists and insufficient financial and institutional resources for data collection in the late 1950s and early 1960s.

As the scientific revolution gradually took place and methodological training reached more faculty and graduate students in political science departments, the late 1960s and 1970s saw a dramatic surge in quantitative research in political science (Franklin 2008). This is also reflected in conflict studies. As demonstrated in Figure 21.1, the proportion of empirical analysis published in *JCR* has increased sharply since 1964, reaching 70 percent in the early 1970s and remained steady at that level thereafter. In addition to the dramatic growth in quantity, more fundamental changes took place in the quality of empirical conflict analysis in terms of both data collection and methods.

While government and commercial data, and data from other disciplines were essential for the takeoff of empirical analysis of conflicts, they had serious limitations: most of these data were compiled to serve purposes other than the research of military conflicts. It was always difficult for researchers to find information to operationalize and measure key concepts in conflict studies such as power, conflict, or foreign policy behavior. Therefore, as more institutional and financial resources became available (Harty and Modell 1991) political scientists started constructing databases tailored to the specific needs of conflict studies. Their efforts resulted in a number of landmark research projects and data sets – the Correlates of War (COW) project, Conflict and Peace Data Bank (COPDAB), the World Event/Interaction Survey (WEIS), and the Stockholm International Peace Research Institute (SIPRI) databases, US Arms Control and Disarmament Agency (ACDA) data, just to name a few – that were widely utilized in later studies. Moreover, a computer program named EUGENE (the Expected Utility Generation and

Data Management Program) was developed to make quantitative data management easy. The program is a Windows-based data management tool. It facilitates the creation of data sets for use in the quantitative analysis of international relations by merging multiple data sets to generate new dyadic data sets, including variables used to test rational choice theories.

Of all the data sets created during this period, perhaps the most influential is the COW project by J. David Singer and his colleagues at the University of Michigan. The COW data have been used in 118 *JCR* articles through 2009. Founded in 1963, the COW project aimed to offer comprehensive data on all international conflicts and wars after the end of the Napoleonic War. The project marked an important milestone in our theoretical exploration of conflicts and wars. Its conceptualization of war, its collection of various "correlates" of war guided generations of scholars in their quests for causes of wars. The COW definition of war and state, and its classification of war have basically become the standard in conflict studies and are still commonly taught in courses of international relations. Over the years, the project has been continuously updated and expanded into new territories of research. It currently offers 11 major databases on various issues and topics of conflicts between 1816 and 2007 to scholars and the public.

Great progress has also been made in research methods. Two major changes are noticeable: extensive use of inferential statistics and the variety of statistical methods. In Figure 21.2, we listed the percentage of articles that used descriptive and inferential statistics. The trend is clearly noticeable: starting from the late 1960s, the number of studies using inferential statistics continuously increased. Another conspicuous change is the variety of statistical methods used in the literature, which include ANOVA (Analysis of Variance), Student's *t*-test, factor analysis, time series ARIMA (Autoregressive Integrated Moving Average) modeling, multiple regression, logit/probit analysis, Vector Autoregression, Error Correction Model, distributed-lag model, and simultaneous equation model. Although, as King (1991) pointed out, these imported methods (mostly from economics, statistics, and psychology) may not be well suited to political data and research, their contributions to the development of empirical conflict studies were significant. These research methods also heightened our ability to process empirical data to a new

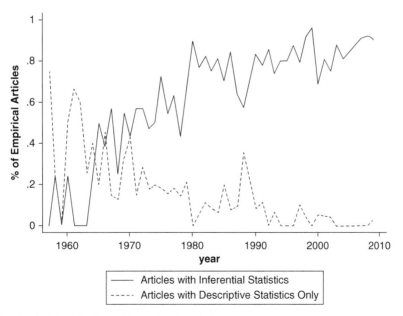

Figure 21.2 Statistical methods used in empirical analysis

level, which in turn motivated more systematic data collections. In addition, applications of these methods highlighted the role of quantitative methods in conflict studies – including both what they are able and unable to achieve – and effectively stimulated the demand among faculty and graduate students for more advanced methods training.

The end of the Cold War brought another transformation in conflict studies. As the bipolar rivalry faded away along with the demise of the Soviet empire, scholars shifted their focus to more urgent threats to international security, such as conflicts between small states, civil wars, ethnic conflicts, and after the September 11 terrorist attack, terrorism. To empirical analysis of conflicts, the immediate impact was the end of the dominance of systemic-level analysis as well as the obsession with great powers. Researchers started embracing a multilevel approach that allowed them to probe state- and individual-level explanatory variables. In addition, studies started forming "standard" variables that are almost required to be included in quantitative conflict analysis. The study by Oneal et al. (2003) shows a list of variables that typically appear in quantitative analysis of conflicts.

However, previous data sets, because of their preoccupation with systemic-level variables, were unable to offer enough information to test the new hypotheses. Therefore, the most notable development in empirical conflict analysis occurred in data collection. Over the years, scores of new data sets were created, expanding empirical analysis to fields where only qualitative research was conducted in the past. For instance, in our review of *JCR* publications after 1990, data sets like the Minority at Risk (MAR) project, Polity project, International Crisis Behavior (ICB) project, UCDP/PRIO Armed Conflict Dataset, International Terrorism: Attributes of Terrorist Events (ITERATE), and Global Terrorism Database (GTD) were applied to topics such as ethnic conflicts, civil wars, international crises, and terrorism.

The most remarkable progress in this period was the usage of game-theoretic approach in conflict studies. Compared to other analytical methods in conflict studies, the most distinguished feature of game theory rests on its emphasis on the interactive nature of conflicts. One party's behavior is affected by the opponent's move. The analysis of equilibrium – i.e. the stabilized status of interactions – generates insights and testable hypotheses about the initiation, duration, and termination of conflicts. It should be noted that game theory is nothing new in conflict studies. Thomas Schelling's (1957) seminal study on bargaining and war was published in the first issue of *JCR*. The study attempted to explain interstate wars and bargaining process from a game perspective between two nations. Nevertheless, game theory did not become a fruitful approach until the 1980s when political studies emphasized dyadic analysis in conflict studies (Levy 2000). Since the pioneer studies by Bueno de Mesquita and Lalman (1992), Fearon (1995), and Powell (1999), a myriad of game-theoretic studies has been designed to investigate various issues of international and domestic conflicts. Between 1990 and 2009, 64 articles that employed game theory were published in *JCR* – as opposed to 23 between 1970 and 1989 – involving a wide range of topics, such as international conflict and crisis, domestic constrains on states' war behavior, economic sanctions and war, civil and ethnic conflicts, terrorism, etc. These achievements have manifested the potential of this powerful and rigorous analytical approach to our understanding of conflicts.

Our literature review has sketched out the development of empirical analysis of conflicts in the past half-century. As one of the most vibrant subfields in international studies, conflict studies always stand out for its ability to absorb the most advanced methods and theories and echo the most recent changes in the real world. Their findings help scholars, policy makers, and the public to better understand the world. That said, the achievements should not blindfold us to the challenges we are facing. The future success of this approach will ultimately depend on whether these challenges are properly addressed. Next, we turn to the basics of empirical analysis of conflicts, and discuss its rationale, major steps, the current debate on its drawbacks and limitations, and possible solutions.

Reflections on empirical analysis of conflicts

Why empirical analysis of conflicts?

To every student of conflict studies, this comes naturally as the first question to be addressed. The answer includes at least two parts. The most direct response is because many research questions on conflicts are empirical. Questions like "What is the relationship between the likelihood of war and the power ratio between the two confronting countries? Do democracies tend not to go to war against another democracy? Or does domestic disturbance prompt a state's external use of force?" are difficult to answer without empirical data and proper statistical techniques. The second part is more contentious, which has divided the study of conflicts between the so-called "traditional qualitative" and "scientific quantitative" communities. Advocates of the scientific approach argue that the merit of empirical analysis over traditional qualitative method (such as historical analysis and case study) in conflict studies lies in its ability to accumulate our knowledge. As demonstrated in the renowned "wheel of science" diagram (Wallace 1971), while our observations of some conflicts can help us reach some generalized conclusions, or theories, about the nature and causes of the conflicts in interest, these theoretical propositions must be verified by systemically collected observational data before they are accepted as being useful. Furthermore, as new observations and data become available, we will repeat this process and put existing theories to new tests. As a consequence, the wheel rolls forward and our knowledge about conflicts is accumulated.

Since Wright (1942) and Richardson's (1960) pioneer studies, impressive progress has been made in our knowledge of war and conflict. Compared to the beginning years of empirical analysis of conflicts, we have a much better understanding of conflicts. Now we know that, as opposed to the popular Balance-of-Power theory, war is more likely to occur when there is parity of power between disputants. But when a war breaks out, it is more likely to be started by the stronger side (Bueno de Mesquita 1980); although democratic states are generally as war-prone as non-democracies, war rarely takes place between democratic states because of normative and structural reasons (Oneal et al. 2003; Rousseau et al. 1996); autocratic leaders are more likely to employ diversionary tactic – when a nation experiences domestic political and/ or economic difficulties, the leader of the nation may employ risky foreign policies including using force to divert public attention from domestic issues – than democratic leaders (Oneal and Tir 2006); democratic leaders are selective in the wars they are willing to fight, whereas autocratic leaders tend to fight longer wars (Bueno de Mesquita and Siverson 1995). We also know what factors help deterrence work or fail (Huth 1988); insurgency and civil war are more likely triggered by economic adversity and political instability rather than ethnic and religious characteristics (Fearon and Laitin 2003).

Nevertheless, these accomplishments do not necessarily mean empirical analysis is the only valid approach in conflict studies. Statistical analysis with quantitative data is not much helpful in addressing normative issues, such as just causes to go to war or right behavior in the war. Neither do they suggest the inconsequentiality of other methods – most notably, qualitative methods – in the analysis of conflicts. Quite the contrary, we believe the relationship between the quantitative and qualitative approaches should be complementary each other rather than competitive. Just as Leng (2002: 423) insightfully contended, "the most interesting research questions often are those that require the integration of quantitative and qualitative methods."

While a complete review of qualitative methods in conflict studies is beyond the scope of this chapter (several chapters in this volume are devoted to various qualitative methods), two facts are crucial for students of empirical analysis of conflicts. First, after decades of advance in methodology and research design, qualitative analysis has grown into a significant part of scientific inquiry in conflict studies. In our literature review of *JCR*, a growing number of comparative analysis and case studies, like their quantitative counterparts, generated both insights into and cumulative knowledge about conflicts. Generally speaking, quantitative research is good at identifying the broad pattern between the dependent variable and independent variables, whereas qualitative research enables us to delve into their particular causal mechanisms (Fearon and Laitin 2002). Second, in those fields where large-N analysis cannot be conducted because of the lack of systemic data or variables, case study and/or small-N analysis remain our only choice. In fact, many data generation enterprises began with comparative case studies. In-depth analysis and comparison of historical events not only generate the first batch of observational data, but also offer the initial theoretical propositions that guide the following data collection efforts.

How to design an empirical analysis of conflicts?

Typically, an empirical analysis of conflicts starts with a clearly defined **research question**. Because an empirical research article is supposed to explicate a real issue in the world, a research question typically involves "why," "how," or "whether." The principal function of a research question is to specify the phenomenon the author attempts to explain, namely, variance of the dependent variable. For instance, in our classical study presented in the textbox, the research question is "whether . . . trade, institutionalized democracy, and joint memberships in international governmental organizations affect the likelihood of militarized interstate disputes" (Oneal et al. 2003: 372). The dependent variable is the "likelihood of militarized interstate disputes." At this stage, the author does not have to propose an explanation. But it is always helpful to discuss the significance of the research question, a justification of the research project.

The second step of empirical research is to conduct a **literature review**. The purpose of literature review is to summarize findings of previous studies concerning the research question. Since empirical research aims to accumulate knowledge, it is crucial to recognize what we have learned, what data sets have been created, and what methods have been employed to process the data. According to Johnson and Reynolds (2005: 132), a literature review is also used "to develop general explanations for observed variations in a behavior or phenomenon; to identify potential relationships between concepts and to identify researchable hypotheses; to learn how others have defined and measured key concepts . . . and to discover how a research project is related to the work of others." In our illustrative research example, Oneal et al. (2003) provide a literature review on democratic peace and the effects of trade on interstate conflicts. Their literature review points out how previous studies failed to show the causal relationship between trade and war, that is, whether trade prevents war or is merely an outcome of peace. Obviously, the analysis of the accomplishments and deficiencies illustrates the current status of our knowledge and what their research is going to achieve and how to accomplish it.

After presenting the research question and assessing the current status of the literature, the following step is to propose an answer to the research question, or the author's **theory**. Simply put, a theory is a generalized explanation for some social phenomena. In an empirical analysis of conflicts, the proposed theory could be derived from a well-established theory, inspired by a particular study, or generated from the author's own observations. A theory is usually expressed as a statement about the relationship between a dependent variable and explanatory variables. For example, the proposed theory in our classical study is based on the famous Kantian theory of perpetual peace that asserts "international peace could be established on a foundation of three elements: republican constitutions . . . free trade and economic interdependence, and international law and organizations" (Oneal et al. 2003: 371). The three independent variables are bilateral trade, the political character of regimes (democracy), and joint international organization memberships.

To test a theory, **hypotheses** are developed. A hypothesis is an educated guess regarding the relationship between a dependent variable and an independent variable. The function of a hypothesis is to test whether or not a theory is supported by empirical data. Each hypothesis is a prediction about the effect of an independent variable on the dependent variable with the direction of the relationship: positive or negative. In our classical study (Oneal et al. 2003), based on the Kantian theory, the authors expected a negative relationship between all three independent variables (bilateral trade, democracy, and IO memberships) and the dependent variable (the likelihood of war).

To test the hypotheses, an empirical model has to be specified based on extant literature. Since many variables affect social phenomena, inclusion of all the theoretically relevant variables, the so-called control variables, in the model is crucial because statistical analysis is based on the assumption that the model is fully specified. Under-specified models due to omitted variables can lead to incorrect results in the statistical analysis.

All the variables included in the model specification also need to be operationalized in order to quantify the corresponding concepts. Fortunately, international relations scholars have developed a notable number of data sets by operationalizing a cohort of core concepts in conflict studies. As a result, most empirical studies can resort to existing data sets for variable measurement. In our classical study (Oneal et al. 2003), for instance, all the variables are directly drawn from existing data sets: the likelihood of interstate war is calculated using the Dyadic Militarize Interstate Disputes from the COW project (Maoz 1999); bilateral trade from Maddison's (1995) and Gleditsch's (2002) trade data sets; democracy from the POLITY project; and international organization memberships from the *Yearbook of International Organization*. Nevertheless, operationalizing and measuring new variables is still a big challenge.

The last step is to put hypotheses to an empirical test with the data. **Data analysis** serves two purposes. One is to find out whether to accept or reject the null hypothesis – that there is no relationship between the dependent and independent variables – at a certain statistical significance level. If the null hypothesis is rejected, then researchers want to know what the direction of the relationship is to see whether the prediction of the hypothesis is confirmed. As discussed earlier in our review of articles published in *JCR*, progress in research methods has provided plenty of choices in data processing. However, a caveat is that the research question and the particular type of data at hand should determine the selection of a proper method. In this regard, our classical research presents a good example. Traditional studies rely on a system of structural equations to investigate the reciprocal relationship between trade and conflict. However, as Oneal et al. (2003) indicated, this method only considers contemporaneous terms, that is, the bilateral trade in a year only affects the likelihood of conflict in the same year and vice versa. To include the long-time effects between trade and conflict on each other, they employed a distributed-lag model, which includes lagged values in the model.

Finally, the main research question, and the author's theory, and all the empirical findings are summarized in the conclusion. In addition, theoretical and policy implications of the findings are discussed. Future research can also be suggested to conclude the empirical study.

Limitations and future developments

There are two issues in the recent literature of empirical conflict studies. These two issues are pertinent to many ongoing research projects and pivotal for the future development of this approach. The first issue concerns the integration of multiple levels of research. The "unexpected" end of the Cold War exposed the weakness of neo-realism, especially its preoccupation with systemic-level analysis. As a result, more and more theoretical quests have employed a multilevel framework that includes variables at the systemic, domestic and individual levels. The reason is that multilevel analysis is required for the analysis of hierarchically structured data as Goldenberg and Soeters (2014) argue in Chapter 18. This change in approach generated a new wave of empirical research in conflict studies. However, most of the multilevel models are, using Levy's (2000: 322) term, "additive in nature." That is, they simply put variables from different levels in the same regression model without inspecting the real interactions between them. This is more than a model specification problem (therefore cannot be resolved by including some interaction terms). The nature of the relationship between hierarchically structured variables must determine how empirical models should be specified. Simply adding variables would not grant meaningful findings.

The second problem, which is related to the first issue, is the absence of a theoretical framework that can systemically incorporate different levels of analysis in the analysis. A series of questions need to be addressed before such a framework can be established. What is the unit of analysis? Should we take it as a monadic issue of decision-making or a dyadic problem of interaction? In the former case, how do the decision maker, a state, a domestic organization, or a national leader, balance interests at different levels? For the latter, how can interactions between two decision makers be modeled and empirically tested? Substantial progress has been made in the theoretical probe into decision-making approach with growing research interests in the link between domestic politics and foreign policy (Bueno de Mesquita et al. 2005). But our empirical investigation in these fields gained limited ground, mainly because of the lack of data at the individual level, not to mention the tremendous gap in our knowledge of multilevel dyadic models.

Conclusion

At the turn of the century, after reviewing the development of conflict studies, Vasquez (2000: xvii) asserted, "while we still have a long way to go, it is clear that we know a great deal more today than we did thirty-five years ago" about international conflicts. A decade later, this comment is still cogent. On the one hand, considerable progress has been made in theories, research methods, and data collection; on the other hand, there still are many questions to answer, many problems to address, and many challenges to overcome.

As for the future, the healthy development of the discipline hinges on its three kinds of ability. The first is the discipline's ability to capture changes in the real world. Due to the uniqueness of its subject matter, conflict studies should be able to identify the most pressing threats to global peace, unveil their nature, and recommend their solutions. After all, the real world is not only where the research questions and data are found, it is also the *raison d'être* for this discipline. Our ability to serve the world is vital for the discipline to attract best brains and secure more resources.

The second is the ability to assimilate the achievements in the subfields of political science and other disciplines. The history of the empirical study of conflicts reveals a pattern of absorbing and integrating the theoretical developments and methodological innovations from other fields. In many places of this chapter, we have urged the integration between quantitative and qualitative, between systemic, state, and individual levels of analysis, and between formal and statistical models. Part of the reason is the interdisciplinary nature of conflicts. Yet the deeper root is the belief in the value of diverse approaches and methods to our knowledge of conflicts.

This belief is the reason the pioneers began the empirical inquiry into conflict, the driving force for the discipline to keep growing and expanding in the past decade, and we are convinced, the secret for empirical conflict studies to continue to thrive in the future.

Finally, a rich source of data is available at the operations level (e.g. situation reports). Researchers should follow the lead of early COW scholars and construct these types of databases. The point is to extend the use of databases into new areas of research.

References

Bueno de Mesquita, B. (1980) "An Expected Utility Theory of International Conflict," *American Political Science Review*, 74: 917–931.

Bueno de Mesquita, B. and Lalman, D. (1992) *War and Reason: Domestic and International Imperatives*, New Haven, CT: Yale University Press.

Bueno de Mesquita, B. and Siverson, R. (1995) "War and the Survival of Political Leaders: A comparative study of regime types and political accountability," *American Political Science Review*, 89: 841–855.

Bueno de Mesquita, B., Smith, A., Siverson, R., and Morrow, J. (2005) *The Logic of Political Survival*, Cambridge MA: MIT Press.

Fearon, J. (1995) "Rationalist Explanations for War," *International Organization*, 49: 379–415.

Fearon, J. and Laitin, D. (2002) "Integrating Qualitative and Quantitative Methods," in J. Box-Steffensmeier, H. Brady, and D. Collier (eds) *The Oxford Handbook of Political Methodology*, Oxford: Oxford University Press.

Fearon, J. and Laitin, D. (2003) "Ethnicity, Insurgency, and Civil War," *American Political Science Review*, 97: 75–90.

Franklin, C. (2008) "Quantitative Methodology," in J. Box-Steffensmeier, H. Brady, and D. Collier (eds) *The Oxford Handbook of Political Methodology*, Oxford: Oxford University Press.

Geller, D. and Singer, J.D. (1998) *Nations at War: A Scientific Study of International Conflict*, Cambridge: Cambridge University Press.

Gleditsch, K. (2002) "Expanded Trade and GDP Data," *Journal of Conflict Resolution*, 46: 712–724.

Goldenberg, I. and Soeters, J. (2014) "Cross-national research in the military: Comparing operational styles," in J.M.M.L. Soeters, P.M. Shields, and S.J.H. Rietjens (eds) *Routledge Handbook of Research Methods in Military Studies*, Abingdon: Routledge.

Harty, M. and Modell, J. (1991) "The First Conflict Resolution Movement, 1956–1971: An attempt to institutionalize interdisciplinary social science," *Journal of Conflict Resolution*, 35: 720–758.

Huth, P. (1988) "Extended Deterrence and the Outbreak of War," *American Political Science Review*, 82: 423–443.

Johnson, J. and Reynolds, H.T. (2005) *Political Science Research Methods*, 5th edn, Washington D.C.: CQ Press.

King, G. (1991) "On Political Methodology," *Political Analysis*, 2: 1–30.

Leng, R. (2002) "Quantitative International Politics and Its Critics," in M. Brecher and F. Harvey (eds) *Millennial Reflections on International Studies*, Ann Arbor, MI: University of Michigan Press.

Levy, J. (2000) "Reflections on the Scientific Study of War," in J. Vasquez (ed.) *What Do We Know about War?*, Lanham, MD: Rowman and Littlefield.

Maddison, A. (1995) *Monitoring the World Economy: 1820–1992*, Paris: OECD.

Maoz, Z. (1999) Dyadic Militarized Interstate Disputes (DYMID 1.1). Available at Dataset ftp:// spirit.tau.ac.il/zeevmaos/dyadmid60.xls.

Oneal, J., Russett, B., and Berbaum, M. (2003) "Causes of Peace: Democracy, interdependence, and international organizations, 1885–1992," *International Studies Quarterly*, 47: 371–393.

Oneal, J. and Tir, J. (2006) "Does the Diversionary Use of Force Threaten the Democratic Peace? Assessing the effect of economic growth on interstate conflict, 1921–2001," *International Studies Quarterly*, 50: 755–779.

Powell, R. (1999) *In the Shadow of Power*, Princeton, NJ: Princeton University Press.

Richardson, L. (1960) *Arms and Insecurity: A Mathematical Study of the Causes and Origins of War*, Pittsburgh, PA: Boxwood Press.

Rousseau, D.L., Gelpi, C., Reiter, D., and Huth, P. (1996) "Assessing the Dyadic Nature of the Democratic Peace," *American Political Science Review*, 90: 512–533.

Rubinstein, A. (1982) "Perfect Equilibrium in a Bargaining Model," *Econometrica*, 50: 97–110.

Schelling, T. (1957) "Bargaining, Communication, and Limited War," *Journal of Conflict Resolution*, 1: 19–36.

Vasquez, J. (ed.) (2000) *What Do We Know about War?*, Lanham, MD. Rowman and Littlefield.

Wallace, W. (1971) *The Logic of Science in Sociology*, Chicago, IL: Aldine-Atherton.

Wright, Q. (1942) *A Study of War*, Chicago, IL: University of Chicago Press.

Zinnes, D. (2002) "Reflections on Quantitative International Politics," in M. Brecher and F. Harvey (eds) *Millennial Reflections on International Studies*, Ann Arbor, MI: University of Michigan Press.

22

COMPUTATIONAL MODELING TO STUDY CONFLICTS AND TERRORISM[1]

Joseph K. Young and Michael G. Findley

J. M. Epstein (2002) "Modeling civil violence: An agent-based computational approach," *Proceedings of the National Academy of Sciences of the United States of America* **99(Suppl 3): 7243–7250.**

Epstein provides two general computational models of civil violence. The first examines a government attempting to suppress a decentralized rebellion and the second investigates government efforts to quash communal violence between rival ethnic groups.

Model I or the rebellion vs. state model involves two broad categories of actors: the state vs. the population or what Epstein terms the *Cops* vs. *Agents*. Like other computational models, each category of actor includes a heterogeneous mix of types. Members of the population (Agents) vary according to their (H) hardship and (L) legitimacy. H is a parameter to capture social and economic grievances. L is the perception of legitimacy of the government. While one could argue about the distribution of types in society (how many people are highly aggrieved, what proportion feel the government is not legitimate), computational models make this assumption clear and allow the analyst to shift this distribution and show the implications for the growth of phenomena, such as rebellion or intercommunal violence. Additionally, Epstein builds in local rationality (a limited bounded form) that is missing in many other formal or verbal models of similar processes. Epstein makes clear that the ideas are general and not meant to predict any single case and that the parameters are not direct measurements of actual grievance or legitimacy. Epstein provides a table showing the different experiments he undertakes and the values for key parameters that he seeds the model with.

One of the most important findings from computational models is an outcome that *emerges* from the interaction of agents. One critique of these models is that properly programmed, the model can tell the analysts anything they want to know. When results are counterintuitive or macro outcomes emerge from micro decision rules that are non-obvious, the model provides microfoundations that

(continued)

(continued)

are unlikely to be unearthed using other methods. Epstein finds deceptive behavior by Agents that were active rebels to hide from the Cops and parade around as normal citizens (something we know occurs). Epstein also finds important tipping points outlined in game models, such as work by Kuran (1991), that occur when parameters move beyond a particular threshold.

In the second model, members of two ethnic groups can choose to target each other. L is still a parameter in the model, but it refers to the belief that the other side has a right to exist. Cops are also included and attempt to reduce ethnic killings. Stylized facts that emerge from the model include: when legitimacy is high, Cops are completely unnecessary. Reductions in L lead to episodes of ethnic cleansing even when force levels are high. Variance in genocide episodes increase as force levels do suggesting that increasing guardianship will work in some cases and not others.

Both models highlight the strengths and weaknesses of this modeling approach. The models are general enough to make predictions about a wide array of phenomena, such as ethnic cleanings, genocide, rebellion, and the emergence of public preferences. To be useful for predicting specific cases of interest for policymakers and the military, initial modeling parameters should be seeded with values consistent with the local context. The equilibria that develop can then be tested using dyadic events data (see for example Findley et al. 2010). Utilizing a lattice with actual GIS information consistent with the context of interest can also help match the model to reality. One danger though is to build such a complex model that it becomes *too real*. In short, with too many parameters (Miller and Page 2007), it is unclear which one is influencing the equilibria in the observed way. Models must strike a balance between being specific and thus actionable and yet parsimonious and as a consequence tractable.

Introduction

A randomized experiment is the gold standard for establishing causality in the sciences. If researchers want to understand how a change in an actor's behavior can be attributed to a stimulus, random assignment to the treatment and control group is an absolute prerequisite (see Chapter 20). While this premise is mostly accepted across the social sciences, it is challenging to implement such a design when studying many applications involving military conflict, such as the dynamics of insurgency, counterinsurgency, and terrorism.

First, the ability to randomly assign interventions to treatment and control is difficult if not impossible in most cases. Many strategies affecting war and peace are typically not practical or ethical to implement. Second, most experiments need to be replicated to ensure their reliability and validity. Yet, it is impossible to rerun history. Third, we cannot directly observe outcomes that did not occur. What would have happened to the trajectory of the World War II had Hitler been successfully killed by coup plotters? Would the post-Iraq War reconstruction have been more stabilizing had the US and its partners not disbanded the Iraqi Army? Both of these questions are what social scientists term counterfactuals. In short, a counterfactual is an attempt by an analyst to reference a condition where the outcome of an event would have been different had a key causal factor been absent (Fearon 1991). Fourth, even when we use controlled experimentation, we want to know how an individual would have reacted in both a treatment or control condition. Yet, we generally only observe them in one of those states (Holland 1986).

These four fundamental problems with experimentation in military science applications suggest a potentially dismal outlook for research in this area: we can undertake studies in this domain, but we can never approximate the ideal study to make valid causal inference. With recent breakthroughs in field experiments applied in comparative and international politics notwithstanding (Fearon et al. 2009; Findley et al. 2013), we argue that computational modeling is a research methodology that can address some of these problems and lead to the development of sound theory in social and military sciences that informs policy choices by political and military strategists.

In the chapter that follows, we first outline the methodology of computational modeling. We explain how to develop a model, how to use computational modeling to assess counterfactuals, how to integrate with data, and how to interpret the final results. We also identify the strengths and weaknesses of the approach and the appropriate domain and usages of this methodology. In the next section, we provide an application to military science focusing on insurgency and counterinsurgency dynamics. We highlight the ability to model many different kinds of actors in a dynamic, interactive, laboratory-like framework. After discussing a more general use of this technique, we focus on particular social science applications, including prominent models that can inform future applications. Next, we discuss the application to policy and how this theoretical approach can be merged with other more empirical tools. Following this discussion, we identify and compare the various tools analysts use to design and implement models. In the conclusion, we summarize key discussion points, outline some best practices for using computational modeling, discuss the preparation needed to become a modeler and suggest some potentially fruitful avenues for future research.

Modeling war and terrorism dynamics

Schelling's (1960) revolutionary work that applied the tools of game theory to conflict helped develop a more dynamic and strategic study of conflict. There are many benefits of game theory to the study of violent conflict (Bueno De Mesquita 2002). Potentially most important, however, is the general framework for finding the equilibrium strategy of violent actors that depends on the incentives of each actor but also on the *strategy of the opponent*. Game theory helped devise a nuclear deterrence strategy even when no nuclear conflict ever actually occurred (Schelling 1960; Powell 1990). Game theory also captures some of the foundational features of the international system making it a useful tool for understanding conflict that spills across borders and engulfs multiple states (Snidal 1985).

Computational modeling builds on game theory in a number of core ways and even extends some of the benefits of a formalized way to generate theory that overcomes some of the limitations of game theory. Two limitations are of particular note for military and conflict applications. First, game theory assumes rational agents with generally fixed preferences. Computational models allow agents to adapt over the course of the interactions. These actors can be rational, boundedly rational, Bayesian, or endowed with other decision rules that allow them to change, adapt, die, or proliferate (Macy and Willer 2002).[2] In an application to ethnic conflict Epstein (1999: 49) notes:

> Game theory may do an interesting job explaining the decision of one ethnic group to attack another at a certain place or time, but it doesn't explain how the ethnic group arises in the first place or how the ethnic divisions are transmitted across the generations

Second and related, most games have a minimal set of actors to make solving the models tractable. A government against an insurgent group, or a homogeneous population and a government, are two actor pairings likely to be modeled in a game theory approach. As experiences from Vietnam to Afghanistan have demonstrated, insurgent conflicts have many kinds of participants, with a variety of interests that change over time, based on conditions and interactions with other actors. Game-theoretic models are ill-equipped to handle this type of heterogeneity as solving these games becomes increasingly difficult with the inclusion of each additional actor, parameter, and distributions of characteristics.

Case studies and more descriptive approaches can handle this heterogeneity and richness of data. Case studies, like both game theory and computational models, can be a tool for generating theory and subsequent testable hypotheses (Gerring 2004). Especially when dealing with a single case over time, the logic of control allows for an analyst to examine a particular unit that should be nearly identical between periods except for the identified intervention. For example, a question, such as, "Was the rule of law affected in the US after the attacks of September 11th?" can be examined using case methods that should help develop more specific hypotheses about the relationship between these attacks and the implementation of law inside the United States. Like the limitations discussed at the outset, however, case studies also do not allow for a different outcome of the case. In sum, we only examine the effect of the treatment on the actual outcome rather than the effect of non-treatment (or the control condition) on another possible outcome.

Statistical modeling has proliferated in the study of civil violence and terrorism over the past 15 years. Statistical models have tremendous advantages in that they allow the inclusion of a large number of cases and established techniques to control for alternative explanations. In large statistical studies, there is scope for many different values of independent and dependent variables. Unfortunately, however, most statistical models rely on observational data for which the data generating process produces systematic and difficult-to-solve biases. To draw on the experimental analogy introduced at the outset, most observational studies are effectively broken experiments where analysts are trying to use statistical fixes to approximate the theoretical experiment. While many statistical approaches are possible, instrumental variables and matching to name a few, they all typically have a number of limitations that prevent strong counterfactual and causal analysis.

We thus turn to computational modeling as a way to address some of these limitations. Clearly computational modeling does not fully solve all limitations in other studies. Instead, it provides a different way of addressing the problem that may illuminate poor conclusions from other approaches. Early computational approaches modeled structural relations using primarily differential and difference equations (see discussion in Cioffi-Revilla and Rouleau 2010). In the last two decades there has been a turn to computational models that are less structural and more generative; most models now capture *bottom-up* processes in which large numbers of interacting agents produce various emergent outcomes (Epstein and Axtell 1996; Axelrod 1997; Epstein 1999; Miller and Page 2007). We now turn to a discussion of how agent-based, computational models (ABM) are typically set up and executed.

The methodology of computational modeling

Computational modeling is a generic name for a wide variety of modeling practices. Social scientists typically use agent-based, computational models (Gilbert 2008)—also referred to as complex adaptive systems models (Miller and Page 2007) a deeper field of study from which Agent Based Modeling (ABM) originated—that share a number of features. In particular, nearly all models specify several basic components: the agents or actors, the environment, and the overall model or mapping to some real-world phenomenon. Furthermore, most models are executed in a similar way: through a variety of controlled, computational experiments. A chapter of this length does not permit an adequate explanation of all parts of an ABM. We will briefly discuss some of the tradeoffs, but refer interested readers to much lengthier treatments of ABM elsewhere (see for example Holland 1998; de Marchi 2005; Miller and Page 2007; North and Macal 2007; Gilbert 2008).

Agents

A first crucial step in any ABM is to specify the agents. At its simplest, agents are the decision-making components in some complex system (North and Macal 2007). The agents can represent any sort of decision-maker the researcher decides. An agent could be an individual militant, a militant organization, a state fighting against a militant, a citizen affected by a militant, or many others. Agents could be specified at different levels as well. In one model, an agent could be an individual and in another model the agent could be some aggregation of individuals. Both could occur in the same model as well.

Of course, some representations may be more sensible than others and the researcher needs to be cautious about how complicated the agents are. Existing agent-based models of insurgency and terrorism have specified agents in most of the ways discussed (see for example Axelrod 1997; Bennett 2008; Cederman 1997; Cederman 2002; Findley 2008; Findley and Young 2006). A hallmark of agent-based models is that collections of agents have heterogeneous attributes (Page 2007). That is, rather than only assuming that agents hold one or two types, as in many game-theoretic models, agents can each take on different values from some distribution. In the Epstein (2002) model discussed previously, for example, agents take on a full range of hardship and legitimacy levels drawn from a uniform distribution.

Environment

Agents are situated in some environment, which they affect and are affected by. The environment refers to the virtual world within which agents are situated and interact (Gilbert 2008). Modelers face a number of decisions about the appropriate environmental setup. Some environments are abstract and agents are simply matched with each other for various types of interactions. Other environments are more complex with some explicit spatial landscape on which agents interact.

In models where there is no explicit spatial representation, agents typically interact in some hypothetical space similar to game-theoretic models in which agents are simply matched without saying how or where. Thus, agents could interact on the basis of some random matching specification (as in works such as Riolo et al. 2001). Alternatively, the non-spatial setup could be modeled according to a network, for example a small-world network (Watts 1999), in which other actors may exist in neighborhoods but not necessarily being overlaid onto a grid or GIS landscape. And some applications to the realm of insurgency and violence have coupled random matching with network structures (for example Bhavnani et al. 2009).

In models with an explicit spatial component, the landscape can be artificial or it can be based on real-world data. Artificial landscapes include representations such as a square grid or a torus where there are no artificial edges (see for example Findley and Young 2006, 2007; Bennett 2008). Although artificial, some implementations also populate the landscape with attributes intended to represent actual terrain (Cioffi-Revilla and Rouleau 2010). Real-world representations include the use of geographic information on factors such as state boundaries, ethnicity, population, or other factors (see for example Girardin and Cederman 2007; Findley et al. 2013).

The agents and environment represent part of the simplification of some realistic phenomenon into a model. In practice, researchers create models in a variety of ways. The question of just how abstract a model should be is not an easy one to answer. Modelers must decide how many agents to include, how many characteristics to ascribe to each agent, how many rules should govern the interactions of agents, how realistic the environment should be, and many more. While some prominent modelers have leaned towards simpler representations (Miller and Page 2007), others are in favor of more complex possibilities (Girardin and Cederman 2007). An alternative is to specify a model's complexity based on the research or policy question at hand (Lustick and Miodownik 2009) with an eye towards one's ability to analyze the model in some tractable way (de Marchi 2005).

Outcomes

Modelers are typically interested in some aggregate outcome. For the topic of this volume, the occurrence and intensity of violence are two frequent outcomes of interest. Popular turnout or participation is another common dynamic or outcome. These outcomes are typically captured in the form of emergent properties (Holland 1995, 1998). The idea of an emergent property has been much debated, but the essence, even if somewhat trite, is that some outcome is more than the sum of its parts. The division is related to the distinction between a complex system and a complicated system. In the former there are dependencies among the various elements of the system that are key to the behavior of that system. In the latter, the various elements maintain a greater degree of independence and therefore dynamics of such systems are easier to reduce (Miller and Page 2007).

Once a model's agents and environment are fully specified, the model is executed as a computer simulation composed of a set of experiments. In each of the computational experiments, a high degree of control can be achieved by holding constant all of the parameters except one. The researcher thus begins by varying a single parameter across reasonable values of its parameter space. After varying one parameter, the researcher then varies a different parameter holding all else constant, including the parameter previously varied. Once all relevant parameters have been varied, then two or more parameters are often varied together to explore the implications of covariance in sets of parameters. In all contexts, the researcher tracks the dynamics and aggregate outcomes (emergent properties) to learn whether there are systematic relationships. Nonlinear relationships are not common, especially as different sets of parameters interact with each other in various ways. Not unlike a carefully controlled experiment in the lab or real-world, this approach allows one to vary key parameters in a way that enables a better understanding of each part of the overall system.

Social science applications

In the international relations literature, early computational models captured interstate war, peace, and system structure. Modeling of violence has since become more common, in the study of insurgency, civil war, and ethnic conflicts. In most cases, these three categories overlap extensively. There are not many computational models of terrorism, which is likely an area ripe for future research.

In these social science applications to violence, researchers set up their models described above: political violence is modeled as the outcome of a complex set of interactions among a set of actors ranging from government leaders to ordinary citizens. The set of actors is typically heterogeneous in motivations for violence and capability to carry out such violence. Other models of strategic interaction largely miss the diversity and resulting emergent dynamics.

Computational models of violence have followed several paths. One distinction is between highly abstract models capturing cooperation and conflict. These models are intended to be applicable, to some extent, to a wide variety of animal and insects species. Prominent examples examining how cooperation and conflict evolved appear in journals such as *Nature* and *Science* including Nowak and Sigmund (1998) and Riolo, Cohen, and Axelrod (2001). Of course much of this literature had its origin in Axelrod's (1984) well-known *Evolution of Cooperation*.

Axelrod followed up with a collection of essays specifically applied to conflict and cooperation within the realm of international relations. About this time, a whole series of works, primarily by Cederman, followed and computationally modeled the dynamics of the international system. These works included models of the development of the international system (Cederman 1997; Cederman 2002), the spread of democracy and the democratic peace (Cederman 2001; Cederman and Gleditsch 2004), and the dynamics of wars (Cederman 2003). While some attention continues to be devoted to interstate wars, much of the literature has now shifted to the dynamics of ethnic and insurgent wars.

A number of works have modeled the role of identity and ethnicity in civil wars. These various works have captured: the construction of ethnic identities (Lustick 2000), the scale of ethnic violence (Bhavnani and Backer 2000), the diffusion of ethnic norms (Bhavnani 2006), ethnic polarization (Bhavnani and Miodownik 2009), ethnicity and nationalism (Cederman and Girardin 2005), and rumor diffusion in ethnic conflicts (Bhavnani et al. 2009). This work took seriously the importance of capturing subnational dynamics of ethnicity while the rest of the field was fixated on national level empirical measures such as ethnic fractionalization (Fearon and Laitin 2003). Indeed, much better empirical work on ethnicity followed this rigorous modeling (Cederman et al. 2010).

A closely related literature uses computational models of civil violence, but with less emphasis on ethnicity and identity. In this set of models, scholars have examined the role of commitment to insurgency that could be a function of identity or other factors (Findley and Young 2006, 2007), emotional attributes of agents including anger and fear (Bennett 2008), heterogeneous contextual factors such as hardship and legitimacy (Epstein 2002; more on Epstein below), government structure and dynamics (Cioffi-Revilla and Rouleau 2010), systemic factors of an insurgent ecology (Bohorquez et al. 2009), and actor-specific dynamics such as the emergence of social movements and the occurrence of splintering (Findley 2008; Findley and Rudloff 2011).

Models of terrorism have received considerably less attention than have models of insurgency and ethnic conflict dynamics. With few exceptions (Leweling and Nissen 2007), this area is almost unexplored. And yet there is reason to believe that models of terrorism could be very fruitful. For one, militants that utilize terrorism are often organized in networks, something that agent-based models can capture well. Moreover, terrorists vary dramatically in their group size, motivations, constraints, and so forth. The heterogeneity afforded by computational models could directly capture these characteristics.

Policy applicability

Over the past decade, computational modeling has been implemented in diverse arenas ranging from military needs (Keller-McNulty et al. 2006; Pew and Mavor 1998) to academic applications (Macy and Skvoretz 1998; Cederman 2003; Findley and Young 2007). In this section, we discuss the costs and benefits of using this methodology as well as other practical issues that need to be taken into account before scaling up the use of computational models. We also discuss the challenges of integrating real-world data with simulated assumptions and data in an agent-based model.

In a review of the difficulty of merging academic quantitative research with the policy community, Mack (2002) argues that there are many barriers to communication between the groups. Some that relate to computational models and demonstrating their utility to the policy community and military include: different ways of communicating, the notion of probabilistic theory, and debates in academia.

First, as Mack (2002) notes, many quantitative scholars speak a different language and do not attempt to translate their results to busy policymakers. Computational modeling can be at least as complicated and theorists in this tradition should strive for communicating their results in as non-technical and non-jargon-filled ways as possible.

Second, computational modeling produces empirical predictions that are probabilistic. Single cases that counter the equilibrium of a model do not destroy the entire enterprise. Policymakers, however, often think of cases that refute a claim as deadly to the claim. If COIN doesn't work in Iraq, then this approach is often thought as a failure across other cases. Computational models are often more general and should apply to numerous cases. If users want a more tailored model to a particular case, then it can be seeded with relevant parameters, data from the case, and other factors that will increase fit. If the model still does not accurately predict a particular outcome, this does not destroy the model. Academics working in this tradition generally prefer models that predict better than other models and that predict better than a random guess. Perfectly determined outcomes are not the goal using this methodology.

Third, academics and modelers do not always agree about the best way to do research and how it will be used by policymakers. They also have major theoretical divisions. Policymakers wanting a single piece of advice about the best course of action can be easily frustrated by trying to sort through the academic arguments and deciding which is more powerful (Mack 2002).

There are major debates about the best ways to use computational modeling. Without outlining all the dimensions, there is at least one major division worth noting. Modelers struggle with whether to be complex and more realistic or parsimonious. A recent computational model by Cioffi-Revilla and Rouleau (2010), for example, makes an entire simulated society with different structures and processes. Other models include just a few parameters and have a small number of actor types, although their values on parameters vary according to some predetermined distribution (e.g. Epstein 1999, see textbox). Each decision has costs. More complex simulations can accurately apply to particular cases, but they lose their generalizability. Another important cost of complex models is that the so-called parameter space becomes prohibitively large. De Marchi 2005 discusses just how quickly the parameter space can get too large to adequately analyze fully.

Findley et al. (2010) simulate insurgency in the context of India from 1998 to 2008. Using GIS information from India, they build a lattice model that operates in the geographical boundaries of this country to generate predictions about the growth or decline of insurgency. Briefly, they seed the model with a large number of agents that can be insurgents, counterinsurgents, or members of the population that have varying values for key parameters. The agents move through the India-shaped landscape. When the agents meet on the board, they interact and can influence each other. These interactions can lead to moving a member of the population into becoming an insurgent, insurgents being killed, or several other outcomes. After these interactions occur over a fixed time period (100, 1,000 iterations, etc.), the analyst can examine changes in numbers of actors, distributions of key parameters, and a host other factors.

Using dyadic events data, they then test the predictions of the computational model. This research design holds promise for merging complicated theory and large data sets. The initial model can be quite simple, and the results can be tested using the events data. When the two do not match, the analyst can adjust the model. To avoid constraining and fitting the model to predict the data, the model can be taken to other locations and other time periods to test out of sample. The assumptions and parameters then can be informed by real-world values and tested to examine fit and prediction.

Technical needs

Learning to use computational models requires some theoretical training as well as some practical skills. The theoretical background to computational modeling is well developed and many resources exist from which to learn about the methodology. Among the available texts, Epstein and Axtell (1996), Holland (1998), de Marchi (2005), Miller and Page (2007), North and Macal (2007), and Gilbert (2008) are all great sources to get broad exposure to the methodology.

On the practical side of using agent-based models, users need to have some exposure to a computer programming language. Not all agent-based models require a computer, of course (see Schelling's [1971] pioneering work). Most current agent-based models, however, are carried out on a computer and thus require some ability to program the agents, environment, rules, and then graph the outcomes. Programs vary in how much background they provide.

Two toolkits are currently most developed: Repast and Netlogo. Both were developed many years ago and have increased the scope of what they can accomplish while decreasing the barriers to entry. While there is much information readily available for non-programmers, in order to design models to accomplish certain user-specific needs, programming is needed to customize the models. A more recent program, Mason RebeLand, provides a platform specifically for modeling the dynamics of violence.

While these toolkits can be useful for many purposes, they can also be far more complicated than what some social science applications require. Many political science applications are not complicated and require no more than a few hundred lines of code. When political science scholars (and others) are unfamiliar with lower-level programming languages such as Java or C#, many can still use programs such as R or Matlab to program simple models. Many applications using all of these various approaches are available online. Downloading and running others' existing models can be a useful way for beginners to get started.

Some resources provide both a theoretical and practical training. For instance, Kendrick, Mercado, and Amman (2006) develop a number of computational models applied to economics and for each chapter provide the source code for different programs including Excel, Mathematica, GAMS, Access, and Matlab.

Conclusion

Over the past 20 years, computational models have become increasingly common in studies of conflict and violence. Computational models offer some important advantages over other methodological approaches. Perhaps most importantly, they provide a way to approximate a controlled experiment in a context that would otherwise not permit experimental methods. Modelers can develop computational experiments that allow the careful and systematic investigation of a large number of possible explanations. Moreover, whereas such models used to be highly abstract, it is now easier than ever to incorporate real-world assumptions, data, and match against observed outcomes.

The allure of computational models is also a challenge. It is tempting to see computational models as a complete solution to data woes. Unfortunately, computational models are best used to generate and refine theory as opposed to providing empirical tests. For this reason, it is difficult to point to a refined and concrete set of conclusions that has emerged from this research. They have been tremendously useful in generating theory about the connections between micro-level behavior macro-level outcomes in contexts such as insurgency, violence, ethnicity, and beyond.

Although the topics of insurgency and ethnic conflict have received much attention, there is still much room for continued work. Notably, very few models attempt to explain the dynamics of terrorism. It is possible that the explanations for terrorist events follow logics similar to domestic political violence. But we do not know at this stage. Computational models could thus be applied fruitfully in identifying the similarities of differences with other forms of political violence.

Although there are some barriers to entry for computational modeling research and practice, this approach has become more accessible in recent years due to a large number of toolkits, programs, and resources for learning. Computational modeling, we hope, will supplement the already useful tools that social scientists and practitioners are using to understand violence. When used in tandem with these other approaches, we expect that many more useful insights will be possible.

Notes

1 This material is based upon work supported by the National Science Foundation Grant No. 0904883.
2 Some game theoretic models allow for learning among agents (see, for example, Camerer 2003), but this is not the norm.

References

Axelrod, R. (1984) *The Evolution of Cooperation*, New York: Basic Books.
Axelrod, R. (1997) *The Complexity of Cooperation: Agent-Based Models of Competition and Collaboration*, Princeton, NJ: Princeton University Press.
Bennett, D. (2008) "Governments, Civilians, and the Evolution of Insurgency: Modeling the early dynamics of insurgencies," *Journal of Artificial Societies and Social Simulation* 11(4): 1–7.
Bhavnani, R. (2006) "Ethnic Norms and Interethnic Violence: Accounting for mass participation in the Rwandan genocide," *Journal of Peace Research* 43(6): 651–669.
Bhavnani, R. and D. Backer (2000) "Localized Ethnic Conflict and Genocide Accounting for Differences in Rwanda and Burundi," *Journal of Conflict Resolution* 44(3): 283–306.
Bhavnani, R. and D. Miodownik (2009) "Ethnic Polarization, Ethnic Salience, and Civil War," *Journal of Conflict Resolution* 53(1): 30–49.
Bhavnani, R., M. Findley, and J. Kuklinski (2009) "Rumor Dynamics in Ethnic Violence," *Journal of Politics* 71(3): 876–892.
Bohorquez, J.C., S. Gourley, A.R. Dixon, M. Spagat, and N.F. Johnson (2009) "Common Ecology Quantifies Human Insurgency," *Nature* 462: 911–914.
Bueno de Mesquita, B. (2002) "Accomplishments and Limitations of a Game-Theoretic Approach to International Relations,' in M. Brecher and F. Harvey (eds) *Evaluating Methodology in International Studies*, Ann Arbor, MI: University of Michigan Press, pp. 59–80.
Camerer, C. (2003) *Behavioral Game Theory: Experiments in Strategic Interaction*, Princeton, NJ: Princeton University Press.
Cederman, L.-E. (2004) "Articulating the Geo-Cultural Logic of Nationalist Insurgency." Paper prepared for presentation at the workshop on "Origins and Patterns of Political Violence I: Violence in Civil Wars," held at the Santa Fe Institute, California, January 15–19, 2004.
Cederman, L.-E. (1997) *Emergent Actors in World Politics: How States and Nations Develop and Dissolve*, Princeton, NJ: Princeton University Press.
Cederman, L.-E. (2001) "Modeling the Democratic Peace as a Kantian Selection Process," *Journal of Conflict Resolution* 45: 470–502.
Cederman, L.-E. (2002) "Endogenizing Geopolitical Boundaries with Agent-Based Modeling," *Proceedings of the National Academy* 99 (suppl. 3): 7796–7303.

Cederman, L.-E. (2003) "Modeling the Size of Wars: From billiard balls to sandpiles," *American Political Science Review* 97: 135–150.

Cederman, L.-E. and K. Skrede Gleditsch (2004) "Conquest and Regime Change: An evolutionary model of the spread of democracy and peace," *International Studies Quarterly* 48(3): 603–629.

Cederman, L.-E. and L. Girardin (2005) "Beyond Fractionalization: Mapping Ethnicity onto Nationalist Insurgencies." Paper read at Disaggregating the Study of Civil War and Transnational Violence Conference, at San Diego, California.

Cederman, L.-E., A. Wimmer and B. Min (2010) "Why Do Ethnic Groups Rebel? New data and analysis," *World Politics* 62(1): 87–119.

Cioffi-Revilla, C. and M. Rouleau (2010) "MASON RebeLand: An agent-based model of politics, environment, and insurgency," *International Studies Review* 12: 31–52.

De Marchi, Scott (2005) *Computational and Mathematical Modeling in the Social Sciences.* Cambridge: Cambridge University Press.

Epstein, J.M. (1999) "Agent-based Computational Models and Generative Social Science," in *Generative Social Science: Studies in Agent-Based Computational Modeling*, Princeton, NJ: Princeton University Press, pp. 4–46.

Epstein, J. (2002) "Modeling Civil Violence: An agent-based, computational approach," *Proceedings of the National Academy of Sciences* 99(3): 7243–7250.

Epstein, J. and R. Axtell (1996) *Growing Artificial Societies: Social Science from the Bottom Up*, Washington, DC: Brookings Institution Press.

Fearon, J. (1991) "Counterfactuals and Hypothesis Testing in Political Science,' *World Politics* 43(2): 169–195.

Fearon, James D. and David D. Laitin (2003) "Ethnicity, Insurgency, and Civil War," *American Political Science Review* 97(01): 75–90.

Fearon, J., M. Humphreys, and J. Weinstein (2009) "Can Development Aid Contribute to Social Cohesion after Civil War," *American Economic Review: Papers and Proceedings* 99(2): 287–291.

Findley, M. (2008) "Agents and Conflict: Adaptation and the Dynamics of War," *Complexity* 14(1): 22–35.

Findley, M., and J.K. Young (2006) "Swatting Flies with Pile Drivers? Modeling Insurgency and Counterinsurgency." Paper presented at the International Studies Association Annual Meeting, San Diego, California, March.

Findley, M., and J. Young (2007) "Fighting Fire with Fire? How (not) to neutralize an insurgency," *Civil Wars* 9(4): 378–401.

Findley, M. and P. Rudloff (2011) "Combatant Fragmentation and the Dynamics of Civil Wars," *British Journal of Political Science* 42(4): 879–901.

Findley, M., J. Young, and S.M. Shellman (2010) "Modeling Dynamic Violence: Integrating events, data analysis and agent-based modeling." Paper presented at the American Political Science Association Annual Meeting, Washington, DC, September.

Findley, M., D. Nielson, and J. Sharman (2013) "Using Field Experiments in International Relations: A randomized study of anonymous incorporation," *International Organization* 67(4) (forthcoming).

Gerring, J. (2004) "What Is a Case Study and What Is It Good For?," *American Political Science Review* 98(2): 341–354.

Gilbert, N. (2008) *Agent-Based Models: Quantitative Applications in Social Sciences Series*, Thousand Oaks, CA: Sage.

Girardin, L. and L-E. Cederman (2007) "A Roadmap to Realistic Computational Models of Civil Wars," in S. Takahashi, D. Sallach, and J. Rouchier (eds) *Advancing Social Simulation: The First World Congress*, New York: Springer, pp. 59–69.

Hollard, J H. (1995) *Hidden Order: How Adaptation Builds Complexity*. New York: Basic Books.

Holland, J.H. (1998) *Emergence: From Chaos to Order*, New York: Basic Books.

Holland, P. (1986) "Statistics and Causal Inference," *Journal of the American Statistical Association* 81(396): 945–960.

Keller-McNulty, S., K.L. Bellman, and K.M. Carley (2006) *Defense Modeling, Simulation, and Analysis: Meeting the Challenge*, Washington, DC; National Research Council.

Kendrick, D., R. Mercado and H. Amman (2006) *Computational Economics*, Princeton, NJ: Princeton University Press.

Kuran, Timur (1991) "Now Out of Never," *World Politics* 44(1): 7–48.

Leweling, T.A. and M.E. Nissen (2007) "Defining and Exploring the Terrorism Field: Toward an inter-theoretic, agent-based approach," *Technological Forecasting and Social Change* 74(2): 165–192.

Lustick, I. (2000) "Agent-Based Modelling of Collective Identity: Testing Constructivist theory," *Journal of Artificial Societies and Social Simulation* 3(1): 1–6.

Lustick, I. and D. Miodownik (2009) "Abstractions, Ensembles, and Virtualizations: Simplicity and complexity in agent-based modeling." *Comparative Politics* 41(2): 223–244.

Mack, A. (2002) "Civil War: Academic research and the policy community.' *Journal of Peace Research* 39(5): 515–525.

Macy, M.W. and J. Skvoretz (1998) "The Evolution of Trust and Cooperation between Strangers: A computational model," *American Sociological Review* 63: 638–660.

Macy, M.W. and R. Willer (2002) "From Factors to Actors: Computational sociology and agent-based modeling." *Annual Review of Sociology* 28: 143–166.

Miller, J.H. and S.E. Page (2007) *Complex Adaptive Systems: An Introduction to Computational Models of Social Life*, Princeton, NJ: Princeton University Press.

North, M. and Ch. Macal (2007) *Managing Business Complexity: Discovering Strategic Solutions with Agent-Based Modeling and Simulation*, Oxford: Oxford University Press.

Nowak, M.A. and K. Sigmund (1998) "Evolution of Indirect Reciprocity by Image Scoring," *Nature* 393: 573–577.

Page, S. (2007) *The Difference: How the Power of Diversity Creates Better Groups, Firms, Schools, and Societies*, Princeton, NJ: Princeton University Press.

Pew, R.W. and A.S. Mavor (eds) (1998) *Modeling Human and Organizational Behavior: Application to Military Simulations*, Washington DC: National Academies Press.

Powell, R. (1990) *Nuclear Deterrence Theory: The Search for Credibility*, New York: Cambridge University Press.

Riolo, R., M. Cohen and R. Axelrod (2001) "Evolution of Cooperation without Reciprocity," *Nature* 414: 441–443.

Schelling, T. (1960) *The Strategy of Conflict*, Cambridge, MA: Harvard University Press.

Schelling, T. (1971) "Dynamic Models of Segregation," *Journal of Mathematical Sociology* 1(2): 143–186.

Snidal, D. (1985) "The Game Theory of International Politics.' *World Politics* 38(1): 25–57.

Watts, D. (1999) *Small Worlds: The Dynamics of Networks between Order and Randomness*, Princeton, NJ: Princeton University Press.

23

EVALUATING PEACE OPERATIONS

Challenges and dimensions

Daniel Druckman and Paul F. Diehl

Paul F. Diehl and Daniel Druckman (2010) *Evaluating Peace Operations.*
**Boulder, CO: Lynne Rienne Publishers [Also Druckman and Diehl
(2013)].**

Methodological issues for performing evaluations of peace operations include taking into account the role of stakeholders, the time perspective for evaluating outcomes, the importance of establishing baselines, defining evaluation criteria in terms of types of operations, and the importance of the larger conflict environment.

The question asked regarding stakeholders is, "success for whom?" The varied perspectives and interests of actors with stakes in the outcome may collide, with pernicious effects on both the conduct of the operation and the criteria used to define success. As well, the independent and dependent variables may be defined differently for short- and long-term evaluations: reduced conflict at the time of exit may resurface during the year following departure. Assessments also address the question, "compared to what?" Longitudinal and cross-sectional comparisons present different evaluation challenges. Changes that occur over a short period facilitate imputing causation. But the observed changes may be misleading if they miss the larger, and more important, changes that take more time to develop. Imputing causation is also problematic when alternative operations are compared. The operations must be sufficiently similar to ascertain reasons for the same or different outcomes.

With regard to defining evaluation criteria, the type of mission must be considered. For example, mission goals are undoubtedly different for missions that place an emphasis on containing violence versus those that aim to protect human rights. But, even with these contingencies, evaluations would be incomplete if the larger conflict environment were not considered. That environment consists of elements that vary in terms of their malleability. However, taking the environment into account complicates the task of inferring the direction of causation: Effects may be circular, with the operation both influencing and being influenced by the conflict environment.

(continued)

(continued)

These considerations add value to the conduct of evaluation research. More practically, they inform the development of a decisionmaking template used to aid judgments about operation success. The decision process proceeds in a sequence of steps: identifying the primary goals of the mission (step 1), identifying key questions that must be answered to achieve the goals (step 2), constructing measures of progress to answer the questions (step 3), identifying the benefits and limitations of those measures (step 4), and ascertaining the extent to which the goals have been accomplished (step 5).

This sequence was elaborated by Diehl and Druckman (2010) in their attempt to specify the dimensions of traditional peacekeeping, new missions, and post-conflict peace-building goals. They applied this framework to the case of the Bosnian civil war and its aftermath, with the various peace operations following the end of that war and the Dayton Peace Agreement signed in 1995. The evaluation framework was then applied to four other cases presented in Druckman and Diehl (2013): the Cambodia, Côte d'Ivoire, Liberia, and East Timor peace operations. These applications called attention to both the strengths and limitations of the approach. An evident strength is that it facilitates comparative analysis. Limitations lead to suggesting extensions and making refinements of the evaluative framework.

Introduction

Evaluating the impacts of peace operations is a vexing challenge. The literature on peacekeeping is not well developed with regard to evaluation methodologies. One problem is that most studies focus attention on the factors thought to influence success (the independent variables) rather than on the criteria for assessing those outcomes (the dependent variables). Another problem is the lack of a broad conceptual framework to guide evaluation efforts. An attempt is made in this chapter to fill these lacunae by specifying the dimensions of evaluation and calling attention to issues that any assessment must address.

Peace operations refer to a variety of types of missions including traditional peacekeeping, robust peacekeeping, peace-building, peace observation. (See the taxonomy of peace operations developed by Diehl et al. 1998.) These operations are performed by troops with a mandate from national or international organizations, regional organizations, or multilateral groupings. Traditional military operations are not included under this rubric. We place more emphasis in this chapter on types of missions than on types of sponsoring organizations. This decision is based on the observation that the various missions occur in each type of organization. Moreover, the evaluation focus is directed at dimensions of the operation rather than the organization. We discuss five dimensions to be considered in evaluations.

Improved evaluations of peace operations have clear policy implications. These include knowing when to exit a mission, to increase or decrease troop levels, to chart progress toward achieving mandated goals, and generally to anticipate critical junctures where changes are likely to occur. Informed decisions along these lines should improve mission effectiveness. But, it is also the case that some features of the conflict environment are difficult to change. These features may be largely beyond the control of a peace operation. The distinction between more or less malleable aspects of the environment is important in evaluating mission success and in the design of operations. It is discussed in a concluding section.

The evaluation challenge

How to evaluate peace operations is far from the simple matter that is implied in most studies. In those works, scholars and policymakers typically select one or more indicators and then apply them to the case(s) at hand. Implicitly, however, those analysts have already made a series of choices, most often because these decisions represent the paths of least resistance; even when the analyses are explicit about criteria, the chosen standards are those most obvious, and indicators are those more readily available. Yet looking behind those decisions reveals a series of issues that impact the way we view the peace operation and define success. These issues are both conceptual and methodological. Confronting them is a step toward reducing the extent to which path-dependent trajectories are followed and old mistakes repeated.

Evaluation decisions turn on a number of elements. Understanding these elements reveals the complexity of evaluating peace operations. They include a variety of objectives and types of missions and, for each objective, key questions asked, indicators of progress, as well as benefits and limitations of those indicators. This complex rendering of the evaluation task is developed in Diehl and Druckman (2010). The evaluation turns on the particular dimensions and indicators chosen for analysis. An emphasis on the core mission goals of violence abatement, containment and settlement is likely to result in a different conclusion about success than when such goals as democratization and humanitarian assistance are highlighted. These differences may also help to explain the divergent conclusions about success coming from different studies. The evaluation framework developed in a final section is based on the specification of broad goals, development of key questions related to those goals, and measurable indicators that would assist in answering those questions. It is informed by five dimensions of peace operations.

Dimensions of peace operation evaluation

The five dimensions of evaluation decisions are: the stakeholders, time perspectives, baselines, "lumping," and mission types.

Success for whom? Stakeholders in peace operations

When conceptualizing peacekeeping success, the question arises: success for whom? Although rarely addressed directly, there are several sets of stakeholders in peace operations, each of which might generate different standards for success: the international community, states contributing personnel, the main protagonist states or groups, and the local population (Druckman and Stern 1997). These actors often have different goals or assign different priorities to shared goals.

The international community, and by this we mean third-party actors including states, international organizations, and NGOs, have different perspectives on the conflict than those directly involved. This set of actors has a number of goals. One might be a desire to stop the conflict from spreading to new regions or across international borders. Negative externalities that extend beyond fighting affect new populations and states, but also include refugees and attendant economic and political costs. Global society also has a concern with maximizing a number of international norms embedded in organizational charters and international agreements. These include peaceful change and security, human rights protections, and economic wellbeing. As outsiders to the conflict, the international community has goals that extend beyond the reach of the fighting.

Macro level concerns would lead one to concentrate on success standards that refer to how well the peace operation promotes world values. This is not to say that the international community is unconcerned with death and dislocation in the conflict area, but rather that its priorities are likely to concern public goods at a higher level of analysis. Thus, indicators of success from the vantage point of the international community could be conflict containment and human rights protection, among others.

Referring to the international community is something of an abstraction. While the different actors that make up this community do share some goals, each has some specific interests in the conduct of a peace mission. Individual states have private interests in the conduct of a peace operation that might or might not comport with other members of the international community. Most obviously, certain states may have a political interest in advantaging one side or another in the outcome of a conflict. Interstate rivalries sometimes intersect in a conflict region, and a peace operation has the potential to affect such competitions depending on the conditions for its deployment and its effect on stability in that area. Success from the perspective of one state could mean failure in the eyes of another.

Peace operations might also influence the flow of resources from the area of conflict to interested external states. Neighboring states to the Congo benefited from the flow of diamonds from the Kasai region. The oil resource dependence of China on Sudan raises another set of interests for resolution of the conflict in the southern part of the latter country and in Darfur. In the first case, actors have an interest in limiting the impact of the peace operation on smuggling; yet such smuggling could be one of the elements fueling the violence. In the latter instance, strong actions against the Sudanese government might undermine Chinese interests and thus mitigation, rather than a total elimination, of violence could be seen as successful for that emerging global power.

A particularly relevant subset of interested states contains those that assume leading roles in peace operations and/or contribute personnel to the peace operation. Leading states are interested in gaining legitimacy for the actions (especially enforcement) taken in a peace operation, a primary reason why such operations are often channeled through international organizations (Coleman 2007; see also Claude 1966). There is some debate over whether states contribute troops for altruistic, power and status, or pecuniary reasons (Neack 1995), but once deployed, contributors have vested interests in protecting those troops. Success for the contributing state might have little to do with changes in local conditions, but rather with minimizing the number of casualties that occur and the quality of training and experience received. The former is especially critical for states whose foreign policies have attentive domestic audiences, and therefore are sensitive to costs; western democracies with extensive media penetration are thought to be those states most vulnerable to such effects, although those same states are most likely to participate in such operations (Andersson 2000).

Organizations also have specific bureaucratic interests in operations (see Barnett and Finnemore 2004). NGOs compete with each other for funds and resources. They also might regard international governmental organizations as rivals for influence in carrying out tasks such as humanitarian assistance. A peace operation that preserves or enhances the roles of a certain NGO could be considered more successful than one in which its power is diminished, regardless of which arrangement is best for ending the conflict or alleviating the suffering of the local population. International organizations, such as the UN and NATO, have similar bureaucratic interests. They also have reputational concerns in that many organizations in the political and security area (as opposed to the economic and social areas) depend on persuasion and legitimation to be effective. When peace operations denigrate the reputation of an organization, their other missions may suffer.

The interests of the primary protagonists in the conflict involve private goods and almost certainly diverge from one another. If all sides agree to a cease-fire, one might presume a common interest in stopping the fighting, but for some this could only be a temporary goal in order to rearm rather than signaling a sincere desire for conflict resolution (Richmond 1998). Furthermore, presumably actors entered into the conflict in order to win. The outcomes are construed in terms of winners and losers or at least partly zero-sum and thus no outcome from a peace operation can leave all parties fully satisfied. Thus, actors will assess peace operation success according to how it affects the distribution of the pie among protagonists. As the number of actors increases, and this can be substantial in a civil or internationalized civil war, the different perspectives on success also swells.

Often left out of calculations are the interests of the local population in the area of conflict (Johansen 1994). It is often presumed that the cessation of violence improves the lives of citizens in the local area, and this is largely correct. Yet there is a wide range of other effects, including those that are unintended, from peace operations that might not be positive (Aoi et al. 2007). For example, peace operations may limit the ability of refugees to return to their homes even as the missions facilitate food and medical care to those displaced populations. Peace operations may also impact the local economy (Ammitzboell 2007) by affecting local markets; this may be positive in providing opportunities for indigenous business or it may distort those markets by creating parallel economic structures. Socially, the presence of peace soldiers might increase the incidence of rape and the spread of AIDS (Kent 2007), although such soldiers could play a role in combating disease as well (Bratt 2002).

As may be obvious from the discussion above, although stakeholders may share some interests (e.g. limiting violence), their interests are not completely coterminous. For example, a contributing state may have as one of its goals limiting casualties to its personnel. Succeeding in that goal, however, may necessitate actions that undermine the international community's goal of protecting the human rights of the threatened population. Evaluating a peace operation according to certain criteria implicitly takes the perspective of one or more actors in the conflict. Thus, there needs to be recognition that success is defined in different ways by the various stakeholders with political and economic interests in the same operation.

Time perspective

Defining success will also vary according to whether one adopts a short- versus long-term perspective (Weiss 1994; Bellamy and Williams 2005). From a short-term perspective, success may be conceptualized as achievement of goals that occur during the course of a peace operation or in some timeframe immediately following the withdrawal of the peacekeeping force. An example of the former is alleviation of starvation and improvement of medical conditions during a humanitarian operation. In this perspective, it is often easiest to tie the actions of the peace operation to the observed outcome. An example of the latter is the absence of violent conflict for several years following the operation (e.g. Enterline and Kang 2002; Heldt and Wallensteen 2006). Although the time frame can vary, the assumption is that peace operations have a substantial influence on ground conditions for some period following the withdrawal of troops. The contention is that the actions of the peacekeepers during deployment laid the groundwork for longer-term effects.

An alternative to short-term concerns is assessing peace operations from a long-term perspective. This generally means looking at conditions for more than a few years after the operation, perhaps as much as decades. The assumption is that policy interventions influence various behaviors and many of their effects are not manifest for many years to come. An example would be considering how life-expectancy improved a decade or more after a peace-building operation ended; such improvements may not show up for a period of time as new facilities and practices take time to have an impact on the local population.

Taking a longer-term perspective often leads to a different assessment of an operation's success or failure than short-term evaluations. For example, various peacekeeping efforts in East Timor were almost universally considered a success in the immediate aftermath, only to prompt a reassessment when violence and instability returned in 2006. This is not merely a case of the same indicators changing over time. As with different stakeholders, there may be significant differences in the predictor and outcome variables for short- and long-term success. It is also the case that different standards are appropriate for short- and long-term success. For example, slowing refugee flows is a short-term indicator of success whereas refugee repatriation is a process more appropriate for long-term evaluation.

In making long-term assessments, at least two problems arise. The initial problem is determining how long a window should be considered in assessing outcomes. Given path dependency (what happens in an earlier phase, or phases, of conflict has an impact on the dynamics of subsequent phases) and other effects, peace operations can have consequences that extend for decades. Yet, extraordinarily long time frames make it impossible to assess ongoing and recently concluded operations (Bellamy and Williams 2005). Thus, policymakers do not have the ability to make mid-course adjustments easily in ongoing operations if years must pass before strategies can be evaluated. The "shadow of the recent past," the perceived success or failure of recent peace operations, has an influence on decision makers' willingness to launch new operations as well as the configuration of those operations. Problems in Somalia in the early 1990s are often cited as the rationale for the slow and inadequate international response to the genocide in Rwanda not much later. Thus, policy decisions are based on recent, formative events. Long-term assessments of distant operations do not provide decision makers with clear cues on immediate policy decisions and will be discounted in any case because they occurred under different circumstances – former leaders, administrations, or policy contexts. Whatever its validity, long-term success assessment does not meet policy making needs, at least in terms of how foreign policy is typically made.

Second, the longer the time period that passes between the end of the operation and the assessment, the more difficult it will be to draw causal conclusions about the impact of the operation per se; intervening factors are likely to have as great or greater impact on future conditions (Bingham and Felbinger 2002). For example, regime change or a global economic downturn could influence local conditions more than the legacy of a peace operation a decade before. Indeed, there is a difference of opinion on whether long-term failure should even be used as an indictment of the mission (see Druckman and Stern 1997).

Although short- and long-term time horizons differ in a number of ways, they are also related. In most cases, the failure of peace operations to meet short-term goals all but precludes a need to understand its long-term impact. Of course, one could imagine scenarios of how short-term failure produced long-term success (e.g. continued armed conflict produces a stable victory), but these are unlikely scenarios or even when they occur long-term positive effects cannot be effectively traced back to operational failures. More probable, short-term success has downstream consequences. For example, the successful conduct of elections might contribute either to long-term conflict resolution (e.g. Namibia) or to a renewal of violence between forces winning those elections and the opposition (e.g. Angola).

The research challenge is to decide, prior to collecting data, on the time span for evaluation. It pays to adopt both short- and long-term criteria, or to institute multiple assessments of the dependent variables, for evaluation. The alternative is to accept a myopic view of peace operations that will be abandoned in the long run. Considering only the long term, however, will miss important short-term impacts and not provide the necessary feedback to policy makers in order to make timely and informed decisions.

Beyond a short- or long-term perspective, further complicating the evaluation task is the issue of temporal dynamics. Missions change through time, often in unexpected ways. Peacekeepers must adjust their strategies to circumstances. This suggests that the mission may be defined and evaluated differently at various points in time.

The above suggests that assessments taken only at one juncture may be misleading and likely different from other fixed-point evaluations. Yet there are other implications as well, especially for inferences about causation. The independent variable(s) is (are) not a static, but rather a moving target. Changing assessments of success could be the result of alterations in approach to a mission. The research challenge is to coordinate definitions of the independent variable – considered to be dynamic – with assessments of success, the dependent variable. For example, what are the impacts of changes in force size, deployment area, and mission goals on progress toward a cease-fire or toward the initiation of peace negotiations? Expanding operational goals may also lead to standards that are not only different, but more difficult to reach. Yet another wrinkle in the evaluation task is the way that mission alterations interact with changes in context, increasing the difficulty of separating causal factors. For example, changes in host country cooperation because of a mission shift might influence decisions about the size and deployment of the peace operation. Those decisions, in turn, are likely to alter the prospects, positive or negative, for conflict reduction or resolution.

Baseline for assessment

A third consideration is developing a baseline against which to assess peacekeeping's effects. That is, when one asks whether a peace operation is successful, there is an implicit query – "as compared to what?" – contained therein. Even studies with specific success criteria usually lack a baseline for comparison. There are several different baselines possible, but all have some limitations.

One standard is that peace operations be compared against a situation in which no action was taken by the international community (Druckman and Stern 1997). This is what we refer to as, somewhat derisively, the "better than nothing" yardstick. Others refer to it as utilizing "absence-based criteria" in the sense of a no-treatment control group (Stiles and MacDonald 1992). A more sophisticated version is using a simple time series in which actual outcomes are compared to those projected based on past trends, the latter assuming no peacekeeping intervention (Bingham and Felbinger 2002).

The "better than nothing" standard is misleading from methodological and policymaking perspectives. It is extremely difficult to measure, or make a projection based on, something that did not happen (Menkaus 2003). Furthermore, the standard employed could also be too low in that peace operations automatically get labeled as successful for any improvement in the situation. Decision makers' choices are also rarely between just peacekeeping and inaction (Diehl 1994). Accordingly, some scholars suggest that analysts consider opportunity costs imposed by the choice of peacekeeping (Druckman and Stern 1997). Rather than "better than nothing," this standard asks "better than what alternative?" Problems with this standard, however, are several. It first requires an adequate specification of alternative policies. A complete menu of choices for an international organization might include diplomatic initiatives, sanctions, and collective enforcement through traditional military means. Yet many of these options are not mutually exclusive and thus it is difficult to determine the extent to which the selection of the peace operation option affected other choices on the decisionmaking menu. In addition, the adoption of other options is probabilistic; that is, not all of the other alternatives would have been chosen had a peace operation not been deployed. Thus, assessing specific opportunity costs would have to be weighted by the probability of another option, something that is a priori difficult to determine. Assessing opportunity costs also necessitates an accurate counter-factual or scenario-based analysis of what would have happened if other alternatives had been selected (Menkaus 2003).

Another standard is one in which the conditions prior to deployment are compared to those during and following the operation (e.g. Kaysen and Rathjens 1995). The design of this assessment is a relatively simple "before versus after," pretest-posttest, or interrupted time series design (Bingham and Felbinger 2002; Druckman 2006) in which the deployment of the peace operation represents the key dividing line. This standard has the advantage of making comparisons across missions possible or "normalizing" the baseline, as moderate levels of violence during peacekeeping might be considered progress in some contexts (e.g. deployment during full-scale civil war), but backsliding in others (e.g. deployment following a cease-fire). A variation is merely to compare "early after" with "later after," in which the analyst tracks the trends (whether in the positive or negative direction) following deployment (Stiles and MacDonald 1992). This allows the analyst to control for the initial conditions at the time of deployment, a concern noted by Heldt and Wallensteen (2006).

This standard would produce either positive or negative assessments depending on when the operation was deployed. Many operations are sent to the most violent conflicts (Gilligan and Stedman 2003), with various attendant problems of refugees, economic disruptions, and the like. For these operations, the initial baseline is likely to be near the peak of any conflict or at least on the high side of severity.

A third baseline of effectiveness is achieved by comparing effectiveness across peace operations, a cross-sectional rather than longitudinal comparison (Ratner 1995; Bingham and Felbinger 2002 refer to this as "benchmarking"). For example, an operation with fewer shooting incidents than another would be judged as more successful. This may be suitable for some scholarly analyses in that it allows the analysts to assess why some operations are more or less successful than others, presumably by reference to variations in some key independent or predictor variables. Yet this approach generates only relative or comparative assessments. A relatively successful operation might still have significant flaws, which are masked when the baseline is composed largely of failed missions. Recent policy evaluation practice has been to use the "best in class" case as the standard for evaluation (Bingham and Felbinger 2002). This baseline also likely leads to negative evaluations, as all other cases will necessarily fall short by definition, even as the standard accurately reflects appropriate aspiration levels for policymakers.

Lumping

By "lumping" we refer to the way that interventions, including peace operations, are packaged. Practically all conflict-reducing interventions, and especially peace operations, are combinations of multiple procedures and processes. For example, any peace operation can be characterized in terms of its size, training of peacekeepers, strategy and tactics, time horizons, clarity and change of the mandate, and extent of involvement with civil society, as well as host country and constituent support, among other features. This panoply of factors complicates the task of determining which ones are specifically responsible for which outcomes: What parts of a peace operation have been successful or unsuccessful and what factors are responsible for that success or failure? From a policymaking standpoint this is vital, as lessons learned from success and failure need to be at the micro level so that adaptations and modifications can be made without throwing out an entire strategic or operational framework.

Lumping is somewhat less problematic when the interest resides in evaluating a particular mission. Similar to many school-based interventions, the question asked is whether the whole package makes a difference in that particular country (or school). Practitioners and consultants are often interested in the summative issue of whether the complete set of actions, with all its parts, worked. This is what is known as an "impact evaluation," in which the end results or measurable impacts are the object of scrutiny (Bingham and Felbinger 2002). It is more problematic when the object of the evaluation focuses on any of the several facets of the lumped package. Although primarily of interest to theorists and researchers, this question also has practical implications. Knowing which factors were responsible for outcomes contributes in important ways to the design and implementation of future operations (see Druckman 2005).

Types of peacekeeping missions

Different kinds of missions require, at least in part, different criteria for evaluating success. Most missions have as their goal the reduction of violent conflict. Others have more specific aims, such as supervising elections, providing human rights protection, or contributing to the building of new societal institutions. The various missions have been shown to differ on a variety of characteristics, particularly with regard to the role of peacekeepers and the type of conflict management outcome emphasized by the mission (Diehl et al. 1998). For example, some missions assume primary or direct roles for peacekeepers. These include collective enforcement, state/nation building, and protective services. Others place peacekeepers in third-party roles. Examples are the supervision of elections, arms control verification, and observation (information collection and monitoring). Missions also divide between whether they emphasize benefits to the peacekeepers themselves or to both the mission and the host country. The former conflict management outcome is evident in collective or sanctions enforcement, interventions in support of democracy, and protective services. The latter outcome is prevalent in such missions as traditional peacekeeping, observation, and election supervision. Some missions have multiple and mixed roles, namely humanitarian assistance and pacification. Thus, the dimensions of missions influence the way we assess effectiveness.

For this reason, the questions asked about success and the indicators used to diagnose progress are specific to the mission's goal. For example, if the goal is to contain violence, we would ask whether the violence levels have decreased and measure the number of shooting incidents and casualties both for members of the disputing parties and for the peace force. If, however, the goal is to protect human rights, we would ask, at one level, whether atrocities have been reduced or genocidal incidents avoided and, at another level, whether a judicial system is in place and functioning. Progress in achieving the goal of human rights is indicated by both a significant reduction in atrocities on the ground and by an institutional system that insures due process.

Not surprisingly, most analysts advocate using guidelines provided in the operations mandate, the authorizing document (e.g. Security Council resolution) provided by the organization carrying out the mission (e.g. Howard 2008; Bellamy and Williams 2005; Ratner 1995). Mandates often contain specific tasks to be completed or benchmarks that should be reached. In one sense, this is appropriate as a particular mission is only judged according to the tasks with which it was assigned. On the other hand, there are a number of drawbacks associated with using mandates to define success. The mandates given for operations, especially those directed by large membership international organizations, are the products of political deliberation and compromise, and the result is that they are frequently vague. For example, the UN Security Force (UNSF) in West Guinea was charged with maintaining law and order. UNIFIL was asked to "restore international peace and security" and "assist the Government of Lebanon in ensuring the return of its effective authority in the area."

There is much room for debate on the scope and detail of the operation's mission. What does "restore peace and security" mean? If the context is a failed state, such a term may be meaningless, as the status quo *ante* involved no such peace or security. There are also various levels that might be established as to whether this mandate has been met or not. That a more precise mandate could not be specified and approved is evidence that there is disagreement over what the operation was supposed to achieve. The analyst cannot merely impose his or her own interpretation of the meaning of a mandate. This problem alone makes it difficult to assess whether the designs of the mandate have been achieved (Druckman and Stern 1997). We should acknowledge, however, that over time, peace operation mandates have become more detailed and more precise, although there is still room for dispute in interpretation.

Mandates could also be inflexible in the face of changing conflict conditions, and thus what peace-keepers are attempting to do may no longer reflect the standards present in the mandate (Bellamy and Williams 2005). Thus, the Multinational Force in Beirut (MNF) was originally designed to supervise the withdrawal of PLO forces from Beirut, but subsequently became involved in supporting the Lebanese government army and other activities that seemed to belie its neutral mandate. "Mandate clarity" is an indicator of peacekeeping success in the literature (Mackinlay 1990; see also Diehl 1994 on this point), again confounding the inputs or influences with the outcomes.

The conflict environment

A focus in this chapter on overall mission effectiveness highlights dimensions at a macro level of analysis: for example, stakeholders in the international community, mission mandates, relations with the host country, and involvement with civil society and local cultures. These factors are considered to be part of the conflict environment that is confronted by a peace operation, contributing to its effectiveness in the short and long term. It is important to distinguish among factors in the environment that are more or less subject to being influenced by the operation: for example, the difference between internal geography or infrastructure (low malleability) and mobilization potential or skills training (high malleability). This distinction has implications for defining the possibilities and limits of any peace operation. These implications are discussed in this concluding section.

The many features of the conflict environment that may influence or be influenced by a peace operation can be divided into three categories: characteristics of the conflict, local governance, and the local population. Somewhat more malleable conflict characteristics include the ease of crossing borders in the host country, involvement of external actors in the host country's dispute, and the phase of the conflict when deployment occurs. These features are variables more likely to be influenced by the operation than to have an influence on it. Less malleable features include internal geography, the stability of neighbors' regimes, and the intractability of the conflict. These features are more likely to influence the operation than to be influenced by it.

Similarly, some aspects of local governance are more malleable than others: compare service provision and host country support with the condition of the country's infrastructure and its economic health. And, with regard to the local population, mobilization potential and organizational attributes are more malleable than the size and density of the population in the area of deployment and the pattern of cleavages between groups in the host country. The more or less malleable distinction has strategic implications, contributing to the design and implementation of operations. By focusing attention on the more malleable features of the conflict environment, peacekeeping forces may be more efficient and effective.

This distinction can also be incorporated in training programs by increasing the sensitivity of peacekeepers to those aspects of the environment that can be altered. Among the relevant skills are gathering and processing information, using the information to perform situation analyses, learning how to manage impressions through tactical posturing, and timing moves when implementing tactical scripts. These skills would help peacekeepers to deal with the challenges of coordinating with the host country regime, working with external actors, mobilizing moderate citizens, and bridging differences among local organizations and in-country NGOs. Design, implementation, and evaluation of training programs that develop these tactical skills are discussed elsewhere. (For example, see Druckman et al. 1997 on the distinction between contact and combat skills; see Druckman and Ebner 2013 on differences between conceptual and tactical learning.) However, whether enhanced tactical skills and performance increase overall mission effectiveness is less clear.

The distinction between more and less malleable aspects of the conflict environment raises issues about the extent to which training contributes to mission effectiveness. Even well-trained and organized forces may not be able to overcome barriers imposed by the conflict environment: for example, the geographical context, a legacy of violence, type of conflict or the phase of conflict during which the mission is deployed. For the policy analyst, this means striking a balance between the different types of factors in performing evaluations, i.e. recognizing the factors over which the operation has little control. For the peacekeeper, this means learning to distinguish among those factors. Another kind of skill – referred to as monitoring situations – is helpful. More generally, learning to recognize opportunities for effective action within a larger environment is likely to contribute in important ways to mission success.

Two types of peacekeeper roles with corresponding skills are suggested: as an agent for change (actor) and as a monitor of changing situations (reactor) (see Diehl and Druckman 2010 and Whalan 2012 for more on this distinction). Both roles form part of the overall evaluation of mission effectiveness.

References

Ammitzboell, Katarina (2007) "Unintended Consequences of Peace Operations on the Host Economy from a People's Perspective," in Chiyuki Aoi, Cedric de Coning, and Ramesh Thakur (eds) *Unintended Consequences of Peacekeeping Operations*, Tokyo: United Nations University Press.

Andersson, Andreas (2000) "Democracies and UN Peacekeeping Operations, 1990–1996," *International Peacekeeping* 7(2): 1–22.

Aoi, Chiyuki, Cedric de Conging, and Ramesh Thakur (2007) *Unintended Consequences of Peacekeeping Operations*, Tokyo: United Nations University Press.

Barnett, Michael N. and Martha Finnemore (2004) *Rules for the World: International Organizations in Global Politics*, Ithaca, NY: Cornell University Press.

Bellamy, Alex J. and Paul Williams (2005) "Who's Keeping the Peace? Regionalization and Contemporary Peace Operations," *International Security* 29(4): 157–195.

Bingham, Richard D. and Clairee L. Felbinger (2002) *Evaluation in Practice: A Methodological Approach*, 2nd edn, New York: Seven Bridges Press.

Bratt, Duane (2002) "Blue Condoms: The Use of International Peacekeepers in the Fight against AIDS," *International Peacekeeping* 9(3): 65–86.

Claude, Jr., Inis L. (1966) "Collective Legitimization as a Political Function of the United Nations," *International Organization* 20(3): 367–379.

Coleman, Katharina P. (2007) *International Organisations and Peace Enforcement*, Cambridge: Cambridge University Press.

Diehl, Paul F. (1994) *International Peacekeeping*, revised edn, Baltimore, MD: Johns Hopkins University Press.

Diehl, Paul F. and Daniel Druckman (2010) *Evaluating Peace Operations*, Boulder, CO: Lynne Rienner Publishers.

Diehl, Paul F., Daniel Druckman, and James Wall (1998) "International Peacekeeping and Conflict Resolution: A Taxonomic Analysis with Implications," *Journal of Conflict Resolution* 42(1): 33–55.

Druckman, Daniel (2005) *Doing Research: Methods of Inquiry for Conflict Analysis*, Thousand Oaks, CA: Sage Publications.

Druckman, Daniel (2006) "Time-Series Designs and Analyses," in Peter Carnevale and Carsten K.W. de Dreu (eds) *Methods of Negotiation Research*, Leiden, the Netherlands: Martinus Nijhoff Publishers.

Druckman, Daniel and Paul C. Stern (1997) "The Forum: Evaluating Peacekeeping Missions," *Mershon International Studies Review* 41(1): 151–165.

Druckman, Daniel and Paul F. Diehl (eds) (2013) *Peace Operation Success: A Comparative Analysis*, Leiden, the Netherlands: Brill.

Druckman, Daniel and Noam Ebner (2013) "Games, Claims, and New Frames: Rethinking the Use of Simulation in Negotiation Education," *Negotiation Journal* 29(1): 61–92.

Druckman, Daniel, Jerome E. Singer, and Harld Van Cott (1997) *Enhancing Organizational Performance.* Washington DC: National Academy Press.

Enterline, Andrew and Seonjou Kang (2002) "Stopping the Killing Sooner? Assessing the Success of United Nations Peacekeeping in Civil Wars." Paper presented at the Annual Meeting of the Peace Science Society, Tucson, Arizona.

Gilligan, Michael and Stephen John Stedman (2003) "Where Do the Peacekeepers Go?" *International Studies Review* 5(4): 37–54.

Heldt, Birger and Peter Wallensteen (2006) *Peacekeeping Operations: Global Patterns of Intervention and Success, 1948–2004*, 2nd edn, Sandoverken, Sweden: Folke Bernadotte Academy Press.

Howard, Lisa Morjé (2008) *UN Peacekeeping in Civil Wars*, Cambridge UK: Cambridge University Press.

Johansen, Robert C. (1994) "U.N. Peacekeeping: How Should We Measure Success?' *Mershon International Studies Review* 38(2): 307–310.

Kaysen, Carl and George Rathjens (1995) *Peace Operations by the United Nations: The Case for a Volunteer UN Military Force*, Committee on International Security Studies, Cambridge, MA: American Academy of Arts and Sciences.

Kent, Vanessa (2007) "Protecting Civilians from UN Peacekeepers and Humanitarian Workers: Sexual Exploitation and Abuse," in Chiyuki Aoi, Cedric de Coning, and Ramesh Thakur (eds) *Unintended Consequences of Peacekeeping Operations*, Tokyo: United Nations University Press.

Mackinlay, John (1990) "Powerful Peace-keepers" *Survival* 32(3): 241–250.

Menkhaus, Ken (2003) "Measuring Impact: Issues and Dilemmas." InterPeace (previously War-Torn Societies Project – International), Geneva, Occasional Paper Series.

Neack, Laura (1995) "UN Peace-Keeping: In the Interest of Community or Self?" *Journal of Peace Research* 32(2): 181–196.

Ratner, Steven R. (1995) *The New UN Peacekeeping: Building Peace in Lands of Conflict after the Cold War*, New York: St. Martin's Press.

Richmond, Oliver (1998) "Devious Objectives and the Disputant's View of International Mediation: A Theoretical Framework," *Journal of Peace Research* 35 (6): 707–722.

Stiles, Kendall W. and Maryellen MacDonald (1992) "After Consensus, What? Performance Criteria for the UN in the Post-Cold War Era." *Journal of Peace Research* 29(3): 299–311.

Weiss, Thomas G. (1994) "The United Nations and Civil Wars." *Washington Quarterly* 17 (4): 139–159.

Whalen, Jeni (2012) "Evaluating Peace Operations: The Case of Cambodia," *Journal of International Peacekeeping* 16 (3–4): 226–251.

24

BUSINESS ANALYTICS RESEARCH IN MILITARY ORGANIZATIONS

*Jan-Bert Maas, Paul C. van Fenema
and Jan-Kees Schakel*

D. Soban, J. Salmon and A. Fahringer (2013). 'A visual analytics framework for strategic airlift decision making', *The Journal of Defense Modeling and Simulation: Applications, Methodology, Technology* 10(2): 131–144.

Soban et al. (2013) present a trade study of a strategic airlift decision-making environment that has been developed around the US Air Force Lockheed C-5A and C-5M aircraft. They pose that it is not enough to rely solely on information sharing to induce effective decision-making, but that business analytics (BA) has an emerging role in improving decision-making. With the use of BA methods and tools, analysts engage in tasks such as forecasting and pattern recognition in order to form judgments about a situation, thus contributing to better-informed decision-making. Soban et al. (2013) focus on visual analytics, which represents a method within the broader field of BA, aimed at visualizing complex data relations to support interactive reasoning (Wong and Thomas 2004). The field of visual analytics has been considered as a key enabler for decision-making under data-intensive situations, because it promises increased contextualization and understanding of data presented.

To gain more specific insight in the opportunities and challenges of visual analytics, Soban et al. (2013) conducted a trade study on strategic airlift decision-making. The practical objective was to assess whether the improved performance characteristics of a C-5M aircraft would provide value in an operational scenario, like delivering a fixed amount of cargo between two locations with a given number of aircraft. To this end data was collected on missions, payload, fleet size, aircraft repair rates, and flight paths. Moreover, several mission scenarios were included. Each mission scenario included airports of embarkation and disembarkation, and a payload to deliver at minimum. In order to observe differences between the types of aircraft, trade-off capabilities were included as well. For example, the trade-off of payload for range, aircraft repair rates and logistics metrics (costs of fuel, flight hours). The main methodological challenge Soban et al. (2013) faced, was the volume and disparate nature of data. In order to solve this issue, the authors designed their analytics tool in such a way that it could predict the missing parts of the data.

(continued)

(continued)

The visual analytics environment provided insight in differences between the types of aircraft. The payload-range curve of the aircraft indicated that the C5-A could fly a payload of 175,000lbs from A to B, while the C5-M could only deliver a payload of 125,000lbs. However, the C5-A would need a stopover for refuelling while the C5-M could directly fly from A to B. Using the visual analytics tool, Soban et al. (2013) show that this balances the additional payload, since the time for landing, refuelling, taking off and other resources would make a flight with a C5-A less efficient than performing the flight with a C5-M. All the curves with the different trade-capabilities could be presented by the visual analytics tool, facilitating effective and timely decision-making. Next to that, other important but more complex characteristics like break and repair rates and utilization metrics could be compared in real time. Moreover, Soban et al. (2013) indicate that visual analytics reveal findings that are relatively less intuitive. For instance, the visual analytics environment showed how many additional legacy C5-A were required to equal the time to deliver a fixed amount of cargo, as compared to the modernized C5-M. As such the decision-making environment offers the US military capabilities for supporting and defending the need for upgrading the existing C-5As into C-5Ms, amidst budget cuts and increased scrutiny. The authors conclude that visual analytics is a powerful enabler to significantly improve decision-making in the military. By combining analytical reasoning with the human capability to ingest and understand visual data, visual analytics facilitates rapid and well-informed decision-making in the face of disparate data, uncertainty and time pressure. However, the authors argue that more research is necessary to disentangle all the opportunities of BA in the military, and to overcome barriers to the acceptance and use of visual analytics in a military context.

Introduction

In this chapter we explore opportunities and challenges for researchers in a military context related to business analytics (BA). BA refers to the collection, storage, analysis and interpretation of data with the use of software and tools, in order to make better decisions and improve organizational performance (Davenport and Harris 2007). From a military point of view, BA offers opportunities to increase efficiency, economies of scale and flexibility (Hammond 2008). Operationally, September 11 and trends such as network centric warfare and cyber warfare have encouraged the military to collect, combine, and leverage information regardless of military service organization or technology. Since 2010, the US President, the Pentagon and the Department of Homeland Security strongly invest in analytics to address national security challenges.[1] New opportunities emerge when fusing knowledge, data, and BA-technologies in a military context, which could provide benefits like faster decision-making and increased situational awareness.

BA tools and methods can be aptly combined with military thinking. Especially the Observe, Orient, Decide and Act (OODA) loop (Boyd 1976) may be complemented with the use of BA. The OODA loop originates from Boyd's analysis that American planes won more battles because the pilot's field of vision was far superior. This gave the pilot a clear competitive advantage, as it meant he could assess the situation better and faster than his opponent (Osinga 2005). The OODA loop has been applied to the combat operations process, but also in other military

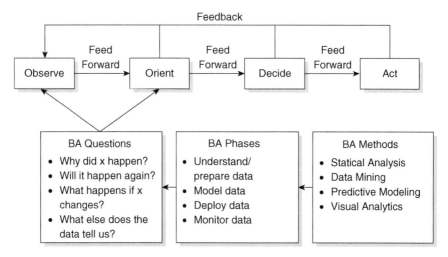

Figure 24.1 Business analytics and the OODA loop

disciplines later on. The OODA loop outlines a four-point decision loop that supports effective and proactive decision-making. The four stages include Observation (collecting information), Orientation (analysing the information), Decision (determine a course of action) and Action (follow through on a decision). BA can enhance this loop by enabling military organizations to make better-informed decisions based on a myriad of sources and databases. As Figure 24.1 illustrates, typical BA questions, phases and tools (Brown 2013) impact phases preceding and following the decision and action phases in the (ongoing) OODA loop.

However, both the application of BA in a military context as well as related research is scarce. The application of BA within a military environment tends to be complex. The example study by Soban et al. (2013), involving stakeholders from industry, academia, and the military, illustrates this. These groups all have different agendas and approaches. Moreover, the unique characteristics of military organizations pose challenges and difficulties when studying BA and its applications in a military context. With the unique aspects of military organizations we refer to features like the public nature of military organizations (e.g. political pressures), danger-settings, time pressure, and the task of dealing with unfriendly opponents in unfamiliar environments (Soeters et al. 2010). The goals of this chapter include explaining what BA entails, and in which way it can be applied to military organizations. Next to that we will cover how to get started with BA research and we indicate different challenges that emerge when applying BA in a military context.

What is business analytics?

BA has become *en vogue* since major successes have been reported in the media such as President Obama's election campaigns (Siegel 2013). BA is the combination of skills, technologies, applications and processes used by organizations to gain insight in to their business, based on data and statistics (Davenport and Harris 2007). From a military perspective, BA is used to inform decision-making on operations in a (near) real-time fashion across sites. An example of this combination of sensors, knowledge, intelligence and command and control is the US Army Distributed Common Ground System – Army (DCGS-A). Utilizing three core functionalities (Intelligence Surveillance and Reconnaissance (ISR), network-enabled capability to exploit information with common analyst tools, and feeds from multiple sensors), the system is intended to enhance situational awareness, reduce risk, and provide commanders at multiple levels with access to information and intelligence (US Army 2009). This is illustrated in Figure 24.2.

This approach increasingly combines short-term support of operations and long-term reuse of intelligence and knowledge. That is, BA also supports long-term evaluation of organization-wide operations, uncovering patterns and trends on which the impact of decisions.

BA can improve the performance of an organization by providing data rich real-time data-bases and providing tools and methods to give more insight in the business and to make superior decisions drawing on available data.

BA solutions typically use data, statistical and quantitative analysis and fact-based data to measure past performance to guide an organization's business planning. Examples of BA methods include (Laursen and Thorlund 2010):

- data mining: exploring data to find new relationships and patterns;
- statistical analysis: explaining why a certain result occurred;
- predictive modelling: forecasting future results;
- visual analytics (of which the example study offers an illustration): reasoning facilitated by interactive visual interfaces.

A well-published example of BA is the way the BA team of the US President Obama applied their tools to make a success out of the electoral campaigns of 2008 and 2012. The team applied different BA methods to inform strategizing aimed at retaining or persuading voters. For instance, when a voter was contacted by the team in a door-to-door campaign, the particular interests of that voter were recorded in a huge database (Siegel 2013). Next to that, the campaign's call centres conducted 5,000 to 10,000 so-called short-form interviews in order to gauge voter's preferences, and 1,000 interviews in a long-form version that was more like a traditional poll (Issenberg 2012). To even further derive individual-level predictions and obtain a detailed voter database, algorithms trawled for patterns between these interview opinions and the data points the campaign had assembled for every voter – as many as one thousand variables each, drawn from voter registration records, consumer data warehouses, and past campaign contacts (Siegel 2013). In this way the BA team could understand the proclivities of individual voters likely to support Obama or be open to his message, and then seek to persuade them through personalized contact via social media, email, or a knock on the door. The data richness combined with real time updates of the BA applications greatly enhanced the ability to pinpoint messaging and made it easier to sway voters.

Civilian and military applications of business analytics

Civilian applications of business analytics

BA is used to optimize processes of many different types of civilian organizations. For example, supermarket chains rely heavily on BA solutions (Davenport and Harris 2007). They use BA to make strategic decisions, such as what kind of new products to add to their assortments and which underperforming stores to close. They also use BA for tactical matters such as renegotiating contracts with suppliers and identifying opportunities to improve inefficient processes. Likewise, banks employ BA to enable fine-grained analysis of customers, products, channels and transactions. Table 24.1 presents several common applications of BA within different organizations.

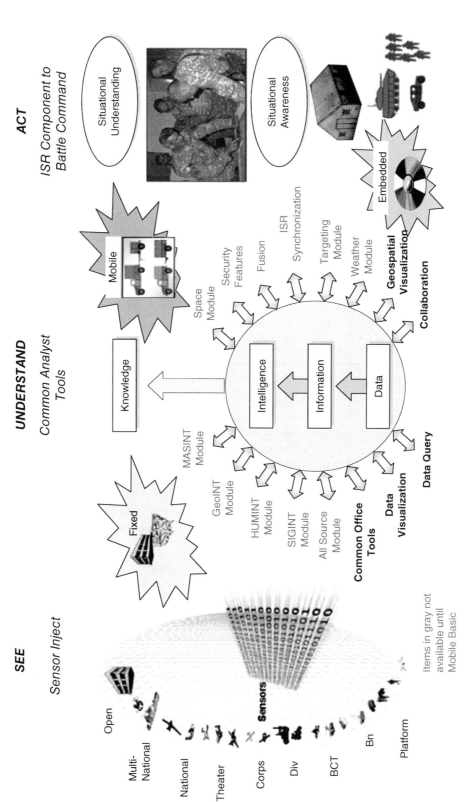

Figure 24.2 Overview of DCGS-A (US Army 2009: 3)

Table 24.1 Common applications of BA in different types of organizations (Davenport and Harris 2007)

Business function	Description	Corporate examples
• Supply chain	• Simulate and optimize supply chain flows; reduce inventory and stock-outs	• Dell, Wal-Mart, Amazon
• Customer selection, loyalty and service	• Identify customers with the greatest profit potential; increase likelihood that they will want the product or service offering; retain their loyalty	• Harrah's, Capital One, Barclays
• Pricing	• Identify the price that will maximize yield, or profit	• Progressive, Marriot
• Human capital	• Select the best employees for particular tasks or jobs at particular compensation levels.	• New England Patriots, Oakland A's, Boston Red Sox
• Product and service quality	• Detect quality problems early and minimize them	• Honda, Intel
• Financial performance	• Better understand the drivers of financial performance and the effect of nonfinancial factors	• MCI, Verizon
• Research and development	• Improve quality, efficacy, and, where, applicable, safety of products and services	• Novartis, Amazon, Yahoo

BA may lead to a competitive advantage by permitting more accurate costing and pricing of products and services and providing an accurate assessment of customer profitability. BA adds value for different types of organizations as well as for different types of departments within these organizations. For instance, Kohavi et al. (2002: 47) describe BA applications in marketing to 'reduce customer attrition, improve customer profitability and increase the response of direct mail and email marketing campaigns'. BA tools are used to increase the quality of human resource management (HRM) (Kohavi et al. 2002). BA software is able to identify work force trends such as attrition rates, and it can perform HRM tasks like compensation and benefits analyses. Other departments like sales and quality and resource planning are known to apply BA solutions to improve efficiency and productivity.

Business analytics in military cold environments

Before, during and after operations in the theatre, military organizations organize their resources and processes as part of their 'cold' side (Soeters et al. 2010). This cold side focuses on prevention, facilitation and preparation for actual operations and missions. Increasingly, BA permeates this cold domain to support adaptability, responsiveness and risk management. We highlight the military's environment, resources and deployment.

- *Military's environment*. Military organizations may analyse social and other web-based media to monitor public perception of their organization and operations. Potential threats of extremism can be mapped and even countered by using BA to support military intelligence (Berger 2013). Using BA, military organizations locate possible extremist individuals and provide for the prevention and detection of cyber warfare intrusions (Lavigne and Gouin 2011). This includes applications for analysing service usage in a network to detect Internet attacks, and investigate hosts in a network that communicate with suspect IP addresses.

- *Military's resources.* Military organizations can also adopt BA to analyse the composition, well-being and effectiveness of their work force, e.g. through measuring the quality of military healthcare (Hudak et al. 2013) or by calculating the ratio of occupying forces to population levels in order to forecast the number of troops needed during operations (Davenport and Jarvenpaa 2008). Similarly, BA offers insight in resources such as IT infrastructure, supply chains, and major military assets. The illustrative study shows the strengths of visual analytics for military decision-makers regarding a specific weapon system.

- *Military's deployment.* BA for military decision-making can also be viewed from the perspective of the deployment cycle. First, BA may be used for force planning and defining future technology needs and costs. Then, when political decisions on an operation have been made, deployment, sustainment and redeployment may draw on BA for analysis of costs and logistics (van Kampen et al. 2012). In an era of budget restrictions for the military, the latter category gains in importance. Military organizations often integrate BA solutions in dashboard tools to make standardized analyses more accessible by providing at-a-glance views of key performance indicators relevant to a particular objective or business process. For example, commanders can quickly observe the condition of their materiel and assess the level of employability of the materiel for exercises or missions. This enables commanders to swiftly gain oversight and insight in the continuity and capabilities of their organization at any given moment, at any chosen aggregated level.

Business analytics in military hot environments

BA can also enable military organizations when they are acting in hot environments. 'Hot' refers to actual operations and missions and is also known as the primary process of military organizations. In these primary processes BA are indispensable for intelligence cells supporting command and control (C2), i.e. the observe and orient phases in the OODA loop.

Before an actual operation, BA can be used to comb through massive amounts of sensor data and other intelligence, elicit patterns, and develop strategies and tactical plans. During actual operations the need for (near) real time information for command and control increases. For example, data on location and movement of friendly and opposing forces, weather, and social media are collected, fused, and analysed (Lavigne and Gouin 2011). During patrol and regular surveillance BA can be used to monitor enemy lines based on remotely sensed patterns of behaviour. By using a broad spectrum of BA applications military organizations are enabled to sustain information superiority, effective intelligence cycles, and command and control that out-speeds and out-smarts opposing forces (Osinga 2007). After a military operation, with increasingly large amounts of data available, BA is being used to (re-) assess and monitor the strengths and weaknesses of opposing forces, and to analyse the organization's own performances. Moreover, experiments can be conducted through simulations or during training missions.

Throughout these phases, data are being combined and analysed to improve insight. An example is Starlight software[2] (Kritzstein 2003). This is a visual BA solution that supports the integration of geospatial data including weather, vegetation, infrastructures, and the locations of civilian institutions. In the Starlight visual analytics platform, viewers can interactively move among multiple representations of the data. This platform enables the visualization of multiple data collections simultaneously in order to uncover correlations that may span multiple relationship types, including networks, geographical data and textual information (Lavigne and Gouin 2011). An example is the Combat Management System (CMS) aboard of US Navy ships (Kooman 2013), which improves the situational awareness and performance of these vessels significantly. Such CMSs are being used in operations against piracy in the Gulf of Aden to analyse movements of ships and identify trends by combining electronic charts and data of civil and military shipping databases (Lavigne and Gouin 2011). Due to the visual analytics interface, military analysts can decide to take action when particular anomalies emerge in these trends in a quick and optimized way. The strength of BA systems like these is their ability to combine data of sensors, weapon and communication systems and the ability to present the data in a clear and uncomplicated ways, giving way to rapid and better-informed decision-making.

Getting started with business analytics research

In order to get started with BA research a project-based approach is recommended. Such a BA research project progresses through five steps, often iteratively (Gangadharan and Swami 2004). Once an opportunity for BA research is identified the researcher should position the study in the BA research field. We distinguish three categories:

- *Researcher (co)develops BA tool.* In this category of studies, BA applications are being developed by the researcher, often in cooperation with organization members and with the aim of supporting the organization. An example is our example study. In these tool-centric studies, academic researchers combine their strengths with military practitioners to develop a BA algorithm, method, or tool to support a given practical decision-making issue. Examples of approaches and methods are design and (participatory) action research. In the example study, practitioners and academic researchers jointly developed a strategic airlift decision-making environment for the US Air Force (Soban et al. 2013). This type of work tends to directly benefit organizations as well as serve academic communities interested in developing tools and designing organizations.
- *Researcher studies BA development and use in organizations.* Studies with BA as their main subject represent the largest part of the BA literature, where the researcher studies BA as an actor interested in, yet distant from, the organization and tool. The aim of these studies is to understand BA and contribute to socio-technological theories. Methods often include case studies, surveys, and participatory research (Bergold and Thomas 2012). This type of BA research includes studies of BA tools and the way they impact organizational phenomena. Lavigne et al. (2011) for example show to what extent visual analytics can increase maritime domain awareness, while Trkman et al. (2010) indicate the impact of BA on supply chain performance.
- *Researcher uses BA to study organizational processes.* Finally, BA may be used as a means to study organizational phenomena. Pentland et al. (2011) use data from an invoice processing workflow system to create event logs which they analyse to uncover patterns of different work routines of employees, and to determine whether these patterns of action were stable or changing over time (Pentland et al. 2011). These studies seek to exploit advances in BA to better process and understand organizational data, for instance by visualizing idiosyncratic patterns of business processes and relating these to organizational effectiveness. In contrast to the first category, theories in non-BA domains – e.g. organizational control and routines – are extended.

Thus, before starting with the research design, one should determine which role BA plays within the study. Next to greatly influencing the design of the research, it also has implications for the potential audience (i.e. academics, analysts, tool developers, or military commanders). Since the example study of Soban et al. (2013) falls in the first BA research category we demonstrate the project-based approach of a researcher (co)developing a BA tool. However, the five steps are also (partly) applicable for the other two defined categories of BA research.

Step 1: Focusing and designing BA research

The design depends on the category of BA research that is selected by the researcher and the associated stakeholders. What expectations have to be met? Is it possible to distinguish layers of core and complementary goals? In our example study, current planning and maintenance of the airplanes gave rise to concerns. Their core focus was to develop a relevant tool, with a complementary benefit for the organization. The secondary goal for the tool's creation was to provide a pilot deployment in the form of a relevant example for 'the use of visual analytics within the corporate and professional culture' (Soban et al. 2013). Formulate the – possibly layered – goals of the BA research, including the scope, conceptual background, and the research design. If military and academic stakeholders play a role, one must think about synergies and articulate a project that is understandable and relevant to both.

Step 2: Developing the BA tool

The researcher will have to select methods, algorithms and tools that support the processing and analysis requirements of the BA project, or develop a system.[3] This may involve several iterations, as the meaningfulness or results of specific methods, algorithms or tools on a given data sets cannot always be predicted. This iterative process starts with identifying the required data and assessing its particularities. The example study included both a model with algorithms and a visual interface. Professional organizations use tools from companies such as SAS, Oracle, and COGNOS. Increasingly, organizations build a comprehensive set of interrelated tools, requiring an architectural approach to systematically collect and process data (Pant 2009: 12). In any case, it is important to consider the organizational context. The researcher may initially experience some resistance as people are not familiar with BA or might be concerned about the results of the study. Gaining legitimacy may be achieved by explaining the work, highlighting benefits for those involved and training users. BA may require a cultural change of the organization (Davenport and Harris 2007). This step is crucial to ensure data access and long-term support.

Step 3: Using the BA tool

In this step the required data is being retrieved. This includes the identification of actual data sources (rather than types), gaining a deeper understanding of its specific meaning, assessing the currency, structure, completeness, and errors and omissions in the data. Data that has been collected may have to be transformed, (re)structured, and cleaned to be used in the BA tool. This may include the creation of new or adjusted categories or classes to enable comparison and integration of multiple data sources. Next, using the tool, one must analyse the data in an iterative fashion, experimenting with different algorithms, methods, and modes of presentation (Soban et al. 2013). Because the analysis process may require highly specialized skills, tools, and expensive software licenses and hardware, increasingly, data analysis is conducted at a centralized department or even outsourced. For instance, UAV data processing from Pakistan is performed in the US (Wall and Monahan 2011).

Step 4: Presenting and leveraging BA results

Once the BA process is finished, the findings or BA application can be transferred to the key stakeholders. This is an important step to prove the usefulness of the study. The researcher should be able to explain their findings in easy and understandable terms. In our example study, unexpected insights were found: 'One example of a relatively unintuitive insight that the visual analytics environment did reveal was how many additional legacy aircraft are required to equal the time to deliver a fixed amount of cargo, as compared to the modernized aircraft under relatively likely circumstances' (Soban et al. 2013). By clearly articulating findings and conclusions of the research, stakeholders may become more energized and motivated about the usefulness of the study.

Step 5: Evolving BA research

Finally, in order to improve the results of the study, critical and forward-looking questions have to be asked. Does the BA tool developed by the study make a difference? How would one reflect on the original design? Opportunities may exist to improve the tool, cover more business processes (Gangadharan and Swami 2004), and raise the BA maturity level of the organization (Davenport 2013).

Challenges in military business analytics research

When initiating BA research in a military context, several challenges have to be addressed. These challenges relate to the methodology and to the context.

Methodological challenges

Information overload. A common challenge relates to the giant amount of data that can be generated and stored in BA databases or tools. Although this is one of the cornerstones for BA success, it may also cause problems. The sheer amount of data is not directly the problem, but the amount of time to analyse the data and the necessary skills to handle the data certainly are. When conducting a study using the data of a BA tool, researchers should take into account that the data warehouse of an average organization quickly holds tens of terabytes of data, not to mention the amount of data the databases hold in a large public organization like the military. The US Air Force already reported to cut back on the amount of drones they use and invest in, because they cannot keep up with analysing all the generated data constructively (Peck 2012). Therefore researchers should frame the specific area of BA they would like to include in their research very carefully in order to prevent 'drowning' in all the data provided by BA solutions. This starts at the very beginning of the project: selecting relevant areas and data before collecting; starting small and adding data (both breadth and depth) incrementally.

Data quality. As stated earlier, the quantity of data from a wide spectrum of sources is vast; however the quality of the data is a more problematic feature. Correa and Ma (2011) indicate that data in BA tools and solutions are inherently uncertain and often incomplete and contradictory. Measured data contains errors, introduced by the acquisition process or systematically added due to computer imprecision (Correa and Ma 2011). For analysts and researchers, it is important to be aware of the sources and degree of uncertainty in the data. For instance, before data can be used in visual analytical tool like in the example study it has to be pre-processed, transformed, and mapped to a visual representation. This uncertainty is compounded and propagated, making it difficult to preserve the quality of data along the reasoning and decision-making process. Thomson (2005) defines a data uncertainty typology, identifying key components of uncertainty such as accuracy/error, precision, completeness, consistency, lineage, credibility, subjectivity, and interrelatedness. In order to overcome or reduce problems of uncertainty and data quality, different (statistical) solutions may be applied. Methods that may be applied to deal with uncertainty include regression, principal component analysis and k-means clustering. To gain more insight in these methods we strongly recommend further reading work that tackle these specific problems in detail (Correa and Ma 2011; Zuk and Carpendale 2007).

Lack of cognitive cues. Like stated previously, some studies use BA as a means to collect data. Van der Aalst (2012) uses process mining to create event logs. For example, the transaction logs of an enterprise resource planning system are used to discover changes in routines and processes (Van der Aalst 2012). Although these kinds of studies do not state anything about BA as a subject, they do use a BA database as a method for their data collection. However, because this BA data has an archival nature, it is hard to test whether changes or alterations in these events or processes can be attributed to cognitive changes among participants (e.g. learning), notwithstanding which changes in processes are deemed most important by organizational members. So, studies using BA as a way to collect data should somehow have to include the cognitive or emotional aspects of their respondents. A solution to this challenge could include enriching the research data by conducting detailed interviews or surveys, thus including cognitive cues in BA research.

Context-related challenges

Sensitivity of the data. Data may be used and misused. We define the sensitivity of data as the chance that it is being misused, 'multiplied' by the harmfulness of misuse, and reasoned from the perspective of the data owner. If data is highly sensitive (e.g. in terms of privacy, politics, or intelligence), measures are often taken to protect the data. The protection measures (e.g. access restrictions, encryptions) present an important challenge for researchers in general and for BA projects in particular. Denying researchers access causes less harm than military information falling into the wrong hands. Especially data related to the hot environment of military organizations are often highly classified. In order to access and handle such data and disseminate scientific results, researchers will need clearance and agree upon dissemination procedures before the project starts.

Besides military sensitivity it is good practice in research projects to anonymize the names of practitioners involved. In order to guarantee anonymity, codes should be used when analysing personal data of, for example, a military health care system (Hudak et al. 2013). When disseminating the results of the study, researchers should make sure that the sensitive data is presented carefully with respect to confidentiality and anonymity. In the illustrative study this challenge is tackled by using fictive or simulated data to demonstrate the 'strategic airlift decision-making environment' that has been developed by the authors. However, BA research concentrating on the output of BA solutions cannot adopt such a method and have to take the described measures of confidentiality and anonymity into account.

Time-dimension and required accuracy. Another context-related challenge concerns the different requirements regarding the time-dimension and accuracy within hot and cold sides of a military organization. Within a mission in a hot military environment, the use of BA is aimed at maximizing 'strike power', while BA applied in a cold military environment is aimed at maximizing resilience and endurance of e.g. administrative and logistic services. The information requirements of BA in these different types of environment differ accordingly. Not only in terms of sources being used, but also in data visualization and the weight of timeliness, accurateness and source reliability. For example, the data presentation and analysis in a hot environment often requires geographical technologies, while in a cold environment tabular data may often be sufficient. Moreover, in a hot military environment time is ultimately expressed in seconds: applied sensing technologies and platforms are synchronized with atomic clocks. In contrast, within a cold military environment, where many processes are performed between '8am and 5pm', time is more lenient. With respect to accuracy and source reliability: in unfamiliar environments (e.g. behind enemy lines), working with data with low accuracy (from reliable sources) is considered better than working with no data at all. In such situations high accuracy is a luxury that cannot always be afforded. The cold environment (own terrain, own forces) is more predictable, allowing for detailed data to be collected, thus allowing high levels of accuracy and thorough checking of source reliability. Researchers should bear these differences in time and accuracy in mind when they develop a tool for the military or when researching BA phenomena in such contexts.

Concluding remarks

In this chapter we provided an overview of the different applications of BA that are available for military organizations. We described six steps to get started with a military BA study and indicated several challenges to take into account when conducting such a research in a military environment. Since the amount of research in this field is still limited, we would like to encourage researchers to explore interesting venues of BA research within the military. Most of the current BA work concerns the tactical-technical (in business studies: operational) level, i.e. where tasks are executed. At this level, researchers are interested in adaptation of BA tools and the interfacing between BA tools and human users (Soban et al. 2013). According to many of these studies, BA tools improve micro-level awareness of patterns, productivity and decision-making. Further research could extend this work, and address the validity of these claims, as well as the interfacing of human workers – often with limited BA expertise – with BA tools.

Moreover, BA and enterprise software such as ERP are used increasingly to connect many processes and sites, both relating to the cold and hot environment. When considering the OODA loop at higher aggregation levels (i.e. operational-strategic), military strategic leaders can be seen as users of (output of) multiple BA tools. Yet they also have a role in shaping what they want (commander's intent), what architectures they consider fitting, and how they adopt BA in their daily practice (Azvine et al. 2006; Negash 2004). Researchers could appoint attention to different ways commanders use BA, and to what extent they try to shape BA tools to their wishes and needs, catering to a military organization's sense and respond capabilities (Bunn et al. 2012; Hammond 2008). Finally, researchers can study interaction processes between BA analysts (who have the skills to handle the data and the tools) and non-BA professionals. These include commanders (who have the knowledge and experience to interpret the data), given differences in jargon (epistemology), hierarchical status, and location.

Notes

1 See for instance www.bigdatafordefense.com/ and www.whitehouse.gov/sites/default/files/microsites/ostp/pcast-nitrd-report-2010.pdf/
2 For more information, see www.futurepointsystems.com/
3 For more information, see e.g. www.processmining.org/tools/start/

References

van der Aalst, W. (2012). Process Mining. *Communications of the ACM*, 55(8), 76–83.
Azvine, B., Cui, Z., Nauck, D. and Majeed, B. (2006). Real Time Business Intelligence for the Adaptive Enterprise. Paper presented at the E-Commerce Technology.

Berger, J. (2013). Fringe Following. *Foreign Policy*. Retrieved June 16, 2013 from www.foreignpolicy.com.

Bergold, J. and Thomas, S. (2012). Participatory Research Methods: A Methodological Approach in Motion. *Forum Qualitative Sozialforschung / Forum: Qualitative Social Research*. Available at: www.qualitative-research. net/index.php/fqs/article/view/1801/3334, 13(1).

Brown, A. (2013). How Does Data Visualization Fit into the Predictive Analytics Process? *SAS Knowledge Exchange*, www.sas.com/knowledge-exchange/business-analytics/innovation/how-does-data-visualiza tion-fit-into-the-predictive-analytics-process/index.html.

Bunn, J., Chandy, K.M., Faulkner, M., Liu, A. and Olson, M. (2012). Sense and Response Systems for Crisis Management. In S. Das, K. Kant and N. Zhang (eds), *Securing Cyber-Physical Critical Infrastructure*. Waltham, MA: Morgan Kaufmann.

Correa, C. and Ma, K.L. (2011). Visualizing Social Networks. In C. Agarwal (ed.) *Social Network Data Analytics*. New York Springer (pp. 307–326). US: Springer.

Davenport, T. (2013). *Enterprise Analytics: Optimize Performance, Process, and Decisions through Big Data*. Upper Saddle River, NJ: Pearson.

Davenport, T. and Harris, J. (2007). *Competing on Analytics: The New Science of Winning*. Boston, MA: Harvard Business School Press.

Davenport, T. and Jarvenpaa, S. (2008). *The Strategic Use of Analytics in Government*. Washington, DC: IBM Center for the Business of Government.

Gangadharan, G.R. and Swami, S.N. (2004). Business Intelligence Systems: Design and Implementation Strategies. Paper presented at the 26th International Conference Information Technology Interfaces ITI, Cavtat, Croatia.

Hammond, M.F. (2008). Sense and Respond: Military Logistics in a Global Security Environment. *Army Logistician*, 40(5): 6.

Hudak, R.P., Julian, R., Kugler, J., Dorrance, K., Ramchandani, S., Lynch, S. et al. (2013). The Patient-Centered Medical Home: A Case Study in Transforming the Military Health System. *Military Medicine*, 178(2), 146–152.

Issenberg, S. (2012). How President Obama's Campaign Used Big Data to Rally Individual Voters, Part 1. *Technology Review*, December 16, 2012. Available at http://www.technologyreview.com/ featuredstory/508836/how-obama-used-big-data-to-rally-voters-part-1/

van Kampen, T., van Fenema, P.C. and Grant, T.J. (2012). Getting There and Back: Organizing Long-Distance Military Logistics with Customers in Mind. In R.M. Beeres, J. van der Meulen, J.M.M.L. Soeters and A.L.W. Vogelaar (eds), *Mission Uruzgan: Collaborating in Multiple Coalitions for Afghanistan*. Amsterdam: Amsterdam University Press/Pallas Publications.

Kohavi, R., Rothleder, N. and Simoudis, E. (2002). Emerging Trends in Business Analytics. *Communications of the ACM*, 45(8), 45–48.

Kooman, I. (2013). Muisklikkend op missie (Dutch). *Defensiekrant* [Dutch Ministry of Defense]. Available from www.defensie.nl/actueel/defensiebladen/defensiekrant/2013/46207406/Defensiekrant_nr_16_2013.

Kritzstein, B.D. (2003). Starlight, the Leading Edge of an Emerging Cass of Information Systems that couples Advanced Information Modeling. *Military Geospatial Technology*, 8(4).

Laursen, G. and Thorlund, J. (2010). *Business Analytics for Managers: Taking Business Intelligence beyond Reporting*. Hoboken, NJ: Wiley.

Lavigne, V. and Gouin, D. (2011). Applicability of Visual Analytics to Defence and Security Operations. *Proceedings of the 16th International Command and Control Research and Technology Symposium*, 4–27.

Negash, S. (2004). Business Intelligence. *Communications of the AIS*, 13, 177–195.

Osinga, F.P.B. (2007). *Science, Strategy and War: The Strategic Theory of John Boyd*. London: Routledge.

Pant, P. (2009). Business Intelligence (BI): How to Build Successful BI Strategy. *Deloitte Consultancy*. Available from www.deloitte.com/assets/Dcom-SouthAfrica/Local%20Assets/Documents/Business%20 intelligence%20that%20aligns%20with%20enterprise%20goals.pdf.

Peck, M. (2012). Why Can't the U.S. Air Force Find Enough Pilots to Fly Its Drones? *Forbes*, August 22, 2012. Available at http://www.forbes.com/sites/michaelpeck/2013/08/22/why-cant-the-u-s-air-force-find-enough-pilots-to-fly-its-drones/

Pentland, B.T., Hærem, T. and Hillison, D. (2011). The (N) Ever-Changing World: Stability and Change in Organizational Routines. *Organization Science*, 22(6), 1369–1383.

Siegel, E. (2013) *Predictive Analytics: The Power to Predict Who Will Click, Buy, Lie, or Die*. Hoboken, NJ: Wiley.

Soban, D., Salmon, J. and Fahringer, A. (2013). A Visual Analytics Framework for Strategic Airlift Decision Making. *The Journal of Defense Modeling and Simulation: Applications, Methodology, Technology*, 10(2), 131–144.

Soeters, J.M.M.L., van Fenema, P.C. and Beeres, R.J.M. (2010). Introducing Military Organizations. In J.M.M.L. Soeters, P.C. van Fenema and R. Beeres (eds), *Managing Military Organizations: Theory and Practice*. London: Routledge.

Thomson, J. (2005). A Typology for Visualizing Uncertainty. Paper presented at the Proceedings of SPIE.

Trkman, P., McCormack, K., De Oliveira, M. and Ladeira, M. (2010). The Impact of Business Analytics on Supply Chain Performance. *Decision Support Systems*, 49(3), 318–327.

USArmy (2009). *Commander's Handbook Distributed Common Ground System Army (DCGS-A)*. Pentagon: Army, March 20, 2009.

Wall, T. and Monahan, T. (2011). Surveillance and Violence from Afar: The Politics of Drones and Liminal Security-Scapes. *Theoretical Criminology*, 15(3), 239–254.

Wong, C. and Thomas, J. (2004). Visual Analytics. *IEEE Computer Graphics and Applications*, 24(5), 20–21.

Zuk, T. and Carpendale, M. (2007). Visualization of Uncertainty and Reasoning. *Smart Graphics*, 164–177.

PART IV

The end

25

A NEW APPROACH
TO DOING MILITARY ETHICS

Celestino Perez Jr.

Celestino Perez Jr. (2012) "The soldier as lethal warrior and cooperative political agent: On the soldier's ethical and political obligations toward the indigenous Other," *Armed Forces & Society* 38(2): 177–204.

This article explores the soldier's ethical and political obligations toward the indigenous other, a term signifying those persons who live and work where soldiers are deployed. The argument, a work of applied political theory, employs multiple methods to justify a cosmopolitan conception of the role of the soldier and the military.

The author argues that war entails destructive and constructive components. Although the soldier's destructive, lethal work is well understood, the soldier's constructive, political work is insufficiently appreciated and theorized. Since a war's successful conclusion must include a satisfactory confluence of governmental, economic, cultural, and ethical conditions, the policymaker and military professional must appreciate that politics is not an engineering project with specific timelines and outcomes. Politics is more an adventure full of uncertainty and unpredictability. This strategic and tactical situation, which relies ultimately on the realization of a set of developments that are hoped for yet unspecifiable beforehand, has ethical consequences for how soldier's intervene amidst an unknown population as well as for how soldiers prepare themselves ethically for such interventions.

The author first juxtaposes two contrasting views of the American military's professional ethic. One view, which is creedal in form, encompasses a set of obligations pertaining to the soldier's four roles: soldier, leader of character, servant of the nation, and member of the profession of arms. This patriotic view is strictly oriented on the United States, the U.S. Constitution, and the hardships and integrity of the American soldier. In contrast to this navel-gazing approach, a second view describes a cosmopolitan ethic, developed in the context of a counterinsurgency campaign, that is outward-looking. This view seeks to cultivate respect, trust, and an expectation of shared hardship between the soldier and the indigenous other as they strive to create suitably durable and humane conditions amidst conflict and violence.

(continued)

(continued)

The author next employs the political theorist Hannah Arendt's distinction between Work and Action to show that war, a subset of politics, is not properly understood to be a variant of Work akin to the act of building a chair or engineering a water system. Action, to include significant dimensions of war and politics, entails collective efforts toward an unspecifiable end. Moreover, Action is the realm of uncertainty and unpredictability. Action is undertaken *for the sake of*, not *in order to*. It is the realm of cooperative political action, not domination or violence.

The author concludes by applying William Connolly's political theory to explore how best to think about strategic and tactical interventions in politics. Connolly's work also suggests how scholars and soldiers might think about the problem of ethical cultivation, especially in light of the political roles soldiers must perform.

The article's strengths are methodological. The research question arises from the real-world difficulties soldiers have encountered in Iraq and Afghanistan. The paper employs multiple sources, to include survey data, military leaders' statements, and official military documents. The author conducts a textual analysis of two contrasting views of a soldier's obligations and evaluates these views using the work of two prominent political theorists. The result is a new, empirically informed articulation of a military ethic. The article is informed by traditional approaches to military ethics, such as the combatant/non-combatant distinction, while introducing other concepts not usually employed in the field.

Introduction

This chapter advances a methodological ethos intended to guide enquiry into the quotidian and extraordinary problems soldiers confront in their organizations, training, and deployments. The aim is to encourage scholars of ethics to fold this ethos, which comprises the values of problem-driven research, analytic eclecticism, and attention to causality, into their habits of problem and method selection. Scholars who adopt this ethos strive to confront the messiness of real-world problems as illuminated – in varying and contestable ways – by scholars in other fields and disciplines.

If there is no single way to study and write about ethics, perhaps there are compelling, if arguable, criteria. Martin Cook and Henrik Syse, who edit the *Journal of Military Ethics*, observe that too many scholars and practitioners are confused about what military ethics is. The editors insist that the best submissions to their journal – however varied in approach and method – seek to inform real-world military practice and evince a granular understanding of soldiers' interactions (Cook and Syse 2010: 121–122).

While the editors value scholarship that is practically informative and informed, scholars such as Roger Wertheimer, who led the military ethics program at the United States Naval Academy from 2001 to 2003, demonstrate that an adequate exploration of the soldier's moral predicament must extend beyond rarefied debates over the just-war framework. Wertheimer, for instance, includes in his edited volume of just-war articles two of his own chapters that deliver a thoroughgoing critique of the presuppositions and practices that permeate the profession of arms and military education (Wertheimer 2010).

This chapter, following the example of Cook, Syse, and Wertheimer, advocates for research that energetically seeks to inform military practice, appreciates the soldier's context, and extends beyond the just-war framework to other topics. In the wake of exciting developments in the normative and empirical social sciences related to strategy, war, and ethics, swaths of territory are open for exploration.

This chapter argues that the scholarly treatment of military ethics should be philosophically and scientifically informed as well as politically aware and engaged. The study of military ethics should evince an appreciation not only for the philosophic tradition (e.g. Michael Walzer's and Jeff McMahan's just-war theorizing), but also for cutting-edge work in the social sciences as it relates to both violent conflict (e.g. Stathis Kalyvas's empirical work on civil wars) and real-world exigencies (e.g. proposed interventions into ongoing civil wars, counterinsurgency campaigns, strategic rebalancing, sexual assault, post-traumatic stress disorder, suicide).

Ethical evaluation must penetrate more deeply into the sociopolitical interactions and contexts in which soldiers participate. A longstanding and necessary component of ethical enquiry relates to philosophical arguments about the proper definition and application of conceptual terms such as legitimate authority, proportionality, and intentionality. Such studies implicitly ask: does the soldier properly construe and apply Distinction X to a tightly bracketed Situation A?

Yet ethics extends beyond the syllogism, the right application of terms, and intentional action. The messiness of a soldier's context is attributable to the complex intermingling of material and biological structures, manmade rules and organizations, psychological hardwiring, as well as ideas, practices, and identities. These forces, in the aggregate, routinely corrode the links between intention, deliberate action, and actual outcomes. Hidden forces, counterintuitive dynamics, and unintended consequences permeate politics and war. Philosophic terms and their application are just a small part of the unbounded, fog- and friction-filled confluence, which – really – generates the force that drives newspaper headlines from day to day.

The first three sections describe the values of problem-driven research, analytic eclecticism, and attention to causality, respectively. Moreover, each section briefly suggests how a scholar might realize these values and identifies the values' attendant challenges. The chapter periodically illustrates these points by referencing the illustrative article, described in the text box, entitled, "The Soldier as Lethal Warrior and Cooperative Political Agent: On the Soldier's Ethical and Political Obligations toward the Indigenous Other" (Perez 2012).

Problem-driven research

Shapiro distinguishes between theory- and method-driven research on the one hand and problem-driven research on the other. Scholars who pursue theory- or method-driven research allow their approach to guide problem selection. A scholar might have a favorite theory about, say, the equality of combatants, or the combatant-noncombatant distinction, or the criteria for what constitutes legitimate authority. Another scholar may have a favorite method, whether it be definitional slicing and dicing, case studies, ethnography, discourse analysis, or genealogical enquiry. The prioritization goes not to illuminating real-world problems, but to scoring points over competing theories and methods. Shapiro instead recommends problem-driven research, which means "starting with a problem in the world, next coming to grips with previous attempts that have been made to study it, and then defining the research task by reference to the value added" (Shapiro 2005: 180).

Shapiro's advice is to foreground the problem, not the theory or method. He wants to avoid a state of affairs wherein "normative theorists spend too much time commenting on one another, as if they were themselves the appropriate objects of study" (Shapiro 2005: 179). The scholar's object of enquiry is not Michael Walzer, the political theorist, or Jeff McMahan, the philosopher, but real-world soldiers, the militaries in which they serve, and the civilians with whom they interact.

Applying problem-driven research

In some cases, problem-driven research points to real-world problems that a scholar of ethics, given her skills, can pursue immediately. For instance, "The Soldier as Lethal Warrior and Cooperative Political Agent" (hereafter *illustrative article*) is a work of applied political theory that explores the situation of soldiers serving as constructive, political agents in Iraq and Afghanistan. It entails a textual analysis of two military leaders' conceptions of the military profession in light of the work of two prominent political theorists. Given the political tasks soldiers at all levels have performed in Iraq and Afghanistan (political agenda-setting, governmental capacity-building, economic development, and reintegration of former adversaries), the article explores the soldier's ethical and political obligations to the indigenous other and dismantles the notion that nation-building is akin to an engineering project from which, with the right inputs and procedures (e.g. robust interagency coordination), a durable polity might arise. In fact, these themes accord with William Maley's contribution in Chapter 6 of this volume, "Studying Host-Nationals in Operational Areas: The Challenge of Afghanistan."

In other cases, problem-driven research requires the employment of unfamiliar methods or collaboration with other departments' colleagues. For instance, the monetary waste in Iraq and Afghanistan is well-documented (confer the work of the Special Inspector General for Afghanistan Reconstruction and its Iraq counterpart). The ethical imperative to avoid massive waste is clear; however, if the ethicist is to understand how such waste occurs and propose recommendations, she might usefully collaborate with a political scientist or economist whose expertise is in institutional analysis. An institutionalist can describe how the various stakeholders within the contracting process respond rationally to perverse incentives that, in the aggregate, lead to enormous waste. The ethicist, seeking to advise soldiers who participate in or supervise contracting processes, must gain some understanding of the rules, principal-agent situations, and routine pathologies that plague the distribution of public goods and common pool resources (Gibson et al. 2005). Ethical action requires not simply the application of a conceptual distinction to a case, but also fine-grained understanding about how to identify, diagnose, and improve sub-optimal institutions.

Another problem relates to how military professionals have come to understand "culture." The military asserts that "leaders must be proficient in a variety of situations against myriad threats and with a diverse set of national, allied, and indigenous partners" (U.S. Army 2013: 5). Hence, soldiers have identified a need to attain some granular knowledge of the identities, institutions, and material structures that compose the world soldiers encounter during deployments. Unfortunately, military professionals tend to construe culture as a nebulous umbrella term that includes the sociopolitical and economic factors that compose foreign lands (e.g. Salmoni and Holmes-Eber 2008). Moreover, many anthropologists have denigrated the military's understanding of culture as outdated, static, and weaponized (Albro 2010). How soldiers, individually and corporately, come to see the "other" is ethically relevant.

Scholars of ethics might choose to collaborate with culture experts to theorize alternative conceptions of culture that are more favorable ethically and operationally. An ethicist might seek out Lisa Wedeen, who writes about "semiotic practices" (Wedeen 2002); or Jason Glynos and David Howarth, who write about "social, political, and fantasmatic logics" and their relation to ethical enquiry (Glynos and Howarth 2007); or Rogers Smith, who writes about "stories of peoplehood" and the exclusions these stories leave in their wake (Smith 2003).

Scholars might also take notice of soldiers' "practices." To observe "practices" means to focus on "patterned actions that are embedded in particular organized contexts and, as such, are articulated into specific types of action and are socially developed through learning and training" (Adler 2011: 7). Since "practice rests on *background knowledge*, which it embodies, enacts, and reifies all at once" (Adler 2011: 8), observing practices can reveal the ethical presuppositions that inform military planning, the evaluation of courses of action, and everyday conversations about news events, scandals, families, units, and experiences.

A soldier's background knowledge is accessible also via the written or spoken word, to include military orders, commanders' letters to troops, professional journal articles, military doctrine, intelligence reports, speeches, etc. The scholar might apply Stephen White's concepts to these texts. One concept is the *lifeworld*, which he describes as "the unthought of our thought, the implicit of our explicit, the unconscious background of our conscious foreground" (White 2000: 54). White employs a second, related concept, which he calls an *ontology*. By using this term, which has a contested pedigree, he means to put his finger on a person's "most basic sense of human being" (White 2000: 8) or a person's "most basic conceptualizations of self, other, and world" (White 2000: 6).

An ethicist might employ White's methodology to examine, say, a doctrinal manual or a commander's speech in order to determine "whether ontological refiguration of a certain sort is in fact occurring, and how it is related to ethical-political judgments" (White 2000: 13). Put otherwise, the ethicist might read between the lines to uncover the presuppositions and assumptions a soldier possesses about the world, its dynamics, right conduct, and desired future states. The ethicist might then begin to think about the connections between the soldier's implicit ontology and the ethical aspects of the assessments the soldier renders (Perez 2009).

An examination of practices and ontologies might also illuminate the relationship between "the fact of pluralism" and a soldier's ethical formation, education, and training. The fact of pluralism captures the reality that the world comprises heterogeneous populations with a multiplicity of political, economic, religious, philosophical, and ethical commitments. This heterogeneity exists within the military and in those places to which soldiers deploy.

The fact of pluralism, which has had a significant impact on debates about the normative bases of liberal democratic polities (e.g. the work of John Rawls, Jürgen Habermas, Amy Guttmann, Dennis Thompson, and Chantal Mouffe), matters also to the military's efforts to craft a unifying table of professional ethics. Unfortunately, scholars of military ethics and military professionals have neglected the "fact of pluralism." It follows that scholars should explore the connections between a soldier's personal beliefs, his military's code of ethics, and the hegemonic and suppressed beliefs that exist in those places where he deploys.

Challenges in doing problem-driven research

Problem-driven research has the merit of addressing real-world problems, including monetary waste, inadequate conceptions of culture, deleterious ontologies and practices, and the failure to account for the fact of pluralism.

Challenges inherent in doing problem-driven research include the potential requirement to learn new skills (e.g. researching as a participant-observer) or collaborate with scholars from other disciplines (e.g. seeking out experts in institutional analysis or culture). Moreover, some objects of analysis are more difficult to access than others. Gaining access to active-duty units is difficult; however, access to observe the practices of mid-career officers attending professional military education is likely easier to attain. In all cases, access will require approval from the military institution, the establishment of human-subjects safeguards, and time spent gaining background knowledge. Of course, other objects of study are easily accessible via the Internet, including military doctrine, professional military journals, ceremonial speeches, investigative reports, biographies, etc.

Analytic eclectism

This chapter's methodological ethos includes also analytic eclecticism. Rudra Sil and Peter Katzenstein advocate for research that integrates the perspectives, concepts, and units of analysis employed across multiple research traditions. The authors distinguish between analytic eclecticism and multi-method research:

> The combinatorial logic of analytic eclecticism depends not on the multiplicity of methods but on the multiplicity of connections between the different mechanisms and social processes analyzed in isolation in separate research traditions. In principle, such a project can be advanced by the flexible application of a single method – be it formal modeling, multiple regression, historical case studies, or ethnography – so long as the problem and the explanandum feature efforts to connect *theoretical* constructs drawn from separate research traditions.
>
> (Sil and Katzenstein 2010: 415)

Analytic eclecticism invites the scholar to find ways to integrate unfamiliar concepts and unfamiliar units of analysis, albeit using the scholar's own familiar, well-trained methods to conduct the research.

Suppose a scholar adheres to Shapiro's call to explore a real-world problem. This scholar decides to supplement her *jus in bello* splicing and dicing with insights from, say, the practice turn in international-relations theory, or discourse analysis, or cognitive psychology, or the ethnographic study of soldiers in action. The just-war scholar need not become an expert in these fields or methods, but she can consider how their concepts and findings might reveal new aspects of the ethical problem she is interested in addressing.

The illustrative article employs analytic eclecticism by integrating multiple scholarly and practitioner inputs. The concepts and objects of enquiry come from many sources, including existing survey research on combat veterans' attitudes towards civilians and adversaries; the just-war framework's traditional distinction between combatant and noncombatant; the content of official military documents, military leaders' statements, and commanders' wartime decisions; textual analysis of a military historian's proposal for a professional code of ethics; textual analysis of a commanding general's counterinsurgency guidance to his troops; Hannah Arendt's political theory on the distinction between Work and Action; and William Connolly's adoption of complexity science to inform strategic and tactical interventions.

Applying analytic eclecticism

Political science provides the scholar of military ethics with a rich bank of templated interactions and contextual webs that, when explored through the lenses of the just-war framework, civil-military relations, and the professional military ethic, generate important research questions conducive to analytic eclecticism.

For instance, Stathis Kalyvas suggests that it is a fundamental error to simply consider the salience of the driving (or master) cleavage separating civil war adversaries into North versus South, Sunni versus Shi'a, Christian versus Muslim, or Communist versus Mujahadeen. In civil wars, the concrete actions that soldiers, civilians, and political leaders take are likely motivated not primarily by the war's master cleavage, but by local, specific grievances unrelated to the civil war's onset (Kalyvas 2003). The consequence for the strategist and the expeditionary soldier is that new, tactical variants of *jus ad bellum* considerations arise, albeit this time for ground-level military commanders who are usually – according to Walzer – excused from such considerations. In the course of deciding which armed group leaders to ally with, flip, or kill, the soldier must account for not only the war's driving cleavage at the national level, but also the byzantine, political cleavages at the local level. The commander risks, because of neglect or error, being duped into supporting unjust local actors and causes.

Fotini Christia (2012) describes a similar amoral dynamic in civil wars. Scholars of politics seem to divide along two dominant modes of research. One mode explains a person's action in terms of rationality and a structural or institutional obstacle course. The second mode interprets a person's actions as a function of meaning-soaked symbols and stories (Smith 2003). Scholars of ethics mine these stories for justificatory language, and military leaders – presuming that "culture matters" – order soldiers to be sensitive to persons and their narratives. Yet, Christia argues, these meaning-infused stories are less drivers of justly waged conflicts than post-hoc justifications for purely strategic moves taken to maximize an armed group's security and power (Christia 2012). The ground commander, who desires to be culturally aware and ethically consistent, will surely encounter a certain amount of ethical disturbance as he witnesses a dizzying series of alliance formations and break-ups, each rationalized with persuasive tales of grievance. This ethical disturbance should be of interest to scholars of ethics.

A third example is Paul Staniland's study of wartime political orders. It is not uncommon for military professionals to define war as a clash of wills and a desire to triumph through "decisive action." The presumption is that war is a clash of wills that ends with one side's succumbing to the other side's will. This view of war informs *jus ad bellum* considerations as well as tactical calculations relevant to defining a war's successful progress and the specification of military end states. Yet Staniland finds that it is not uncommon for wartime adversaries to adopt – sometimes simultaneously – one of six accommodations with each other. These accommodations may include varying degrees of agreed-upon coexistence, cooperation, and collusion in some areas while simultaneously engaging in lethal combat in others (Staniland 2012). These possibilities prompt the military professional to consider – especially over the course of a long war – the point at which mere stability, in contradistinction to more ambitious and principled aims, becomes acceptable as an end state.

Aaron Rapport's study, which examines how political and military leaders planned for postwar Iraq, finds that persons, as part of their psychological hardwiring, tend to evaluate short-term objectives in terms of nuts-and-bolts feasibility, whereas persons tend to evaluate long-term objectives in terms of desirability (Rapport 2012). The theory that our psychological hardwiring predisposes us toward a lack of due diligence when planning long-term strategic and tactical objectives should be of interest to scholars of ethics.

These studies point to a larger but less discernable ethical problem. Although the foregoing scholarship is directly relevant to the work military professionals do, professional military education neither requires nor invites sustained exposure to the social sciences. These studies not only provide templates for how politics, economics, and culture affect and are affected by lethal power, they also raise serious ethical questions. Hence, military professionals who neglect the ethical and empirical potentialities raised by these studies are at a disadvantage when asked to offer military advice or imagine the tertiary and hidden boomerang effects of contemplated actions.

For instance, if a president asks a military commander whether the state should intervene militarily in another state's affairs, the commander and his staff should include among their considerations Patricia Sullivan's finding that the nature of an objective significantly affects the chances of a powerful state's success. If an objective can be attained by military means alone (e.g. taking territory or destroying an army), the likelihood of success is great. However, if the objective entails securing the cooperation or compliance of a certain population, the strong state, despite its impressive military power, will likely lose (Sullivan 2007). These considerations are obviously relevant to *jus ad bellum* insofar as a just war must have a reasonable chance of success.

If a president asks about the possibility of a negotiated settlement in a certain country, the military commander should have in his mind Monica Duffy Toft's finding that negotiated settlements to civil wars often lead – when the horizon extends beyond five years – to renewed fighting and increased bloodshed (Toft 2010). Although these findings should by no means dictate action or advice, they should – as an ethical and operational imperative – cause soldiers to consider the norm, "First, do no harm."

If political leaders expect soldiers to operate among and understand communities comprising a kaleidoscope of linguistic, ethnic, religious, secular, and political identities, might it not be useful to familiarize soldiers with unfamiliar and uncomfortable modes of thinking about ethics? Yet military ethics instruction within the United States and among the force has become an ancillary duty of the Army's chaplaincy, whose members' formal (and possibly religious) study of ethics has likely not included sustained engagement with nonfoundationalist approaches like those of William Connolly, Richard Rorty, Chantal Mouffe, or Friedrich Nietzsche. Those American soldiers who do study ethics likely restrict their efforts to classically foundationalist approaches and the just-war framework. It follows that the soldier, who exists at the nexus of several ethical systems and beliefs, learns only about Kant, Mill, and Aristotle on the one hand and a strawman relativism on the other. The notion that nonfoundationalist thinkers might have something insightful to instruct about ethics never arises.

Since commanders and staff officers operate under the condition of bounded rationality, they are, as a routine practice, engaged in abductive reasoning. This form of reasoning occurs when a person attempts to discern and explain the causal dynamics of an existing or anticipated state of affairs (Shapiro and Wendt 2005; Cox 2011; Friedrichs and Kratochwil 2009). If abductive reasoning is to be done well (by both soldiers and scholars alike), it requires that the person's explanatory attempts be informed by a bank of mature (and often contradictory) theories, such as Arendt's, Connolly's, Kalyvas's, Christia's, Staniland's, Sullivan's, Toft's, and Connolly's. Taking a different but related tack, Patricia Shields and Joseph Soeters draw upon Morris Janowitz and the pragmastist tradition to recommend that soldiers employ theory to inform their peacekeeping operations (Shields and Soeters 2013). In any case, an ethical problem arises insofar as military professionals know neither that they conduct abductive reasoning nor that their work is inescapably intertwined with political, economic, and cultural factors that established scholarly theories can help illuminate.

Challenges inherent in practicing analytic eclecticism

Analytic eclecticism conduces to an increased appreciation for ethically relevant factors all too often ignored in military ethics; e.g. tactical *jus ad bellum* (Kalyvas 2003), strategic, amoral decisionmaking (Christia 2012), battlefield compromise (Staniland 2012), psychological hardwiring (Rapport 2012), strategic disadvantage (Sullivan 2007), deleterious negotiating (Toft 2010), nonfoundationalist ethics (Connolly), and abductive reasoning (Shapiro and Wendt 2005).

The principal challenge inherent in analytic eclecticism is the need to spend precious hours reading cutting-edge literature in other fields and consulting with colleagues in other departments. This chapter focuses mostly on the contributions of political science and political theory;

however, other fields, to include cognitive science (e.g. Steve Pinker's study of violence and Joshua Greene's and his colleagues' functional neuroimaging and genotyping) and behavioral economics (e.g. Dan Ariely's study of dishonesty), are also relevant to ethical enquiry.

Of course, another challenge to analytic eclecticism is the fact that interdisciplinary work, which is more often lauded than practiced, is a problematic endeavor for most young scholars whose tenure committees favor disciplinary over interdisciplinary approaches.

Ethics and conventional causality

A third value prompts the scholar of military ethics to be attuned to problems of causality. An appreciation of causal complexity accords nicely with both analytic eclecticism and problem-driven research. Sil and Katzenstein, like Shapiro, desire for scholars to address "problems of wide scope." They propose an "intellectual stance" whereby scholars confront "more of the complexity and messiness of particular real-world situations." The authors advocate an approach that "complements existing traditions by seeking to leverage and integrate conceptual and theoretical elements in multiple traditions." The aim is to relate "academic debates to concrete matters of policy and practice" (Sil and Katzenstein 2010: 412). Such engagement will require scholars to confront "greater complexity," which is "precisely what policymakers and ordinary actors contend with as they address substantive problems in the course of everyday politics" (Sil and Katzenstein 2010: 421).

Explaining human action requires more than an analysis of moral judgment, which is the favored approach in much just-war scholarship. Not all of the forces acting upon a soldier are known to him. Some forces that prompt a soldier to action include error-inducing psychological hardwiring, heuristics, and biases of the sort that Dan Kahneman (2011), Dan Ariely (2008), and Blair Williams (2010) identify. A second set of causal forces is attributable to persons' ideas and identities. A third set of forces is attributable to structural factors such as terrain, income distribution, natural resources, and the formal and informal rules that bound interactions. Finally, to the extent that manmade institutions generate perverse incentives, some human action is attributable to the unintended, path-dependent consequences of persons behaving rationally within a sub-optimal institutional regime. Craig Parsons, a scholar who specializes in comparative politics, has denominated these discrete and comprehensive causal logics as, respectively, psychological, ideational, structural, and institutional (Parsons 2007).

Parsons's relevance to ethical enquiry is twofold. Since human action is not solely a cognitive endeavor wherein purely intellectual considerations are determinative, the scholar who evaluates such actions must strive for a fuller appreciation of the contextual forces that influence action. To identify that the alcoholic drunk driver breaches some Kantian, Aristotelian, or consequentialist principle fails to capture the ethically relevant confluence of physical, social, psychological, and neurobiological forces at play in the drunk driver's actions. Similarly, the scholar who investigates military ethics should strive to account for a fuller range of structural and institutional (exogenous) factors influencing ethical choice as well as the influence of affective, cognitive, and often undetected ideational and psychological (endogenous) factors that shape human action.

Ethics amidst causal complexity

Military commanders and staff officers routinely craft explanations for why a certain region is unstable. They must explain also why the actions they propose will lead to a better state of affairs. Were soldiers to use Parsons's logics to craft more nuanced and cogent explanations, efficacy and ethics might improve.

Yet soldiers, like all political actors, often encounter a gap between the intended and actual effects of their actions. In politics, complexity accounts for the inability to – with confidence – trace the causal connections from a set of initial conditions to a final state and vice versa. This problem is central to ethical assessment, but it is relatively unexplored.

A commander can do nothing other than to think through – using something like Parsons's conventional causal logics – how best to employ his troops, resources, relationships, and speech to achieve a better state of affairs. Given the stakes, political leaders and civilian populations should encourage their military commanders and staff officers to propose tightly crafted causal explanations for why a set of actions will engender favorable results. The problem is that, in the realm of politics and war, intended action seldom achieves – in simple and clear ways – the hoped-for result. Predictability does not belong to the realm of politics and war.

The illustrative article addresses the gap between intentions and outcomes by bringing to the fore Connolly's notion, adapted from complexity theory, of spiraling (also "resonant" or "emergent") causation. Connolly understands the world to comprise open systems of various kinds, each of which has a certain degree of "agency" insofar as it can and does affect the world. Open systems are as varied as a virus, a climate pattern, an economic system, a religion, a neural-muscular network, and a soldier. Emergent causation, as Connolly understands it, occurs when two or more open systems come into contact and prompt embedded potentialities within one or more systems to become active in new, unforeseen ways. The effect is that one or more of the systems undergoes fundamental change or – most dramatically – engenders the existence of a wholly new system (Connolly 2011).

Emergent outcomes are unpredictable, yet they are ethically relevant. The illustrative article describes General Petraeus's intent to counter the downward "spiral" of violence in Afghanistan with an upward "spiraling" effect to be achieved through multifarious security, governance, and development efforts. Petraeus's approach suggests that no single action (describable in Parsons's conventional terms) can achieve success in Afghanistan. This fact, coupled with the reality of emergent causality, obliges the soldier to conceive of his tasks in a new light and with a reformed ethical sensibility. The unpredictable nature of causation in politics and war has ethical implications related to *jus ad bellum*, *jus in bello*, the laws of armed conflict, the self-understanding of the profession of arms, and a soldier's ethical formation.

Ethical enquiry should situate human decision and action amidst a richer context such that the soldier is not simply a philosophic agent weighing deontological commitments, anticipated consequences, or tables of virtue. The soldier is a thinking, moral agent, but she is also much more. Countless micro and macro systems impinge upon the soldier to engender their thoughts and deeds. It follows that causation, complexity, uncertainty, and unpredictability are at the very heart of ethical and political decision, and discerning these forces is never easy. Nevertheless, robust ethical enquiry is impossible without the attempt.

Challenges inherent in studying causality and complexity

Accounting for causality and complexity presents the same transaction costs inherent in problem-driven research and analytic eclecticism. The researcher needs to enter into face-to-face discussions with persons from unfamiliar research communities, perhaps including scholars from the natural sciences. It will require also the skill of wading through unfamiliar methodologies – some positivist and others interpretivist – to identify the sorts of causal claims scholars are making.

Most importantly, appreciating causal complexity entails the unique challenge of adopting a shift in how one views the world and the moral agent. The scholar of ethics must learn to see the world as comprising a multiplicity of dynamic, interacting open systems giving rise to unpredictable results. The scholar must appreciate the connections that exists between lower-level and perhaps linear causal mechanisms on the one hand and their contribution, via emergence, to system-level causal mechanisms and feedback loops. To see the world in this way is not to see metaphorically, but to appreciate how the world really does comprise a heterogeneous mix of micro and macro systems.

The scholar of ethics must switch between two views of the soldier. In some cases, the scholar may view the soldier as nothing more than a philosophic agent who, focusing on a single bracketed problem, weighs and applies the proper conceptual distinctions. In other cases, the scholar must begin to see the soldier as a single, partially agentic open system amidst a field of countless, partially agentic open systems. Ethical enquiry of this sort requires a sensitivity to the notion that the soldier is not simply a philosopher consumed with making and applying conceptual distinctions. On the contrary, the soldier is only one among multiple open systems, and the soldier's agency is only partial and oftentimes inefficacious.

Conclusion

This chapter argues for the adoption of a threefold methodological ethos. Every now and then, scholars should fearlessly allow real-world problems to dictate methods as opposed to allowing their favorite theory or method (or imagination) to restrict what they can study. The scholar interested in ethics might also become interested in other disciplines' perspectives, concepts, and objects of study since – given the world's complexity – the factors and dynamics these disciplines study are undeniably connected to more familiar, ethical factors. Finally, scholars should confront more of the world's complexity by expanding beyond conceptual slicing, dicing, and evaluation. An appreciation for the world as a mix of animate, inanimate, and immaterial open systems (of which the human person is only a part) promises a fruitful approach to ethical enquiry and the rise of important research questions.

References

Adler, E. and Pouliot, V. (eds) (2011) *International Practices*, Cambridge: Cambridge University Press.
Albro, R. (2010) "Writing Culture Doctrine: Public anthropology, military policy, and world making," *Perspectives on Politics*, 8: 1087–1093.
Ariely, D. (2008) *Predictably Irrational*, New York: HarperCollins Publishers.
Christia, F. (2012) *Alliance Formation in Civil Wars*, Cambridge: Cambridge University Press.
Connolly, W.E. (2011) *A World of Becoming*, Durham, NC: Duke University Press.
Cook, M.L. and Syse, H. (2010) "What Should We Mean by 'Military Ethics'?" *Journal of Military Ethics*, 9: 119–122.
Cox, M. (2011) "Advancing the Diagnostic Analysis of Environmental Problems," *International Journal of the Commons*, 5: 346–363.
Friedrichs, J. and Kratochwil, F. (2009) "On Acting and Knowing: How pragmatism can advance international relations research and methodology," *International Organization*, 63: 701–731.
Gibson, C.C., Anderson, K., Ostrom, E. and Shivakumar, S. (2005) *The Samaritan's Dilemma: The Political Economy of Development Aid*, Oxford: Oxford University Press.
Glynos, J. and Howarth, D. (2007) *Logics of Critical Explanation in Social and Political Theory*, Abingdon, UK: Routledge.
Kahneman, D. (2011) *Thinking Fast and Slow*, New York: Farrar, Straus, and Giroux.
Kalyvas, S.N. (2003) "The Ontology of 'Political Violence': Action and identity in civil wars," *Perspectives on Politics*, 1: 475–494.
Parsons, C. (2007) *How to Map Arguments in Political Science*, Oxford: Oxford University Press.
Perez, C. (2009) "The Embedded Morality in FM 3–24 Counterinsurgency," *Military Review*, 89: 24–32.

Perez, C. (2012) "The Soldier as Lethal Warrior and Cooperative Political Agent: On the soldier's ethical and political obligations toward the indigenous other," *Armed Forces & Society*, 38: 177–204.

Rapport, A. (2012) "The Long and Short of It," *International Security*, 37: 133–171.

Salmoni, B.A. and Holmes-Eber, P. (2008) *Operational Culture for the Warfighter: Principles and Applications*, Quantico, VA: Marine Corps University Press.

Shapiro, I. (2005) "Problems, Methods, and Theories in the Study of Politics: Or, what's wrong with political science and what to do about it," in I. Shapiro (ed.) *The Flight from Reality in the Human Sciences*, Princeton, NJ: Princeton University Press.

Shapiro, I. and Wendt, A. (2005) "The Difference That Realism Makes: Social science and the politics of consent," in I. Shapiro (ed.) *The Flight from Reality in the Human Sciences*, Princeton, NJ: Princeton University Press.

Shields, P.M. and Soeters, J. (2013) "Pragmatism, Peacekeeping, and the Constabulary Force," in S.J. Ralston (ed.) *Philosophical Pragmatism and International Relations: Essays for a Bold New World*, Plymouth: Lexington Books.

Sil, R. and Katzenstein, P. (2010) "Analytic Eclecticism in the Study of World Politics: Reconfiguring problems and mechanisms across research traditions," *Perspectives on Politics*, 8: 411–431.

Smith, R.M. (2003) *Stories of Peoplehood: The Politics and Morals of Political Membership*, Cambridge: Cambridge University Press.

Staniland, P. (2012) "States, Insurgents, and Wartime Political Orders," *Perspectives on Politics*, 10: 243–264.

Sullivan, P.L. (2007) "War Aims and War Outcomes: Why powerful states lose limited wars," *The Journal of Conflict Resolution*, 51: 496–524.

Toft, M.D. (2010) "Ending Civil Wars: A Case for Rebel Victory?," *International Security*, 34: 7–36.

U.S. Army (2013) "Army Leader Development Strategy, 2013." Available online at http://usacac.army.mil/cac2/CAL/repository/ALDS5June%202013Record.pdf.

Wedeen, L. (2002) "Conceptualizing Culture: Possibilities for political science," *The American Political Science Review*, 96: 713–728.

Wertheimer, R. (2010) "The Moral Singularity of Military Professionalism," and "The Morality of Military Ethics Education," in R. Wertheimer (ed.) *Empowering Our Military Conscience*, Farnham: Ashgate Publishing Limited.

White, S. (2000) *Sustaining Affirmation: The Strengths of Weak Ontology in Political Theory*, Princeton, NJ: Princeton University Press.

Williams, B.S. (2010) "Heuristics and Biases in Military Decision Making," *Military Review*, 90: 40–52.

26

THEORY BUILDING IN RESEARCH ON THE MILITARY

Eyal Ben-Ari

Edward A. Shils and Morris Janowitz (1948) "Cohesion and disintegration in the Wehrmacht in World War II," *Public Opinion Quarterly* **12(2): 280–315.**

This article – one of the classics in military sociology – uses the case of the German Army in World War Two to explore the question of why, despite horrendous losses, its troops continued to fight until the end of the conflict. The authors answer this question by carefully analyzing alternative explanations for soldierly motivation that focused on the following factors: the social structure and dynamics of the organization and especially of small groups, the symbols and ideology that ostensibly moved the troops and the ways in which morale was bolstered or broken, among others by Allied propaganda. By exploring and rejecting alternative explanations, Shils and Janowitz posit that the cause for soldiers' behaviors and attitudes regarding continued participation in combat was the interpersonal relationships of the primary group within which they were embedded (concretely, groups the size of no more than a company). The article is based on a review of empirical data gathered by the Allied armies during the war: front-line interrogations of prisoners of war, intensive interviews in rear areas, captured enemy documents, statements of recaptured Allied personnel and reports of combat observers. Well aware of the methodological difficulties of using these sources they nevertheless state they can be used fruitfully and convincingly.

Shils and Janowitz conclude that the relationship to the primary group is the strongest predictor of why soldiers went into combat and continued fighting and, in the same vein, why they stopped and surrendered. There are two key arguments here. First, is the extent and manner by which the primary group meets the major personal needs of the individual (including basic organic needs, offering troops affection and esteem from both officers and comrades, providing a sense of power and adequately regulating his relations with authority). Second, primary group behavior, whether deviant or desirable from the organization's point of view, results from norms formed by primary group interaction. Hence, as long the primary group, usually the squad or the section, fulfilled their needs, Wehrmacht soldiers were bound by the expectations and demands of its members.

(continued)

(continued)

Theoretically, Shils and Janowitz recognized the impact of secondary groups on individual soldiers, but maintained – in contrast to previous studies – that when compared to primary groups their influence is slight. Their argument, which is akin to the one found in much of the scholarship of the time, emerged out of dissatisfaction with commonly explaining motivation in ideological terms. Their perspective was generalized after World War II when a number of research teams drew attention to cohesion as the primary factor in the motivation of American soldiers (Stouffer et al. 1949). Yet in contrast to a romantic explanation of "a band of brothers" fighting for the military, Shils and Janowitz clearly pointed out that cohesive primary groups may produce behaviors that are not congruent with the goals of the military organization. Thus they showed that units that surrendered as a group were led by "soft-core," non-Nazi comrades to whom organizational goals were relatively unimportant. To reiterate, the idea at base of their article was to contend with and rule out alternative explanations.

This article has led to many theoretical extensions, critiques and debates (see Ben-Shalom et al. 2005; King 2013; Segal and Kestenbaum 2002; Siebold 2011). Among the critiques directed at it were first that it was difficult to causally demonstrate how cohesion contributes to military performance and effectiveness; second, that it was complicated to conceptualize group cohesion; third, that there is a gap between cohesion under conditions of routine garrison duty or maneuvers and the cohesion that develops under conditions of combat; and fourth, that there are factors contributing to soldierly motivation other than cohesion. Nevertheless this classic essay continues to be part of a long theoretical debate about soldierly behavior decades after its writing and thus persists in the processes by which scholars theorize about the motivation and conduct of troops.

Introduction: Theory construction as process

There has always been a duality to theorizing within the social scientific study of the military. On the one hand, scholars have treated the armed forces as "just" like any other large-scale organization to be described and analyzed by appropriate theoretical constructs. On the other hand, other researchers have focused on its uniqueness as "the" organization charged with the handling of organized (if at times contested) violence and attempted to create theories pertinent to this character of the armed forces (Boëne 1990). It is this duality that has dictated theoretical developments about the armed forces, specifically the application or testing of theories developed in other areas to the military or the development of theories that specifically relate to its particular violent character. Examples of the latter include studies of soldiers in combat that have been rooted in psychology, social-psychology or organizational science or the sophisticated literature on civil-military relations emanating from the potential of the armed forces to take over polities. The article by Shils and Janowitz that opens this chapter is a good example of developing and testing alternative theoretical formulations about the behavior of troops in battle. But the reason for choosing this publication is also because seen against the background of previous and subsequent research it is an excellent example of the processes – the emergent concepts, unforeseen developments, blind alleyways and debatable contentions – by which theories are created over time.

What is theory? What is theorizing? A good starting point is Weick's (1989; also Eisenhardt 1989; Layder 1993) definition of a theory as "an ordered set of assertions about a generic behavior or structure assumed to hold throughout a significantly broad range of specific instances." Whetten (1989) suggests that a complete theory must contain the following essential elements: the factors (variables, constructs, concepts) that should be logically considered part of the explanation of the social or individual phenomenon of interest; the relations between these factors as they are ordered into patterns or causality; and the underlying assumptions about the (psychological, economic, social or other) dynamics that justify the selection of factors and proposed relationships or patterns. Whetten's idea is that in essence, theory represents a set of demonstrated relationships between selected variables or constructs. In other words, with a proposed theory, the researcher aims to capture and demonstrate the missing relationship(s) in the observed patterns or regularities or to highlight relationships, connections and interdependencies in the phenomenon of interest (Weick 1989).

In a more practical vein, Shields and Rangarajan (2013) suggest that a theory is a way to organize inquiry: a theory refers to the way ideas are organized in order to achieve a project's aims. Hence, in a later essay, Weick (1995) suggests that for practical reasons – that is, for social scientists as practicing researchers – it is useful to think of theory not as a product but as a process: a constant unfolding of systematically formulated concepts and contentions, and an active engagement or dialogue among scholars. Cibangu (2012: 98; Campbell 1988) adds that theory constitutes a core body of a discipline's literature which is criticized, evaluated, and revamped over time in a logically articulated manner. In fact, the processual character of theory building should be understood as taking part on two analytically distinct levels: the wider dialogue in a discipline and the particular study carried out. The construction of concepts, hypotheses, linkages to data or revisions of thoughts are practices that involve – at the same time – ongoing engagements in wider scholarly debates *and* a specific emergent research project. To emphasize, theory construction takes place within an individual research project and the iterative cycles of theory building in which a community of scholars participates.

There are a number of advantages to seeing the processual character of constructing theories. First, we can begin to appreciate that this is not a mechanistic process, but rather involves intuitive, blind, and wasteful elements (Weick 1989). Second, if we understand theory construction as thinking-in-action and reflecting-in-action we can be clearer about how and from where we derive our contentions (Carlile and Christensen 2005; also Sarafino 2005). That is because all observations are shaped, consciously or unconsciously, by cognitive structures, previous experience or some theory-in-use. And third, we realize that much of what we do involves progressively clearer approximations of theory. Indeed, many products that are labelled theories are actually "rough" theory. Merton (in Weick 1995: 385) proposes that approximations may take a number of forms: general orientations in which broad frameworks specify variables to be taken into account without specification of relationships among them; analyses of concepts in which concepts are specified, clarified, and defined but not interrelated; post-factum interpretations in which *ad hoc* hypotheses are derived from a single observation but alternative explanations or new observations are not explored; or empirical generalization in which an isolated proposition summarizes the relationship between two variables, but further interrelations are not attempted. In a closely related manner, categorization can also be seen as a vital part of theorizing. While none of these are full-blown theories, they can serve as means to further *development*.

But how does one go about constructing theories? In the following I have set out the various stages of theorizing based on an amalgam of sources (De Jong 2010; Carlile and Christensen 2005; George and Bennett 2005; Jaccard and Jacoby 2010). However, two points are important. First, since the construction of theory is a practical endeavor undertaken by scholars, in what follows I introduce a variety of techniques and procedures – actionable suggestions – that scholars have found to be useful. Second, because research is set of interactive components it is usually not linear (Creswell 2009): researchers find themselves going back and forth between the different stages even within one project.

Explication and scholarly positioning

Many of the projects undertaken by researchers emanate or are posed by the military field. Commanders and soldiers may face a variety of problems ranging the whole gamut between soldierly motivation to new challenges for units and on to civil-military ties. In order to find answers to these problems, they often turn to social scientists. As many chapters in this volume show, there is a long history of close ties between the armed forces and researchers in and around problem-driven studies. But at other times, researchers undertake investigations deriving from questions posed within their various academic disciplines or from the data itself, as sometimes happens in qualitative studies. In any case, once a problem has been identified (and may change along the route a study takes) researchers must make sense of it in theoretical terms. It is in this manner that explication should be seen, since it involves identifying the theory or theories researchers intend to use and clarifying their assumptions and causal scheme or interpretative framework.

The aim is to spot their gaps, disparities or surprises so that alternatives can be offered. A useful technique that I have developed for such identification is to clearly think about who or what kinds of assertions one's research is *engaged* with. Accordingly, when teaching (or thinking about) a certain book or article, I often ask students the following (for them at times somewhat odd) question: "Who is the author 'arguing' with?" By such a question I attempt to steer students away from explicating what the author's main contentions are towards understanding the kind of dialogue the author is engaged with in terms of other scholars' concepts, contentions, assumptions, or methods. Indeed, once we are clear about this point the publication's own theoretical contentions are better understood. To be fair, however, many people have told me that such understanding may emerge at a later stage of research when they have a "eureka moment," when they realize who their research is engaged with and what kind of alternative they are proposing.

This move, of making clear our engagement with other scholars' contentions is what underlies the "literature review." The aim of such reviews is not to "ornament" one's text with citations of famous essays in the field. Nor is the aim simply – as one finds in many students' papers or even in doctoral theses – to show that someone is conversant in a pertinent scholarly literature. The aim of such reviews is to clearly position one's research within, and thus to make clear its potential contribution to, a scholarly field: for example, the development of a new concept, testing a key hypothesis, or exploring a hitherto understudied set of phenomena (Whetten 1989). Thus the literature review is aimed at detecting and addressing the disparities, insufficiencies, and weaknesses in relevant literatures to propose newer and tighter conceptualizations of (say) relationships about selected phenomena or to apply existing theories to new populations. Shils and Janowitz do this by arguing with the then prevalent emphasis on the purported power of propaganda disseminated by the Western Allies as the factor that helped disintegrate the Wehrmacht. After positioning themselves vis-à-vis this, the propaganda argument, they then go on to show its deficiencies and offer their own alternative.

This part of theory building cannot be overemphasized. When asked to situate their work within a stream of scholarship, beginning scholars can often recite long lists of articles in "the literature," but may have difficulties in explaining what kind of problem their research is aimed at addressing. In some cases, they may be able to explain that their work exemplifies or demonstrates a concept, relationship or contention proposed by other scholars. But this is not enough, because for research to be significant it should make clear what is new about it. In fact, this point goes for cases in which researchers apply theory rather than develop a new one because in such cases the application itself – to a new data set, a hitherto understudied group, or a novel aspect, for instance – represents the contribution of the study. On a practical level, the need is to master the expertise of being able to organize citations in a way describing the gaps in prior research, to give readers a sense for how theory has or has not been built *or* applied to date. Thus the aim is not to provide a simple list of prior research. Rather researchers need to explain why testing hypotheses or applying an already existing theory is important because it concerns a new data set and thus breaks new ground. Or, alternatively, researchers must show that they are interested in new explanations, that is, new forms of linking phenomena (Weick 1995). The process of explication therefore requires a broad-based groundwork in the theories attendant on the key concepts of the selected social science research whether they be qualitative or quantitative projects (Goertz and Mahoney 2013).

In terms of the study of the military a key distinction may be fruitful. Researchers may ask themselves how they are using the case of the military (or cases from the military): are they using it, and data derived from it, for exploring wider theoretical questions (say leadership), or, alternatively, are they using theories developed outside of the military to illuminate the special character of the armed forces and thus extend understanding of its dynamics (leadership in combat and the perpetration of violence, for instance). Thus, probably because of the easy accessibility of soldiers (they are after all, like students in psychology programs a captive population), scholars have often used them to explore various questions developed in a scholarly field. This kind of move has been at the heart of some general studies such as ones about small group dynamics or organizational bureaucracies. But if researchers want to understand the "uniqueness" of the military then they have to show how concepts used outside are applicable (or not) to its context. Thus a reading of Shils and Janowitz reveals that while they were engaged with prior and theorizing about motivation and primary groups, what they developed was a formulation about the *specific* factors promoting motivating soldiers in battle, in a violent environment. Another attempt is Collins' (2009) chapter on combat in his volume on violence. Explaining that organized violence is part of a small family of human behaviors he goes on to chart out what is unique to the perpetration of violence in battles. Thus when focusing on the armed forces, it may be helpful to ask if the relations of the armed forces to violence is pertinent to the kind of scholarly literature researchers are engaged with and the theorization they are undertaking.

Evaluation and integration

Again keeping in mind that theoretical statements are often approximations, evaluation entails examining the degree to which the theoretical ideas fit the empirical evidence, the data (Carlile and Christensen 2005). But what is good data? The dichotomies of subjective-objective or quantitative-qualitative are often used by scholars to distinguish different types of data – and other chapters in this handbook address this point – but much like theory, the only way to judge the value of data is by their usefulness in helping understand how the world works, identifying categories, making predictions and finding anomalies and surprises (Creswell 2009; Johnson and Christensen 2008). These insights are apt for deductive, inductive and abductive modes of research. In deductive reasoning researchers first move toward the development of a logical explanation or theory and then gather evidence (always based on a literature review) while inductive reasoning moves with a systematic observation of the world and then seeks a logical explanation or theory to develop (Shields and Rangarajan 2013). Abductive reasoning typically begins with an unfinished or partial set of observations and proceeds to the likeliest (or best) possible explanation for the set under the conditions of incompleteness (Feilzer 2010). While this chapter emphasizes the inductive method, in reality all research involves a continuous circle of deductive, inductive and at times abductive inquiries. For instance, in inductive research, once tentative explanations are created the move back to the empirical data is done in a deductive manner and so on.

The first practical move in inductive processes is to develop abstractions from the messy detail of the empirical data by classifying it into categories. At this stage the classifications are most typically defined by the attributes of the phenomena and are tentative. While we do not have access to the theorizing process of Shils and Janowitz their detailed categorization of modes of disintegration would most probably have evolved over time. Hence, they present a detailed typology of types and categories of military disintegration based on their empirical data and then go on to use it to develop their theoretical contentions. Once such a classification is done, we can think about the relations – our initial ideas about emerging patterns – between the category-defining attributes and the outcomes that have been observed.

In the end one ends up with a sort of hierarchy of categories that looks like a picture of an organizational tree – with this sub-category answerable to that and so on (Carlile and Christensen 2005). And this is exactly the type of tree that one finds in Shils and Janowitz. More generally, the idea is to recognize and make as clear as possible what differences in attributes and magnitude of these attributes, correlate most strongly with the patterns in the outcomes of interest. In quantitative studies, techniques such as regression analysis are often useful in defining these correlations although they are generally only probabilistic statements of association representing average tendencies. In qualitative oriented work or interpretative studies similar techniques are used, for example, linking the observed phenomena to interpretative hypotheses and then placing them in sort of provisional models that are then tested back against the data. Making these linkages is a form of theorizing in that researchers seek to connect this with that, to look for patterns.

Now researchers can begin to integrate findings, classifications and conjectures. Often during this process the concepts that emerge will still not be well-defined elements of an explicit theory. Rather they will take the forms of "sensitizing concepts" (Blumer 1954 in Hammersley and Atkinson 2004: 180) that are often an important starting point for theorizing. As various analytical categories emerge, researchers try to build or fit them into a theoretical scheme – to integrate ideas. At the same time, along the whole process, researchers should be on the lookout for anything that is surprising, unusual or stands out; whether there are any conflicts and contradictions between the various results obtained (Hammersley and Atkinson 2004). This is the stage where integration takes place: namely that phase when researchers try various explanations (in an often messy and time-consuming process) to make things come together, to put together separate, if cumulative, analyses. Indeed, the juxtaposition of conflicting results forces researchers into a more creative, framebreaking mode of thinking than they might otherwise be able to achieve. The result can be deeper insight into the emergent theory and the conflicting literature, as well as sharpening of the limits to generalizability of the focal research.

Emendation and application

Theory begins to improve when researchers continuously cycle between the empirical data, its classifications and the more abstract contentions about the relations between them. The improvement sought is when initial formulations are corrected and approximations are made clearer. This is done by continuously trying to further "test" the hypothesis that had been inductively formulated (Carlile and Christensen 2005). This most often is done by exploring whether the same correlations or patterns exist between attributes and outcomes in a different set of data than the data from which the hypothesized relationships were induced. If researchers find that the attributes of the phenomena in the new data correlate with the outcomes predicted or expected, then this "test" confirms that the theory is of use under the conditions or circumstances observed. When they don't, researchers need to think further about their explanations. In this way surprises or anomalies – or unexpected connections between phenomena – continue to be valuable throughout the process of building theories. In Shils and Janowitz we see remains of this process in the way they begin with data and contentions about the regular units of the Wehrmacht and then need to explain the much higher rates of desertion among members of the units comprising soldiers (Czechs, Yugoslavs, Poles and Russians, for example), who were coerced into the Wehrmacht. They explain the higher desertion rates of these units as being due to the multiple languages used by these troops and the obstacles this situation created for creating cohesive groups. Alternatively, they explain that the Germans in the Channel ports fought for much longer than those on the mainland since there were constantly with each other and not seconded or amalgamated constantly into new units. This is a very good example of the application of theory because in this way their initial formulations are further tested in regard to other data and their theory is extended.

To continue, when researchers use statements of association or causality to predict what they will see, they are often surprised since they observe something that the theory did not lead them to expect; thus identifying an incongruity, something the theory could not explain. Becker (1998: 95) suggests that if we reach an impasse, it would be worthwhile to use the following procedure: try to find the question that goes with the answers, information or patterns you already have. In fact, he proposes that for theorizing to be fruitful that researchers should deliberately look for extreme cases that are most likely to upset their ideas and predictions. It is these discoveries that force theory builders to cycle back into the categorization stage with a problem such as "there's something else going on here" or "these two things that we thought were different, really aren't." As Weick (1989) puts it, a disconfirmed assumption is an opportunity for a theorist to learn something new. The results of this constant effort at cycling back between explanation and data can typically include more accurately describing and measuring what the phenomena are and are not: changing the definitions by which the phenomena or the circumstances are categorized; adding or eliminating categories; and/or articulating a new theoretical statement of what is associated with, or what causes what and why, and under what circumstances (Carlile and Christensen 2005). The objective of this process is to revise theory so that it still accounts for both the anomalies identified and the phenomena as previously explained. However, many times researchers who aim to "prove" a theory's validity are likely to view the discovery of an anomaly as a failure. Too often in quantitative projects they find reasons to exclude outlying data points in order to get more significant measures of statistical fit. There typically is more information in the points of outlying data than in the ones that fit the model well, however. Understanding the outliers or anomalies is generally the key to discovering a new categorization scheme.

In this respect, scholars have found many techniques to be useful for the processes of emendation and application. C. Wright Mills (1959), in what has turned into a classic volume, proposed a number of practical suggestions as to how to stimulate our (sociological) imagination. Here I only provide a few examples. First, try rearranging your files (today electronically): disconnected folders placed side by side, or mixing up contents and then sorting them out again may lead to unforeseen or unplanned linkages. Second, and admittedly this may be more difficult, is to undertake an attitude of playfulness towards the words and phrases with which various issues are defined. One of my personal favorites is using a thesaurus (or technical dictionary) to look up synonyms or antonyms for each of my key terms. Doing this, I have found, prods me to elaborate the terms of the problem and hence to define them more precisely, because only if you know the several meanings which might be given to a term can you select the exact one with which you want to work. A third example from Mills is placing all of your contentions in a comparative perspective: that is actively looking for comparable cases, parallel situations or historical instances (even based on secondary literature).

Becker (1998) in another highly recommended text about "tricks of the trade" offers other techniques. For example, describing the information researchers have without using any of the specific words found in the data. I adopted his idea and when teaching (or thinking) about a certain publication, I ask students to come up with a new title that, while not using any of the words used in the existing name, describes the key components of the idea at base of the article or book. Another favorite of Becker is what he calls the "machine trick." The idea is to think of all of the parts of a phenomenon one wants to explain and then take out each part in turn to see if the whole "machine" still remains. Another technique that I often use is to purposely try to explain a phenomenon using different theories: conflict them. My favorites are classic sociological theories of functionalism and conflict theories. Because they have very different assumptions they can explain or make sense of different aspects of the same social phenomena. To reiterate, all of these techniques can be used once researchers reach an impasse or anomaly that gets them "stuck" in the process of theorizing.

Validity and generalization

Now take a step back from the process of constructing theories to two questions that bear upon the value of the constructs researchers are building. Yin (1984; also Carlile and Christensen 2005) sums up the scholarly consensus about two types of internal and external validity of a theory, that is, the criteria used to appraise its power for explaining or interpreting a variety of phenomena. In general, validity has to do with the strength of conclusions made about research, but both kinds of validity are not all-or-none, present-or-absent dimensions of a research design. Validity varies along a continuum from low to high. A theory's internal validity is the extent to which its conclusions are logically drawn from its premises, and researchers have dealt with all plausible alternative explanations that may explain the relations between the phenomena researched. Much of this chapter has been devoted to issues related to this point, to the various procedures or practices through which we examine the events, behaviors, or texts we are studying through the lenses of as many analytical viewpoints as possible. In short, researchers have made every effort to show the negation or limitation of alternative accounts.

The external validity of a theory is the extent to which a relationship that was observed between phenomena and outcomes in one set of circumstances applies in different circumstances as well. In other words, the extent to which researchers can generalize to other contexts or populations. When researchers have defined what causes what or what is related to what (*and* why) and that the causal mechanism or interpretative link differs by circumstance, then the scope of the theory, or its external validity, is established. As Carlile and Christensen (2005) explain, one can only say that a theory is externally valid when the process of seeking and resolving anomaly after anomaly results in a set of categories that are collectively exhaustive and mutually exclusive. At the same time, Weick (1989) urges prudence because theorists often write trivial theories because their process of theory construction is hemmed in by methodological structures that favor validation rather than usefulness. Too much validation takes away the value of imagination and selection in the process. Hence, he argues, a theorizing process that produces lots of conjectures is better than one producing only a few.

This last point is related to the kind of generalization researchers are interested in: generalization to theory or to populations. In other words researchers need to be clear about explaining if and why their research question is better addressed by theory building rather than theory-testing research. A useful way to understand this distinction is via Eisenhardt and Graebner's (2007) discussion of a strategy of theory building from cases. Such a strategy involves using one or more cases to create theoretical constructs, propositions, and/or midrange theory from case-based, empirical evidence. What is crucial to understand is that in such case studies, the theory building process occurs via recursive cycling among the case data, emerging theory, and later, extant literature. Although sometimes seen as "subjective," well-done theory building from cases is surprisingly "objective," because its close adherence to the data keeps researchers "honest": The data provide the discipline that mathematics does in formal analytic modeling (Eisenhardt and Graebner 2007).

Along these lines, when using data within such a research strategy, researchers must explain that they are generalizing to theory rather than to populations. This entails clarifying why the research question is significant, and why there is no existing theory that offers a feasible answer to it. This is also the logic of theoretical sampling: we choose cases because they are particularly suitable for exploring certain theoretical questions. Just as laboratory experiments are not randomly sampled from a population of experiments, but chosen for the likelihood that they will offer theoretical insight, so too are cases sampled for theoretical reasons, such as revelation of an unusual phenomenon, replication of findings from other cases, contrary replication, elimination of alternative explanations, and elaboration of the emergent theory (Eisenhardt and Graebner's 2007). In regard to the study of the military these distinctions are important. In statistical research that has long been dominant in the study of the micro-sociological or psychological studies of the armed forces, the interest is often generalizing findings to a universe or a population. But in the field of civil-military relations where so many studies are based on a single case or a small number of multiple cases, case studies do not produce statistically representative data but are used in order to develop or extend theory. Theory then can be used to address new research questions, structure future empirical investigations, understand phenomena, resolve problems and perhaps inform policy.

For all of this, however, one must not confuse the logical presentation of "theory-data-conclusions" as they appear in publications with the actual process of theorizing. What may appear in published texts as a linear presentation or delineation of theoretical deficiency followed by a justification of a case or multiple cases or an explanation for the reasons of studying a population may in reality have worked the other way. Researchers at times find themselves with findings "in search of a question" as I have detailed above.

Conclusion: Never-ending processes

This chapter has argued that researchers take *building* or *applying* theory seriously, as a set of practices and techniques that are actively (and constantly) used in the process of theorizing. Constructing theories is a practical endeavor. Building of theory is undertaken both within a specific project - and hence the constantly shift between the different stages of the process – as well as within a wider community of scholars that deliberate and contest the most appropriate theory for explaining distinct phenomenon (consequently the importance of constantly clarifying researchers' position within a scholarly field). While the armed forces have been (and continue to be) used to explore wider theoretical questions, the particular character of the military as the legitimate handlers of organized violence has colored all the theories particular to this field. As explained, this point does not mean that external theories should not be applied to explanations or interpretations of the military but rather that in applying such frameworks researchers take into account the uniqueness of the armed forces. More generally, if we take a long-term view of theory construction we can appreciate that it is never ending. The ways in which we continue to debate about and dialogue with the classic essay by Shils and Janowitz attest to this point. Weick (1995: 35) has the final word here:

> The process of theorizing consists of activities like abstracting, generalizing, relating, selecting, explaining, synthesizing, and idealizing. These ongoing activities intermittently spin out reference lists, data, lists of variables, diagrams, and lists of hypotheses. Those emergent products summarize progress, give direction, and serve as placemarkers. They have vestiges of theory but are not themselves theories. Then again, few things are full-fledged theories. The key lies in the context – what came before, what comes next?

References

Becker, Howard S. (1998) *Tricks of the Trade: How to Think about Your Research While You're Doing It*, Chicago, IL: University of Chicago Press.

Ben-Shalom, Uzi, Zeev Lehrer and Eyal Ben-Ari (2005) "Cohesion during Military Operations: A Field Study on Combat Units in the Al-Aqsa Intifada," *Armed Forces & Society* 32(1): 63–79.

Boëne, Bernard (1990) "How Unique Should the Military Be? A Review of Representative Literature and Outline of Synthetic Formulation," *European Journal of Sociology* 31(1): 3–59.

Campbell, Donald T. (1988) *Methodology and Epistemology for Social Science*, Chicago, IL: Chicago University Press.

Carlile, Paul R. and Clayton M. Christensen (2005) *The Cycles of Theory Building in Management Research*, Harvard Business School Working Paper 05–057.

Cibangu, Sylvain (2012) "Qualitative Research: The Toolkit of Theories in the Social Sciences," in Asuncion Lopez-Varela (ed.) *Theoretical and Methodological Approaches to Social Sciences and Knowledge Management*. InTech downloaded February 27, 2013. Available at www.intechopen.com/books/theoretical-and-methodological-approaches-to-social-sciences-and-knowledge-management.

Collins, Randall (2009) *Violence: A Micro-sociological Theory*, Princeton, NJ: Princeton University Press.

Creswell, J. W. (2009) *Research Design: Qualitative, Quantitative, and Mixed Methods Approaches*, Thousand Oaks, CA: Sage.

De Jong, L.H. (2010) "From Theory Construction to Deconstruction: The Many Modalities of Theorizing in Psychology," *Theory & Psychology* 20(6): 745–763.

Eisenhardt, M.K. (1989) "Building Theories from Case Study Research," *Academy of Management Review* 14(4): 532–550.

Eisenhardt, Kathleen M. and Melissa Graebner (2007) "Theory Building from Cases: Opportunities and Challenges,' *Academy of Management Review* 50(1): 25–32.

Feilzer, Martina Yvonne (2010) "Doing Mixed Methods Research Pragmatically: Implications for the Rediscovery of Pragmatism as a Research Paradigm," *Journal of Mixed Methods Research* 4(1): 6–16.

George, L.A. and A. Bennett (2005) *Case Studies and Theory Development in the Social Sciences*, Cambridge, MA: MIT Press.

Goertz, Gary and James Mahoney (2013) *A Tale of Two Cultures: Qualitative and Quantitative Research in the Social Sciences*, Princeton, NJ: Princeton University Press.

Hammersley, Martyn (2006) *The Sage Dictionary of Social Research*. Downloaded April 3, 2013. Available at http://srmo.sagepub.com/view/the-sage-dictionary-of-social-research-methods/n205.xml.

Hammersley, Martyn and P. Atkinson (2004) *Ethnography: Principles in Practice*, London: Routledge.

Jaccard, J. and J. Jacoby (2010) *Theory Construction and Model-building Skills: A Practical Guide for Social Scientists*, New York: Guilford Press.

Johnson, Burke and Larry Christensen (2008) *Educational Research: Quantitative, Qualitative and Mixed Approaches*, Thousand Oaks, CA: Sage.

King, Anthony (2013) *The Combat Soldier: Infantry Tactics and Cohesion in the Twentieth and Twenty-First Centuries*, Oxford: Oxford University Press.

Layder, D. (1993) *New Strategies in Social Research*, Cambridge: Polity.

Mills, C. Wright (1959) *The Sociological Imagination*, New York: Oxford University Press.

Sarafino, Edward (2005) *Research Methods: Using Processes and Procedures of Science to Understand the World*, Thousand Oaks, CA: Sage.

Segal, David R. and Meyer Kestenbaum (2002) "Professional Closure in the Military Labor Market: A Critique of Pure Cohesion," in Don M. Snider and Gayle L. Watkins (eds.) *The Future of the Army Profession*, New York: McGraw-Hill, pp. 441–458.

Shields, Patricia and Nandhini Rangarajan (2013) *A Playbook for Research Methods: Integrating Conceptual Frameworks and Project Management Skills*, Stillwater, OK: New Forums Press.

Siebold, Guy L. (2011) "Key Questions and Challenges to the Standard Model of Military Group Cohesion," *Armed Forces & Society* 37(3): 448–468.

Stouffer, Samuel A., Edward A. Suchman, Leland C. DeVinney, Shirley A. Star, and Robin M. Williams, Jr. (1949) *The American Soldier: Adjustment during Army Life*, Vol. 1 of *Studies in Social Psychology in World War II*, Princeton, NJ: Princeton University Press.

Weick, Karl. E. (1989) "Theory Construction as Disciplined Imagination," *Academy of Management Review* 14(4): 516–531.

Weick, Karl. E. (1995) "What Theory Is Not, Theorizing Is," *Administrative Science Quarterly* 40(3): 385–390.

Whetten, David A. (1989) "What Constitutes a Theoretical Contribution?," *Academy of Management Review* 14(4): 490–495.

27

DOING PRACTICAL RESEARCH AND PUBLISHING IN MILITARY STUDIES

Patricia M. Shields and Travis A. Whetsell

Risa A. Brooks (2008) *Shaping Strategy: The Civil–Military Politics of Strategic Assessment.* **Princeton, NJ: Princeton University Press.**

Shaping Strategy examines the mechanisms civilian and military leaders use as they decide to engage in war. Specifically it explains success and failure in strategic assessment – the processes and practices nations use to evaluate their strategies in interstate conflict. Brooks carefully lays out a theory, which identifies four key types of strategic assessment. When military and civilian leaders are free to share information privately information sharing (1) is effective. Strategic coordination (2) includes structures compatible with political objects that effectively evaluate military operational plans and military strategies. Authorization (3) incorporates decision processes that follow assessment. Militaries with the ability to be self-critical exhibit structural competence (4). Military promotion mechanisms are a key component here.

Success or failure in strategic assessment depends on whether military and civilian preferences diverge and how the balance of power is distributed (civilian, military or shared). Brooks develops five hypotheses, to explain the quality of the strategic assessment. For example, the best strategic assessments occur when civilian and military agreement is high and civilians dominate the balance of power (H1). The author demonstrates clarity of purpose and then supports her framework with appropriate literature, well-reasoned arguments and tables that clarify and emphasize key concepts and relationships. She sets the stage so that subsequent case study analysis is organized, coherent, and practical.

Brooks tests her hypotheses using eight case studies. The cases include Great Britain during WWI, Pakistan and Turkey in the late 1990s, the US in Iraq, Egypt in the 1960s and 1970s, and Great Britain and Germany before WWI. These cases demonstrated significant variation in strategic assessment effectiveness. For example, Egypt in 1962–67 was rated very poor overall and negative across all types of assessments. Conversely, Turkey (1996–1999) was rated fair overall and negative on strategic coordination and information sharing, and positive on authorization (pp. 262–263).

This is clearly an ambitious effort. Brooks uses accessible data such as historical records, government documents, transcripts, press reports, historical scholarship, records of interviews, and reports in the scholarly literature as sources of evidence to test her hypotheses. Her data sources provide a variety of information including behind the scenes deliberation that illustrate how the militaries of different countries act as they approach war. We see, for example, how corrupt promotion systems can result in faulty information reaching military and civilian leadership at critical times.

Brooks uses the key concepts developed in her theory section to organize the discussion of each case. Early in the case discussion information about the degree of divergence between the civilian and military leadership and whether power was held by the military, civilians or shared is presented. Subsequently, each type of strategic assessment (information sharing, strategic coordination etc.) is analyzed.

The strength of her findings across the eight cases is impressive and documented in an easy to interpret table. She shows that the challenging art of strategic assessment is enhanced when there is agreement between civilians and the military about strategy and when civilians are clearly in control. Further, strategic assessments are compromised more by a shared balance of power than by military control because agreement is difficult to attain.

The many meanings of practical research

There is nothing more practical than a good theory.
(Lewin 1952: 169)

Kurt Lewin's well known quote about the practicality of theory certainly applies to Brooks' study of strategic assessment. Without her carefully crafted conceptual framework it would have been almost impossible to make sense out of eight such disparate cases and sift through the myriad of data available on these conflicts. Brooks' (2008) definitions of strategic assessment and clear development of the four types of strategic assessment made key concepts easier to recognize and operationalize in their many manifestations. Further, her key explanatory factors (preference divergence and balance of power) draw from existing civil–military theory and have intuitive appeal. This framework enabled her to make sense of critical processes as countries face war. The reader leaves with fresh insight into the causes of strategic assessment breakdown.

This chapter examines practical research in its many dimensions. First, we look at purpose driven, practical research, which explicitly uses theory-as-tool to achieve the purpose and to provide coherence across methods of data collection and analysis. This discussion draws upon a pragmatic philosophy of science informed by the works of Charles Sanders Peirce (1877) and John Dewey (1938). This practical orientation is richly illustrated with military studies examples. Second, if military scholarship is to be practical, it needs to be published. So, we shift gears and examine the military studies journals. We identify top military studies journals and present their focus and disciplinary orientation. Third, we briefly review publication processes in scholarly journals and close with practical tips for navigating this process.

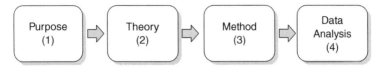

Figure 27.1 Research process model

The typical research process

A common research process model applied to empirical inquiry begins with the articulation of a purpose. Theory is then incorporated along with methodology/data collection and finally analysis of the findings (see Figure 27.1). In practice, this process is often blurry. The link between research purpose, theory, method(s) and findings is often obscured or nonexistent. In many cases theory is so abstract that it is difficult see its applicability to either the purpose or data collection. Further, this problem deprives the research itself of wider theoretical application.

The practical research model developed in this chapter is designed to clarify and bring coherence to the links between research purpose, theory, method and data analysis. To accomplish this task examples of military studies research, which like Risa Brooks "connect purpose, theory, method and data analysis," are provided. It should be noted that we are not making the case that the practical research orientation presented here is better than others. Rather, an important facet of theoretically informed, empirical research is highlighted.

Practical research has a clear purpose

Practical approach to research underscored by the philosophy of pragmatism clarifies the links in the research process by emphasizing theory as a useful tool to achieve the research purpose (Dewey 1938; Rescher 2012). Further, when theory and purpose are explicitly connected they bring coherence to data collection and analysis.

The link between research purpose and theory can become problematic when notions of theory used in empirical research ignore the research purpose. Stephen Van Evera (1997) defines theory as "general statements that describe and explain the causes or effects of classes of phenomena. They are composed of causal laws or hypotheses, explanations, and antecedent conditions" (8). Similarly, Earl Babbie (2007: Glossary 11) claims theory provides "a systematic explanation for the observations that relate to a particular aspect of life." Babbie (2007) identifies three types of research purposes (exploration, description, and explanation) and does not link them explicitly to theory.

The unstated assumption is that the hypotheses of a given theory may achieve only explanatory purposes. This connection is explicit and useful in *practical* research, but it is not the only connection. Much research conducted under the umbrella of military studies is purely descriptive (Kümmel 2002; Hussain and Ishaq 2002) or exploratory (Hendrickson 2002; Ruiz 2010; Whetsell 2011). The explicit message of theory as the rationale underlying a set of hypotheses is that neither exploratory nor descriptive studies use theory.

The Deweyan approach to practical research widens the scope of theory to include ideas and abstractions outside of explanation, prediction and causation. The singular notion of theory as explanatory or predictive hypotheses is rejected. Instead Dewey's (1938) theory-as-tool of inquiry is used to broaden the notion of theory so that it applies more explicitly to description, exploration and other research purposes. For example, categorization is a type of theory.

The periodic table of elements, and plant and animal taxonomies are examples of categories in science. In military studies, Gerhard Kümmel (2002: 559) used categories to describe "male soldiers' opinions and images on the issue of women in the military."

Just as a map is a tool that helps a traveler navigate the terrain, theoretical tools facilitate empirical inquiry. Theories like maps should be judged by their usefulness (ability to achieve the purpose). There is no expectation that a map is a true representation of reality. Rather, the expectation is that a map represents the relationship between a small set of important features, selected because they are relevant to the traveler, which ultimately enables the traveler to reach the destination (achieve a purpose). The research purpose itself can be conceptualized as a problematic situation to be resolved. Hence, in the final evaluation, theories are judged not by how well they describe, explain and predict reality, but how well they help resolve given problems (Laudan 1977).

Conceptual frameworks

Theory construction is often challenging because it crosses scale. Theory can be used to understand something large (causes of war) or narrow (reenlistment motivation in Canada). Brooks' (2008) set of hypotheses (or theory) began fairly broad and then narrowed to provide explicit clues or directions for data analysis. She hones strategic assessment into four clear manifestations – strategic coordination, information sharing, authorization process and structural competence. Further, her explicit hypotheses logically and clearly link to her overall purpose. In this chapter we focus on theory development at this level. We call this type of intermediate theory a conceptual framework. And, define conceptual framework as *the organization of ideas to achieve a purpose* (Shields and Rangarajan 2013).

Borrowing a metaphor from traditional notions of ground warfare. The responsibility for winning a war lies at the top. Strategy is the theory used to achieve the goal of winning the war. Tactics move the focus to the battlefield and close to the ground maneuvers. Tactics would vary depending upon whether the goal was to cross a river, jungle, hill, valley, or siege a city. Tactics make little sense outside the immediate purpose. Strategy informs tactics yet strategy and tactics are distinct. Likewise, the big picture of civil–military relations theory informs Brooks' (2008) more narrowly defined data-linked, strategic assessment conceptual framework. In this chapter, we focus on building and using conceptual frameworks as a practical tool of empirical research.

Because tactics are so close to the ground, they inform a host of other considerations – size of force, equipment, how to take into account weather, appropriate weapons, etc. Likewise, conceptual frameworks guide on-the-ground decisions like variable construction, statistical technique, sampling technique, who to interview, etc. Hence, for practical research studies conceptual frameworks become the connective tissue of the research enterprise. Conceptual frameworks are a kind of "intermediate theory" because they mediate between concrete research questions and data collection choices (Shields and Tajalli 2006).

From here forward we replace the term theory with conceptual framework because we wanted to denote this special type of intermediate, closer-to-the-data theory. By replacing causation/explanation with "organizing ideas to achieve a purpose" the applicability of theory is broadened beyond explanation and hypotheses. The link between purpose and framework is imbedded in its definition of "conceptual framework"; this connection *is* the overarching characteristic of practical research. The next step is to identify common research purpose/framework pairings. Shields and Tajalli (2006) identify purpose/framework pairings often found in social science and applied research (see Table 27.1).

Table 27.1 Research purpose conceptual framework pairing

Research purpose	Conceptual framework
Exploration	Working hypotheses
Description	Categories
Decision-making	Models of operations research
Explanation/prediction	Formal hypotheses

Table 27.1 begins with preliminary or early stage – exploratory research. This kind of inquiry occurs as a topic is being uncovered. It might be used in the problem formation stage or as a new policy or management approach is being considered. *Exploration* is linked with the flexible *working hypothesis*. Description is a way to make sense of a phenomenon. *Categorization* is the most common and ubiquitous way to approach *description*. Description also focuses on *what* questions and is often used in attitudinal survey research. In the 1960s in the United States, Robert McNamara introduced decision-making tools from private industry to the armed forces (Hitch and McKean 1960). The goal was to make the institution more efficient through the tools of operations research such as cost effectiveness analysis. These tools are commonly used to address questions about weapon systems or large investments like base road construction. Hence, *decision-making* and *operations research* are paired.

Explanation/Formal hypothesis is the final purpose/framework pairing. We use the term formal hypothesis to distinguish between working (which may or may not be relational) hypotheses and formal (always relational) hypotheses. Explanation and its mirror image prediction are the research purpose that represents the type of military studies research most commonly found in academic journals.

Examples of practical research from military studies

Explanatory research is by far the most common empirical methodology found in scholarly journals. One would expect that there would be a clear link between purpose and formal hypothesis. This is often not the case because the purpose statement is muddled, the hypotheses are disconnected from the purpose, the hypotheses are muddled or all three. Most of these studies, of course, do not reach the pages of a journal. But with acceptance rates for top journals running between 2 and 20 percent, it is not surprising that a foggy purpose statement, weak literature review and missing theoretical framework is a common criticism for manuscripts that never see publication.

Given the emphasis in practical research on achieving a purpose, it is not surprising that the introduction and setting for the paper's purpose is of particular importance. A clear statement of what the study plans to accomplish should occur early in the paper and be easy to find. In their study of children's adjustment to parental deployment Andres and Moelker (2011: 419) a two-part purpose used: "The purpose of this study is twofold: (a) to delineate the experiences of Dutch children and their parents in the course of service members deployment to Bosnia or Afghanistan and (b) to examine factors that predict children's adjustment difficulties during parental absence and upon reunion." The first part of the research question explicated something like a descriptive purpose. During the discussion of the results the authors used loose categories (subheadings) loosely based on a timeline (prior to departure, absence . . . reunion and perspective (child or parents) to examine the "experiences of Dutch children and their parents in the course of service members deployment." The second purpose was explanatory and asked what predicted (or explained) children's adjustment to deployment. They developed a coherent set of hypotheses to achieve this purpose.

Adres, Vanhuysse and Vashdi (2012: 93) provide another example of a clear purpose statement: "This article aims to connect two of the most often studied social science phenomena in recent decades – the social consequences of globalization and contributions to national public goods. We explore a possible causal link between these phenomena in one salient case: the tendency to evade military conscription in Israel." This purpose statement takes into account the author's multiple imbedded agendas. Big questions about the influence of globalization and public service values are narrowed to the case of conscription evasion in Israel. (For other examples of clear purpose statements in military studies research see Ben-Dor et al. 2002; Wombacher and Felfe 2012; and Hogan and Seifert 2010.)

Explanatory research generally seeks the answer to a "*why* question." "Why questions" seek causes. An answer to a "why question" often begins with *because*. Hypotheses are expected and testable answers to "why questions." Van Evera (1997: 8) argues that hypotheses in their most general form can be reduced to "*if X then Y*" or "*If X then Y with probability A.*" In other words X explains Y. The answer to the "why question" is X. Brains et al. (2011: 29) identify three characteristics of formal hypotheses. Formal hypotheses are (1) declarative sentences; (2) identify a relationship (often directional); and (3) are specific. Adres et al. (2012: 98) develop five hypotheses to explain a tendency to evade conscription. Their first hypothesis fit the characteristics of a hypothesis quite well: "The greater the individual's level of individualism, the greater will be his/her tendency to evade military service" (2012: 98).

Exploratory research and working hypotheses are some of the most basic kind of research in military studies. Historically, military leaders relied on scouts to bring back information about the enemy or the terrain. If they carried with them a more or less uniform set of assessment criteria they would have a framework akin to working hypotheses. This example shows the usefulness of exploratory research – one must begin somewhere and if possible be systematic and purposeful about it. On the other hand, exploratory research usually is incomplete and suggestive. Many a battle was lost because a scout missed something.

Ryan Hendrickson (2002) used the term proposition in lieu of working hypotheses to study diversionary use of force under President Clinton. Previously, the research on diversionary use of force employed aggregated time series data and examined "many uses of force, testing for the relevance of factors such as the domestic economy's strength" (Hendrickson 2002: 309). Hendrickson wanted to explore presidential behavior to "discern whether the military action was 'diversionary' in specific cases" (309). Clinton at the time was embroiled in the Monica Lewinski scandal and would have had a great incentive to engage in a military strike as a way to divert public attention away from this scandal. Were Clinton's strikes on Bin Laden and Operation Desert Fox diversionary or were they a strategic response to real security threat?

To answer this question Hendrickson (2002) articulated a clear purpose statement "This article explores four propositions regarding diversionary employment of force to examine two military strikes by Clinton in 1998 ..." He makes the case that the propositions and case study approach are a "novel way to assess this question" (310). Two of his propositions take into account decision-making conditions prior to the use of force. For example, Proposition 1 states, "*Prior to a diversionary use of force, the president's group of advisers is purposively kept to a minimum and the strike is conducted unilaterally*" (310). Each of his propositions were developed using carefully crafted arguments that are connected to the theoretical and historical literature. The propositions were also constructed so that supporting or disconfirming evidence was relatively clear. This made evidence collection and analysis of the data relatively straightforward. Finally, the case's evidence was systematically presented and organized by the propositions. All research components (purpose, framework, data collection, data analysis) were coherently connected – the hallmark of practical research.

Academic journals of military studies

As indicated in the introduction, practical research is also used for that to happen, it should be published. The next section focuses on the top journal outlets for military studies research. There are many outlets to publish empirical research in military studies. Unfortunately, up until only recently, a select few military studies journals had metrics with which to evaluate their merit. Further these journals were subsumed within the rankings of related fields such as international studies, political science, sociology, history and psychology. There was no easy, straightforward way to locate the top military studies journals. Recently this has changed with the advent of Google Scholar's ranking of military studies journals.

We have used the Google Scholar ranking to organize the top 20 journals in military studies (see Table 27.2). In addition, other useful information such as their Journal Citation Report two- and five-year impact factors is presented as well as the journal's focus and audience, and publisher. There should be enough information in this table to give a military studies scholar a good sense of the top journals in the field.

Table 27.2 Military: Top 20 rankings

Journal title	Google Scholar "Military Studies" H-stat ranking	Journal citation reports: 2-Year and 5-Year impact factor	Journal's focus and audience	Publisher
International Security	1	2.333 3.529	**Security Studies.** Traditional topics such as war and peace, as well as more recent dimensions of security, such as demographics of humanitarian issues. **International Audience.**	MIT Press
Security Dialogue	2	1.032 2.021	**Security Studies.** Marries theory and new empirical findings relevant to security. Multidisciplinary. **International Audience.**	Sage
Washington Quarterly	3	0.775 0.742	**Broad International Affairs.** Analyzes global strategic changes and their public policy implications. U.S. role in the world, missile defense, implications of political change. **International Audience.**	Routledge

Survival	4	0.613 0.583	**Strategic Studies.** Analysis and debate of international and strategic affairs. Policy relevant in approach. **International Audience.**	Routledge
International Peacekeeping	5	0.585 Not available	**Peace Studies.** Peacekeeping and peacekeeping operations. **International Audience.**	Routledge
Military Review	6	Not measured	**Military Science Studies.** Provides a forum for the open exchange of ideas on military affairs; focuses on the concepts, doctrines, and combat at the tactical and operational levels of war. **International, Professional Military Audience.**	U.S. Command and General Staff School
Security Studies	7	0.864 1.11	**Security Studies.** International security studies, including historical, theoretical and policy articles on the causes of war and peace. **International Audience.**	Routledge
Military Psychology	8	0.72 1.244	**Military Psychology Studies.** Psychological research and practice within a military environment **International, Psychology Profession Audience.**	Routledge
Journal of Strategic Studies	9	0.933 0.725	**Strategic Studies.** Multidisciplinary, forward-looking articles concerning military and diplomatic strategy in terms of strategic studies. **International Audience.**	Routledge
Armed Forces & Society	10	0.815 0.918	**Civil–Military Relations.** Military institutions, civil-military relations, arms control and peacemaking and conflict management. Interdisciplinary **International Audience.**	Sage
Orbis: A Journal of World Affairs	11	Not measured	**International Relations.** U.S. foreign policy. **International Audience.**	Elsevier

(continued)

Table 27.2 (continued)

Journal title	Google Scholar "Military Studies" H-stat ranking	Journal citation reports: 2-Year and 5-Year impact factor	Journal's focus and audience	Publisher
Small Wars and Insurgencies	12	Not measured	**International Relations and Conflict Studies.** Directed at providing a forum for the discussion of the historical, political, social, economic and psychological aspects of insurgency, counter-insurgency, limited war, peacekeeping operations and the use of force as an instrument of policy **International Audience.**	Routledge
Joint Forces Quarterly	13	Not measured	**Security and Military Studies.** Topics include joint and integrated operations, whole of government contributions to national security policy and strategy, homeland security and developments in training and joint military education. **U.S., Professional National Security Audience.**	National Defense University Press
Contemporary Security Policy	14	Not measured	**Conflict and Security Studies.** Research on policy problems of armed violence, peace building and conflict resolution, including: war and armed conflict, strategic culture, security studies, defense policy, weapons procurement, conflict resolution, arms control, disarmament. **International Audience.**	Routledge
European Security	15	Not measured	**Security Studies.** Forum for discussing challenges and approaches to security within the region as well as for Europe in a global context. **European Audience.**	Routledge

Nonproliferation Review	16	Not measured	**Peace and Security Studies.** Concerned with the causes, consequences, and control of the spread of nuclear, chemical, biological, and conventional weapons. Debates issues: state-run weapons programs, treaties and export controls, terrorism, and the economic and environmental effects of weapons proliferation. **International, Policy-oriented Audience.**	Routledge
RUSI Journal (Royal United Services Institute)	17	Not measured	**Defense and Security Studies.** Forum for the exchange of ideas on national and international defense and security issues. Topics include war and conflict, the UK's and other states' armed forces and defense and security policies, and military history. **International Audience.**	Routledge
Defense and Security Analysis	18	Not measured	**Security Studies.** Defense theory and analysis. Sample topics include: comparative defense policies, economies of defense, historical patterns in defense, and terrorism studies. **International Audience**.	Routledge
Parameters	19	Not measured	**Military Science Studies.** Art and science of land warfare, joint and combined matters, national and international security affairs, military strategy, military leadership and management, military history, ethics, and other topics of significant and current interest to the US Army. **International, Professional Military Audience.**	U.S. Army War College
International Journal of Intelligence and Counterintelligence	20	Not measured	**Intelligence Studies.** Issues and challenges encountered by both government and business institutions in making contemporary intelligence-related decisions and policy. **International Audience.**	Routledge

The steps to submitting a journal article

Academic journals use a blind peer-review process to select the articles that appear in their pages. A potential author should carefully consider which journal to submit to. The list in Table 27.2 is a good place to start. All of these journals have websites, which should be reviewed to learn the specifics of the submission process. Many journals use a web-based manuscript management system while others seek manuscripts by email or in a disk using regular mail. Regardless of the method of arrival, a new manuscript will be reviewed using a consistent set of procedures.

The process is known as blind peer review because the author and the reviewers are unknown to each other. This process is designed to ensure objectivity in the review process. So, the manuscript itself should be scrubbed of information that would identify the author(s). Once the manuscript has been reviewed for consistency with the form proscribed in the submission guidelines it is passed to the editor for review. The editor often rejects the manuscript at this point. One of the most common reasons for rejection is a manuscript that does not fit the mission or scope of the journal. If a manuscript gets through the editors initial screen, it is sent out for review. The editor contacts potential subject matter expert reviewers asking them whether they would be available to review the manuscript. Most manuscripts have three anonymous reviewers. The reviewers are generally asked to return the reviews within 30–45 days.

The reviews generally contain two items. One is the overall assessment of the manuscript (reject, revise and resubmit, and accept). Second, reviewers make suggestions to improve the paper. Most of the time, even if the manuscript is rejected, the reviewer comments provide the author with useful ways to improve the paper, which enable subsequent success. If the author received a revise and resubmit it is very important to carefully consider and respond to all of the reviewer comments. If the comments are lengthy and call for rethinking parts of the paper, authors should give the undertaking the reflective thought needed to take the review seriously. Nothing gets a reviewer more annoyed than a superficial response to suggested changes. Sometimes the reviews are short and easy to implement. Although nothing should be taken for granted, reviews of this nature often signal that the paper is on the road to acceptance. If the reviews contradict each other, the author should seek advice from the editor. It is very rare for a manuscript to be accepted the first round. In these rare cases, reviewers often have a few suggestions for improvement that should be taken into account.

When submitting a revised manuscript, authors should be sure to include a way for the reviewers and editors to know how the reviewer comments were addressed. Sometimes the editor asks for a letter that details their response; other editors want the changes made with track changes. The revised manuscript along with response to the reviewer comments is returned to the original reviewers for their assessment. Most of the time the decision is (accept or reject). Sometimes it takes three or more rounds. Each time the author response is repeated.

If the manuscript is accepted the author usually is asked to submit a "final" draft that adheres to the publishers checklist for accepted manuscripts. The publisher is responsible for copy-editing the manuscript and ensuring all of the references in the bibliography and text match. When the copy-editor has completed their changes and identified any questions, the edited paper along with author queries are sent to the author. The author, of course, should respond quickly. Once the paper is copy-edited it moves to typesetting; the author will get a chance to review the typeset version for a final approval. The manuscript is now an accepted article ready to be assigned to an issue.

Tips for successful publication

Generally high-quality journals have acceptance rates under 20 percent. What can an author do to improve the likelihood of success? While there is no substitute for a strong, quality, manuscript that makes an important new contribution, there are ways to increase the likelihood for acceptance. The first and perhaps most important is the question of "fit." The authors should try and ensure that the manuscript fits well within the scope of the journal. The best way to get a sense of fit is to look closely at several issues of the journal. Is the subject matter broadly compatible? Look at the bibliography. What kinds of references are common? For example, if the bibliographies are weighted toward journal articles, it is a mistake to have most of the references government reports and newspaper articles. Likewise, a journal that publishes mostly empirical, quantitative studies is less likely to consider a normative, policy essay.

If the manuscript's topic is frequently discussed in recent issues (past 5 years) the likelihood of a good fit increases. If not, a persuasive yet subtle argument needs to be made that the topic works. Most of the time it makes sense to discard the journal as a choice and move to another more appropriate fit. Keep in mind that publishing a journal article is entering into a conversation about the topic. A paper should add something to the conversation and it should be respectful of the ongoing conversation. This means that the proper literature should be cited and if possible, sources from the journal should be included.

Technical methodological issues such as the appropriate statistical technique, an adequate sample size and hypotheses that are presented in testable form should be considered. Journal editors are interested in papers with external validity. Their journal's audience extends well beyond the walls of an organization like the US Army or a single country. Further, the higher the quality the writing the greater the chances of success. Quality writing includes organization, clarity, grammar, paragraph cohesion/coherence and proper citations.

The extensive array of expertise and knowledge necessary for a successful journal article perhaps explains why so many articles are co-authored. Two or three authors may have the set of strengths and sufficient time unavailable to a single author. Since so many authors in military studies have professional military duties time could easily be an even more problematic issue. Further, senior authors can act as mentors. Perhaps more importantly, co-authoring helps to build a network of colleagues interested in the same field of study. A successful ongoing scholarly agenda depends on ideas, data and enthusiasm for the enterprise. Sharing work and ideas with colleagues helps these ideas grow and direct new fruitful inquiry. In addition, a set of colleagues can provide support and direction when confronted with a complicated revise and resubmit letter or a devastating reject letter. It is useful to share work widely and present papers prior to submission. That way, the merits of the work can be gauged using the feedback of a still wider audience.

Conclusion

This chapter began with a positive evaluation of Risa Brooks' research design, as both an excellent work of military scholarship and an example of practical research. Practical, purpose oriented scholarship uses theory as a tool that coherently connects purpose to methods, data collection, and results. Several examples of practical research were presented in their many manifestations. In addition the typology of Shields and Tajalli (2006), connecting research purpose to conceptual framework, was presented as a way to think about producing practical research. This chapter has argued that a pragmatic approach to research design, in the tradition of John Dewey and C.S. Peirce, allows differing conceptual frameworks to satisfy varying research purposes, in distinction to traditions in philosophy of science that accept only explanatory and predictive endeavors.

The final section of the chapter presented practical information, which may demystify the art of publishing in scholarly journals. Perhaps the most important practical tip this chapter can offer is the role of the introduction, problem statement and purpose in setting the stage for an accepted article. In addition, a short list of the top journals in military journals was identified along with their focus and audience. In general, editors of these journals will evaluate research based on whether they can find a clear and compelling purpose and whether a clear framework for accomplishing the research goal is presented. Does the framework help to make sense of variable definition and statistical or qualitative data analysis techniques? Emerging scholars need to ask themselves if they have designed their research in such a way as to allow for coherence between purpose, theory, methods, and results. If the field of military studies finds that the answer to this question is increasingly yes, then, as this chapter has argued, it will maintain and further develop coherence as an interdisciplinary, applied field in the service of both theory and practice.

References

Adres, E., Vanhuysse, P. and Vashdi, D.R. (2012) "The individual's level of globalism and citizen commitment to the state: The tendency to evade military service in Israel," *Armed Forces & Society*, 38(1): 92–116.

Andres, M.D. and Moelker, R. (2011) "There and back again: How parental experiences affect children's adjustments in the course of military deployments," *Armed Forces & Society*, 37(3): 418–447.

Babbie, E. (2007) *The Practice of Social Research*. Belmont, CA: Thompson Wadsworth.

Ben-Dor, G., Pedahzur, A. and Hasisi, B. (2002) "Israel's national security doctrine under strain: The crisis of the reserve army," *Armed Forces & Society*, 28(2): 233–255.

Brains, C., Wilnat, L., Manheim, J. and Rich, R. (2011). *Empirical Political Analysis: Quantitative and Qualitative Research Methods* (8th edition). Upper Saddle River, NJ: Pearson.

Brooks, R. (2008) *Shaping Strategy: The Civil–Military Politics of Strategic Assessment*. Princeton, NJ: Princeton University Press.

Dewey, J. (1938) *Logic: The Theory of Inquiry*. New York, NY: Holt, Rinehart, and Winston.

Hendrickson, R.C. (2002) "Clinton's military strikes in 1998: Diversionary uses of force?' *Armed Forces & Society*, 28(2): 309–332.

Hitch, C. and McKean, R. (1960) *The Economics of Defense in the Nuclear Age*. Santa Monica, CA: Rand Corporation.

Hogan, P.F. and Furst Seifert, R. (2010) "Marriage and the military: Evidence that those who serve marry earlier and divorce earlier," *Armed Forces & Society*, 36(3): 420–438.

Hussain, A. and Ishaq, M. (2002) "British Pakistani Muslims' perceptions of the armed forces," *Armed Forces & Society*, 28(4): 601–618.

Kümmel, G. (2002) "Complete access: Women in the Bundeswehr and male ambivalence," *Armed Forces & Society*, 28(4): 555–573.

Laudan, L. (1977) *Progress and Its Problems*. Berkeley, CA: University of California Press.

Lewin, K. (1952) *Field Theory in Social Science: Selected Theoretical Papers by Kurt Lewin*. London: Tavistock.

Peirce, C.S. (1877) "The fixation of belief," *Popular Science*, 12(1–15)

Rescher, N. (2012) *Pragmatism: The Restoration of its Scientific Roots*. New Brunswick, NJ: Transaction Publishers.

Ruiz, V. (2010) *A Knowledge Taxonomy for Army Intelligence Training: An Assessment of the Military Intelligence Basic Officer Leaders Course Using Lundvall's Knowledge Taxonomy*. Applied Research Project. San Marcos, TX: Texas State University.

Shields, P. (1998) "Pragmatism as philosophy of science: A tool for public administration," *Research in Public Administration*, 4, 195–225.

Shields, P. and Tajalli, H. (2006) "Intermediate theory: The missing link in successful student scholarship," *Journal of Public Affairs Education*, 12(3): 313–334.

Shields, P. and Rangarajan, N. (2013) *A Playbook for Research Methods: Integrating Conceptual Frameworks and Project Management Skills*. Stillwater, OK: New Forums Press.

Van Evera, S. (1997) *Guide to Methods for Students of Political Science*. Ithaca, NY: Cornell University Press.

Whetsell, T. (2011) The HEROES Program: *Child Support Enforcement among Veterans of War*. Applied Research Project. San Marcos, TX: Texas State University.

Wombacher, J. and Felfe, J. (2012) "United we are strong: An investigation into sense of community among navy crews," *Armed Forces & Society*, 38(4): 557–581.

SELECT BIBLIOGRAPHY

Brooks, R. (2008). *Shaping Strategy: The Civil–Military Politics of Strategic Assessment,* Princeton, NJ: Princeton University Press.

Bryman, A. (2012). *Social Research Methods* (4th edn), Oxford: Oxford University Press.

Carreiras, H. and C. Castro (eds) (2012). *Qualitative Methods in Military Studies: Research Experiences and Challenges,* London and New York: Routledge.

Diehl, P.F. and D. Druckman (2010). *Evaluating Peace Operations,* Boulder, CO: Lynne Rienner Publishers.

Epstein, J. (2002). 'Modeling civil violence: An agent-based, computational approach', *Proceedings of the National Academy of Sciences,* 99(3): 7243–7250.

Erikson, R.S. and L. Stoker (2011). 'Caught in the draft: The effects of Vietnam draft lottery status on political attitudes', *American Political Science Review,* 105(2): 221–237.

George, A.L. and A. Bennett (2004). *Case Studies and Theory Development in the Social Sciences* (BCSIA Studies in International Relations), Cambridge and London: MIT Press.

Giustozzi, A. (ed.) (2009). *Decoding the New Taliban,* New York: Columbia University Press.

Goertz, G. and J. Mahoney (2012). *A Tale of Two Cultures: Qualitative and Quantitative Research in the Social Sciences,* Princeton, NJ: Princeton University Press.

Griffith, J. (1995). 'The Army Reserve soldier in Operation Desert Storm: Perceptions of being prepared for mobilization, deployment, and combat', *Armed Forces & Society,* 21(2): 195–215.

Hynes, S. (1997). *The Soldiers' Tale: Bearing Witness to Modern War,* New York: Penguin.

Moore, B. (1996; pbk. 1998). *To Serve My Country, To Serve My Race: The Story of the Only African American WACs Stationed Overseas during World War II,* New York: New York University Press.

Morjé Howard, L. (2008). *UN Peacekeeping in Civil Wars,* Cambridge and New York: Cambridge University Press.

Moskos, Charles (1977). 'From institution to occupation: Trends in military organization', *Armed Forces & Society,* 4(1): 41–50.

Oneal, J., B. Russett and M. Berbaum (2003). 'Causes of peace: Democracy, interdependence, and international organizations, 1885–1992', *International Studies Quarterly,* 47(3): 371–393.

Perez, C., Jr. (2012). 'The soldier as lethal warrior and cooperative political agent: On the soldier's ethical and political obligations toward the indigenous Other', *Armed Forces & Society,* 38(2): 177–204.

Rietjens, S.J.H. (2008). 'Managing civil–military cooperation: Experiences from the Dutch Provincial Reconstruction Team in Afghanistan', *Armed Forces & Society,* 34(2): 173–207.

Ruffa, C. (2013). 'What peacekeepers think and do: An exploratory study of French, Ghanaian, Italian, and South Korean armies in the United Nations Interim Force in Lebanon', *Armed Forces & Society,* Online before print, 28 March 2013.

Schaubroeck, J.M., S.T. Hannah, B.J. Avolio, S.W.J. Kozlowski, R.G. Lord, L.K. Trevino, N. Dimotakis and A.C. Peng (2012). 'Embedding ethical leadership within and across organizational levels', *Academy of Management Journal,* 55(5): 1053–1078.

Shields, P. and N. Rangarajan (2013). *A Playbook for Research Methods: Integrating Conceptual Frameworks and Project Management*, Stillwater, OK: New Forums Press.

Soban, D., J. Salmon and A. Fahringer (2013). 'A visual analytics framework for strategic airlift decision making', *The Journal of Defense Modeling and Simulation: Applications, Methodology, Technology*, 10(2): 131–144.

Soeters, J.M.M.L., P.C. van Fenema and R. Beeres (eds) (2010). *Managing Military Organizations: Theory and Practice*, London: Routledge.

Stouffer, S.A., E.A. Suchman, L.C. DeVinney, S.A. Star and R.M. Williams Jr. (1949). *Studies in Social Psychology in World War II: 'The American Soldier'; Vol. 1: Adjustment during Army Life*, Princeton, NJ: Princeton University Press.

Tosh, J. (2009). *The Pursuit of History*, London: Routledge.

INDEX